LEADING
THE
WAY

THE STORY OF ED FEULNER AND THE
HERITAGE FOUNDATION

LEADING THE WAY

Lee Edwards

CROWN FORUM
NEW YORK

Published in the United States by Crown Forum, an imprint of the Crown Publishing Group, a division of Random House, Inc., New York.

www.crownpublishing.com

CROWN FORUM with colophon is a registered trademark of Random House, Inc.

All photographs courtesy of The Heritage Foundation.

Library of Congress Cataloging-in-Publication Data is available upon request.

ISBN 978-0-7704-3578-3
eISBN 978-0-7704-3579-0

Printed in the United States of America

Book design by Elina Nudelman
Jacket design by Joe Rusenko
Jacket photographs: (center, far left) White House; (all other photos) Chas Geer
Author photograph: David Hills Photography

10 9 8 7 6 5 4 3 2 1

First Edition

TO THE PHILOSOPHERS, POPULARIZERS,
POLITICIANS, AND PHILANTHROPISTS
WHO MADE HERITAGE POSSIBLE

CONTENTS

LEADING
THE
WAY

INTRODUCTION

In the early evening of November 13, 1980, barely a week after Ronald Reagan was elected the fortieth U.S. president, seven conservatives met in a private dining room on the lower level of the venerable Hay-Adams Hotel, facing the White House.

Present were the top members of President-elect Reagan's transition team, who would subsequently hold major positions in the Reagan administration: Edwin Meese III, Richard V. Allen, Martin Anderson, and E. Pendleton James. The others represented The Heritage Foundation, a new kind of Washington think tank.

While Meese and the other Reagan aides watched curiously, the Heritage men—president Edwin J. Feulner, Jr., executive vice president Phillip N. Truluck, and special projects director Charles L. Heatherly—carried into the wood-paneled room four heavy Xerox boxes.

With a flourish, Ed Feulner lifted the cover of a box to reveal the giant manuscript, weighing thirty pounds, of a study unprecedented in Washington policy making: *Mandate for Leadership: Policy Management in a Conservative Administration.*

In the past other research organizations, like the liberal Brookings Institution and the conservative Hoover Institution, had produced transition studies, suggesting a general solution for a serious domestic issue or a vexing foreign policy problem. The authors were invariably knowledgeable and experienced. The study was usually published after a new administration had taken office. It received a few respectful mentions in the establishment media, perhaps an editorial in *The New York Times* or a column in *The Washington Post,* and then it quietly died.

No one before had brought forth a thousand pages of policy recommendations two months prior to the inauguration. And no one before had been so far-ranging in their analysis, proposing a 30 percent cut in all personal income taxes, the building of a six-hundred-ship navy, a new undersecretary of the treasury for tax policy to shepherd things like tax cuts through the bureaucracy, the establishment of urban enterprise zones in the inner cities, the rescinding of affirmative action quotas in government hiring and contracting, and the firing of air traffic controllers if they went on strike.

Ed Meese, Reagan's deputy campaign manager, had a general idea of what was coming—he had visited Heritage in the spring and had been briefed on *Mandate for Leadership.* Dick Allen, who had brought Ed Feulner to Washington in the mid-1960s and had kept in touch, also knew about the study.

Meese was the point man because he had been given responsibility by Reagan to oversee the presidential transition. In late summer Meese had been a surprise guest at a private dinner for the chairmen and co-chairmen of the twenty teams writing the Heritage study. He gave *Mandate* his blessing and in effect that of candidate Reagan. But even Meese was not prepared for the magnitude of *Mandate,* which contained 1,270 policy proposals to move the federal government at all levels in a conservative direction.

Only The Heritage Foundation, the master of the rapid response, could have produced a volume the size of Tolstoy's *War and Peace* in just ten months.

Only Heritage, with its extensive contacts throughout the conservative movement, could have persuaded more than 250 scholars, former federal officials, and experts in and out of government to volunteer their time and expertise to write a programmatic blueprint for a conservative administration.

Only Heritage, among all the Washington think tanks, believed, as Ed Feulner put it, that "major fundamental changes in the size, scope, and direction of the federal government are possible."[1]

Only Heritage was prepared to show precisely how the changes could be effected. Other studies, for example, had suggested the acceleration of offshore oil-leasing programs, but Heritage's unique analysis specified particular lease parcels—numbers 53 and 68 in California and number 68 in the Gulf of Mexico—that should be moved up in the schedule.

Heritage understood that the hundreds of recommendations in *Mandate for Leadership* would remain recommendations unless they were marketed aggressively. Unlike think tanks of the past that published a study and hoped someone would pay attention to it, Heritage strategically regarded its publications as products to be delivered to the right policy makers and news media at the right time. "Ideas do have consequences," explained Ed Feulner, "but only if they become part of the public policy dialogue."[2]

The foundation conceived a special media strategy for *Mandate*. Senior Washington writers and editors were invited to attend a by-invitation-only press briefing at Heritage on November 14, when the details of the study were discussed and copies of a 150-page executive summary were distributed. In advance of the exclusive briefing, select portions of *Mandate* were leaked to targeted journalists. The chapter on national defense was given to reporters who covered the Pentagon, the chapter on the environment to those who wrote about the Environmental Protection Agency (EPA).

Media interest in the Heritage study was heightened when Godfrey Sperling of *The Christian Science Monitor* invited Ed Meese to his weekly breakfast meeting of journalists and policy makers after Reagan's victory. Now that you have won, Sperling asked, how are you going to govern? We're going to look to Heritage's *Mandate for Leadership*, Meese replied.[3] With that imprimatur, articles about the Heritage study soon began appearing in major newspapers and magazines.

At the same time, members of Heritage's legislative department met with each new Senate committee chairman (Reagan's decisive victory had helped Republicans capture the Senate for the first time in thirty years) as well as key House Republicans and Democrats and their senior staff.

Faced with a new administration about which they admittedly knew little, the mandarins of the media conceded *Mandate*'s importance. *The New York Times* wrote that "a team of little-known academics and congressional aides has produced a thousand-page plan for conservative government and has emerged . . . as a major force in Ronald Reagan's transition to the Presidency." United Press International described it as "a blueprint for grabbing the government by its frayed New Deal lapels and shaking out 48 years of liberal policies." "Feulner and the Washington think-tank firm he heads," said Media General News Service, "emerged from the relative obscurity of conservative wishful thinking into the coziness of the Presidential inner circle."[4]

That prospect alarmed some. Senator Birch Bayh (D-IN), defeated for reelection, described *Mandate for Leadership* as "most disturbing," while the outgoing head of the EPA attacked its recommendations as "out to lunch, totally impractical." Reacting to *Mandate*'s call to rescind affirmative action in government hiring, the black columnist Vernon Jarrett snapped, "I have been most pleased that the avowed right-wingers have taken off their verbal bedsheets."[5]

Seeking to capitalize on the extensive media coverage, Heritage rushed into print a 1,093-page paperback edition of *Mandate for Leadership*. It rose quickly to number nine on the *Washington Post*'s bestseller list as Washington power brokers combed it for clues to the new administration's intentions. Based on telephone calls he received, *Mandate* editor-in-chief Heatherly estimated that the foundation could have sold advance copies to desperate lobbyists for $1,000 or more.[6]

One individual in particular was impressed by *Mandate*—Ronald Reagan. The president asked that the study be given to every member of his cabinet at their first meeting in the Cabinet Room of the White House. T. Kenneth Cribb, Jr., then working in the Office of the Cabinet, made certain they saw it by placing the mammoth book on the seat of every chair. Meese recalls that at the meeting Reagan termed it "a valuable document" that each secretary should read and "use . . . for their agenda."[7]

Taking his cue from his boss, Meese said publicly that *Mandate for Leadership* "is very impressive" and that "the Reagan Administration will rely heavily on the Heritage Foundation."[8]

Representative Newt Gingrich (R-GA), the future House Speaker who was then a Republican backbencher, heaped praise on the foundation's research capability, saying, "The Heritage Foundation can recognize an issue before it becomes an issue, analyze it, and distribute it to those who will make policy."[9]

Ed Feulner knew that governing would not be easy for conservatives accustomed to playing defense in Washington and deeply suspicious of and even hostile to government. "In the past," he said, "so many of our activities have been against things. Now how do you start thinking more positively in terms of conservative initiatives?"[10]

Mandate was overflowing with conservative initiatives and ideas—like tuition tax credits and education vouchers—that had been accumulating within the conservative movement for decades. Now was the time to put them to the test. That was why Heritage had gambled—at a total cost of $250,000—on producing *Mandate for Leadership* when it wasn't certain in late 1979 whether Ronald Reagan would win the Republican presidential nomination, let alone the presidency.

• • •

Speaking in early 1980 at separate Heritage events, two of conservatism's most influential intellectuals—traditionalist Russell Kirk and libertarian Milton Friedman—drew the same conclusion: American conservatism had arrived at a critical point.

Kirk called the present time "an hour of conservative opportunity." Thirty years before, he noted, there were no public policy organizations like The Heritage Foundation.

It would have been inconceivable then that "two economists believing in a free economy [F. A. Hayek and Milton Friedman] would be awarded Nobel Prizes."

It would have been improbable for both national political parties to nominate those candidates "who seemed the more conservative of the lot."

Kirk predicted that America was "entering upon a period of conservative policies" and that "the conservative political imagination will set to work to allay our present discontents and to renew our order."[11]

Milton Friedman was equally optimistic, declaring, "Today our side—the side of truth, the side of freedom, the side of individual rights—has a strength and appeal which thirty years ago one would have hardly imagined."[12]

Many people inside and outside Heritage contributed to *Mandate*'s success, but one person was more responsible than any other for its extraordinary impact—Ed Feulner. It was Feulner and another young congressional aide—Paul Weyrich—who conceived the idea of a conservative think tank that would concentrate on providing timely, concise, reliable analysis to members of Congress and their staff.

It was Feulner who brought Phil Truluck with him from the Republican Study Committee in the House and asked him to build a new kind of research department committed to rapid succinct response. Truluck soon became the foundation's chief operating officer, its COO, forming with Feulner a unique, long-lasting partnership in Washington's think tank world.

It was Feulner who hired the veteran public relations man Hugh Newton to fashion a proactive communications department that would work with all sectors of the mass media—left, right, and center—not just with those on the right, as most conservative organizations were wont to do.

It was Feulner who exponentially expanded the direct-mail fund-raising started by his predecessor Frank Walton: by the end of 1980, there were some 120,000 Heritage donors (called "members" by the foundation). The expanded membership gave Heritage a financial independence that assured policy independence. If any individual, foundation, or corporation threatened to withdraw its support if Heritage did not amend its position on a particular issue, Heritage could and did reply, "We're not for sale."

It was Feulner who instructed personnel whiz Willa Johnson to form a national network of conservative groups and individuals—the Resource Bank. "We wanted Heritage," he explains, "to identify conservative policy experts on and off the campus and connect them to the Washington policy community."[13] Many of the experts served as the authors and editors of *Mandate for Leadership*.

Mandate was a true reflection of The Heritage Foundation—principled and pragmatic, innovative and conservative, optimistic and realistic—just like the foundation's president.

But who was Ed Feulner? Who had shaped him? What had shaped him? How did he come to be the president of what the liberal *New Republic* called "the most important think tank in the nation's capital"?[14]

CHAPTER I

GROWING UP RIGHT

Edwin John Feulner, Jr., was born on August 12, 1941, in Evergreen Park, a tiny suburb on the far southwest side of Chicago, the broad-shouldered city of the Daley political machine and the University of Chicago school of economics. He was the first child and only son of Edwin John and Helen Joan (Franzen) Feulner, also born on the South Side. His grandparents came to America from Germany in the 1870s. Ed Jr.—he was called "Bud" within the family—would be followed by three sisters—Mary Ann, Joan, and Barbara.

Tall and an outstanding athlete in his youth, Edwin Feulner, Sr. ("E.J."), was outgoing and easy with people, always ready with a story in the office or at a party. He had a good position in the real estate department of the Continental Illinois Bank and a promising future there. Pretty and as gregarious as her husband, Helen Feulner ran the household with a firm but loving hand. Eddie was her favorite child, according to his sisters.

The Feulners were members of America's largest self-identified nationality: German Americans represented about one-sixth of the population. Since Baron von Steuben and the American Revolution, Americans of German descent had been influential in every aspect of U.S. society. There had been military leaders like Jack Pershing, business leaders like John D. Rockefeller, renowned scientists like Albert Einstein, and presidents like Herbert Hoover.

Like all immigrants, the Feulners had been enticed by the promise of the American Dream, to have the freedom to be whatever they wanted to be, to rise as fast and as far as their talents and ambition could take them. Because they worked harder and longer and with more purpose, German Americans prospered more than almost any other ethnic group.[1]

The Feulners were different in one aspect from many other German Americans—they were devout Roman Catholics. All three of Helen Feulner's brothers were parish priests, whose examples deepened the Catholicism of their family members. Uncle Peter's parish was on the South Side, and he would visit his sister and her family several times a month. For the Feulners, saying grace before meals and praying the rosary were as natural as going to mass on Sunday, which they did without exception. In fact, Ed and Helen usually went to Saturday-morning mass as well. "Mom and Dad had a great love of Mary," recalls Barbara Lackey. "When the clouds would start to come and it would start to rain, we took the rosary out. When we were in the car, we took the rosary out. It was very much a natural part of our growing up," says Joan Barry.[2]

Edwin Feulner, Sr., was the first in the family to receive a college degree, earning a BS from DePaul University in the late 1930s by attending classes at night while working at the Continental Bank during the day. He endured without complaint the long days and nights, understanding that a degree would advance his career and help him provide for his family. During World War II he got a draft deferment because of his family status.

Shortly after the end of the war, E.J. left the security of his bank job and started his own realty firm located on State Street and later on Wabash Avenue on the near North Side. (His office was above a go-go club.) He decided to deal primarily in commercial real estate. It was a risk but a calculated one. The war was over, Chicago was beginning to boom, and office space was at a premium. He played a significant part in assembling the parcels of land that became Water Tower Place and Marina City, two of downtown Chicago's most important developments. "You would ride up or down a street with him," remembers his son, "and he could tell you the history and the ownership of just about every building. But he never lost his South Side roots, so we all grew up loving the White Sox, not the Cubs."[3]

E.J.'s quiet charity made a lasting impression on his son. For many years the senior Feulner paid the rent of two relatives who otherwise might have been homeless. No one knew he was helping them until after his death. He would hire a friend down on his luck to work in his office, causing his practical wife to sigh: "There goes more overhead and not much more productivity." "That was the kind of person he was," says his son. "He didn't need or expect accolades for his good deeds."[4]

The senior Feulner was innately conservative—grateful for the rewards of free enterprise—but he was not politically active. He rarely expressed an opinion about any politician, although it came out in family talks around the kitchen table that he and Helen had voted for Dwight D. Eisenhower in 1952. They voted for John F. Kennedy in 1960 mainly because he was a Catholic. E.J. focused on running his modest-sized but highly successful firm and providing a comfortable living for his wife and four children.

By 1950, the Feulners were doing well enough to move to the prosperous suburb of Elmhurst, which had so many elms and other trees it was known as Tree City, USA. Its annual Memorial Day and St. Patrick's Day parades were among the largest in the county. Elmhurst was a Norman Rockwell town in which a boy could ride a bike and join the Boy Scouts and deliver the local newspaper and go to church every Sunday and wonder what was on the other side of Lake Michigan.

It was also a good town for making friends. When twelve-year-old Bruce McEvoy and his family moved from Brooklyn to Elmhurst in 1955, they knew no one. On the day they moved in, Bruce noticed several boys riding by on their bikes, but no one stopped until one boy pulled his bike up to the sidewalk in front of their house. Sticking out his hand, he said, "Welcome to Elmhurst. My name's Eddie Feulner. What's yours?" The two boys talked for thirty minutes, beginning a close friendship that would last for the rest of their lives.

Bruce was soon invited over to Eddie's house to meet his parents, who quickly accepted the likable young New Yorker who shared the senior Feulner's love of sports. On that first visit, McEvoy recalls, Eddie invited him downstairs to see his room. "I thought it was a wing of the New York City Library," he says. "It was filled with all kinds of books on history, geography, railroads, photography, all the things that interested Ed. It was clear from the start that Ed was a little different from the rest of us."[5]

What impressed McEvoy was his new friend's thoroughness. When Eddie took up something, "it [was] 100 percent," like the model trains that seemed to occupy every inch of the Feulner basement. Proud of the complex of tracks, bridges, stations, gates, and lights he had constructed, he insisted on referring to them as model railroads, not model trains.

Although happy in Elmhurst, Edwin and Helen Feulner never

forgot they were from the South Side. Every week, along with Eddie and his sisters, they visited their parents, who had remained in the city. Helen's father owned a hardware store at 102nd and Vincennes, which the grandchildren loved to explore. "We could play with putty or watch our grandfather cut glass or sell paint or cut keys," recalls Ed Feulner. "You don't make a key, you know—you *cut* a key."[6]

Their paternal grandfather died when Eddie was only four, but his widow lived for another thirty years, working as a factory cook on the South Side within a mile of the stockyards. "We used to go there Sunday evenings for dinner," Feulner remembers, "and on the way home we'd see the trucks with cattle, hogs, sheep lined up—hundreds of them in a row—waiting for the opening of the stockyards Monday morning. That was back when Chicago was the hog butcher of the world."[7] E.J. would explain the law of supply and demand to his fascinated son sitting beside him in the front seat.

E.J. had been an altar boy, and so starting in the fourth grade, Eddie was an altar boy at Immaculate Conception, their large parish church in Elmhurst. In those pre–Vatican II days you fasted from midnight Saturday, taking only water until receiving communion at Sunday morning mass. That could be hard on a growing boy, as it was for Eddie one Christmas morning at high mass, when he fainted while serving. But that did not deter him from showing up the next Sunday.

Because he and Bruce McEvoy, who was also Catholic, lived close to the church, they were often drafted to fill in as altar boys when other boys fell sick or there was a special mass, presided over by the bishop. "Ed was very good at ceremony," says McEvoy, "and had pretty good Latin. He was devout without calling attention to it." He gave some thought to becoming a priest but, as his sister Joan puts it, "no more than most good Catholic boys in the fifties and sixties."[8]

As a boy, Eddie was fascinated by the giant steam engines and freight cars of the Northwestern Railway, the Illinois Central, and the Chicago and Great Western Railway, all of which passed through Elmhurst, "a big train town." Elmhurst was the last stop for the commuter trains coming from Chicago that would pull off on a siding about two blocks from the Feulner house. "I could go over on my bicycle and watch the engine go down the track, run around a Y, do a switch, and turn itself around so that it was ready to run back into the city. I had notebooks to keep track of cars going in and out."[9] He and his father built a model Elmhurst and Western Railroad, complete with passenger passes that Eddie printed on his own small press.

From an early age, Eddie possessed boundless energy and was curious about everything, in and out of school. While maintaining a high grade average at Immaculate Conception High School—which earned him a commendation from the Illinois State Scholarship Commission—he appeared in the classic farce *Charley's Aunt*. He was the official photographer of the yearbook, developing pictures in his darkroom in the basement of the Feulner home, and the head of the debating society. He organized a model United Nations, resulting in a trip to New York City.

His class picture reveals an earnest young man in a dark suit and white shirt with black horn-rimmed glasses with thick Coke-bottle lenses. The glasses were essential—without them, he had 20–1200 vision in one eye and 20–1150 in the other, a condition formally classified as "severely impaired," almost legally blind. His exceedingly poor eyesight meant he couldn't play on any of the school teams, but he was at every ICHS football game, snapping pictures of the players. And his eyesight did not prevent him from reading and reading and reading, starting with the wall of books in what the Feulners called the library in their home. "Dad loved Mark Twain," remembers Barbara Lackey, "*Huckleberry Finn* and all the rest."[10]

"Mom and Dad instilled the entrepreneurial spirit in me from an early age," Ed says.[11] He did it all—washing windows at a penny a pane, selling cucumbers and tomatoes from a backyard vegetable garden, mowing the neighbors' lawns. He delivered the *Elmhurst Press* twice a week and was a salesclerk on the weekends at the Elmhurst Camera Shop. In the summers, he and Bruce McEvoy parked cars for a summer stock theater. He was a Cub Scout and then a Boy Scout, attaining First Class. His scouting experience taught him not only to tie knots and read a compass but also to take oaths seriously. To this day, he writes approximately two thousand letters a year congratulating young men who have made Eagle Scout.

Barbara remembers sitting around the kitchen table with her brother and sisters after dinner when their father would talk about what had happened that day—" 'this deal went through,' he'd say, or 'we had better pray that I close this deal.' He would explain something to us if we didn't understand it. And he instilled in us a sense that we could do anything we wanted to if we put our mind to it, and we could be successful at whatever we do as long as we really concentrated on it."[12]

In the 1950s a good Catholic high school offered a liberal arts education equivalent to that of many of today's colleges. Immaculate

Conception was one of the best and one of the few coed schools in the diocese, with solid instruction by the Sisters of Saint Agnes of Fond du Lac, Wisconsin. "They were tough, but they were fair," says Joan Barry.[13]

Fifty years later, when he received Immaculate Conception's Distinguished Alumni Award, Ed remarked that the school had equipped him with "a remarkable education . . . a sound faith in good over evil and a deep trust in God." Even then, he said, "I knew I wanted to one day make a difference for the general good of my country by restoring the First Principles I believed it to be founded upon."[14]

After considering a number of Catholic colleges—his father suggested Chicago's Loyola University, of which he was a trustee—Ed surprised his parents by picking Regis College, an all-male liberal arts college in Denver, Colorado. "I wanted," he explains, "a school that was Jesuit, small, and away." Although unknown in secular higher education, Regis University is one of just twenty-eight Jesuit universities in America, and it is highly regarded within the American Catholic Church. In August 1993, Pope John Paul II visited the Regis campus, where he met with President Bill Clinton for the first time.

During Ed's first eighteen years, his father provided an entrepreneurial spirit, his mother gave him her unqualified love, Elmhurst gave him a sense of community and patriotism, and Immaculate Conception High School gave him a good education and deepened his faith. Regis College would introduce him to a world of ideas he did not know existed.

• • •

Ed Feulner entered college at the end of the 1950s, when it seemed that America's center was holding steady, but a series of violent events would soon cause a polarization between generations, races, and social classes.[15] They included the assassination of a dynamic young president, a distant war involving half a million servicemen, and the rise of a radical counterculture.

Most accounts of the 1960s focus on the most visible manifestations of the Left—the antiwar movement, the riotous Democratic National Convention in Chicago, SDS and the Weathermen—but they leave out the rise of a Right that offered an alternative, emphasizing patriotism, free enterprise, and religious faith. Concerned about the course of the nation, conservatives plunged into politics and helped a Silent Majority find its voice.

They nominated Barry Goldwater, an unapologetic conservative, as the presidential candidate of a major political party—a feat not accomplished since Calvin Coolidge headed the Republican ticket forty years before.

They elected Ronald Reagan, a charismatic, principled conservative, to the governorship of California, the second most populous state in the union.

Through organizations like the Intercollegiate Society of Individualists (ISI) and Young Americans for Freedom (YAF), young conservatives confronted leftists on campuses from Columbia to Berkeley.

The 1960s were heady times for conservatives who believed, swept up in the revolutionary spirit of the day, that they could launch a counterrevolution through political action.

• • •

Apolitical like his father when he was in high school, Ed Feulner discovered a political philosophy and a calling at Regis College—conservatism.

His history professor Bernard Sheehan recommended *Liberty or Equality* by Erik von Kuehnelt-Leddihn, a prolific Catholic writer, lecturer, and artist who could speak eight languages and read in another ten. Kuehnelt-Leddihn described himself as a classical liberal in the tradition of the French political scientist Alexis de Tocqueville and the German historian Jacob Burckhardt. He believed that men and women are in their element when they can "savor life's variety, the fruit of human liberty."[16] That made a lot of sense to young Feulner.

For Kuehnelt-Leddihn, the ideal society would be highly federalist and based on "immutable laws" that curtailed the state and protected the rights of the individual, the family, and the smaller political units. But, he conceded, his blueprint rested on "solemn oaths given to [a] Constitution . . . subject to religious convictions." Kuehnelt-Leddihn was echoing the Founders of the American Republic, including John Adams, who insisted that "public virtue is the only foundation of republics. There must be a positive passion for the public good . . . or there can be no republican government, nor any real liberty."[17]

"I was a fairly naïve freshman," says Feulner, "in favor of both liberty and equality. It took me about four hundred pages of Keuhnelt-Leddihn to convince me that in fact there is a big distinction. You're either going to be in favor of liberty or you're going to be in favor of equality and I realized at age eighteen that I favored liberty."[18]

Feulner next encountered the work of the American historian

Russell Kirk, who would have a more lasting influence on him than any other conservative writer. He was enthralled by Kirk's *The Conservative Mind* (published in 1953) and its brilliant overview of Anglo-American conservative thinking over the past 175 years.

Kirk argued that America was not liberal but conservative in its intellectual and political origins. The assertion stunned many liberals, who had accepted without question the liberal critic Lionel Trilling's statement that in America "liberalism is not only the dominant but even the sole intellectual tradition."[19]

In *The Conservative Mind,* Kirk deftly sketched the lives and works of such conservative champions as the British politician Edmund Burke, the founder of "the true school of conservative thinking," and John Adams, the "Atlas" of American independence and our second president. Other Americans he discussed included the novelists Nathaniel Hawthorne and James Fenimore Cooper, and political thinkers Orestes Brownson, Irving Babbitt, Paul Elmer More, and, more recently, Clinton Rossiter and Robert Nisbet.

Feulner paid particular attention to Kirk's statement that the essence of conservatism lay in six canons:

- A divine intent as well as personal conscience rules society.

- Traditional life is filled with variety and mystery, while most radical systems are characterized by narrowing conformity.

- Civilized society requires order and hierarchy.

- Private property and freedom are inseparably connected.

- Man must control his will and his appetite, knowing that he is governed more by emotion than reason.

- Society must alter slowly.[20]

Feulner liked Kirk's inclusion of divine intent and the intimate connection between private property and freedom—tenets of traditional conservatism and libertarianism. Here was an early example of the fusionism that would preoccupy many conservatives in the 1960s and which Ed Feulner adopted and insisted upon as head of The Heritage Foundation.

As revelatory to Feulner as *The Conservative Mind* was F. A.

Hayek's classic work, *The Road to Serfdom*. He was "electrified by [its] relevance, accuracy and eloquence" with the unbridled enthusiasm of a young man discovering who he is and what he believes in.[21]

Hayek wrote that planning leads to socialism, that those who try to control the economy are guilty of a fatal conceit that inevitably dooms planned economies. He described the disturbing signs of collectivism around him in Britain and elsewhere in the West and proposed a different road—the road of individualism and classical liberalism.

The future Nobel laureate in economics described the personal virtues necessary to travel that road: independence and self-reliance, individual initiative and local responsibility, and "a healthy suspicion of power and authority." He emphasized that he was not advocating a dogmatic laissez-faire attitude. Like the classical political economist Adam Smith, Hayek accepted a governmental role, carefully limited by law, which encouraged competition and the functioning of a free society.[22] Feulner would incorporate these concepts into the mission and the vision of Heritage.

With Hayek and Kirk providing a philosophical foundation, Feulner sought a political manifesto to complete his transformation into a committed conservative. Providentially, *The Conscience of a Conservative* appeared in the spring of 1960. Its author was no armchair philosopher but a straight-talking, fiercely independent politician from the West—Barry Goldwater.

In the first pages of *The Conscience of a Conservative*, Goldwater dismissed the liberal's favorite argument that conservatism was out of date. That was like saying, responded Goldwater, that "The Golden Rule or the Ten Commandments or Aristotle's *Politics* are out of date." The conservative approach to politics, he explained, "is nothing more or less than an attempt to apply the wisdom of experience and the revealed truths of the past to the problems of today."[23]

Unlike the liberal, the conservative believed that man is not only an economic but also a spiritual creature and "looks upon the enhancement of man's spiritual nature as the primary concern of a political philosophy." Indeed, Goldwater said, the first obligation of a political thinker was "to understand the nature of man."[24]

The conservative "looks upon politics as the art of achieving the maximum amount of freedom for individuals that is consistent with the maintenance of social order." But, Goldwater wrote, the balance that ideally existed between freedom and order had tipped against freedom "practically everywhere on earth." Even in America the trend against freedom and in favor of order was "well along and gathering momentum."

For the American conservative, therefore, there was no difficulty in "identifying the day's overriding political challenge: it is to preserve and extend freedom."[25]

Feulner was captivated by the crystal-clear rhetoric and the forthright way that Goldwater dealt with the issues that dominated (and continue to dominate) the national political debate.

Taxes? Flatten them.

Government spending? Eliminate programs better handled by the states, private institutions, or individuals.

Social Security? Strengthen it by introducing a voluntary option.

Law and order? The rights of victims should always take precedence over those of criminals.

Communism? Why not victory?

Alarmed by the concentration of power in Washington, Goldwater was convinced that most Americans wanted to reverse the trend. The transition will come, he wrote, when the people entrust their affairs to those "who understand that their first duty as public officials is to divest themselves of the power they have been given." The people, he said, must elect candidates who boldly proclaim, "My aim is not to pass laws, but to repeal them."[26]

• • •

Books like *The Conservative Mind* and *The Road to Serfdom* and publications like *National Review* and *Human Events,* says Feulner, "helped turn my conservative instincts into firm conservative convictions." After reading *The Conscience of a Conservative,* he became a Goldwaterite: "He was the political embodiment of what I believed."[27] Another Regis professor who contributed to his political thinking was philosopher-historian Larry Stepelevich, an authority on the German philosopher Hegel.

Feulner discovered through the Regis student government that he was good at politics. Borrowing from his outgoing father, he developed a firm handshake and a wide smile. Although blessed with a resonant baritone voice, he did not enjoy public speaking. He preferred to speak from text rather than to ad-lib his remarks. With practice, he developed into a competent if not an eloquent speaker. Better organized than any of his college opponents, he was elected sophomore class treasurer, then junior class secretary, and in his senior year student body president. He also served as vice president of Alpha Kappa Psi, the professional business fraternity, signaling an intention to learn all he could about the world of business. In 1962 the Regis chapter of Alpha Kappa Psi was named the best chapter in the nation.

The one complaint, and the only one made about the Feulner "administration," was that the young college leader was too organized. He and his colleagues were so efficient at arranging the dances and other student activities that the other students had scant opportunity to participate. Here was an early example of the micromanagement that Ed Feulner was prone to, even as the CEO of Heritage.[28]

Eager to further conservative thought on campus, Ed organized and served as the first president of the American Society, which became a chapter of the Intercollegiate Society of Individualists, the preeminent student group on the Right. It was the beginning of a lifelong association between Ed Feulner and the ISI that, among other things, would result in his studying at the London School of Economics and meeting fellow conservative Richard V. Allen, who would eventually bring him to Washington, D.C.

Feulner first met Allen, who in his mid-twenties was already an acknowledged expert on Communism, at a one-day ISI conference in the winter of 1962. He approached Allen after his lecture and engaged him in an extended conversation. Allen was impressed with the young conservative's keen mind, energy, and willingness to listen. They promised to stay in touch.[29]

Ed sharpened his writing skills at Regis. He was the news editor and a columnist for the college newspaper, the *Brown and Gold Review,* served as a member of the editorial board and chief photographer of the *Ranger* yearbook, and was secretary-treasurer of the Literary Club. His columns were frequently about topics far removed from campus, such as recommending that the United States stop sending foreign aid to "neutral" countries that did not promote freedom and private enterprise. He wrote reviews of M. Stanton Evans's *Revolt on the Campus* and Milton Friedman's *Capitalism and Freedom,* both of which he praised.

Asked by a student reporter what he had gained from his experience as president of the student senate, Feulner "hesitated for a moment" and then answered:

There were two personal things I acquired. First of all, I learned the valuable advantage of being able to get up and speak before a group and to conduct a meeting. Secondly, I was given the opportunity to see the inner workings of this institution, the functions of this corporation. And Regis is in the full sense of the term a business.[30]

It was a coolly objective comment, probably not shared by many at Regis, but indicative of a mind that liked to analyze and organize—a mind that would be stretched and challenged at a graduate business school.

In the summer of 1961 he and sixteen other Regis College students along with Fr. Edward Maginnis, S.J., a faculty member, spent two months traveling through much of Western Europe with their bedrolls. It was the first foreign visit for the twenty-year-old Feulner, a true child of the twentieth century, always restless and looking beyond the horizon. He was excited about visiting historic Berlin on his birthday, August 12, 1961, when that leg of the trip was abruptly canceled—the Soviets had begun building the Berlin Wall.

In his senior year Ed conceived the idea of a three-day student leadership conference that would meet before classes began to examine issues such as Regis's student government, athletics, freshman orientation, and administration rules. It was an audacious idea, especially for a college where the Jesuit fathers generally ran things as they thought best.

In his conference remarks, Rev. Thomas F. Finucane, S.J., the dean of men, admitted he had been skeptical when Ed Feulner first approached him. "I wasn't too sure," he said, "whether or not we would be successful in getting together a group [of students] before school at their own expense to come and to do this. . . . I must admit I have been most agreeably surprised and impressed. And it just shows what a determined young man and an interested student leadership could do."[31]

The six-foot, 190-pound Feulner was rarely still, physically or intellectually. He was a mailroom attendant at Regis and during the summers a stagehand at the Denver Civic Theater (he became a card-carrying member of the stagehands' union), a headwaiter at the Saga Food Service at Regis serving the students and the Jesuit faculty, and an advertising proofreader for Joslin's Department Store in Denver—all done to "supplement my meager monthly budget."[32] His parents paid his tuition, but the rest of his expenses was up to him. He made the dean's list despite all the extracurricular activities but missed cum laude because of an unexpected B in a senior economics course.

To no one's surprise, he was named a Regis Man of the Year in 1962 and again in 1963, his final year at the school. The young Chicagoan was known off campus as well through his stand on issues like Vietnam. In a letter to the editor of the liberal *Denver Post,* Feulner wrote:

Student's View on War

The basic questions which I, as a college student of draftable age, will ask the women marchers for peace, the ban the bombers, and the other assorted groups of pacifists are:

Can we, as citizens of the leading country of the free world, be satisfied with peace? With the Communists professing the intention of world conquest, shouldn't our goal also be one of world conquest—but world conquest for the free enterprise, republican form of government which enables an individual to express his talents freely, and advance on his own merits?

Isn't it about time that we admit we are in a war, and that given the nature and avowed purpose of the enemy, peaceful coexistence is impossible, and that we must either conquer or be conquered?

E. J. Feulner, Jr.
(Student at Regis)[33]

Feulner was twenty years old when he wrote this bold letter, which anticipates almost all of the basic ideas that guide The Heritage Foundation: limited government, free enterprise, individual freedom, traditional American values, and a strong national defense. Only the idea of traditional American values based on our Judeo-Christian heritage is not mentioned in this early statement by a young conservative willing to challenge the prevailing zeitgeist.

Such countervailing views were bound to elicit a strong reaction, as they did from George Martelon, adviser to the Regis chapter of the Alpha Kappa Psi business fraternity. Writing to congratulate Feulner on winning the outstanding club award, Martelon admitted, in what was meant to be a humorous tone, his disappointment with the young man's politics:

"I find it difficult to justify or reconcile in my own mind the why's or wherefore's of an individual with your capabilities allowing himself to sink to such decadent situation as to allow himself to advocate or even condone the fallacious political theories as expounded by one Barry Goldwater."

Martelon went on to offer his "most sincere congratulations" but could not resist adding: "I deeply regret the complete loss of your leadership abilities in one instance, and yet look forward to working closely with you in another."[34] There is no recorded answer from Ed Feulner, who had already developed an ability to shrug off criticism—unless warranted—preferring to accentuate the positive. Besides, he was occupied with considering what to do after graduating from Regis.

CHAPTER 2

GETTING DOWN TO BUSINESS

The young graduate had several options. He could go into real estate with his father, or work for the Illinois Central Railroad, which offered him a job, or perhaps attend business graduate school in order to teach.

To satisfy his ever-present wanderlust, Feulner decided to spend his post-undergrad summer of 1963 in Scotland, attending the Scottish Universities Summer School at the University of Edinburgh. He earned six graduate hours in history. And he got to know the deceptively dour country that inspired his intellectual hero, Russell Kirk, and the esteemed university—founded in 1583—from which he would later receive a PhD.

He took the LSATs and the business school exams but decided "somewhere along the line" that he didn't want to be a lawyer. It came down to a choice between the Wharton School of Business and Finance at the University of Pennsylvania and the University of Southern California's business school. He considered Harvard but didn't like the case study method it had made so famous, preferring the more traditional approach of Wharton.

Feulner thinks he was accepted by Wharton because "I did fairly well on the admissions test" and because the admissions office decided not to accept one more student from Swarthmore or Penn State but to try something a little different: admit a kid from Regis College ("which they probably had to look up") who had decent grades, was student president, and did well on the entrance exam. "Getting into Wharton," he admits, "was a pretty big deal."[1] Indeed it was: Wharton was the first business school in America and is still ranked in the top five schools.

Over the next fifteen months, he majored in transportation and public utilities, took a reading course in German, and wrote his master's thesis on "The Determination of International Air Fares." (As Heritage president, Feulner would become an expert in such fares, traveling an estimated 150,000 miles annually giving speeches, visiting donors, and attending international conferences.) He would achieve a cumulative GPA of 3.19 and place twenty-third out of a class of eighty, causing him to write to a friend, "Not bad for a small town boy with all the Eastern slickers."[2]

Feulner took full advantage of Wharton's academic diversity. When Robert Strausz-Hupé, the coauthor of the Cold War classic *Protracted Conflict,* lectured, Feulner was there but sat in the back "because I was not officially taking [his] course." The Austrian-born Strausz-Hupé was "a giant intellect" who counseled firmness but not belligerence when dealing with the Soviet Union.[3]

In *Protracted Conflict,* Strausz-Hupé and his coauthors outlined how the Soviets and their allies were conducting a long-range strategy that contained a sphere of peace for the Soviet bloc that was off-limits to the West and a sphere of war in which the United States and its allies were constantly challenged by the Communists. There might be periods of truce, like détente or peaceful coexistence, the authors said, but they were temporary because Communist ideology would never permit a true peace.

Ed Feulner absorbed Strausz-Hupé's realpolitik assessments in class and in his writing, especially that military strength was essential to the preservation of freedom—one of Heritage's five big ideas. When Strausz-Hupé retired in 1989 from the Foreign Service after serving as ambassador to Turkey and several other key U.S. allies, Feulner invited him to join Heritage as a distinguished fellow. The appointment was typical of Feulner, who always tendered due recognition to a conservative for his service to the conservative movement and the nation.

Another major intellectual influence on Feulner while at Wharton was ISI president Victor Milione, a traditional conservative and Catholic. The young graduate student frequently visited the ISI offices in the Public Ledger Building, located a few blocks from Independence Hall and three stops on the subway from the University of Pennsylvania. Feulner describes Milione as "an intellectual mentor in a nonclassroom setting."[4]

Milione's door was always open to young conservatives whom, Socratic-like, he loved to engage in philosophical discourse. In a single meeting, Milione would quote in extenso John Henry Newman, Tocqueville, Seneca, Burckhardt, Ortega y Gasset, James Bryce, and Richard Weaver, his favorite modern conservative writer. An ISI staffer once quipped, "Vic may not [be] the most quoted conservative, but he [is] certainly the most quoting."[5]

Citing Weaver, Milione said that students are not objects but individuals who should be allowed to develop their own intellectual abilities and cultural interests. Milione was confident that a goodly number would choose the conservative rather than the liberal road if given a choice. He viewed Ed Feulner as a leading example of someone who had made the right choice because of his faith, his family, his education, and his association with organizations like the ISI.

On his visits to the ISI, Feulner became involved in the organization's search for a formal in-house publication. After experimenting with a newsletter and a magazine of young conservative writing on and off campus, the institute committed itself to publishing a quarterly journal and titled it *The Intercollegiate Review*. In part, the ISI journal was a response to the recently launched *New Individualist Review*, a libertarian publication out of the University of Chicago. The first editor was Sam Peltzman, who went on to become a professor of economics at Chicago and a member of the Mont Pelerin Society. Years later, at a Mont Pelerin meeting, Feulner and Peltzman exchanged stories about their philosophically dueling journals.

Launched in January 1965, *The Intercollegiate Review* remains after nearly fifty years one of the oldest and most influential intellectual journals on the Right. The first editor was the remarkably mature and well-read Robert Ritchie, a graduate of George Washington University. The associate editor was Edwin J. Feulner, Jr., who filled that post for some twenty years.

An editorial in the first issue explained that the *Review* would be revolutionary and conservative—revolutionary in that it would "challenge ideas which have been unquestioned by the prevailing academic orthodoxy," and conservative in that it would promote an appreciation of those things in Western civilization that are "consonant with the moral underpinnings of the free society."[6] Substitute the word "political" for "academic," and you have a neat summary of The Heritage Foundation's mission.

At the ISI offices, Feulner formed lasting friendships with other young conservatives, like fellow midwesterner and pipe smoker Donald Lipsett. A graduate of Indiana University, where he earned a BS in business and an MBA, Lipsett was a field organizer of unflagging energy and quirky humor, as reflected in the "secret" Stephen Decatur Society, which he founded. The society's red, white, and blue letterhead provided no address, telephone number, or names of officers (because there were none). At the top next to the society's name was an eagle with arrows in both of its talons.

The society collected no dues or fees, it was explained, because it was comfortably financed by an "extensive holding of Imperial Hapsburg Gold Bonds, Imperial Russian Bonds, Chinese Imperial Railway Bonds . . . gold bullion, enriched Uranium (for maximum fallout), numbered deposits in the Liechtensteiner Stattsbank."[7] Perhaps coincidentally, Ed Feulner would later become good friends with Prince Nikolaus von Liechtenstein, a senior member of the ruling family of Liechtenstein.

Another intellectual influence on Feulner was the Foundation for Economic Education (FEE) and its founder and president Leonard Read. He had been reading *The Freeman,* FEE's monthly journal, and was intrigued by its articles that covered not only economics but history as well. Upon receiving a brochure about a seminar at its headquarters in Irvington-on-Hudson, New York, he wrote the foundation asking for a scholarship.

Read promptly replied that because of Ed's commitment to the free-market system, he was confident he was capable of advancing his own education by finding a way to pay the registration fee of some seventy-five dollars. "I thought about that," Feulner recalls, "and admitted to myself that there really is no such thing as a free lunch." He dipped into his own funds for the fee, which included room and board and tuition.

His exposure to FEE lecturers Ed Opitz, Paul Poirot, William Peterson, and Read himself was "a mind-stretching experience for an intellectually inquisitive graduate student" who had been concentrating on marginal vs. average-cost pricing of transportation products and key statutes on labor relations. "It was good to get back to First Principles" at the FEE seminar.[8]

Feulner learned much from Vic Milione but disagreed with his downgrading of politics. His political hero Barry Goldwater was running for president. How could he not get involved in his campaign? Feulner set about organizing a youth group for Goldwater at the University of Pennsylvania, to the dismay of more than a few students. He capped his pro-Goldwater activity by arranging for the Arizona conservative to make a campaign appearance at the university.

In mid-October 1964 he was seated on the stage of a school auditorium, listening intently as Senator Goldwater called for the implementation of conservative ideas such as the partial privatization of Social Security, a phasing out of farm subsidies, and victory over Communism.

Suddenly he ducked as several tomatoes and raw eggs were thrown at the presidential nominee by partisans who thought a conservative shouldn't be allowed to say such crazy things, especially on "their" campus. It was one of Ed Feulner's first public encounters with political correctness in its most hostile form. He took it personally, seeing the assault on Goldwater as an assault on him and their mutual beliefs. Feulner became so engrossed in the campaign—as a volunteer—that he nearly flunked out of Wharton. Carried away by enthusiasm, he said publicly, "If we lost Philadelphia by only 100,000 we'll carry the state!" (In fact, Philadelphia went for Lyndon Johnson by 300,000.)[9]

The nation was not ready for Goldwater's brand of undiluted conservatism. Everything from false charges of racism to allegations he would get America into a nuclear war were thrown at Barry Goldwater and stuck. Buffeted by a hostile media and confronted by a president who believed that extremism in the pursuit of victory was no vice—President Johnson had the FBI bug Goldwater's campaign plane—the Arizona conservative's defeat was certain.[10]

Shortly before Election Day and looking at an uncertain future, Lipsett and Feulner conceived the idea of starting a society of conservative intellectuals. It would be an American version of the Mont Pelerin Society of free-market intellectuals, begun by Hayek twenty years before. It would also serve as an unofficial alumni association of the ISI. "We wanted to keep [ISI graduates] involved in the battle of ideas," Feulner explains.[11]

The two young men decided that to be successful, the organization would need the participation of two conservatives in particular—editor-author William F. Buckley, Jr., representing the traditionalist wing of the conservative movement, and economist Milton Friedman, representing the libertarian wing.

Surprisingly, the two eminent conservatives had never met. Feulner recalls thinking, "How can we bring them together?" Fortunately he and Lipsett had met both Buckley and Friedman through the ISI, and they suspected that the two older men would be willing to help younger conservatives get organized. A meeting was arranged in New York City, and *National Review*'s senior editor Frank Meyer, well known for his efforts to "fuse" the different strains of conservatism, joined them.

Buckley and Friedman readily agreed to endorse the as-yet-unnamed organization. Twenty-three-year-old Ed Feulner was elected treasurer and took on for the first time the responsibility for the finances of a national conservative organization. Bill Buckley wrote a check for $100 so "we could open a bank account," and the Philadelphia Society was born.

"Commodore" Donald Lipsett was named secretary and ran the society to the members' satisfaction for three decades until his early death in 1995. For nearly fifty years, the meetings of the Philadelphia Society have provided an opportunity for conservatives of all persuasions to analyze the present state of conservatism and debate its future. They are guided by a founding statement that says a "fundamental purpose of the Society [shall] be a continuing dialogue between the 'traditionalist' and 'libertarian' emphases of conservatism."[12] Ed Feulner has sought the same balance as president of Heritage, which he calls "an honest broker" among conservatives.

However, at the time, the founding of a society devoted to conservative ideas seemed quixotic at best. Running as an uncompromising conservative, Barry Goldwater had been buried beneath a landslide, winning just 38.5 percent of the popular vote and carrying only six states, including his home state of Arizona. President Johnson's victory enabled Democrats to pick up a net 2 seats in the Senate, giving them a total of 68 out of 100. In the House there were 295 Democratic congressmen as against only 140 Republicans. It was the largest Democratic majority in the House since 1936, the high point of the New Deal.

Pundits and political scientists were unanimous in their analysis of the 1964 election results—conservatism was stone cold dead and ready for burial.

Walter Lippmann, the dean of political commentators, wrote that "the returns prove the falsity of the claim . . . that there is a great silent latent majority of 'conservative' Republicans who will emerge as soon as the Republican party turns its back on 'me-tooism' and offers them a 'choice.' The Johnson majority is indisputable proof that the voters are in the center."

Academics Nelson W. Polsby and Aaron B. Wildavsky stated that if the Republican Party continued "to nominate conservatives like Goldwater," it would continue to lose so badly that "we can expect an end to a competitive two-party system."

Washington bureau chief James Reston of *The New York Times* summed up that "Barry Goldwater not only lost the presidential election yesterday but the conservative cause as well."[13]

There were, nevertheless, dissenting opinions about the fate of conservatism, mostly although not exclusively from the Right.

Frank Meyer, of *National Review,* wrote, "Despite the caricature of Goldwater's position, despite the fact that everything was done to make it appear that the conservative course is extremist, radical, nihilist, anarchic—still two-fifths of the voters saw through the distortions and solidly voted for the unthinkable proposition that there is an alternative to liberal domination."[14]

Writing in the ultra-liberal *Nation,* Dalton Trumbo warned that the defeat of Goldwater did not mean the end of conservatism. How could it, he argued, when never before had conservatives "been able to carry [their] program to the whole people from the platform of a national party; never had a candidate of the Right been so attractive, or aroused such profound devotion; never before had hundreds of thousands of dollars—perhaps millions—flowed to [their] cause from the grassroots."[15]

Ronald Reagan reflected the view of most conservatives, including Ed Feulner, when he wrote, "The landslide majority did not vote against the conservative majority, they voted against a false image our liberal opponents successfully mounted."[16]

The Goldwater candidacy was "absolutely critical" for the conservative movement, Feulner later said, proving that "we could mount a national campaign, albeit thin in spots." Goldwater's and therefore conservatism's showing "proved our political maturity . . . [1964] was our political bar mitzvah, our confirmation in a political sense."[17]

• • •

In December 1964, one month after the Goldwater defeat, Feulner received his MBA from Wharton. Perhaps because of his public efforts on behalf of Barry Goldwater, one of his professors predicted his future: "Feulner, once you're in Washington, you just won't want to go back to Pocatello."[18] The professor was premature—Feulner decided he wanted to study basic economic and political principles in more depth, he hoped at the famed London School of Economics (LSE). He applied to the ISI and received one of the very first Richard Weaver Fellowships, worth $1,500. It was named after the author of the seminal work *Ideas Have Consequences,* which Feulner, in his usual thorough way, took the time to read. The book deepened his appreciation for the importance of faith and tradition.

In *Ideas,* the traditionalist Weaver traced the dissolution of Western thought and culture to the fourteenth century, when many in the West abandoned a belief in transcendental values and accepted man as "the measure of all things." Religious practice declined, and a faith in scientific rationalism ultimately triumphed. Western civilization, Weaver wrote, now faced rampant egalitarianism and the cult of the masses.

But *Ideas Have Consequences* was no jeremiad. The author urged three reforms: a strong defense of private property, a rescue of language from the purely sensational, and a solemn respect for other human beings and the past.

The parallels between the conservative Richard Weaver and the classical liberal F. A. Hayek struck Feulner as instructive. Both attributed the decline of the West to pernicious liberal ideas. For Hayek, it was economic planning; for Weaver, it was moral relativism. Hayek proposed the alternative road of individual freedom within a framework of carefully limited government. Weaver insisted that a good society requires a foundation of certain eternal truths. Together, Feulner thought, the two writers provided a conservative answer to the twin threats of statism at home and socialism abroad.

The London School of Economics accepted Ed Feulner for the Lent and summer terms of the 1964–65 school year, placing him in class from January to March and then May to early July 1965. (April was set aside for the students for vacation and travel.) Feulner was delighted to be accepted but was already looking ahead to what he would do after the LSE.

Writing to a Regis professor in the late fall of 1964, he said he was planning to pursue a PhD in economics at an American university, like the University of Virginia, the University of Pennsylvania, American University, or Johns Hopkins, which had "a very interesting course in economics." Which school depended on "the availability of funds."[19]

Feulner sailed for Southampton and the land of the Magna Carta, Adam Smith, and Parliament, where Edmund Burke defended the American colonies in the 1770s, Benjamin Disraeli pressed for the extension of the franchise to workers in the 1860s, and Winston Churchill issued Britain's defiant response to Adolf Hitler. He carried with him a letter of introduction from William F. Buckley, Jr., to Anthony Lejeune, *National Review*'s London correspondent. Buckley misspelled Feulner's name but got everything else right, describing him as "a fine young man, first-rate scholar, a devoted conservative . . . I have taken the liberty of asking him to call on you."[20]

At the LSE, Feulner was exposed to Kenneth Minogue, a former pupil of the eminent conservative British philosopher Michael Oakeshott, and the author of *The Liberal Mind*. That mind, said Minogue, is committed to the notion that history requires the perfection of society, preferably through government. But the author warned: "A populace which hands its moral order over to governments, no matter how impeccable its reasons, will become dependent and slavish." Feulner placed *The Liberal Mind,* which he bought for thirty shillings, on the shelf next to *The Conservative Mind*. At twenty-eight, Minogue was only five years older than Feulner, who found the British academic easy to talk to.

He was also impressed by the lectures of the economist Peter Bauer, later Lord Bauer of Clare Market, who redefined issues like aid for developing countries, "about which I had previously gotten the conventional wisdom from 'experts' like Walt Rostow."[21] Bauer proved through statistics that outside aid retarded rather than advanced the economy of a developing country, which becomes dependent upon the aid rather than developing its own economy. Feulner also met for the first time a personal hero, Friedrich Hayek, who gave a series of lectures on classical liberalism that spring. Feulner attended every one.

The LSE's chief transportation economist was Michael Beasley, who worked closely with Feulner on the research project that had helped him obtain the Weaver Fellowship—an examination of the nationalization of Britain's railway system. Feulner stated his thesis in the form of a question: "Did the interwar mergers of the British railroads from 240 independent railroads into the five main regional systems make it easier for the Labor government—the government of 1945—to nationalize the British rail system?"

He haunted the LSE library reading *Hansard's*—the British version of the *Congressional Record*—and other documents to discover that "if there had been a thousand railroads, the Socialists would have nationalized them . . . because ideologically they believed in state control of the economy."[22] His paper "The British Method of Pricing Their Rail Transport Product" was published a year later in *Transportation*

Research Forum. It did not win any literary prize—"it's pretty dry and boring"—but Feulner was able to produce a policy prescription from his original topic.[23]

Because he was not working toward a formal LSE degree, Feulner found time to organize and head a student organization, the Old Whig Society, and to affiliate it with the ISI. The name had been suggested by Hayek, who one day had met with the students. (The original Whigs had sought to limit the authority of the king and expand the power of Parliament.) Feulner's fellow officers were from Portugal, India, and Scotland, and a small minority among the predominantly leftist student body; but they were deeply interested "in the basic premises of a free society."[24] His experience at the LSE reinforced his conviction that America's future depended in large part on what happened outside as well as within its borders. Ed Feulner was a globalist long before the term came into popular use.

He kept in touch with old friends like Bruce McEvoy, who had joined the ROTC at John Carroll University in Cleveland and was assigned after graduation to Orléans, France. "We got together in London," remembers McEvoy, "and he seemed to know people everywhere, not just in England, but in Europe." In the summer of 1964 they drove in Bruce's MGB from Bremen to Copenhagen to Oslo, where they spent hours with a Norwegian professor of economics Feulner had met, and wound up in Sweden during the summer solstice, allowing them to enjoy the many attractions of Scandinavia almost twenty-four hours a day.[25]

Aside from giving him the opportunity to interact with Hayek, Minogue, Bauer, and other leading classical liberals, Feulner was grateful to the London School of Economics for introducing him to the most important think tank on the British Right, the Institute of Economic Affairs (IEA), and its two brilliant founders, Ralph Harris and Arthur Seldon. The IEA would provide many of the free-market ideas for Conservative prime minister Margaret Thatcher in the 1970s and 1980s.

Armed with a letter of introduction from Milton Friedman, Feulner went to the IEA offices then on Eaton Square. Like so many others, Harris and Seldon were taken with the intelligent, enthusiastic young American and offered him a part-time post as a research assistant to John Lincoln, who was writing a book on the negative impact of labor unions on the British economy. The stipend was modest—five pounds a day or fifteen dollars—but the opportunity enabled Feulner to observe a think tank up close.

He learned that it was "absolutely essential" for a think tank to maintain the integrity of its research. Because the institute's analysts were so scrupulous, everyone from the media to the liberal opposition accorded the IEA's work attention and respect. If the institute issued a study that challenged the status quo on housing or trade unions, "the other side had to rebut it. Ideas were taken seriously" at the IEA, Feulner recalls, "ideas mattered."[26] He would insist that Heritage practice the same scrupulosity in its research.

That the idea of an American IEA was already floating around in his brain surfaced in a conversation he had with Milton Friedman on his return to the United States in the fall of 1965. After characterizing the influence of the IEA in Britain as "substantial," he asked Friedman why a U.S. organization "has not had a similar impact on American public policy." Friedman responded that it might be because Great Britain was farther down the path toward "dirigisme" than the United States and therefore easier to get back on track.[27] It would be another fifteen years, with the elections of Margaret Thatcher in Britain and Ronald Reagan in America, before both nations would be placed back on the path to liberty—with the help of the Institute of Economic Affairs in the United Kingdom and The Heritage Foundation in the United States.

• • •

Taking advantage of the LSE's April break, Feulner decided to do a little traveling across the Channel, continuing a lifelong pattern of visiting as many countries in as few days as possible. In a letter to a friend at Regis, he outlined an itinerary that would hospitalize any normal traveler.

> *I am leaving on 20 March and sailing to Lisbon; several days there and then fly to Casablanca; train to Rabat, bus to Tangier; ferry to Gibraltar, train to Granada; train to Seville, fly to Madrid where I spend 5 days; fly to Valencia; 3 days relaxing in Palma de Majorca; fly to Barcelona for 2 days; then fly to Nice to change planes; fly to Bastia on the north east coast of Corsica; bus to Ajjacio on the west coast; train to Bonifacio; ferry across to Sardenia and then ferry overnight to Rome where I meet my parents on 10 April. We then spend 3 days in Rome (hence Petosa) then up to Nice, to Avignon, Geneva, Lucerne, St. Gall, Munich, Heidelberg, Koblenz, Cologne, Amsterdam and back here about 26 April.*[28]

After such a frenetic five weeks, an ordinary person would have spent some time catching his breath and perhaps sleeping a little longer, but Feulner was busily weighing his options for graduate school and his pursuit of a PhD. He had applied to the University of Illinois, Northwestern, Pennsylvania, New York University, and Virginia.

In the middle of filling out and mailing forms, he received a life-changing letter from Richard Allen at the Center for Strategic Studies (then affiliated with Georgetown University) saying that the center was "quite interested" in having him as part of a new pilot program that would begin that fall. He would spend one year at the center doing research in a specific area of economics and a second year working on the staff of a congressman.

Allen explained that while it was a full-time position, Feulner would be "perfectly free" to pursue graduate study, preferably at Georgetown. "We have met only once," Allen wrote, "but on the basis of that meeting, and subsequent close scrutiny of both your records and promise I feel certain that you are facing a very successful future." He offered a salary of $6,500 ($45,000 in 2012 dollars), an attractive sum for a young graduate student. Allen added this closing argument: "I think I am correct in predicting that you would acquire experience under circumstances available to only a few today, if available at all."[29]

He asked for an immediate response and got one. Feulner sent a cable the same day he received Allen's letter, followed by a letter in which he said, "I am thrilled that you have given me [this] opportunity." Allen wrote back, "We look forward to welcoming you here at the Center this September."[30] Allen and Feulner agreed to meet later in London to go over the details of the new CSS program.

Dick Allen's letter of invitation would transform Ed Feulner's life, bringing him to Washington, D.C., the center of American politics and public policy, but a city enthralled by the notion of a Great Society, which, according to its creator Lyndon B. Johnson, would give every citizen "full equality," rebuild the urban United States, free every citizen from "the crushing weight of poverty," and make it possible for all nations to live "in enduring peace."[31]

In such a city, conservatism seemed almost absurd, but when the Great Society imploded, the advocates of conservatism were prepared to provide an alternative vision.

CHAPTER 3

THE CAPITAL
OF THE WORLD

The two young Americans sitting down to dinner at the Reform Club in London in the late summer of 1965 had much in common. Ed Feulner and Dick Allen were conservative by reason of their Catholic faith and education, optimistic about the future as only young men who do not believe in barriers can be, active members of a growing political movement on the American Right, and convinced that notwithstanding Lyndon Johnson's remarkable electoral success the previous November, conservatism had a crucial role to play in America. Both would become prominent players in American politics, Allen as foreign policy adviser to Richard Nixon in his 1968 presidential campaign and then to Ronald Reagan in 1980, Feulner as executive director of the Republican Study Committee in the U.S. House of Representatives and then president of The Heritage Foundation.

But on that London evening, while Feulner was still just a comer in the conservative movement, Dick Allen had already arrived. He had helped start the Center for Strategic Studies (CSS) with two senior partners—Admiral Arleigh Burke, the famed World War II naval hero, and David Abshire, a suave West Point graduate at ease in both the academic and the political worlds of Washington. Allen, who had studied under the eminent political theorist Gerhart Niemeyer at the University of Notre Dame, had just been awarded a prestigious Congressional

Fellowship by the American Political Science Association when Abshire invited him to help organize the CSS and serve as its senior research associate.

Now, over dessert and coffee, Allen explained that Ed Noble, a good friend and conservative philanthropist, had agreed to underwrite a new program at the Center for Strategic Studies (later the Center for Strategic and International Studies). Noble and other trustees of the Noble Foundation understood that Republican members of Congress needed more research help in the fields of foreign policy and national security. They were routinely denied adequate staff by majority Democrats, especially on committees.

Allen had devised a fellowship program under which a graduate student would do research at the center for a year and then spend a second year as a research assistant to a senator or congressman, helping to level the policy playing field. He wanted Feulner to be the CSS's first Public Affairs Fellow.[1]

The timing was right for Ed Feulner. He had thought about teaching—Regis College had hinted it would like to have him back as a faculty member—but he knew he would first need a PhD, which would take several years. And as much as he loved Regis, it was far from everything. He could join his father's firm in Chicago, but selling real estate held little appeal. The thought of working in Washington and on Capitol Hill, where the levers of political power and public policy were located, was intoxicating.

• • •

He spent much of the next year researching and writing about U.S. trade policy with the Soviet Union, often in collaboration with Samuel F. Clabaugh, a retired army colonel with a strong interest in economic strategy. They coauthored a well-received CSS monograph, *Trading with the Communists*, which examined the current literature and particularly the report of President Johnson's Special Committee on U.S. Trade Relations with East European Countries and the Soviet Union.

Clabaugh and Feulner pointed out that the Miller Report (named after J. Irwin Miller, board chairman of the Cummins Engine Company) recommended expanding trade with Communist countries but with several caveats. The trade should be limited to nonstrategic goods. Both Mainland China and Communist Cuba were excluded. The granting of most-favored-nation status (MFN) should be selective and conditional: MFN could be revoked for political reasons, such as interfering in the affairs of another country. A prime example of such "interference" was the brutal Soviet suppression of the 1956 Hungarian Revolution.

The authors quoted from a "Statement of Dissent" by Nathaniel Goldfinger of the AFL-CIO, who wrote that he was disturbed that the Miller Report dealt only briefly with "several thorny problems . . . such as goods produced by slave labor, dumping, [and] market disruption."[2]

Feulner monitored congressional proceedings for the center and watched with growing concern as the heavily Democratic Congress routinely passed measure after measure of the Great Society, like federal aid to elementary and secondary education and Medicare and Medicaid. The former dramatically increased the role of the federal government in school financing. The latter changed the nature of health care in America although falling short of national health insurance (which would be signed into law some five decades later by President Barack Obama).

In January 1966 he wrote his father about President Johnson's State of the Union address and its proposal to initiate "nondiscriminatory housing." If passed, he said, "it would simply be another intrusion of the federal government into a new field where it, constitutionally, has no right to be." It was really stretching a point, he said, to claim that the Interstate Commerce Clause would allow such action. He hoped that the National Association of Realtors would oppose the measure.[3]

In addition to his CSS duties—such as sitting in on hearings of the Joint Economic Committee, reading and annotating the *Congressional Record,* reviewing reports and other congressional publications—Feulner kept the accounts of the Philadelphia Society as its treasurer, suggested authors and wrote book reviews for *The Intercollegiate Review,* and served as district director for Virginia of Alpha Kappa Psi, his college business fraternity. He thrived on the multitasking.

And he never stopped networking, as when he wrote Patrick J. Buchanan, Richard Nixon's chief liaison with the conservative movement, while readying himself for a 1968 presidential run, suggesting that they have Sunday brunch "soon." He had just moved into a much larger townhouse on Prospect Street in Georgetown, which was "much more conducive to entertaining."[4] He suggested to Frank Meyer, who was organizing the annual Philadelphia Society meeting in Chicago, that he invite Gary Becker of Columbia University to speak. Feulner said that Becker's new book, *Human Capital,* would provide "an ideal background" for his presentation, a shrewd prediction. Becker would receive the Nobel Prize in Economics in 1992 for "extending the sphere of economic analysis to new areas of human behavior and relations."

The following year Feulner wrote Milton Friedman, the newly elected president of the American Economic Association (of which Feulner was a member), suggesting his friend and mentor Richard Allen as a panelist speaker on the subject of "convergence" between East and West at the annual AEA meeting. He listed Allen's several books and pointed out that he had lectured on the subject at "more than twenty colleges and universities in this country and in Europe."[5] He reached out beyond U.S. borders, welcoming the chairman of the Conservative Party of Sweden to the Center for Strategic Studies and apologizing for not organizing a more extensive program for him.

Still committed to getting a PhD, Feulner enrolled in Georgetown University seeking a doctorate in economics and began taking nine hours of graduate classes at night. Tuition was $1,200, which he paid out of his own pocket because he refused "as a matter of principle" to take out a National Defense Education Act or other government loan.[6]

His favorite professor was Lev E. Dobriansky, "who had his head screwed on straight and was not all wrapped up in numbers."[7] Dobriansky was a committed anti-Communist and originator of the annual Captive Nations Week, authorized by Congress in 1959 and proclaimed by every president since Dwight D. Eisenhower. Feulner admired Dobriansky for his mind-stretching vocabulary—swinging back and forth from one opinion to another was "pendulumic"; a propensity to obey was called "obediential." There was the professor's willingness to challenge conventional Cold War wisdom. Declining to endorse the extremes of détente or nuclear war, Dobriansky declared dismissively, "The Soviets are not ten feet tall."

The Soviet Union would collapse, he argued, if it were separated from the captive nations behind the Iron Curtain as well as the subjugated nationalities like the Ukrainians within its borders.[8] Dismissed at the time by most analysts, Dobriansky's strategy of building up American strength and exploiting the imperial weakness of Moscow was proven correct in 1989, with the fall of the Berlin Wall and the collapse of Communism in Eastern and Central Europe.

Wanting to introduce Dobriansky's creative thinking to the ISI, Feulner suggested that his professor write an article for *The Intercollegiate Review* comparing U.S. trade with Nazi Germany in the 1930s to present U.S. trade with the Soviet Union and Eastern Europe. Both the student and the professor saw parallels between the twentieth century's most deadly isms—Nazism and Communism. Feulner hoped that Dobriansky would expose the thinking of those advocates of East-West trade who believed that "the people in East Europe or the [Soviet Union] can be bought." This is the kind of "idealistic liberal thinking," he wrote, "that has permeated our foreign aid program for so many years" and that has failed of success, as Peter Bauer at the London School of Economics and other scholars had shown.[9]

In the late spring of 1966, Feulner had an opportunity to view Communism up close when he and Edward Chapin III, the Republican candidate for Congress from Georgia's seventh district (who later lost to his Democratic opponent), visited Moscow, Prague, Budapest, Berlin (East and West), and London. It was his first trip to the Soviet Union, which he found to be rigidly Marxist-Leninist. "Those who claim we are heading toward a détente with the Soviet Union," he wrote the president of Regis, "are engaging in idle dreams."[10]

Summing up his impressions, he said that the Iron Curtain "is still very iron." On this trip and one he had made the previous summer, he was "overwhelmed' by the border installations—"machine guns in lookout towers; four or five fences of barbed wire, with mined fields in between; guards on patrol with dogs; etc." For those who have forgotten that "there is still a Church Suffering," he suggested they attend the six a.m. mass at the Gothic cathedral in Prague "to see what the faithful have to put up with" and the suffering the "truly heroic clergy is constantly subjected to."[11]

To strengthen his academic credentials, Feulner reviewed Henry Hazlitt's latest book, *The Foundations of Morality,* in *The Review of Social Economy,* the journal of the Catholic Economic Association (which became the Association for Social Economics), of which he was a member. He commended Hazlitt for his "spirited defense of capitalism" and his rejection of the claim that "the market system is morally indifferent." To the contrary, according to Hazlitt, capitalism is the "only" economic system based on freedom, which is the sine qua non for a moral act.

However, the young Catholic economist disagreed strongly with the last chapter, in which the agnostic Hazlitt offered "the force of someone else's opinion whom the actor deeply respects or admires" as a substitute for a moral code based on a religious framework. Nevertheless, Feulner concluded, "the skillfully constructed defense of capitalism" made *The Foundations of Morality* "a worthy addition" to the library of a serious economist.[12]

In late 1966, at the end of his first year at CSS, Ed Feulner carefully considered his options for his forthcoming year on Capitol Hill. They were Republican Senate leader Everett M. Dirksen, where he would probably "lick postage stamps"; Representative Donald H. Rumsfeld (R-IL), whose primary area of international interest was Latin America, a region of marginal interest to most Americans, including Feulner; and Representative Mel Laird (R-WI), head of the House Republican Conference. Regarded as the "idea man" of House Republicans, Laird offered the greatest opportunity, politically and intellectually.

Meanwhile, Dick Allen had moved from the Center for Strategic Studies to the Hoover Institution on War, Revolution, and Peace at Stanford University, taking the Noble grant with him. Accordingly, Feulner became Laird's public affairs fellow under Hoover's sponsorship. That would lead to his meeting Glenn Campbell, the head of the Hoover Institution, the nation's oldest conservative think tank, and adding to his knowledge of conservative research organizations.

• • •

Feulner spent the next three years working for Mel Laird, one of the shrewdest men in Congress, first as an aide at the House Republican Conference and then, when President-elect Nixon named the Wisconsin congressman his defense secretary, as confidential assistant to the special assistant to the secretary and the deputy secretary. The young conservative operated on two seemingly simple rules: (1) never turn down any assignment, and (2) do everything well and on time. Once Laird and the others in his office, whether on the Hill or at the Pentagon, realized how competent and indefatigable Feulner was, they gave him more and more to do.

In his first year on Laird's staff, when he was still formally a Hoover fellow, the twenty-six-year-old Feulner carried out an amazingly wide variety of assignments. He wrote major floor speeches for the congressman on revenue sharing and foreign policy (Vietnam and Latin America were the subjects). He served as the staffer on the Republican Task Force on East-West Trade, for which he wrote all the press releases and all the staff memos and whose business and staff affairs he generally conducted. He prepared a briefing book on South America for Richard Nixon—flying to Pittsburgh with two senior experts to meet and discuss the report with the former vice president.

To acquaint himself with a part of the world about which he knew comparatively little, he spent two weeks in Central America and submitted a comprehensive report with emphasis on Panama and the proposed Panama Canal treaties (he recommended rejection). He personally raised all the money for his Central America trip, declining Laird's offer to share the cost so as to avoid any semblance of a conflict of interest. (Half came from the Hoover Institution with Dick Allen's approval, the other half from Feulner's pocket.)

He wrote a number of introductory remarks and short speeches for Laird, handled the heavy correspondence resulting from the major floor speeches, and prepared a cost-benefit analysis of the Wood County Project—a $1.5 million vocational rehabilitation program in Wisconsin for the "culturally disadvantaged"—which Laird used in his handling of the project with the Department of Health, Education and Welfare. Feulner discussed revenue sharing with numerous congressional staff, resulting, according to Laird, "in a number of bills being introduced." He also mentored the summer interns of the House Republican Conference, one of them a politically ambitious Wellesley student.

She came to the conference through Representative Harold Collier, who represented Park Ridge, Illinois, and had asked his colleague Mel Laird if he would take on "a bright young woman at Wellesley College who had been a Goldwater girl and who wanted a Washington internship." Laird agreed and called Feulner to say, "Eddie, you have a new intern by the name of Hillary Rodham." Right after Bill Clinton's election in 1992, *The Washington Post* uncovered the thirty-year-old connection and asked Feulner if he remembered her. He responded, "She was very bright, very aggressive and not very Republican." In later years, he would joke, "I was Hillary's first boss in Washington."[13]

Working for Representative Laird, Ed Feulner was in effect a one-man think tank. He did all the things a research organization does—research and write, contact the media, advise public officials, hold meetings, raise money, handle correspondence, mentor interns, and network within the Washington community. It was invaluable on-the-job training for the future president of The Heritage Foundation.

At the same time, he did research for Agatha Schmidt, Bill Buckley's longtime assistant at *National Review*; wrote a "Washington Report" for the pro-national-defense organization the American Security Council; and talked about Richard Cornuelle's innovative new book *Reclaiming the American Dream* at a statewide meeting of the Georgia Young Republicans.

He just hated to say no to anybody, which made a letter he wrote to the director of alumni affairs at the Wharton School very unusual.

Because of his new job with Representative Laird and his PhD studies at Georgetown, he explained, he would not be able to "spend much time on organizing the Washington area Wharton School alumni." He then left the door open by promising "to do what I can as long as the commitment is kept to a minimum." As we have seen, Ed Feulner's "minimum" was an ordinary person's maximum.

Seeking to expand his social life, he and his childhood friend Bruce McEvoy rented a three-story townhouse at 3336 Prospect Street, N.W., in Georgetown, from an elderly lady who was taken with the two young men and their assurances they did not smoke. The monthly rent was a quite reasonable $660. They soon had another housemate, John Lehman, whom Feulner had met at an ISI seminar. Lehman, who would serve as secretary of the navy in the Reagan administration, recalls that "we had a lot of fun. We were always having bull sessions with various people about issues—it wasn't a typical bachelor pad. And we had a lot of good dinner parties—they'd hardly qualify as chic, but they were great fun."

"We hit it off right away," remembers Lehman. "Ed was an intriguing guy and clearly a doer who wanted to get things done. He combined practice and theory like Dick Allen, who introduced me to Ed."

In the 1980s when he was navy secretary, Lehman looked to Heritage for talking points papers and experts who could be used to persuade members of Congress to approve the administration's military buildup. "It was no good having a center for advanced studies with a lot of eggheads who were immersed in theory that no one else could understand. You had to have an organization with the intellectual firepower and the ability to translate its work into usable ideas."[14]

At the end of Ed Feulner's first year, Mel Laird knew that he had the productivity of two or maybe three people in Feulner and offered him a permanent position as a research analyst with the House Republican Conference. In a summary letter to Dick Allen, Laird called the Hoover public affairs program "a very real success" and Feulner's contribution "substantial." He hoped the program would be continued and expanded.[15]

• • •

But the plans of every American were interrupted by a series of unforeseen and violent events throughout 1968. The Vietcong nearly seized the U.S. embassy in Saigon. President Johnson declined to run for reelection, while students chanted outside the White House, "Hey, hey, LBJ, how many kids did you kill today?" The leader of the civil rights movement was foully murdered. The brother of an assassinated president was himself assassinated while campaigning for his party's presidential nomination. Chicago—Ed Feulner's hometown—became a tear-gassed battlefield during the Democratic National Convention. A hundred and one college campuses exploded in frustration and anger.

In his January 1961 inaugural address, President John F. Kennedy had declared that "we shall pay any price, bear any burden, meet any hardship, support any friend, oppose any foe to secure the survival and success of liberty."[16] Eight years later, more than 600,000 people held giant antiwar "moratorium" demonstrations in Washington, D.C., demanding U.S. withdrawal from Vietnam. A nervous populace wondered, "What's happening to America?"

Feulner offered a conservative perspective on the troubled state of the nation at the August 1968 national convention of the Alpha Kappa Psi fraternity. He was nominated for national president but asked that his name be removed from consideration because he could not give the office the time and attention it demanded. He used the occasion to present a tour d'horizon of U.S. and world politics and issue a challenge to his fraternity brothers.

Calling higher education "the cornerstone" of America's cultural heritage, he expressed his concern about the calls of the William Sloane Coffins for civil disobedience, about the Columbia Universities and their civil insurrection, "which is nothing short of guerrilla warfare," about SDS and the other radical groups that call for "academic freedom" for themselves but "trample on everyone else's freedom."[17]

Noting the ever-expanding role of the federal government in education, he reported that the Department of Education was considering a policy of cutting off or slowing down the expenditure of federal funds to a college if a fraternity on its campus discriminated against a minority in the selection of its members. Such a step, he said, would strike at the very heart of the fraternity system and its right to discriminate—"not on the grounds of creed or color which has been against our policy for many years" but on the basis "of who can make the best contribution" to a chapter. He quoted Alexis de Tocqueville: "No sooner does a government attempt to go beyond its political sphere than it exercises, even unintentionally, an insupportable tyranny."[18]

The government's action against the fraternity system, Feulner said, was coming at a time when America's colleges and universities needed fraternities like Alpha Kappa Psi, with their high ideals and strong professionalism that produced "Joe College" students, not "pseudo-intellectual beatniks." "*We* are the real voice of America's students," he declared.

Looking abroad, he noted that the Soviet Union remained a danger to the cause of freedom, as demonstrated by its recent invasion of Czechoslovakia. What does that have to do with Alpha Kappa Psi? he asked, before explaining that that "there can be no Alpha Kappa Psi in Czechoslovakia or the communist half of the world."[19]

Whether at home or abroad, whether considering civil insurrection, governmental intervention, or international Communism, he said, the nation faced a world in crisis that necessitated that "we all take a very active personal part in the American system—the system of free, strong, private institutions" that form the core of a free society. Alpha Kappa Psi and institutions like it are more important than ever before, he concluded, because of "the domestic decay and international disorder" that confront our nation and ourselves.[20]

The insightful analysis—and the decision not to seek the national presidency of his fraternity—marked a milestone in the maturation of Ed Feulner, who at twenty-seven was learning when to say yes and when to say no, although he much preferred the former.

The tumultuous year 1968 ended with one of the closest presidential races in modern times. The final tally was Nixon 43.4 percent, Democrat Hubert Humphrey 42.7 percent, and independent George Wallace 13.5 percent. Nixon's popular margin over Vice President Humphrey was a slim 510,000 votes.

A campaign aide, Kevin Phillips, published a seminal work on Nixon's victory, titled *The Emerging Republican Majority*. He showed that the old Democratic coalition was disintegrating and a new Republican coalition was emerging. He predicted that the new Republican majority would be based in the Midwest, the South, and California, while the Democratic minority would be limited to the Northeast and the Pacific Northwest. Rather than appeal to liberal groups in the inner cities and the traditional suburbs, Phillips argued, the GOP should take advantage of the "populist revolt of the American masses who have been elevated by prosperity to middle-class status and conservatism." The primary target for future elections should be the fast-growth states like California, Arizona, Texas, and Florida.[21]

Phillips's analysis was adopted by Republican strategists and would produce presidential winners like Ronald Reagan and the two Bushes—George Herbert Walker and George W.—and a Republican congressional majority in the 1990s. Those victories would greatly expand the conservative movement and enable The Heritage Foundation to become a major player in public policy in just a few years rather than the decades it had taken other Washington think tanks. From the start the fortunes of Heritage and the conservative movement were inextricably linked.

With Nixon's election, Ed Feulner moved to the Pentagon as confidential assistant to the special assistant to the secretary of defense. His main area of responsibility was to vet the résumés and applications of those seeking a political job in the department. Out of three million people, civilian and military, in various Defense agencies, he noted, "there were about 92 or 93 political slots to fill." The right balance between national security competence and political reliability had to be struck. Feulner found himself frequently explaining to the White House Office of Personnel why his boss had appointed someone "who was right on defense" but had politically irritated almost "everyone else in the administration."[22] His experience would lead him to coin one of his favorite sayings, "People are policy."

The days at the Pentagon were exciting but frustrating. "You had to fill out a requisition form for *everything*, even a pad of paper." The young conservative was also distressed by what was happening within the Nixon administration. Decisions on defining issues, like U.S.-China relations and government regulation, were increasingly veering to the left of center. Abandoned by Nixon was the "New Spirit of 1976" with its liberating language about "the great vital voluntary sector" that he had championed in his campaign speeches. In its stead was a so-called New Federalism that preserved federal control of state spending through bureaucratic oversight of billion-dollar grants. Governors happily took the money and kept the welfare state growing.

Under Nixon, the historian Stephen Hayward points out, social spending exceeded defense spending for the first time, more than doubling from $55 billion in 1970 (Nixon's first budget) to $132 billion in 1975. He approved substantial increases in funding for the Model Cities program and the Department of Housing and Urban Development.[23]

• • •

Feulner's immersion in politics and policy was far from total. Feulner, McEvoy, and Lehman hosted weekend parties, including an annual "big bash," in their Georgetown townhouse on Prospect Street. "Ed got into wine," recalls Bruce, who was working toward a master's in business at

American University, "and before long we had an impressive wine cel-
lar." The two Elmhurst boys bought a twenty-six-foot Chris-Craft and
sailed down the Potomac River without a single lesson, winding up late
at night in what they thought was an empty inlet but turned out to be a
bay of crab traps. They immediately signed up for a crash course in sailing and navigation, and before long "Ed was as good a chart reader as
there is." They soon sold the boat and bought a two-hundred-acre farm
in West Virginia, which, following a Feulner inspiration, they tried
and failed to turn into a Christmas tree farm. "Things were never dull
around Ed," says McEvoy.

It was about this time, in 1967, that Ed Feulner noticed, from the
balcony of his third-floor room, that someone new, and very attractive,
had moved into the basement apartment at 3338 Prospect Street. He
introduced himself to Linda Leventhal, a tall slender beauty from the
East Side of New York City. Also a cradle Catholic, Linda was a graduate of Tufts University with a BS in occupational therapy who had come
to Washington to intern and then work at D.C. General Hospital. Ed
was captivated by her grace, delighted that she shared his faith (she had
attended the Convent of the Sacred Heart in Manhattan), and intrigued
that she rode a motorcycle to work. He was so taken that he began a
regimen of strenuous dieting and reduced his weight to 180 pounds.

He kept an eye on Linda's comings and goings from the third floor,
and soon Ed and Linda got into the habit of talking to each other, late at
night—he from his balcony, she from the stoop of her house—a modern
Romeo and Juliet, but with their positions reversed. Their courtship of
a little more than eighteen months included boat trips on the Potomac,
double dates with McEvoy, and a weekend at the West Virginia farm
cut short by an inquisitive neighbor who peered at the young couple
through the living room window, startling Linda.

Ed proposed to Linda at the Sans Souci restaurant on 17th Street,
N.W., around the corner from the Metropolitan Club. When Linda
went to the ladies' room following dinner, Ed slipped the engagement
ring into her glove lying on the table. They were married on March 8,
1969, in the Gothic-style St. Thomas More Catholic Church on East
89th Street in New York City—the parish church of Jacqueline Kennedy Onassis until her death. Bruce McEvoy was best man. Holley Kil-
cullen, Linda's sister, was the matron of honor.

Linda had hoped that her father—"so kind and debonair"—would
be able to give her away. But Stanley Leventhal suffered from agorapho-
bia, the fear of public places. He was able to come to the church, but

as they stood at the back before the wedding march began, he said to Linda, "I'm sorry, but I can't walk you down the aisle, I just can't." "I was devastated," Linda recalls, "for him." But her mother had Linda's favorite uncle, Myle Holley, standing by. He stepped forward to escort a shaky Linda down the aisle, while her father watched from the rear. "It could have been the worst of days," Linda says, "but it turned out to be the best of days for as soon as I saw Ed waiting for me in front of the altar with his biggest smile, I just knew life would be wonderful."[24]

At the wedding reception, the bride and groom were ready to celebrate with their families and friends. Ed was allergic to champagne, so Bruce McEvoy had arranged, without Linda's knowledge, for ginger ale to be poured into a champagne bottle and served to Ed all evening. "He was his usual ebullient self throughout the reception," recalls Linda. "Bruce told me of the 'big switch' later that night as we left for our honeymoon."[25]

The couple honeymooned in Florida at a condo provided by a friend of Ed Feulner, Sr., taking an excursion to the sunny Bahamas. But after a week on the beach with his bride, Ed was ready to return to Washington and the conservative cause. The young couple took up residence in a two-bedroom apartment at 1200 South Court House Road in Arlington, Virginia, close to the Pentagon.

"From our window on the seventh floor," he remembers, "I could literally see the Pentagon bus coming up Columbia Pike, and when I saw it make the turn at the top of the Pike, I knew it had one more stop to make. So I would shoot out the door of our apartment, run down the seven flights of stairs, turn around and wave up to Linda, and be at the bus stop before the bus got there. I'd be at the Pentagon in about four minutes. That only lasted for about a year, but those early days were kind of fun."[26]

In September 1971, Edwin John III (E.J.) was born, and Emily Victoria arrived in April 1973. Like his father, Ed was a devoted dad who regularly gave the children their baths, put them to bed, and did family errands with them. One of Emily's favorite memories is of Saturday mornings when they would visit the car wash (which she called "the Octopus"), make deposits at the bank ("he let me put everything in the tube"), and drop off his shirts at the dry cleaner. "He made everything so much fun. We would go skipping through the parking lot."[27]

They would usually wind up at the Dixie Pig Restaurant on Route 1 for lunch. One Saturday Emily couldn't decide whether to have a bacon sandwich or a tuna salad sandwich, so the cook put them together and created what Ed called the "Emily Sandwich," which she ordered from then on. A special day for father and daughter is Christmas Eve, when just the two of them have lunch and then go shopping for family presents.

Years later, to her father's delight, Emily decided to study in the United Kingdom, spending her junior year in college at Oxford University, where she discovered she loved political philosophy and especially John Locke. "It opened up a whole new life for her," says Linda Feulner. Asked what she remembers best about her father, Emily replies, "He gave us such a gift by taking us to church every Sunday." In second place are the visits to Europe, where she met Margaret Thatcher and Jacques Chirac kissed her hand.[28]

• • •

Because of his very poor eyesight, Ed could not play catch or kick a soccer ball with his son, but he made it a point to attend E.J.'s games when he wasn't traveling—"whether it was on a Thursday afternoon or a Saturday." E.J. remembers a lacrosse game on the Mall played in a downpour and looking over at the sideline to see his father and Linda's sister huddled under an umbrella and waving him on.[29] When E.J. took up skateboarding, his father built an enormous skateboard ramp in their driveway. When E.J. started dirt biking and then dirt bike racing, his father came to his races.

Ed introduced his son to a sport that had captured his interest—high-performance car driving. They drove his bright red 1982 Mercedes convertible to a West Virginia track rented by the Washington Mercedes Club. They took turns going around the racetrack, which was a road course, not an oval like the Indianapolis 500. Mercedes provided professional drivers who taught participants how to handle the turns and the high speeds. How fast did Ed Feulner go? "We were probably getting up to about 120 or 130," recalls E.J.[30]

Seeking to pass along his love for far-off places, Ed often took his son and daughter with him on his overseas travels—Emily usually to Europe, E.J. to Asia. "Hong Kong is my favorite city in the world," says E.J. "The first time I ever tried waterskiing was there. Dad likes to say that I learned to ski on Repulse Bay."[31]

Ed's favorite poem—tellingly—is Rudyard Kipling's "If," and he began reciting it to E.J. every night when he was one year old and in his crib. As E.J. got older, Ed would lie in bed with him and recite a line or two and then encourage E.J. to say a line. They would go back and

forth until they had recited the whole poem, Linda all the while standing outside E.J.'s room and listening to her husband and her son.

The poem begins, "If you can keep your head when all about you /
are losing theirs and blaming it on you" and it ends:

> If you can fill the unforgiving minute
> With sixty seconds' worth of distance run,
> Yours is the Earth and everything that's in it,
> And—which is more—you'll be a Man, my son!

The poem is framed and hanging today in E.J.'s house.

When E.J. was in the third grade, his father wrote an open "letter to my son" about Independence Day and what makes America so
special—our ability to make choices.

"When I was in Russia a few years ago," he wrote, "just after you
were born, anyone who wanted a car had to pay for it first, and then
wait for a long time to get it. Even then, there was only one kind he
could get, and they all looked the same."

He recounted how when he was growing up, his family had Hans,
a student from Austria, living with them. On his first day with the Feulners, Hans suddenly stopped talking because he had just "seen a bowl
of fresh fruit for the first time in his life." He took pictures of the fruit
bowl to send home because his younger sisters, born during the Second
World War, had never seen oranges or bananas or other fresh fruit.

He recalled how proud he was when E.J. scored his first goal in
the Alexandria soccer league. He reminded E.J. that he had chosen to
play soccer instead of Little League baseball. And then he talked about
the children he had seen in a refugee camp in Vietnam who didn't have
choices like that because their parents had been killed by the Communists. "The only toys these Vietnamese children had were the simple
things they could make themselves out of tin cans and other things we
throw away everyday here in Virginia."

He talked about big choices, too, like voting, and how disappointed
he was that in a recent Virginia election only seven percent of the people bothered to vote. Elections are important, he said, because "we can
choose whether we want people in government who will let us make
more choices or who will take them away."

"Four years ago," on another Independence Day, "Mommy and I"
were in Hong Kong talking to Vietnamese friends who had left their
home and were in a Hong Kong refugee camp. They talked about how

they might help their Vietnamese friends start a new life in Virginia. But it would not be an easy decision. If they came to America, they knew they would have to leave their parents and all their property behind.

A lot of people, he wrote his son, think making choices is easy—just a case of buying a baseball bat or a fishing pole. "But it isn't that easy." Let us remember, he said, that independence means "we have to make choices. Sometimes they are hard choices. But then again, we all learn that anything that is worthwhile isn't easy."[32]

CHAPTER 4

ON THE HILL

As the 1960s came to a close, Ed Feulner would learn that even he could not do it all at the same time. On the surface, his PhD in economics seemed to be going well. He had finished his coursework, passed his German and French exams (Georgetown requiring a knowledge of two foreign languages for a doctorate), and started preparing for the oral examinations that had to be passed before a dissertation topic was assigned.

However, while there was "no overt hostility" among the faculty, Feulner detected subtle derogatory comments about his open conservatism and his work for Secretary Laird, a well-known hawk about the Vietnam War, an emotional issue even at a relatively conservative university like Georgetown.

Feulner also concedes that he became so immersed in Vietnam and other high-profile political issues that it "detracted from my ability to sit down and study rigorous ideas like macro-economic theory." He decided, reluctantly, that a Georgetown PhD was "a no-go" and put aside, at least for the time being, the possibility of a doctorate.[1]

As demanding as his Pentagon job was, Feulner did not neglect the conservative movement, as when in August 1969 he delivered three lectures at the ISI's Western Summer School at Stanford University on "Freedom and Power." His major points were:

- A free economy is a sine qua non for a free society.

- Big government is under attack not only from conservatives but from liberals, so that some, like Harvard's Daniel Patrick Moynihan, noted that the welfare state "has been converted from a means of helping the poor into a method for comfortably employing bureaucrats."

- While both traditional conservatives and libertarians have suggested ways to expand individual freedom, the former's proposals—such as individual income tax cuts rather than the elimination of the federal income tax—are more practical and possible of congressional approval.[2]

The first point is at the heart of one of Heritage's most successful publications—the annual *Index of Economic Freedom,* co-published with *The Wall Street Journal.*

The reference to the liberal Democrat Moynihan anticipates Heritage's willingness to reach out to and work with Democrats as well as Republicans on the right issues.

The third point is an early variation of one of Feulner's most deeply held beliefs—"Do not let the perfect be the enemy of the good," taken from Milton Friedman, who borrowed it from Voltaire.

The Stanford talk prompted Feulner to do some reflecting about his job. Just how much good was he doing at the Pentagon? He was increasingly frustrated by the deliberate pace of the military. As prestigious as it was to work at the Pentagon in the secretary's office, the Department of Defense with its multiple layers of bureaucracy and manifold rules and regulations was just not the right fit for him. His entrepreneurial abilities were of little use. Although he was learning much about "the interaction of ideas and policy" in government—knowledge that he would put to good use at the Republican Study Committee and Heritage—Feulner was receptive when, in December 1969, he received a telephone call about a possible position with recently elected Representative Philip Crane on Capitol Hill.

The groundwork for the call had been laid by Don Lipsett, who had come to know Phil Crane through his frequent talks at ISI events. On November 26, Lipsett wrote Representative-elect Crane strongly recommending that he hire Ed Feulner "to head your Washington office staff." Of greater importance than Feulner's educational and philosophical credentials, Lipsett said, was his administrative ability. "Ed is one of the dozen or so people I know who, when he says he will do something, actually gets the job done."[3]

Crane, a popular and articulate professor of history at Bradley University, had just won a special congressional election (defeating ten other candidates) to succeed Donald Rumsfeld as the representative from Illinois's thirteenth congressional district. Crane had to run again in less than a year in the November 1970 elections and decided to focus much of his personal attention on his reelection campaign. He needed someone in his Washington office who knew "how Washington works" and could help him "do the conservative things he had been promising he would do."

Feulner, who had met the future congressman at an ISI summer school, was just what Crane was looking for. "Ed was very bright," remembers Crane, "a committed conservative, and he understood the legislative process."[4] He was hired as legislative assistant and then became his administrative assistant or chief of staff after Crane was handily reelected.

Demonstrating how small a community Washington can be, Feulner had informally helped Crane win that crucial special election—from Washington. In mid-July 1969 he was having a late dinner at the White House mess with Dick Allen and several other conservatives when Don Rumsfeld walked by. They began talking about the race in Rumsfeld's former district, occasioning Rumsfeld to say there were three candidates out of the ten running whom he did not want to see chosen, including Phil Crane, who he said was an extreme conservative.

Allen and Feulner both quickly responded that Crane was a responsible conservative and not "way out." They pointed to his academic credentials—he held the highest GPA of any student in the history of Indiana University—and his association with the ISI and similar conservative groups. Their defense "seemed to give Don a new outlook on Phil," Feulner wrote a friend. "Phil is a good man and I hope he wins the primary." In that conservative Illinois district, he said, the winner of the primary is "almost automatically the winner of the general election."[5] And so it turned out to be—in part because Rumsfeld did not express a public preference for his successor. Phil Crane went on to serve in Congress for the next thirty-six years, until 2005.

In his January 1970 letter of resignation to Carl S. Wallace, special assistant to the secretary of defense, Feulner stressed how much he had learned working for "the finest politician in Washington"—Mel

Laird. He warmly thanked Wallace for backing him up "under any circumstances" and for his "sympathy with my frustration." All told, he wrote, the last three years had been "the most rewarding period in my life."[6] The next three years would prove to be even more rewarding, and important, for they would culminate in the birth of The Heritage Foundation.

• • •

In the early 1970s there was only a budding conservative movement in Washington. It seemed as though liberals had all the answers and provided all the policies, from détente to Keynesian economics. Young conservatives like Ed Feulner knew that conservatives had better ideas, like limited constitutional government and free enterprise, but they seemed unable to come up with workable legislative proposals.

As legislative and then administrative assistant to Representative Crane, Feulner constantly asked himself: Is this a good bill or a bad bill? Do we have a conservative alternative? Do we have a strategy to pass the good legislation or stop the bad? The answer was almost always no.

"What I needed, as an overworked staffer laboring away in a congressman's office, was nuts-and-bolts legislative research and off-the-shelf policy prescriptions that had a realistic chance of making their way through Congress."[7]

Two pieces of legislation helped convince Feulner and other conservative staffers they had to get organized: the Family Assistance Plan (FAP) and the Child Development Act (CDA). Sponsored by the Nixon administration, both proposals cut sharply against the conservative grain. Nixon called FAP "the flagship" of his legislative program, the "warship from which his colors flew."[8] William F. Buckley, Jr., called it "another tumor on the bulbous welfare body. There is no longer any justification in principle for the bill, and no reason for any congressional bloc to feel enthusiastic enough about it to get it passed."[9]

The FAP aimed to federalize the welfare system and guarantee an annual income for every citizen. It would have enforced a national level of benefits on the basis of need, with few or no work requirements. The CDA contained child-advocacy and child-rights programs that were incompatible with traditional American values.

The FAP seemed on its way to easy House passage in March 1970—the Democratic majority enthusiastically endorsed it—when a small group of Republican congressmen led by Phil Crane, Ed

Derwinski of Illinois, and John Ashbrook of Ohio decided to challenge
it. To help prepare them for the debate, Crane volunteered his administrative assistant Ed Feulner to help research various parts of the bill.
Feulner was joined by Jack Cox, who worked for Representative Barry
Goldwater, Jr., of California; Jerry James with Representative Floyd
Spence of South Carolina; and two aides from the Senate—Paul Weyrich with Senator Gordon Allott of Colorado and James Lucier, a special assistant to Senator Strom Thurmond of South Carolina.

In one of those coincidences of history—which some prefer to call
providential rather than coincidental—three of the aides would later
serve as president of The Heritage Foundation while a fourth would
play a pivotal role in a predecessor organization. These young conservatives were a new breed of staffer not previously seen in Congress: conservative first and Republican second; inspired to enter politics by "Mr.
Conservative," Barry Goldwater; sprung from the Midwest, the South,
and the West rather than the establishment East; committed to rolling
back the welfare state, not to managing it more efficiently; readers of
The Conservative Mind and The Road to Serfdom; aggressive and ambitious, not just for themselves but for what they called The Movement.

Although they came late to the debate, the young conservatives set
to work, contacting, for example, state welfare directors to determine
what impact the FAP would have on state programs. They began writing floor speeches for their bosses. They drafted a "Dear Colleague"
letter for Representative Sam Devine of Ohio, a senior Republican, explaining why he opposed the measure.

On April 15 the House narrowly approved a "closed rule" (no
amendments allowed) for the FAP by a vote of 205 to 183. More Republicans opposed the motion than supported it—a major rebuff to the
Republican leadership, which had lobbied hard for the closed rule as
part of its long-held strategy to get along with the Democratic majority as best as it could. The next day the House passed the legislation,
but the large number of Republican defections on the closed-rule vote
demonstrated that conservatives, if organized and supported by relevant research, could make a difference in a policy debate. Feulner and
Weyrich, who had struck up a friendship during the preparation for the
FAP debate, recognized the necessity of being well prepared.

Conservatives immediately began planning a Senate strategy. Crane
and Derwinski contacted Republican senator Carl Curtis of Nebraska,
a senior member of the Senate Finance Committee, which would consider the legislation. They suggested a meeting of House and Senate

Republican conservatives, which might seem obvious but was unprecedented. Liberals had long coordinated their House and Senate activities, but conservatives had chosen to respect the independence of each house. But now, beleaguered by liberals and with a Republican president turning left, conservatives took Benjamin Franklin's advice and decided to start hanging together.

Jerry James offered a further suggestion. Why not invite Dr. Roger Freeman, a senior fellow at Stanford University's Hoover Institution, to testify before the Senate Finance Committee and privately brief committee members? Freeman was a nationally respected economist who had resigned from the Nixon White House over the FAP issue. He was commissioned—by a conservative research firm—to write a rebuttal to the FAP and to provide an alternative welfare reform program based on block grants to the states. His eighty-eight-page study received official recognition by being published as a committee report of the Democrat-controlled Senate Finance Committee. Freeman concluded that the FAP was "a form of guaranteed annual income" and "would have immediately more than doubled the number of public assistance recipients and lifted welfare outlays to new heights."[10]

The Hoover academic's participation was critical. As the political scientist Allen Schick wrote, "Congress can more easily exploit work done by others than carry the main burden of analysis by itself." That insight would be incorporated into the core mission of The Heritage Foundation, which is never happier than when a member of Congress "exploits" its analysis.[11]

Senator Russell Long, the Democratic chairman of the Senate Finance Committee, invited Governor Ronald Reagan to testify before the committee. Reagan argued forcefully against the proposal, estimating that the FAP's true cost was closer to $15 billion than to the White House projection of $4.4 billion. He said that its work requirement was weak and would make it more profitable for people to remain on welfare rather than to work. "I believe," he said, "that the government is supposed to *promote* the general welfare. I don't think it is supposed to *provide* it."[12]

On November 20, 1972, after months of deliberation and several hearings, the Democrat-controlled Senate Finance Committee rejected the Family Assistance Plan by a vote of 10 to 7, with Russell Long, the chairman of the Senate Finance Committee, among the nos. It was a stunning upset. With modest staff resources but a carefully conceived strategy, conservatives had delayed and then buried the keystone of the Nixon administration's domestic agenda.

Years later a disillusioned liberal Democrat, Senator Daniel Patrick Moynihan of New York, who had conceived the FAP as a White House aide to Nixon, wrote an apologetic letter to William F. Buckley, Jr.:

> I've had a week here, reading and fussing with a great mound of research reports on the guaranteed income experiments which we started in the late 1960s. . . . Were we wrong about a guaranteed income! Seemingly, it is calamitous. It increases family dissolution by some 70 percent, decreases work, etc.[13]

Coalition building, politicking, and delaying tactics all contributed to the FAP's defeat, but Ed Feulner is convinced that research made the difference: "We were able to change the minds of some key people."[14]

Feulner later argued that the conservative victories on the FAP and the Child Development Act "might easily have been the beginning of the end of the [Lyndon] Johnson-type Great Society programs. They provided the base for the formation of the Republican Study Committee."[15] And Ed Feulner's experience as executive director of the RSC enabled him to make a quick start as president of The Heritage Foundation.

• • •

The key congressman in the creation of the Republican Study Committee was Phil Crane, who appreciated the importance of ideas and their impact on public policy. In his bestselling book, *The Democrat's Dilemma,* Crane told the story of the Fabian Society—led by Sidney and Beatrice Webb—and its fifty-year campaign to turn Great Britain into a socialist country, basically by capturing control of the Labour Party. He argued that American Fabians were attempting the same thing in the United States by using organized labor and organizations such as the League for Industrial Democracy to control the Democratic Party.

Crane admitted that while the Fabians had made significant progress toward converting America into a socialist state, the majority of Americans did not hold socialist beliefs but still believed in First Principles like free enterprise, republican government, individual liberty, and private property. He refused to despair and quoted Charles Beard: "When it gets dark enough you can see the stars."[16]

In such an atmosphere, a counterorganization inside the House of

Representatives was urgently needed. Such a group, Crane knew, would require aggressive young House members, the involvement of senior members, and a staff that could produce reliable independent research. Liberal House Democrats had relied on the Democratic Study Group for research help since the 1950s—no such group had ever existed on the Right.

In May 1971, Crane shared his idea with two young conservatives whom he had learned to trust—Ed Feulner and Paul Weyrich. They decided to hold a two-day meeting away from Washington—at the historic Red Fox Inn in Middleburg, Virginia—at which they would discuss how to organize conservatives in Congress. Among the invited were senior staff aides on the Hill, the executive director of the American Conservative Union, and several businessmen who were political supporters of Crane.

Feulner and Weyrich drew up an agenda that included electoral and policy politics. Weyrich argued that conservatives should focus their House political activities on electing a handful of potential leaders who could set a legislative agenda or steer debate in the right direction. This strategy would allow conservative activists to target specific congressional districts. If elected, he argued, such members would feel obliged to participate in conservative efforts, such as a House study group. "The dream was exhilarating," Feulner later wrote, "and the Red Fox group agreed to the concept."[17]

Among the candidates targeted for the 1972 congressional elections were Trent Lott of Mississippi, Steve Symms of Idaho, Robert Huber of Michigan, John Conlan of Arizona, Harold Froehlich of Wisconsin, and David Treen of Louisiana. All six would be elected the following year and would go on to hold important positions in the Congress and advance the conservative agenda over the next two decades.

After Weyrich's presentation at the Red Fox Inn, Feulner and another Hill aide talked about the liberal Democratic Study Group as a model to be studied and imitated by conservatives. Crane, Feulner, and Weyrich were more than satisfied with the results of the initial meeting. For the first time a strategy for organizing conservatives on Capitol Hill had been drawn up and approved. They agreed to hold a second meeting after the November 1972 elections, at which they would brief the new members on how a conservative study group could operate outside the formal Republican Party structure.

With President Nixon running far ahead of his Democratic opponent, Senator George McGovern of South Dakota, and Watergate a tiny cloud in an otherwise sunny sky, the Red Fox group had reason to be optimistic about the 1972 elections. Their optimism was justified Nixon carried forty-nine states against the hapless McGovern. Forty-three House Republican candidates were elected, including thirty conservatives and all six of those singled out at the first Red Fox meeting.

At Red Fox II the six freshman congressmen were briefed on foreign policy, defense, domestic, and economic issues. An entire session was devoted to the nuts and bolts of office organization to help the newcomers set up their office as quickly as possible, with special attention given to staffing. Members were urged to hire staffers with conservative convictions and Washington experience. There was a presentation on electoral politics by political analyst Kevin Phillips, who cautioned against Republican overconfidence. What could possibly go wrong? the new members asked themselves, eager to begin changing the way Washington works.

Looking ahead to the first session of the new Congress, the group stressed the need for a comprehensive tax reform package, with major input from free-market economists. Crane argued strongly for the involvement of conservative academics—a departure for Republicans and conservatives, who tended to regard all professors as members of the enemy camp. Crane and Feulner both knew conservative academics who would be willing to testify before Congress and participate in the shaping of legislation if asked. But they rarely were, leaving the field to liberal academics and liberal institutions like Brookings. Crane and Feulner were determined to include professors who argued for limited government and free enterprise, like Milton Friedman of the University of Chicago.

In early 1973, following the two Red Fox meetings and discussions on and off Capitol Hill, House conservatives formed the Republican Steering Committee (renamed the Republican Study Committee after the 1974 congressional elections). "We described ourselves," Feulner says, "as a group of 'conservatives' in general agreement on policy issues, thus drawing a clear distinction between our group and other Republican Party organizations which had no clearly defined philosophical point of view."[18]

Ed Derwinski of Illinois, the senior congressman of the group, became chairman although no formal election was held. Once again, Phil Crane "volunteered" Ed Feulner to coordinate the start-up. Under his direction a part-time staff was recruited in the fields of energy, economic policy, foreign policy, the federal budget, housing, trade, and social issues. Congressmen and their chief aides both felt that the RSC had to have its own professional staff.

Feulner attempted to run the RSC as well as continue to serve as administrative assistant to Crane, but he could not do justice to both. Crane, Derwinski, and Feulner agreed that the most sensible solution was to hire a full-time executive director for the Republican Steering Committee. In June 1973 the committee appointed Dr. Albert Gilman, a former vice president of Western Carolina University who had been active in Carolina politics, as the committee's director. They found an office in the House Office Building complex and began operations.

But immediately there were conflicting views about the committee's role. Some congressmen expected it to provide information about bills coming to the floor. Others saw it as a real conservative think tank. Still others wanted to use it as an alternative to unreliable and Democrat-dominated committee staffs—the ratio of Democrat to Republican on a committee staff could run as high as ten to one. All the committee members worried about becoming too visible and irritating the Republican House leadership. The first mailings to members were sent in plain orange envelopes.

A major legislative agenda was drawn up, which included the elimination of the Legal Services Corporation and a conservative response to the proposed federal land-use act. But after just a short time, the daily demands of the job overwhelmed the academically trained Gilman, who did not realize that he would have to be policy wonk, office manager, fund-raiser, and diplomat all at the same time. When a worried research analyst asked when he would be paid, Gilman responded cavalierly: "It's okay—if I don't raise it, you can take half of next month off."[19]

It was clear the committee needed a new director without delay. After considering several candidates, the committee selected the thirty-two-year-old Ed Feulner, who became executive director of the Republican Steering Committee in February 1974—after resigning as head of the Robert M. Schuchman Center for the Public Interest, a decision we will discuss in detail in the next chapter. Moving quickly to put the RSC on track, Feulner focused on three things—mission, staff, and finances.

He made a series of courtesy calls on members of Congress to get their ideas about the direction the committee should take. He insisted that every RSC staffer meet with the administrative assistant of RSC members at least twice a month. He reminded his staff that part of their salaries came from the members (the rest from his and the chairman's fund-raising efforts). He reassured RSC staffers that they would be paid by instituting a policy of paying the executive director last.

He set about turning the RSC into a smooth-running effective organization. But he found himself frustrated by the daily visits of congressional aides lobbying for the RSC's help with their favorite piece of legislation. Soon the visits were taking up as much as half of his time. So Feulner went to a warehouse filled with old furniture and picked out the most uncomfortable chair he could find and placed it next to his desk. His office was so small, he had room for only one visitor at a time, and Feulner made sure he always sat in the "special" chair. Few aides now stayed more than five minutes, "since sitting in the one vacant chair was so painful."[20] Soon the daily visits became fewer and shorter, and Ed Feulner could spend his time more efficiently.

With Feulner at the helm, the Republican Study Committee would become a major force in the House of Representatives, the Republican Party, and the Washington political community. By the time Feulner left the RSC in April 1977 to join The Heritage Foundation, the organization consisted of 80 members of the 145 Republican members of the House and a staff of twelve.

The committee was a busy publisher, producing *The Case Against the Reckless Congress,* a lively paperback book setting forth conservative positions on public policy issues such as welfare and food stamp reform; *A Research Guide in Public Policy,* an annotated bibliography of scholarly articles about politics, economics, and national security; and *The Research Directory,* a listing of four hundred Washington-based policy experts, including congressional aides, lobbyists, and academics.

It established the RSC Campaign Fund, which distributed nineteen information packets to nonincumbent Republican candidates during the 1974 elections. Several new House members were introduced to the RSC through the packets and expressed their appreciation of the campaign fund's efforts. They willingly joined the RSC upon arrival in Washington.

The committee devoted itself to several major legislative items during this period. The National Welfare Reform Act of 1975 was the RSC's major business during the 94th Congress. It represented an effective partnership between conservatives in the House and Senate and enabled members, recovering from the GOP trouncing in the 1974 elections, to be *for* something after a long period of opposing almost every pending bill. Key provisions included assistance to the truly needy and a "work program" that encouraged welfare recipients to find employment and leave the system.

Another initiative was the Jobs Creation Act of 1975, introduced by Jack Kemp of New York, an active member of the RSC's executive committee. The bill moved House Republicans away from their traditional position of cutting federal spending in order to reduce taxes. Kemp reversed the equation, proposing a substantial tax reduction for individuals and businesses to encourage savings and create jobs in the private sector. His proposal was an imaginative alternative to the expensive and ineffective federal job programs advocated perennially by liberals. Although it did not gain much traction that first year, the Kemp bill was introduced in 1976 as the Kemp-Roth bill and subsequently became the basis of President Reagan's historic tax proposal of 1981.

The committee also helped House conservatives win a major victory in the battle over federal land use. Feulner assigned RSC research director Phil Truluck full-time to the issue. Truluck briefed members and staff, wrote speeches, arranged for a special order on the House floor that included remarks by over twenty congressmen, and worked on language for an alternative land-use bill introduced by Sam Steiger of Arizona. The Steiger substitute offered incentives to the states to adopt their own land-use plans, demoting the federal government to an advisory role.

At a critical juncture, Truluck briefed White House aides about conservative objections to the Democratic bill sponsored by Morris Udall (D-AZ). Two weeks later the White House sent word to House minority leader John Rhodes of Arizona that the Nixon administration was withdrawing its support of the Udall bill in favor of the Steiger substitute.

In June 1974 the House, despite its 243–188 Democratic majority, rejected the Udall measure by 211–204. It was clear to everyone from Udall to the White House that the Republican Study Committee had mobilized the opposition and was now a significant force in the House legislative process. Feulner noted that allowing a researcher (in this case, Truluck) to focus on a single issue materially affected the outcome.

There was a practical payoff for the committee. Two days after the successful floor vote, Rhodes called RSC chairman Lamar Baker of Tennessee to advise him that the committee had been given new space in the Cannon House Office Building, three times larger than its previous quarters. Ed Feulner was delighted. His current office was a converted and not-very-large kitchen. Many of the RSC's files had been stacked over a bathtub in an old restroom.

• • •

As committed as he was to making the RSC a significant force in the House of Representatives, Feulner did not neglect the conservative movement, an integral part of his political DNA. Much of his activity had to do with fund-raising, agreeing with California Democratic politician Jesse Unruh that "money is the mother's milk of politics."

He obtained a $10,000 grant for the Philadelphia Society from the Scaife Family Charitable Trusts through his close relationship with President Richard Larry of the Scaife Trusts; he corresponded with Richard DeVos of the Amway Corporation, whose representative had expressed a keen interest in promoting "free enterprise in an effective manner"; he urged Milton Friedman to visit Washington soon to give "the troops" a needed shot in the arm; he invited Bill Buckley to speak at a dinner meeting at the Capitol Hill Club (the favorite club of congressional Republicans); and he asked Irving Kristol to help place an essay by Representative Phil Crane on the United Nations in *Commentary,* one of the neoconservatives' favorite journals.[21]

In late May 1974 he traveled to Vietnam—sponsored by a private group, the Vietnam Council on Foreign Relations—with nine other congressional aides for five days of briefings and travel within the country. Flying home, he wrote a long letter to Linda describing what he had seen and explaining why he made such trips even though they took him away for long periods from his family.

The government officials whom they met were "most impressive" and were carrying out their jobs often at great personal sacrifice. He mentioned a Vietnamese friend who had gotten his PhD under Warren Nutter at the University of Virginia and was making $25,000 a year at the International Monetary Fund when he decided to return to Vietnam and work for his country "at about $2,000–3,000 per year, leaving his family behind in D.C."

The Communists, he said, "are still on the offensive—killing, shelling, etc.," but the South Vietnamese people still hang on. The delegation visited a refugee camp of about six thousand people who "voted with their feet" and left everything behind them "rather than live under the VC" (Vietcong). One of their escort officers got tears in her eyes when she talked about Hue, her home, because part of her family was buried alive during the Communist Tet offensive of January 1968.

This trip was important, he wrote, "because these people are counting on us for . . . just enough to see them through" and because "we've already invested so much in blood and treasure that we must see it through." "I hope," he said, that "in some small way, our group will be able to help do that."

He supposed that it sounded idealistic to say he made such trips "not because I want to but because it's my duty to do it," but it really was true. "I and all the guys in our group, are idealistic—we believe in certain things and hope to implement them. If we didn't, we could all be somewhere else making more money and getting off work earlier. But it really wouldn't give us, or at least me, the same satisfaction and the same sense of purpose."

He hoped that she would continue to understand "why these trips are important." When, not if, she had the chance to come to South Vietnam, he was certain that "you'll come away with the same impressions" of "a strong, bright people who've had it really rough and who need support for a while longer so they, too, can have the advantages of freedom that we now enjoy."[22]

• • •

In summarizing Ed Feulner's contributions to the Republican Study Committee, Phil Crane, its godfather, asserted that Feulner's entrepreneurial leadership, his intimate knowledge of the House, and his personal friendship with many RSC members "held the RSC together." What he did in terms of the committee's growth and influence was "awesome."[23] Directing the committee was a decisive experience for Ed Feulner, who ended his tenure as a recognized leader of Washington conservatives and of the movement.

The RSC was a reflection of the coalescing conservative movement in America. Before this time, Russell Kirk has written, "the American intellectual renewal of conservative ideas [had been] perfectly unorganized and undirected." Young conservatives like Ed Feulner, Paul Weyrich, and Phil Truluck sought new ideas, refined them, and pursued them inside and outside Congress.

The Republican Study Committee served as the "inside" organization that advanced the conservative agenda, and it does so to this day in the House of Representatives. It worked alongside Republican leaders on the Kemp-Roth tax cuts of the 1980s and on welfare reform in the 1990s, and it bucked party leadership on Bush 41's tax hike in 1990 and the Medicare Part D battle of 2003. In 2011, in the middle of a debt ceiling debate, the RSC introduced and ultimately won House passage of the Cut, Cap and Balance Act, which cut federal spending, capped future spending, and proposed a balanced-budget constitutional amendment. However, the Democratic Senate rejected it.

So much for the inside operation, but what about the outside organization, the conservative think tank committed to the clear articulation and aggressive promotion of conservative ideas, that could inform and guide the work of conservative members of the House and the Senate?

CHAPTER 5

A NEW KIND OF THINK TANK

The early 1970s were not the most propitious time in which to launch a conservative think tank in Washington, D.C. The conservative movement was a congeries of smallish organizations (the mammoth Conservative Political Action Conferences were far in the future), modest-sized publications (*National Review*'s circulation was less than 100,000, *Human Events*'s less than that), and struggling politicians (Vice President Spiro Agnew was fighting to stay on the 1972 Republican ticket, while Governor Reagan was laboring to pass a tax limitation measure in California).

Conservative ideas were out of public favor and largely ignored by the Nixon administration. President Nixon, faced with large Democratic majorities in both houses of Congress, moved in an increasingly liberal direction on domestic issues. He closed himself off from conservative intellectuals like Richard Allen and Martin Anderson, who had advised him during the 1968 campaign. He now preferred the counsel of big-government Democrats like former Texas governor John Connally and Harvard professor Daniel Patrick Moynihan and practitioners of realpolitik like Henry Kissinger.

At home, Nixon instituted wage and price controls and tried to implement welfare state proposals like a guaranteed annual income for everyone. Proudly he proclaimed, "I am now a Keynesian in economics."[1]

He materially expanded government regulation of the environment, creating the Environmental Protection Agency (EPA), the Occupational Safety and Health Administration (OSHA), the Clean Air Act, and the Endangered Species Act. And he signed Title IX, which banned sex discrimination in higher education, paving the way for affirmative action regarding student admission.

In the field of foreign policy, the president practiced détente from dawn to midnight. Once known as the man who "got" Soviet spy Alger Hiss, Nixon traveled to Communist China to toast Mao Zedong. He signed SALT I, accepting nuclear parity with the Soviet Union, and withdrew U.S. forces from Vietnam, despite warnings about falling dominoes in Southeast Asia.

As to think tanks, the American Enterprise Institute (AEI) and the Center for Strategic Studies at Georgetown University (CSS severed ties with the university in 1987) provided most of the analysis for Washington conservatives, with AEI focusing on economic policy and CSS on foreign policy and national security. And yet there was a real need for authoritative conservative analysis in one crucial place—Congress, where liberals had been king for more years than anyone could remember.

The sharp congressional debate in the spring of 1971 over a now-forgotten issue—the supersonic transport plane—was the catalyst for the creation of a conservative public policy organization that could get the right information to congressmen and their staffs at the right time, before a floor vote.[2]

Most conservatives felt that the funds for the SST should come from the private sector rather than the public sector, although some favored continuing the program at taxpayer expense so as to maintain U.S. technological superiority over the Soviets, who had begun SST test flights that year. But they lacked the authoritative analysis that could guide them in a debate.

Shortly after the Senate voted 51–46 to halt government support of a supersonic transport plane, two rising stars in the conservative movement met for one of their frequent breakfasts in the basement cafeteria of the U.S. Capitol. Twenty-eight-year-old Paul M. Weyrich was press secretary to Republican senator Gordon Allott of Colorado; Edwin J. Feulner, Jr., just turned thirty, was administrative assistant to Representative Philip Crane of Illinois.

The two young men had much in common and a history of working together. But they came from far different backgrounds. Feulner's father was a successful businessman; Weyrich's father stoked the furnace at a Catholic hospital for fifty years. Feulner had a MBA from Wharton; Weyrich never graduated from the University of Wisconsin. They also differed in their personalities. Feulner was relentlessly upbeat, the perennial optimist; Weyrich was ever skeptical, an ingrained pessimist. Both were fed up with the go-along Republicans in Congress and were eager to advance a conservative agenda of less government, free enterprise, and a strong national defense.

Weyrich had barely seated himself at breakfast when he waved aloft a monograph from a right-of-center think tank that carefully examined both sides of the SST funding question. It was long, but it embodied the kind of thoughtful research that made it something busy Hill staffers could use to prepare their members for debate. But the study had arrived in Senator Allott's office several days *after* the debate. A perplexed Weyrich contacted the organization's president, a member of his church.

"Great study," Weyrich said. "Why didn't we get it sooner?"

"We didn't want to try to affect the outcome of the vote," the president responded. Weyrich was speechless for one of the few times in his young life.

"Paul and I decided then and there," recalls Feulner, "that conservatives needed an independent research institute designed to influence the policy debate as it was occurring in Congress—*before* decisions were made."[3]

And they had a ready model for their enterprise—the Brookings Institution.

• • •

Brookings was the catalyst for many of the legislative successes of liberals in the 1960s and 1970s. The process was familiar to Washington insiders. A prominent professor would write an article in an academic journal suggesting a new federal program. The idea would be cited approvingly in *The New York Times* or *The Washington Post*. Studies of the suggested program would be underwritten by the Ford or Rockefeller foundation. Brookings scholars would meet with members of Congress and their staffs to discuss how the program might be legislatively framed. Special interest groups would endorse the program and contact their senators and congressmen. A broad-based coalition would emerge—seemingly out of nowhere—backing the bill. The liberal idea would become law, a new government office would be created, a new social experiment would begin, and taxes would be raised to pay for it.

A key moment in this alchemy occurred when Brookings's experts transmuted the academic's theoretical plan into an acceptable legislative proposal.

Such legislative legerdemain was old hat to Brookings, which, as a creature of the Progressive Movement, had long been an advocate for expanding the federal government. In 1921 Brookings's predecessor, the Institute for Government Research (IGR), engineered passage of the Budget and Accounting Act, establishing the Bureau of the Budget. According to historian James Allen Smith, the IGR drafted House and Senate versions of the budget reform bill, organized congressional testimony, and arranged publicity to generate public support. It even housed the new bureau and provided staff until "it could secure its own offices and personnel."[4]

Brookings performed the same service for the John F. Kennedy transition in the late fall of 1960, supplying offices, a library, and meeting rooms at the institution's downtown headquarters on Massachusetts Avenue. According to Smith, the Kennedy people "relied heavily" on nearly one hundred scholars who were working on policy issues for Brookings.[5]

The liberal think tank's direct influence was also evident in the Carter years. A 1976 Brookings study recommended that the B-1 bomber be dropped from the Pentagon's arsenal. Six months after taking office, President Carter announced his decision to scrap plans for producing and deploying the B-1. Another Brookings report urged the United States to withdraw its ground troops from South Korea. Carter declared his intention to effect just such a withdrawal but later changed his mind.

"The Left had a finely tuned policy-making machine," Feulner later explained, "and the Right had nothing to match it."[6]

The idea of a conservative research organization began to take form in 1968, when Dr. James Lucier, an assistant to Senator Strom Thurmond (R-SC), introduced Paul Weyrich to Victor Fediay, a veteran analyst at the Library of Congress. They agreed that conservative senators were often unable to get a grip on key issues for want of information while liberal senators could always depend on the Brookings Institution.

Fediay argued that the answer lay in a for-profit research firm—not a think tank—that would provide conservatively oriented material gratis to members of Congress but would charge corporations a fee for the same material. Believers in free enterprise, the three conservatives set about expounding their idea to Washington corporate representatives, who showed little or no interest. (At this point, Ed Feulner and Weyrich had not yet met.)

Frustrated by the lack of response and the continued ineffectiveness of conservatives in Washington, Weyrich contacted a Wisconsin friend and mentor, J. Frederic (Fritz) Rench, and asked for his help. Rench was a successful businessman and Republican activist. In the spring of 1969, Weyrich, Lucier, Fediay, and Dr. William Roberts, a tenured professor of law at the Catholic University of America, flew to Racine, Wisconsin, to confer with Rench about their lack of success.

After listening to Weyrich and the others complain loudly about the shortsightedness of the U.S. business community, Rench asked quietly, "Where is your business plan?"

They admitted they didn't have one.

"What is your budget?"

They hadn't prepared one.

"How can you expect businessmen," Rench asked, "to support something that doesn't have either a business plan or a budget?"

Weyrich quickly replied: "Fritz, you're right. Will you write one for us?"

Unwilling to say no to a good friend who had a good idea, Rench spent several days that summer in Senator Thurmond's hideaway office in the lower depths of the U.S. Capitol, writing and rewriting a business plan (including salaries, rent, telephone, printing, and office equipment) for a new venture called Analysis and Research Associates, Inc. (ARA). Its annual budget was a modest $80,000.[7]

But even with their new business plan, the would-be entrepreneurs were still unable to find any takers. The future of ARA—and The Heritage Foundation—now turned on the high temperature and scratchy throat of Barbara Hughes, who handled the mail in Senator Allott's office. One morning in the summer of 1970, Barbara called in sick.

The same day a letter addressed to Allott arrived in his office. Ordinarily it would have been directed to his administrative assistant, who would have referred it to the legislative assistant George Will, who later became one of the nation's preeminent columnists and commentators. Instead, an intern gave it to press secretary Weyrich. The letter was from Jack Wilson, who had just become the assistant for political affairs to Joseph Coors, the president of the largest brewery west of the Mississippi and a proud conservative. Coors had told Jack Wilson to conduct a national search for the right "investment" in the conservative movement. Wilson wrote to a number of prominent political figures, including Colorado's senior senator, Gordon Allott, asking for suggestions.

Weyrich's hands trembled as he read the letter. He immediately called Wilson and said, "We need to talk—I have an opportunity in mind for Mr. Coors."[8]

Wilson traveled to Washington, where Weyrich, Lucier, and the others explained the urgent need on Capitol Hill for an independent for-profit research operation. "We razzle-dazzled him" so well, remembered Weyrich, that Joseph Coors subsequently came to Washington for an in-depth briefing. Weyrich laid on an impressive program for the Colorado millionaire, featuring Senator Cliff Hansen of Wyoming, Senator Thurmond, Representative Henry C. Schadeberg of Wisconsin, Representative Ed Foreman of New Mexico, and Walter Mote, aide to Vice President Agnew. Senator Hansen recounted how "the other side" controlled the information flow in Washington and asserted that Weyrich and his associates were "the guys" who could counter the liberals.[9]

Weyrich was excited at how well the presentation had gone until he learned that Coors was also considering "investing" in the American Enterprise Institute. His high hopes collapsed. How could an unknown, untested research firm compete with a respected think tank that had been operating for nearly thirty years?

Weyrich, with the help of Ed Feulner, arranged for Coors and Wilson to visit Lyn Nofziger, a deputy assistant to President Nixon for congressional affairs. They met in Nofziger's large pastel-blue office in the Old Executive Office Building next to the White House.

But first they arranged a little artifice. Nofziger took some of the cigar ashes from the ashtray on his desk and sprinkled them on a thick AEI study in his bookshelf. With a wink, he said he was ready if asked about the institute.

Nofziger had scarcely begun talking when Coors asked, "So what about AEI?"

"AEI?" repeated the White House aide, who strolled over to the bookshelf, removed the AEI study, and blew the "dust" off it. "That's what they're good for—collecting dust. Sure they do great work, but they're not timely. What we need are studies for Congress while legislation is being considered."[10]

Coors later told Weyrich that two things made him decide to back Analysis and Research Associates, despite the youth and inexperience of its principals: Lyn Nofziger's dismissal of AEI as too academic and ARA's "tremendous business plan." And he was not impressed when he was invited to the Pentagon to meet Defense Secretary Laird, who wound up talking about AEI and the wonderful research it was doing. Coors did not think it appropriate for a secretary of defense to make a pitch for a private think tank on government property.[11]

Without ARA and its successor, the Robert M. Schuchman Memorial Foundation, there would have been no Heritage Foundation.

• • •

Analysis and Research Associates, Inc., started as a joint business venture with the Adolph Coors Company, with Coors investing some $250,000 for 1971–72. James Lucier was ARA's president, Jack Wilson its treasurer. Its first office was in a basement apartment behind the Supreme Court. The small staff included a quiet but bright South Carolinian who had been working for Senator Strom Thurmond—Phil Truluck.

Immediately ARA began researching and analyzing key issues on Capitol Hill, including the Family Assistance Plan. It played an important part in its defeat by contracting with Roger Freeman to write an anti-FAP report that was subsequently published by the Senate Finance Committee. And it was Freeman who helped persuade Governor Reagan to testify against the FAP before the Senate Finance Committee in February 1972. Weyrich recalled that Senator Russell Long, the committee chairman, told Senator Carl Curtis that if Reagan came out publicly against the FAP, "we can kill it." At the conclusion of Reagan's statement, Senator Long praised it as "truly magnificent" and the "most eloquent" of any testimony before the committee.[12]

Despite Joe Coors's faith and generosity, ARA had problems from the start. Lucier was an analyst, not a manager. Weyrich was a political activist. Fediay was often out of the city and the country. Roberts was knowledgeable about issues but unpredictable as to performance. ARA was unable to attract other major sponsors. "They were dedicated," recalled Coors, "but not unified." In the fall of 1972, Wilson told Weyrich to find another vehicle—ARA wasn't working.[13]

A concerned Weyrich mentioned his predicament to conservative Hill staffer Dan Joy, who suggested a dormant tax-exempt organization—the Robert M. Schuchman Memorial Foundation, named after the brilliant first president of Young Americans for Freedom, who had died a few years earlier at the age of twenty-seven of a brain embolism. The foundation's board was receptive. In short order, a

reconstituted, Coors-funded Schuchman Foundation opened offices on
the second floor of a townhouse behind the Supreme Court.

The new foundation president was Paul Weyrich; Weyrich, Joseph
Coors, Jack Wilson, and Ed Feulner were elected to the board of directors. Richard M. Scaife, a generous backer of many conservative and
anti-Communist causes, joined Coors as a supporter of the Schuchman
Foundation. Other conservative businessmen, like industrialist William
Brady of Milwaukee, also contributed to the new research organization,
which seemed, with the additional financing and personnel changes, as
if it might find a niche in Washington.

It was decided to divide the foundation, forming the Schuchman
Center for the Public Interest and creating a new as-yet-unnamed public policy research foundation. Paul Weyrich would head the new research organization. Ed Feulner would be president of the Schuchman
Center, which would operate as a public-interest law group, a field long
dominated by Ralph Nader and "other advocates of consumerism and
environmentalism." Writing to Joe Coors, Feulner promised that when
crucial public policy questions were raised, the Schuchman Center
would make certain that "the case for free enterprise will be heard" in
the courts of law as well as the court of public opinion.[14]

After nearly four years with Phil Crane, Feulner was ready to move
on—he did not want to be a permanent Hill staffer. The Schuchman
Center would afford him the opportunity to test his entrepreneurial
skills. He submitted his resignation as Crane's administrative assistant
effective August 20, 1972, but promised he would stay on as a special
assistant through the end of the year to "wrap up several long-range
projects."[15]

Joe Coors's lawyers, led by Edward McCabe, who had directed
much of the research in the 1964 Goldwater presidential campaign,
began preparing the papers for the new 501(c)(3) organization. But they
needed a name for the new entity.

Paul Weyrich studied a list of possibilities. The James Madison
Foundation? One already existed. The Commonwealth Foundation?
Too vague. He considered the name of a Wisconsin congressman whom
he had long admired, but the family objected. Finally one evening an ex-
asperated Joe Coors telephoned Weyrich and told him, "You *will* have
a name by tomorrow."

The next morning, with the foundation still nameless, Weyrich and his
wife Joyce took their usual walk near their Annandale home in northern

Virginia. As they strolled along, a brooding Weyrich lifted his head and suddenly saw a new sign on a vacant lot: "Coming Soon: Heritage Townhouses." He turned to Joyce and said triumphantly, "That's it! The Heritage Foundation!" Lawyers confirmed the availability of the name, and Joe Coors enthusiastically endorsed it.[16] Future Heritage employees would note, wryly, that the foundation owed its name to urban sprawl in northern Virginia created by an ever-expanding federal government.

The Heritage Foundation was formally incorporated in the District of Columbia on February 16, 1973. The three original trustees were Marvin H. (Mickey) Edwards, later a Republican member of Congress from Oklahoma; businessman John Perrino of Rhode Island; and the ever reliable Fritz Rench. On March 23 the board of trustees was expanded to include Paul Weyrich, Ed Feulner, Jack Wilson, and Forrest Rettgers, a veteran conservative who would soon become executive vice president of the National Association of Manufacturers.

Rettgers was elected chairman of the board, and Weyrich became the first president of The Heritage Foundation. He was a logical choice, having the full confidence of Joe Coors, the foundation's leading benefactor. In a staff memorandum, Jack Wilson, Coors's personal representative, explained that Weyrich and Feulner each had "their own areas of responsibility and management" at Heritage and the Schuchman Center. He predicted they would build "the most sophisticated and effective conservative organizations this city has ever seen."[17]

• • •

But the board of directors of the parent foundation became increasingly divided over the direction of the two new groups. Pre-Coors members preferred a more traditional approach to public policy, relying on formal conferences and book-length publications. The new members, led by Weyrich and Feulner, wanted to affect the legislative process promptly with timely studies and legal challenges to pending cases in the federal courts. There were intense discussions turning into disputes about how to spend the funds raised, particularly those obtained through Coors's efforts. In addition, the foundation's often-casual bookkeeping did not meet the high standards Coors was used to. As Dan Joy recalled, "Divorce became inevitable."[18]

The split came to a head at a heated board meeting on January 23, 1974. The primary issue was money, specifically Joe Coors's money. After being told repeatedly by the old board members what he could and could not do with the tens of thousands of dollars he had contributed,

Coors finally stood up and said that was not the way the real world operated.

Saying it was "impossible to continue" under such conditions, he resigned from the Schuchman board but remained in the meeting. When a director later admitted, "We are broke," Coors offered to cover the cost of the February payroll. The generous offer had little effect on the loud accusations and counteraccusations regarding bank statements and fund-raising costs. Deciding there was little chance of reconciling the differences, Feulner and Weyrich also announced their resignations as board members, with Feulner also resigning as president and CEO of the Schuchman Center.[19] The board meeting abruptly ended, said one participant, "in the coldest fashion possible and no one spoke to anyone as they headed out the door."[20]

As frustrating and unpleasant as the Schuchman experience was, Ed Feulner drew from it important lessons that he later applied at The Heritage Foundation. The board of trustees and the senior management of a nonprofit organization must agree as to the organization's mission and work together to advance it. There must be constant and open communication between the board and the CEO and other senior managers. There must be a strict accounting of all receipts and expenditures of the organization—otherwise confusion, misunderstanding, and even chaos were bound to occur. Was it feasible, Feulner wondered, to run a nonprofit organization like a business—or as much like a business as possible?

During the tempestuous January board meeting, Feulner had said he would be willing to take all the various documents, including the bank records, back to the office that night to prepare for an orderly transition. Back in the foundation offices on Second Street, N.E., behind the Supreme Court, the four conservatives who had resigned looked at one another.

"What are we going to do now?" someone asked.

Unsure how to answer, Weyrich began sorting idly through the mail on his desk. Suddenly he stopped. There was an official-looking letter from the IRS. He opened it eagerly. On November 27, 1973, tax-deductible status had been granted to The Heritage Foundation.

"Gentlemen," said Weyrich, "I have the answer." Waving the IRS letter, he said, "Tomorrow, we begin operating as The Heritage Foundation."

They stayed up much of the night, separating the files, papers, and financial accounts of Heritage and the Schuchman Foundation, leaving a modest balance for Schuchman. The next morning Weyrich told the staff of ten they were now working for The Heritage Foundation, which moved to three small offices on the third floor of 415 Second Street, N.E., next to a Gulf gasoline station (and around the corner from the present Heritage headquarters). Jeffrey B. Gayner, who would work for Heritage in a variety of senior research positions for nearly twenty years, recalls a "seamless change" from Schuchman to Heritage. The separation of the two organizations was effective January 31, 1974.

Ironically, the Schuchman split occurred just three days after it had sponsored a successful, well-attended conference on "The Energy Crisis," featuring a sparkling luncheon dialogue between Senator James L. Buckley (C-NY) and Senator William Proxmire (D-WI). During an afternoon panel Milton Friedman argued that the market, not the government, should determine oil prices. "What we need," Friedman said, "is not a specific, detailed [government] blueprint for the future but an adaptable, adjustment machine." Ronald Reagan would adopt just such a policy in the first weeks of his presidency, deregulating oil and gas prices.

Plans for another conference, with Friedman again a featured speaker, were drawn up, but without Coors's support they were abandoned. Within eighteen months the Robert M. Schuchman Memorial Foundation had quietly faded from view.

For its part, The Heritage Foundation would undergo major changes over the next three years before finding the right combination of dynamic leadership and timely research that would turn it during the Reagan years into what liberals and conservatives agreed was the most influential think tank in Washington.

The first months were difficult for the fledgling foundation, including its skeptical reception by fellow conservatives. Fritz Rench recalls a telephone call from a distressed Paul Weyrich, who said that conservative organizations and individuals "are trashing our initiative as divisive and counterproductive. What can we do?"

Understanding that the criticism might be generated by members of the old Schuchman board, Rench calmly proposed that Weyrich send a personal letter to the critics sharing Heritage's mission, inviting them to partner, and closing with a polite "This is where we are headed." In a month, Rench says, "the uproar subsided." Ever since, Heritage has reached out to and shared with all conservative groups—functioning as an "honest broker," in Ed Feulner's phrase.[21] In the early days of a still-inchoate conservative movement, such selfless cooperation was rare.

Just how different Heritage was from the usual conservative research organization of the 1970s can be seen from a Fritz Rench memorandum (written years later) that summed up the foundation's operating philosophy:

It was "socially acceptable" for conservative groups to promote their agendas and positions aggressively.

Such organizations should be managed "adhering to business principles"—an unheard-of idea then.

"Timely" aggressive marketing was necessary and would work. Even hostile elements of the media would respond to reasoned dialogue.

Hands-on "public action" was necessary to successfully promote the conservative agenda and ideas.

A "sane," logical, and well-crafted presentation of ideas—as contrasted with a shouting-from-the-rooftops, lapel-grabbing style—was a must.[22]

Heritage would follow this revolutionary (for think tanks) outline in the ensuing decades, ultimately achieving a public success unimagined by its founders.

CHAPTER 6

WATERGATE WAVES

No other American president in modern history experienced so swift and steep a fall in public favor as Richard Nixon, who won forty-nine states and almost 61 percent of the popular vote in his 1972 reelection but was forced to resign his office in disgrace less than two years later. Yet most conservatives, still remembering Nixon as the young congressman who had exposed Soviet spy Alger Hiss in the 1940s, supported the president through the early stages of the growing Watergate scandal.

When Senator James Buckley in March 1974 publicly urged Nixon to resign in order to preserve the presidency, fellow conservatives did not back him. John Ashbrook said he did not consider resignation "practical," while Phil Crane declared he was just plain opposed to the president resigning. In the Senate, six leading conservatives, including Barry Goldwater, declined to join Buckley. But privately they were dismayed at the mounting evidence of Nixon's involvement in Watergate.

Already badly damaged, the Nixon presidency suffered telling blows in July with the Supreme Court's ruling ordering the release of another sixty-four White House audiotapes and the House Judiciary Committee's formal approval of three articles of impeachment. Any possibility that Nixon might evade impeachment disappeared with the release of his June 23 "smoking gun" conversations with presidential aide Robert Haldeman. Nevertheless, Nixon clung stubbornly to the mast of the White House, hoping the Senate would vote to acquit him.

A distraught Senate Republican leadership decided that someone had to tell Nixon it was time for him to go. They picked a senator who had never hesitated to do what he thought was right for his party and his country—Barry Goldwater.

On the afternoon of August 7, 1974, Goldwater, Senate Republican leader Hugh Scott of Pennsylvania, and House Republican leader John Rhodes of Arizona walked into the Oval Office to meet with the president. When Nixon asked how things stood in the Senate, Goldwater replied, "You can count on about 12 votes, perhaps as many as 15, but not more." And he added that he was not sure that his vote would be one of them, especially on Article II, the abuse of presidential power.[1] Everyone in the room knew that thirty-four Senate votes were needed to defeat conviction. Nothing more had to be said.

The following evening, August 8, Richard Nixon announced in a national telecast that he was resigning his office. A key factor in his decision was the loss of "Mr. Conservative," Barry Goldwater, the 1964 presidential candidate who had inspired thousands of young people like Ed Feulner to get into politics and policy making.

Like every other institution in Washington, Heritage was affected by Watergate. Even before President Nixon resigned, Paul Weyrich concluded that the fall elections would be a disaster for the Republican Party—and conservatives. Always more activist than intellectual, he resigned as Heritage president in March 1974 and started the Committee for the Survival of a Free Congress—a title that fooled no one. Everyone knew he meant a "conservative" Congress. The committee and its nonprofit educational successor, the Free Congress Foundation, would materially influence Washington politics for the next four decades.

Ed Feulner had just become the full-time director of the Republican Study Committee, so Jerry James, a veteran of many legislative battles and a reliable conservative, succeeded Weyrich as Heritage's second president. James was a talented writer, an experienced analyst, and creative—it was he who had suggested getting Roger Freeman involved in the Family Assistance Plan battle. But he was neither a manager nor a fund-raiser, two necessary abilities of the CEO of a Washington think tank. By the end of the year it was obvious to everyone, including James, that he was not the right person for the job. Besides, he was tired of Washington and wanted to return to his native Oklahoma. Before he left in the spring of 1975, he and his colleagues produced a prospectus that offers revealing insights into the pre-Feulner Heritage.

Pointing to the "disproportionate influence" of the Ford Foundation and "the Brookings Institute" [sic] on public policy, Heritage promised to provide in-depth research based on "traditional American economic and social values" and the Constitution. Its audience would be "the public at large" and members of Congress "who struggle to cope with the initiatives of the liberal/socialist think tanks." Some of the language—such as "traditional American values"—would be incorporated later into Heritage's mission statement. Congress is cited as a core constituency, a guiding Heritage principle. But the latter-day Heritage has yet to describe Brookings or any other liberal think tank as "socialist."

The prospectus mentioned areas that would receive "particular [research] emphasis, including international trade, energy, federal spending, public campaign financing, tax reform, environmental issues, legal services, public education, and Social Security"—an ambitious list for a think tank with a handful of analysts. The projected annual budget of $525,000 was a reasonably ambitious goal, which Joe Coors, Richard Scaife, Ed Noble, and other conservative donors enabled Heritage to achieve.[2]

At about the same time, Ed Feulner wrote to fellow conservative Walter Mote, who worked for Vice President Spiro Agnew, sharing his general impressions of how Heritage was doing, from his perspective as the executive director of the Republican Study Committee and a Heritage trustee. He was encouraged. "I think our original hopes are showing great promise," he said, and then took a large leap: "Given enough resources, I think we will have our answer to Brookings." The statement seemed hopelessly optimistic, but turned out to be prophetic.

Heritage had already made a difference for conservative members of Congress, Feulner continued, by using academic experts like Roger Freeman of Hoover and by assigning an analyst full-time to a major issue. Heritage's publications have made "a good impression on the Hill," Feulner reported, "and have always been timely." At last, Feulner concluded, "we have another [key] component in the system to match what the liberals have had for so long."[3]

But right then the organization needed a new CEO. A search committee was formed, and Frank J. Walton, the former secretary of business and transportation for Governor Ronald Reagan in California, was hired as Heritage's third president. He took up his duties on June 9, 1975, when the conservative movement was undergoing major long-lasting changes.

Walton had a new chairman to work with—Ben Blackburn, an Atlanta trial lawyer and four-term Republican congressman from Georgia, who had lost his bid for a fifth term in November 1974. Blackburn was a dependable member of the Republican Study Committee and had been impressed with Feulner's managerial skill. He also remembers Phil Truluck's hands-on research assistance on a federal land-use bill, which, if it had not been defeated by the House, would have been "a disaster."[4] Blackburn would serve as chairman of the board of trustees for eight years, during which time Heritage evolved from a tiny right-wing research group on the fringes of official Washington into Ronald Reagan's favorite think tank and a go-to resource for conservative members of Congress and much of the mass media.

In order to defray expenses in the early days, Blackburn recalls, he would sleep in Ed Feulner's basement when he came to town for board meetings. It was not an imposition, as the two conservatives had become good friends. There would be an informal trustees' dinner at the University Club Friday night and then the board meeting the next morning at the club.

Blackburn vividly remembers his first visit as chairman to the Heritage offices in late 1974. "They were in what looked like a deserted building next to a filling station. The first floor was used by court reporters and was filled with books, reports, and cabinets. You had to make your way through all the stuff to take the elevator to the [third] floor, where Heritage had a couple of small offices with a few desks and chairs."

Heritage's surpassing influence, says Blackburn, "proves the power of ideas. We needed that kind of research facility, attuned to the heartbeat of Congress. AEI did good work but took too long." "The foundation's most important quality," he argues, is "credibility. Their work is solid."

About Ed Feulner, the former Heritage chairman, congressman, and candidate for governor of his state is to the point. "He had his head screwed on right. He would think things through. He was a good picker of good people. He deserves the great bulk of credit for the success Heritage has achieved. I'm proud of him."[5]

•••

It was during Watergate and the chaotic period following it that two major branches of American conservatism came into being. The New Right was a reaction to the attempted liberal takeover of the Republican Party—epitomized by President Gerald Ford's selection of ultraliberal Nelson Rockefeller as his vice president. The neoconservatives similarly responded to the liberal seizure of the Democratic Party, represented by the 1972 nomination of ultraleft George McGovern.

Political analyst Kevin Phillips described the New Right as true believers, firmly conservative, and resolutely anti-Communist, middle-class, and middle American. They saw as their enemy the four "bigs" of modern America—Big Government, Big Business, Big Labor, and Big Media.

Direct-mail expert Richard Viguerie was rightly called the godfather of the New Right because he raised most of its money, but the chief strategist was Paul Weyrich. With funding from Joseph Coors and direct-mail assistance from Viguerie, Weyrich founded or cofounded conservative organizations such as Heritage, the Committee for the Survival of a Free Congress, the American Legislative Exchange Council, and the Senate Steering Committee, and he had a key role in the formation of the Moral Majority, a major player in the political wars of the 1970s and 1980s. The New Right regarded itself as independent of the Republican Party and respectful of all strains of conservatism. "I think," said Howard Phillips, founder of the Conservative Caucus and a frequent presidential candidate, "both the New Right—the iron fist—and the Old Right—the velvet glove—are necessary."[6]

At about the same time, a series of political events jolted a small but influential group of old-fashioned liberals and forced them to move out of their no-longer-comfortable Democratic digs. These happenings included McGovern's left-wing presidential candidacy; the willingness of modern liberals to let Vietnam and other nations under siege fall into the hands of the Communists; the refusal of Democratic leaders to fault the United Nations for its virulent anti-Israel rhetoric; and the revolution in sexual and social relations that produced what the liberal critic Lionel Trilling called the "adversary culture."

"Mugged by reality"—the aphorism coined by onetime Trotskyite Irving Kristol—the neoconservatives attacked the radicals as despoilers of the liberal tradition. Kristol called for a return to the "republican virtue" of the Founding Fathers and invoked the idea of a good society. He endorsed the notion of a "moral and political order" and conceded—with a nod to Adam Smith—that the idea of a "hidden hand" had its uses in the marketplace. Conservatives, led by Bill Buckley, welcomed Kristol and his colleagues warmly, with Buckley saying that Kristol was "writing more sense in the public interest these days than anybody I can think of."[7]

The neoconservatives were, as the political historian Theodore

White put it, "action intellectuals" with connections to America's leading universities and mass media, direct access to officeholders and the
political elite, good relations with major elements of organized labor,
and strong roots in influential foundations and think tanks with
multimillion-dollar budgets.[8]

The New Right and the neoconservatives were not natural allies.
The New Right was deeply suspicious of government, while the neoconservatives embraced it. The New Right loved the mechanics of politics,
while the neoconservatives preferred the higher plane of public policy.
But both hated Communism and despised liberals—the New Right
for what they had always been, the neoconservatives for what they had
become.

It was the neoconservatives' anti-Communism and resistance to the
counterculture that won the approval of conservatives and led to a marriage of convenience. The minister who presided over the nuptials was
Ronald Reagan, who needed the brainpower of the neoconservatives
and the manpower of the New Right, especially the Christian Right, to
win the presidency.

With the addition of the two new groups, the conservative movement became a national movement, empowering the Heritage Foundation at a critical time in its development. Ed Feulner often said,
"Heritage needs a strong conservative movement just as the conservative movement needs a strong Heritage."[9]

• • •

In his two-year tenure, Frank Walton did much to strengthen Heritage.
In his late fifties when he took the reins of the foundation, Walton had
been a successful California businessman before joining the Reagan
administration in Sacramento. He was tall, charming, and almost as
good a storyteller as Reagan. And there was no question about his conservative credentials: his California license plate read CUT TAXES. To
have someone from Reagan's gubernatorial cabinet as head of Heritage
gave the new foundation instant credibility in Washington and among
conservatives.

Walton delighted in calling on U.S. senators and congressmen and
telling them about Heritage and what it could do for them. He once
remarked to Senator Russell Long, chairman of the powerful Senate
Finance Committee, "Think of us as an extension of your committee staff." Long, who commanded a staff twice the size of Heritage's,
must have been amused. But Walton, because of his Reagan credentials,

could get in to see Long when a Weyrich or a Feulner could not—at least not yet.[10]

Nor was Walton shy about asking for money. During his time as president, Heritage's income more than doubled, from $413,497 at the end of 1974 to just over $1 million in 1976. Also, in one of the most important decisions in its history, Walton introduced direct-mail fund-raising to Heritage by hiring Steve Winchell & Associates. Like so many other young rainmakers, Winchell had been trained by Richard Viguerie, the guru of conservative political fund-raising (still active in the business in 2012 after fifty years).

Written by the talented Mary Elizabeth Lewis, the first Heritage mailing focused on the unionization of the military and featured a photo of a very small Heritage and a very large Brookings Institution, which favored unionization. The message was clear: Help David bring down Goliath. The returns flowed in, producing several thousand donors, the first in an ever-increasing number of individual supporters that would approach 700,000 some thirty years later, making Heritage the most broadly based research organization in Washington and the world. Winchell & Associates has remained the foundation's direct-mail fund-raising agency, a continuous client-agency relationship that probably belongs in *Guinness World Records*.

• • •

Meanwhile Frank Walton's former California boss announced in November 1975 that although a Republican sat in the White House, he would be a candidate for his party's 1976 presidential nomination. Ronald Reagan declared that "the American dream" had been mislaid, and he promised to reduce "the power centralized in Washington."[11] Polls showed Reagan more popular than President Ford among Republicans and independents and running ahead of the presumed Democratic candidate, Hubert Humphrey.

But a favored Reagan narrowly lost to Ford in the New Hampshire primary and lost every succeeding primary, including the one in Illinois, his home state. While everyone on his campaign—including Nancy Reagan—was urging him to withdraw, an aroused Ronald Reagan began hitting the president hard on his deficit spending and détentist foreign policy. With the help of Senator Jesse Helms of North Carolina and his astute campaign director Tom Ellis, Reagan delivered a powerful TV address on the eve of the North Carolina primary, declaring his firm opposition to the proposed Panama Canal treaties. To the amazement of nearly every political analyst, Reagan defeated Ford in the Tarheel State and began a comeback that almost made political history.

The North Carolina primary was the most important primary in modern conservative history, second only to the epic battle between Barry Goldwater and Nelson Rockefeller in the 1964 California primary. Goldwater's win in the Golden State assured his presidential nomination and began the transformation of the Republican Party into the conservative party. If Reagan had not won North Carolina, he would, in all probability, have withdrawn from the race and retired from national politics.

Reagan was now on a roll, winning primaries in Texas and California and gaining momentum. But Republicans are loyalists to a fault. They liked Jerry Ford and felt he had earned the nomination through his years of service to the party. At the 1976 national convention in Kansas City, Ford bested Reagan by a mere 117 delegates—1,187 to 1,070.

After his nomination, a magnanimous Ford asked Reagan to join him on the podium to say a few words. Without notes or a Tele-PrompTer, the defeated challenger spoke of the problems facing the nation—"the erosion of freedom," "the invasion of private rights," "the controls and restrictions" on the economy, the "missiles of destruction" that the great powers had aimed at each other.

What will Americans of the Tricentennial in 2076, Reagan wondered, say about the Americans of the Bicentennial? "Will they look back with appreciation and say: 'Thank God for those people in 1976 who headed off that loss of freedom; who kept us now a hundred years later free; who kept our world from nuclear destruction'? . . . This is our challenge" today, said Reagan to a standing ovation from the delegates.[12]

Four years later Reagan would use the same themes—an unfettered economy, individual freedom, peace through strength—to win the Republican presidential nomination and the presidency, and to launch what came to be called the Reagan Revolution. Guided by his favorite adviser, Ed Meese, he looked to The Heritage Foundation to help him shape the revolution.

• • •

While Reagan was trying to move into 1600 Pennsylvania Avenue, The Heritage Foundation—thanks to a $300,000 gift from Joseph Coors—was moving to 513 C Street, N.E., a former union hall and then adult movie theater facing Stanton Park, six blocks from the U.S. Capitol. The new offices afforded much-needed space, but people were still cramped—one analyst worked out of a onetime broom closet.[13]

There was much for Heritage to do. According to an OMB study, the total cost of federal regulations to the American economy in 1976 was an estimated $130 billion ($525 billion in 2012 dollars). The foundation proposed that the administration remove the price caps on U.S.-produced oil. George Washington University professor Charles Moser reported that the federal budget had grown so large that the percentage of national income taken by all levels of government had reached an alarming 40 percent.

And then there was the American health system. Heritage published a sixty-two-page monograph, *The British National Health Service in Theory and Practice: A Critical Analysis of Socialized Medicine*. The coauthors were Eamonn F. Butler and Stuart M. Butler, who would later become Heritage's vice president of domestic and economic policy. The Butlers found "startling parallels" between British socialized medicine, which had produced "unsatisfied demands and shortages" in every health sector in Britain at an ever-increasing cost, and America's Medicare and Medicaid programs. The authors said that "virtually all [cost] restraint had been stripped away" from the U.S. programs since Congress elected to reimburse users of the system on the basis of "reasonable cost."[14]

The inevitable result, the Butlers said, was "inflationary cost increases, declining efficiency of medical services in terms of their costs, and over-equipping of many hospitals." The only workable solution was "a system of private medical insurance" with tax concessions for those who could provide for themselves and "direct assistance for those who cannot."[15]

Led by Stuart Butler, Heritage would make much the same arguments in the 1990s during the fierce public debate over the Clinton health care plan and the equally controversial Obamacare in the 2000s. In both cases, the most debatable issue was the question of the "individual mandate" or whether everyone should be required to have health insurance. As we will see, Heritage favored such a requirement in its alternative to the Clinton plan but later changed its position in its analysis of the Obama plan.

In these early days, Heritage emphasized its quick-response capability. Elected representatives, Frank Walton asserted in a foundation newsletter, are "quickly and accurately informed on any topic of national consequence." "Any topic" was a stretch, but Heritage did cover many of the major issues with a *Backgrounder*.

The first *Backgrounders* usually ran four pages and were printed on beige paper. They did not yet carry the disclosure that is as much a part of Heritage literature as its Liberty Bell symbol: "Nothing written here is to be construed as an attempt to aid or hinder the passage of any bill before Congress." The language came from Heritage's lawyers but accurately represented the foundation's intention to persuade a member of Congress with the content of their research and analysis. However, these early studies fell short of the fact-filled, fast-moving publications that came to characterize Heritage's research in the 1980s and beyond.

In 1977 the foundation published the transcript of a debate between conservative columnist and author Jeffrey St. John and radical Jeremy Rifkin, head of the People's Bicentennial Commission. In several respects it was a forerunner of the recent debate between the Tea Party and the Occupy Wall Street movement. Rifkin called for a second American revolution against Big Business, which he said was running and ruining the country. St. John responded that the People's Bicentennial Commission wanted not a second American revolution but a replay of the bloody French Revolution that "centralized power in the hands of an elite few who claimed to be acting in the name of the people."[16]

An introduction explained that Heritage was pledged "to the preservation and furthering of traditional American values" and hoped that publication of the debate would contribute "to that goal." The phrase "traditional American values" would be formally added to the foundation's mission statement in 1993.

As a matter of policy, Heritage decided in the late 1970s after Ed Feulner became president that it would concentrate on economic and foreign policy/national security questions, leaving the analysis of social issues like abortion, gay rights, and school prayer to other public policy organizations already dealing with them. "We made it clear," Feulner says, "that we were not going to be a Swedish smorgasbord of things that someone in the movement happened to think was good, reasonable, or worthwhile."[17]

But by the early 1990s, the decline of American culture had become so pronounced that Heritage felt compelled to add a cultural policy studies program. William J. Bennett, former secretary of education, was named a distinguished fellow at Heritage and served as the major spokesman for the program. The foundation favorably analyzed several profamily legislative initiatives, including the Defense of Marriage Act.

Today Jennifer Marshall, described by the *National Journal* as one of twelve "power players" in Washington for her work on school choice and other education reforms, heads the Richard and Helen DeVos Center for Religion and Civil Society.

• • •

As the fireworks of America's Bicentennial faded, citizens speculated about their new Democratic president, Jimmy Carter, looking for clues in the 1976 Democratic platform. For conservatives, it made alarming reading.

It said, for example, that the United States "must set annual targets for employment, production and price stability"—a clear endorsement of national economic planning, a fundamental practice of socialism. The platform also endorsed national health insurance, a guaranteed annual income, "mandatory" school busing, gun control, repeal of Section 14(b) of the Taft-Hartley Law (which allowed state right-to-work laws), a sharp reduction of defense spending, and a new Panama Canal treaty. The estimated cost of the Carter platform was $750 billion—suggesting why workers from the far-left George McGovern campaign of 1972 labored so hard for Carter's victory.

The trustees and staff of The Heritage Foundation, meanwhile, completed a third year with mixed feelings about their performance and future. Yes, the foundation was producing solid work and was often cited in the conservative media. But Heritage was seen by most of the Washington establishment as part of the bumptious New Right and found itself on the fringe of policy making. *The Washington Post* described Heritage as "controlled" by Joseph Coors, who according to the *Post* believed that the United States had to be rescued from liberalism lest it become "another version of godless communism."[18]

Heritage was extremely grateful for Coors's generosity—it wouldn't have existed without him. But neither he nor any other donor controlled it. The foundation's first obligation was to remain faithful to fundamental conservative principles like limited government, free enterprise, individual freedom, and a strong national defense.

The mainstream media stressed the Heritage–New Right connection when the foundation's legal counsel, James McKenna, paid frequent visits to Kanawha County, West Virginia, to help parents who objected to the liberal textbooks chosen for their schools. The struggle of the Kanawha County parents against West Virginia's educational establishment (and the National Education Association union) was prominently featured in *Conservative Digest* and other New Right publications.

Further evidence of Heritage's tilt to the New Right was provided by the publication in late 1976 of a *Critical Issues* study, *Secular Humanism and the Schools: The Issue Whose Time Has Come*, by Dr. Onalee McGraw. The thirty-page pamphlet was described as "a case study of the growth of humanistic teaching in the public schools and the efforts of local parent groups to stymie the humanistic trend."[19] It quickly went into a second printing and was one of Heritage's most popular early studies.

But some trustees wondered whether this was the right direction for the foundation. Wasn't Congress Heritage's primary constituency? If so, then policy analyst Milt Copulos's testimony before the EPA about the potential serious burdens to small- and medium-sized businesses of the Toxic Substances Control Act was more important than the McGraw pamphlet about secular humanism—an issue over which Congress had little if any control.

At this critical moment in Heritage's history, Frank Walton announced at a trustees' meeting in February 1977 that his two years as president would be up in June, and he wanted to go home to California as soon as possible. Trustees were forced to ask: Who should succeed Walton? There was even some question whether they could find someone willing to succeed him.

The distribution of Heritage publications was erratic and unorganized. Richard Odermatt, the longtime director and now senior editor of publications, recalls that twice a week he would make a circuit of about twenty conservative congressional offices, dropping off the latest Heritage study, fresh from the foundation's copying machine.[20] But there was no systematic effort to determine who or if anyone in an office read the study.

In these early days, Heritage was not the imposing flagship of a mighty conservative armada, but a small tanker making its way through uncharted waters. Its staff of twenty-six worked cheek by jowl out of a tiny two-story building. They had one Xerox copier, a couple of electric typewriters, and no computers. But they did have a mandatory prayer meeting every Monday morning.

Heritage needed a president who would take command and enable the foundation to realize the hopes of its organizers.

CHAPTER 7

INTELLECTUAL ENTREPRENEUR

In March 1977, one month after Heritage president Frank Walton announced his determination to return to California, U.S. president Jimmy Carter proposed four radical changes in American election laws that would have materially affected the growing conservative presence in Congress: federal financing of all congressional elections, "instant" voter registration, repeal of the Hatch Act that prevented the active participation in politics of federal employees, and the direct election of the president—that is, the elimination of the Electoral College.

Republican senators met and gloomily decided that little could be done to stop the changes. However, a group of youthful conservative activists outside Congress stepped in with a strategy to block Carter's pseudopopulist plan.

Led by Paul Weyrich and direct-mail expert Richard Viguerie, they sent special mailings to major Republican donors, asking them to call their senators and oppose the Carter plan. They wrote op-ed articles for leading newspapers in key states and held briefings for the news media to explain—sometimes using Heritage studies—why they opposed the changes. And they mailed "millions of letters," urging people to contact their congressman by telephone, postcard, and letter.[1]

Unlike the Old Right, the new conservatives were adroit at the practice of public relations. At a news conference, Representatives Steve

Symms of Idaho and Robert Dornan of California displayed poster-size voter IDs to demonstrate the possibility for fraud inherent in the instant registration proposal. The cards featured photos of Symms and Dornan but carried the names of liberal Democrats on the House Administration Committee who favored the registration plan. The influential *Washington Star* published the phony IDs on its front page. The chairman of the House Administration Committee kept the story going by losing his temper and publicly railing at the Republicans.

Inside the Senate, Senator Paul Laxalt of Nevada organized and led a successful filibuster that blocked the combined efforts of President Carter, Senate majority leader Robert Byrd of West Virginia, liberal icon Edward M. Kennedy of Massachusetts, and other liberal Democrats to pass taxpayer financing of congressional elections.

In August 1977 the liberals gave up, and the election law reforms designed to enlarge the Democratic base were laid to rest. A disappointed *New York Times* wrote that "the New Right . . . is more tightly organized, better financed, more sophisticated and more pragmatic than their predecessors." Lyn Nofziger, the once and future presidential aide, commented that "the Old Right were talkers and pamphleteers. They would just as soon go down in flames as win. But the New Right has moved toward a more pragmatic goal of accomplishing things."[2]

Although not an official member of the New Right, Heritage benefited from its energetic efforts in Washington and across the country. A more conscious conservative force in Congress required more research and analysis. An energized conservative grass roots was receptive to fund-raising appeals and calls to action from a right-minded think tank in Washington.

Four years after it had been launched against long odds, Heritage seemed poised to make a real difference in public policy in the nation's capital. But first it had to select a new president.

• • •

In their search for a successor, the trustees drew up a list of nineteen qualifications of a Heritage president. They knew they were asking for a lot, but they felt strongly he had to be:

> *Philosophically sound . . . knowledgeable in politics/government . . . movement-oriented . . . tough-minded . . . even-tempered . . . articulate . . . a good fund-raiser . . . acquainted with tax-exempt foundation laws and regulations.*[3]

Did such a paragon exist?

"Ed Feulner was our choice from the beginning," remembers Fritz Rench, a member of the search committee that had also considered economics professor Philip Gramm of Texas A&M University (later a Democratic congressman and then a Republican senator from Texas). Joseph Coors concurred: "Ed was the right person for the job."[4] Indeed he appeared to be typecast.

Along with Paul Weyrich, Feulner had conceived the idea of a conservative think tank that got relevant readable research to members of Congress for use in a debate. He had stayed close to the foundation from the beginning, serving as a member of the board of trustees since 1973 and as the corporate secretary since 1975. In the latter capacity he helped arrange the quarterly trustees' meetings in Washington and solicited suggestions for the agenda.

He frequently memoed Walton and other foundation officials about issues such as Social Security reform, a proposed "zero-deficit budget" (an approach he termed "virtually meaningless"), and wage and price controls.[5] He concerned himself with the minute as well as the momentous. Commenting on two Heritage studies he had received, he said that he would "like to see wider margins" and larger type. He countermanded the printing of a revised brochure when he learned that the errors in the first edition were inconsequential and the revisions would have delayed time-sensitive mailings by the Republican Study Committee and two other organizations.[6]

Feulner had immersed himself in the conservative movement since his undergraduate years at Regis College. He had been associated with respected think tanks in America and in Britain: the Center for Strategic Studies in Washington, the Hoover Institution at Stanford University, and the Institute of Economic Affairs in London.

He had nearly a decade of experience on Capitol Hill. As the RSC's executive director, he had supervised a professional staff, raised funds, organized press conferences, built a network of conservative academics willing to advise Congress, and developed enduring friendships with congressmen and senators, applying the management lessons he had learned at the Wharton School.

He was a recognized leader of the core group of young conservatives that guided much of the conservative movement's activities in Washington, D.C. "He had presence," says Phil Truluck, "real presence."[7]

In the 24/7 atmosphere of Washington, he worked harder and longer than almost anyone else, taking at least one bulging briefcase home

and rarely sleeping more than six hours a night. He was always prepared and expected the same of his colleagues. As he put it, "I don't like
surprises."

Some conservatives called him abrupt and gruff, even intimidating,
but for Feulner every minute was precious when the future of the nation
and that of the free world were in question. But he was not too busy to
set aside time each day to write personal notes of appreciation and sympathy to colleagues and friends. Beneath the crusty exterior was a Catholic awareness that without charity life is empty and without purpose.

He was an intellectual entrepreneur who believed that even the best
ideas will have no measurable impact on public policy unless they are
placed in the hands of the right policy makers at the right time and marketed aggressively to the public.

Feulner was definitely interested in the Heritage presidency, but he
had a conflict. The British businessman and entrepreneur Antony Fisher
had approached him about starting an American-style Institute for Economic Affairs in New York City. It would be a scholarly free-market
think tank that produced books and monographs intended to influence
the academic world and the media, and thereby U.S. public policy.

Feulner agreed to help Fisher, and the two of them met with a third
conservative, New York lawyer William Casey (later President Reagan's
CIA director). Fisher, Casey, and Feulner were the original incorpora-
tors of the International Center for Economic Policy Studies (ICEPS),
which later became the influential Manhattan Institute for Policy Research, now headed by Larry Mone. Feulner was leaning toward accepting Fisher's invitation to be ICEPS's founding president when he was
offered the Heritage position.

He had some doubts about Heritage's image—was it New Right,
Old Right, or something in between? But he liked that the foundation
had a defined mission and some money in the bank. He knew from
personal experience that conservatives on Capitol Hill needed the
free-market, limited government, anti-Communist research Heritage
offered. Accepting the presidency of Heritage was a gamble, but it was
a calculated gamble.

Ever the optimist, even he was taken aback when Frank Walton said
during a transition session that he could envision Heritage reaching out
to the states and even the world, becoming "the central institution for
the whole conservative movement." Don Lipsett made almost the same
point, telling Feulner that Heritage could be "the anchor" for the movement."[8] "I thought," Feulner recalls more modestly, "that Heritage, if

properly managed with clarity of purpose, could develop into something really big."[9] His immediate concern was meeting payroll for the
next two months.

The Heritage board elected Edwin J. Feulner, Jr., executive vice
president effective April 1, 1977, with the understanding that he would
succeed Frank Walton as president on June 1, 1977.

Among those who sent their congratulations was Republican senator Orrin Hatch of Utah, who promised "to give you every help [I]
can"—a promise he kept during his decades-long stay in Washington.
From the London School of Economics, Peter Bauer expressed his confidence that "you will make good use of the considerable opportunities
offered by your new position." It had been barely a decade since Feulner
had been an LSE student and attended Bauer's lectures. University of
Dallas professor Steve Pejovich, a fellow member of the Mont Pelerin
Society, wrote, "I would not be surprised if before too long the Heritage
Foundation becomes a real force in the nation's life."[10]

Still, the political climate remained problematic. Conservative
ideas had been repudiated by Republicans in 1976, when Gerald Ford
rather than Ronald Reagan won the presidential nomination. They had
been repudiated again when Ford lost the presidency to Jimmy Carter, a
liberal preaching moderation. Conservative candidates in congressional
races had made something of a comeback in 1976, Feulner conceded,
"but we were really a remnant."[11]

With an annual budget of about $1 million, Heritage was tiny
when compared with liberal giants like the Brookings Institution and
the Carnegie Endowment. Still Feulner believed that "most Americans
agreed with us on most issues." What was needed in Washington, he
later said, was a conservative institution that could compete on an equal
basis with the leading research organizations on the Left.[12] He set to
work implementing a plan he had been developing at the Republican
Study Committee, using people he knew he could rely on.

His very first act was to hire Phil Truluck, his trusted colleague
from the RSC, as the foundation's director of research. Truluck's task
was to build a research department that would take complicated, topical public policy questions and analyze them, using language that could
be quickly read and absorbed by policy makers in Congress and the
executive branch.

The new research director retained Heritage's core publication the
Backgrounder, a fifteen-to-twenty-page paper that could fit in a congressman's briefcase and be read by him on the ride to National Airport

or on the plane to his home district. In Richard Allen's words, "Get inside a person's briefcase and you have a chance to get inside his head."[13]

A Truluck innovation was the *Issue Bulletin,* a two-page commentary that summarized the main arguments for and against a piece of legislation. While all think tanks—including Brookings and AEI—now use a quick-response approach, Heritage was the first to do so.

The first Heritage researchers were not recognized scholars, as many in the established think tanks were, but young analysts striving to build a reputation. The typical Heritage analyst had recently completed a PhD, had a couple of published articles in his portfolio, and had done perhaps some work on a book. "We wanted people who were looking to make a mark," Feulner said, "as opposed to someone who already had made his mark. At Heritage, we build credibility, we don't buy it." Heritage did not want old lions but young tigers who were excited about engaging in a war of ideas, eager to go into battle, and optimistic about the prospect for victory.[14]

Feulner next brought on board Hugh C. Newton as the foundation's senior public relations counsel. Newton, an experienced high-energy PR specialist, set about getting Heritage's product into the hands and minds of opinion makers in Washington and across the country, dozens of whom he knew personally. Before the end of the year, the creative publicist Herb Berkowitz joined Heritage as director of public relations and began developing a national marketing strategy. Like Feulner and Truluck, Newton and Berkowitz became over the next two decades one of Washington's most effective partnerships in mass communications.

They understood that journalists thrive on conflict, so they provided them with conservative studies that refuted liberal claims—and articulate experts who could back up their arguments. Newton and Berkowitz toured the country and met with the editorial boards of dozens of major newspapers. This unglamorous scut work opened up the editorial pages to Heritage analysts and to Ed Feulner. By 1979 his topical weekly column was being carried in some fourteen hundred daily and weekly papers. Leading papers like *The New York Times, The Wall Street Journal,* and *The Washington Post* began quoting Heritage on a regular basis.

However, there was not the same penetration of the three broadcast networks—CBS, NBC, and ABC—which remained skeptical of conservative ideas and spokesmen. CNN (established in 1980) and Fox News (started in 1995) did not yet exist, and talk radio had not been freed from the straitjacket of the Fairness Doctrine, which mandated equal time for differing political viewpoints. That would come in 1987, when President Reagan's Federal Communications Commission abolished the doctrine.

Research was and remains the raison d'être of The Heritage Foundation, but Feulner believed that Heritage had to be more than a respected research organization. He wanted it to be a place "where conservatives could meet for lunches, forums, and roundtable discussions." He wanted it to be "a resource for information on the work of other conservative organizations." He wanted to create a comprehensive roster of conservative experts on university campuses and connect them to the Washington policy community.[15]

To that end, conservative insider Willa Johnson was appointed director of the Resource Bank and given the responsibility of forming a national network of conservative individuals and groups, something Johnson had started at the Republican Study Committee under Feulner's direction. "I wanted Heritage to become a clearing house," Feulner later explained, "not only *for* conservative information but *of* conservative people."[16]

In its first year, the Resource Bank arranged for conservative experts to testify before congressional committees, including social scientist Ernest van den Haag of Fordham University and economists Thomas Sowell of UCLA and Walter Williams of Temple University—both members of a growing black conservative intellectual community. Because of the Resource Bank, Charles Hobbs, an architect of California's welfare reform and author of an early Heritage monograph, *The Welfare Industry,* was invited to appear before the Senate Finance Committee. Hobbs was later named one of President Reagan's senior advisers on domestic policy.

Heritage discovered dozens of conservative organizations and hundreds of conservative scholars across the country who were engaged in public policy research. Even Ed Feulner, who prided himself on knowing everybody worth knowing, had not heard of many of them. So the Resource Bank initiated *The Insider Newsletter,* a monthly bulletin that briefly described the latest and most relevant publications and conferences.

The Resource Bank emboldened conservative academics to be more openly conservative once they realized they were not alone. But it was slow going, particularly at America's most prestigious schools.

Robert Bork tells a story of his days as a professor of law at Yale University. In 1964 the editor of the student newspaper, *The Yale Daily*

News, approached him, explaining the paper was interested in publishing "pro" and "con" articles about Barry Goldwater's candidacy for president. Bork replied that he would prefer not to call attention to the fact that he was for Goldwater and asked if they might find some other professor to write the pro-Goldwater piece.

The editor said he knew of only one other member of the Yale faculty who supported Goldwater, "and he's nuts." Bork thought the editor was engaging in youthful hyperbole but agreed to write the article. He later discovered that the other Goldwater man on the Yale faculty was indeed mentally unbalanced.[17]

While not knowing the reasons for the professor's mental problems, Feulner suggested that had he had "the benefit of a network of conservative academics as provided by the Resource Bank, he could have been saved from going 'nuts.' "[18]

The Resource Bank also published an *Annual Guide to Public Policy Experts,* eventually listing several thousand academics and policy experts. It established a Talent Bank to gather and distribute the résumés of those seeking jobs in Washington policy making, especially on Capitol Hill. Johnson and Feulner knew that congressional staffers would benefit from a training program run by experts, so Heritage started one. A typical session featured up to a dozen Capitol Hill veterans talking to aides about how to handle the press, be an effective legislative assistant, answer constituent mail, and manage an office.

Although Heritage did not have so specific a goal in mind, all of its movement work helped the future Reagan administration enormously. A sizable pool of experienced young conservatives was working in Washington when the Reagan transition team arrived in November 1980. Many of them were named to midlevel and even senior posts throughout the executive branch. After thirty-five years the Resource Bank remains a vital part of the Heritage goal to make the conservative movement a permanent part of the intellectual and political landscape of America.

Research organizations usually have their own publications, and Robert L. Schuettinger, American-born and Oxford-educated and someone whom Feulner had met through the ISI, was named director of studies and editor of the foundation's new quarterly journal, *Policy Review.* Schuettinger, who never quite lost his British accent, had taught at Lynchburg College in Virginia and had then been a visiting lecturer at Yale. The journal was an intellectual agora—a place where thinkers and policy experts and politicians of differing conservative viewpoints could debate ideas and policies. An early issue included a controversial article on why the minimum wage hurt young workers and minorities in particular—it was written by Walter Williams, a brilliant African American economist. The article was widely reprinted and, says Schuettinger, "probably had the biggest impact of any of our [early] articles."[19]

Policy Review would be published under a series of brilliant and independent editors—including John O'Sullivan, later editor of *National Review,* Adam Meyerson, later president of the Philanthropy Roundtable, and Tod Lindberg—until 2001, when Heritage management decided there were so many conservative journals that the funds necessary to underwrite it, a little over half a million dollars annually, could be spent more advantageously on nonprint media. Ownership of *Policy Review* was transferred to the Hoover Institution for a token sum. The decision anticipated the widespread shift by media organizations and think tanks from print to electronic media, which continues to this day.

But in 1977 there was a place and a need for *Policy Review.* The year before he became Heritage president, Ed Feulner presented a paper, coauthored with Robert Schuettinger, at the Mont Pelerin meeting in Paris. Addressing the question of how to transform a conservative idea into a public policy, Feulner said it was necessary not only to make that idea popular with the public but to convince policy makers that by enacting that idea, they were serving their own interest. He counseled patience and perseverance in the pursuit of that goal.

"We ought not to press our ideas to the limits," he told his audience of conservative intellectuals, "but rather proceed one step at a time, always having our ultimate objective firmly in view." We must move toward our goal, he said, "consonant with our abilities, with the temper of the times, and with the instincts and traditions of the electorate." At the same time, he stressed, it is important to keep in mind our "inner basic principles" when and if we temporarily compromise on what he called "day-to-day matters."[20]

Among the early letters of commendation of *Policy Review* was one from Chris DeMuth of the Harvard School of Government, who wrote: "You have obviously gotten off to a spectacular start, and if you can sustain the high quality of the articles in the first two issues you should move very quickly into the top rank of public policy journals."[21] A decade later DeMuth would become president of the American Enterprise Institute when AEI was undergoing severe personnel and financial problems and set it back on course. The two people he sought out for advice were Ed Feulner and Glenn Campbell of the Hoover Institution: "They were the best in the business."[22]

Committed to developing future conservative leaders, Feulner retained the Washington Semester Program, an intensive one-semester course designed to promote an understanding of Congress and the legislative process among college students. Students were required to take a course at a Washington-area university, attend a Schuettinger seminar on political philosophy, intern on the Hill or at Heritage, and attend a variety of congressional and other Washington events. When a number of conservative institutions started, expanded, or improved similar programs, Heritage discontinued the Washington Semester Program, in keeping with its practice of not duplicating what another organization is doing well.

Seeking to strengthen the foundation's performance and morale, Feulner discharged several nonperforming employees, met personally with those whom he asked to stay, and quietly dropped the weekly prayer meeting. He also asked his new general office manager, Kathryn St. John, not to bring her two black Doberman pinschers to work—they made her colleagues a little uneasy when they growled at anyone who walked by her office. As his personal secretary and assistant, he chose Kathy Rowan, who although only in her twenties had already worked in the House of Representatives (with Phil Crane) and the Senate (with Senator George Murphy of California) and on the White House staff. Rowan was Washington-smart, efficient, and imperturbable, required qualities for an assistant to the hyperactive Feulner.

The new president upgraded the board of trustees, adding William E. Simon, former secretary of the treasury; J. Robert Fluor, president of the Fluor Corporation; and Joseph Coors. In keeping with the foundation's entrepreneurial spirit, the new trustees were creative, risk-taking business leaders, not play-it-safe corporate managers.

Heritage passed a critical market test at the end of Feulner's first eighteen months as CEO, when it increased the number of its members to 120,000 and its annual budget to $2.5 million, inspiring Heritage chairman Ben Blackburn and Feulner in a joint message to boast: "We intend to remain the liveliest and the best of the new conservative think tanks."[23]

• • •

To be successful, Ed Feulner had learned, to be a permanent part of Washington, a think tank must perform well in five areas—Mission,

Management, Members, Media, and Money. And the most important of these is Mission.

In the foundation's 1977 annual report—covering Feulner's first six months as CEO—there was no specific declaration of intent, but Chairman Ben Blackburn stated Heritage's firm belief in "market solutions, limited government and maximum free choice." In a separate message, Feulner wrote that the foundation's goal was "to become the voice of those who believe in the free enterprise system, individual liberty, and limited government." He then added: "We will continue to do our best to promote the traditional values of our society."[24]

Here are four of the key principles that would later be listed in the foundation's formal mission statement; the only missing principle is the commitment to a strong national defense. This is a surprising oversight, given the long-standing conservative consensus about the need for U.S. military superiority. It would be corrected in short order.

In 1983 the Heritage chairman and president jointly declared that the foundation would strive "to promote the conservative values of free enterprise, limited government, and a strong national defense." In 1988 they said, "We remain deeply committed to certain principles: limited government, private enterprise, individual liberty, and strong national defense."[25]

Finally in 1993, twenty years after its founding, The Heritage Foundation published the following mission statement, which has been cited over and over again in publications ever since:

> Founded in 1973, The Heritage Foundation is a research and educational institute—a think tank—whose mission is to formulate and promote conservative public policies based on the principles of free enterprise, limited government, individual freedom, traditional American values, and a strong national defense.[26]

Visiting Heritage shortly after the adoption of the mission statement, Rich DeVos, the cofounder of the enormously successful Amway Company, drew Feulner aside and said, "What this organization needs is a *vision* statement . . . if you are going to have a lasting impact on social policy in America. A bold but practical vision will help you to reach those long-term goals you've been telling me about."

Inspired by DeVos, Feulner and the other senior managers worked for almost three years, producing dozens of drafts "until we got it just right." With each revision, they felt they were not just changing words around, "we were shaping the future of our institution." Feulner kept in touch with DeVos throughout the process and presented him with the seventeen-word statement at a national convention one week after its approval by the Heritage board of trustees. "You know, Rich," said Feulner, "this statement of vision is going to guide everything our organization does from now on—and we owe [it] to you."[27]

The vision read: "The Heritage Foundation is committed to building an America where freedom, opportunity, prosperity and civil society flourish."

The words are inscribed in bright letters over the entrance to Heritage headquarters and in all the elevators.

• • •

Although it is a nonprofit research organization, Heritage functions as much like a business as possible, reflecting Feulner's managerial philosophy. "We're not for profit," he says, "but we're not for loss either."[28]

Senior managers meet every Wednesday afternoon for an hour to discuss the current issues and approve any necessary action. They meet every month for half a day to examine pressing issues and to present, when necessary, a mini-review of their departments. There is always a report from John Fogarty, the engaging young vice president for development, on whether Heritage is on track to meeting its fund-raising goal for the year. Every meeting ends with "For the Good of the Order," at which any senior executive—there are now ten Heritage vice presidents plus the top officers of Heritage Action—can bring up anything he wants affecting the foundation and the movement. There is also an annual two-day retreat in the fall for senior management on the isolated Eastern Shore of Maryland, far from the maddening crowds, cell phones, and iPads. The retreats have produced foundation-altering decisions like Leadership for America, which in the late 2000s restructured Heritage's policy-making process, and Heritage Action, the foundation's lobbying offshoot.

Every fall Heritage goes through a rigorous "management by objective" process that becomes its business plan for the next twelve months. Priority issues are debated and agreed upon, and a budget is set. "There is always vigorous, open discussion," Feulner says, "but once a decision is made, everyone accepts it."[29] Both the issues and the budget are submitted to the board of trustees for approval. Along the way, there are quarterly reviews of the business plan by senior management with careful attention paid to the flow of income—always a high-priority matter to an institute that has a relatively modest endowment (less than $100 million in 2012) and that has to raise its multimillion-dollar budget each and every year.

The board of trustees is not a figurehead board. It has a budget committee, an investment committee, a separate audit committee, a development committee to keep the doors open, and in more recent years an executive organization and structure committee responsible for succession issues. "The board stays active and involved," says Feulner, "and has came up with many important ideas like *Mandate for Leadership* and the *Index of Economic Freedom*."[30]

Feulner calls himself an "optimistic entrepreneur" who looks for new opportunities "instead of arguing why something undesirable can't be changed." An entrepreneur, he says, doesn't just develop new ideas and discover new talent; he markets them intensively and effectively to his target audiences. This requires "a clear sense of your priority issues and audiences," which makes Heritage's "management by objective" crucial to its success.

"I hire the best people I can," Feulner says, "and then give [them] a lot of responsibility. . . . I'm proud of the long-term stability of our management team at Heritage." Other conservative organizations suffer, he points out, "because the person in charge tries to do everything himself."[31]

• • •

"Heritage is its people" is one of Ed Feulner's favorite sayings. He is referring not only to the nearly three hundred full-time and contract employees who work for the foundation but the members who respond to Heritage's appeals for support. At the end of 2012, Heritage had approximately 600,000 members, making it the most broadly supported research organization in the world.

Heritage members do more than give—they read its publications online, attend its events, send letters and e-mails to their congressmen and senators, and call upon their representatives in Washington or at home. They are members of a national movement, committed conservatives responding to the powerful message that freedom works for everyone, regardless of race, creed, color, or political philosophy.

There are members like Dr. G. L. Carter, Jr., of Hamblen County, Tennessee, who after a lifetime of teaching graduate programs in agriculture and consulting in Western Europe, Southeast Asia, Africa, and Latin America is able to include Heritage in his estate plans. "It turns out," says Carter, "you can save quite a lot over a lifetime, and suddenly I find myself in a position to make an estate gift that will help preserve our founders' vision for America. . . . There's a lot of satisfaction in making a gift that will make such a big difference in our country's future."[32]

• • •

Heritage has always been media savvy, beginning with Hugh Newton and Herb Berkowitz and including Feulner, who hired them, and now under communications vice president Michael Gonzalez, a veteran *Wall Street Journal* reporter and editor. The foundation reaches out to a wide variety of print, broadcast, cable, and other media. Its analysts appear on Fox News so often, it has been nicknamed Heritage News by some media analysts. The foundation stresses the personal approach. Even in the Age of the Internet, Heritage communications people spend hours daily talking to their contacts at a radio station, a television or cable network, a blog, a daily newspaper, or a weekly journal via phone and e-mail.

Heritage rejects the dictum of the late media guru Marshall McLuhan, "The medium is the message." For the foundation, the mission is the message. And the mission is to formulate and promote public policies based on America's First Principles, as laid down by the Declaration of Independence and the Constitution. "We Americans have the immeasurable benefit, the providential gift," writes Heritage vice president and constitutional scholar Matthew Spalding, "of having inherited a great country, built on the rock of human liberty, with a firm confidence that free men and women are capable of self-government."[33]

The foundation prides itself on using the newest media technology to reach policy makers and their constituents, from talk radio in the 1980s and cable TV in the 1990s to the Internet and social media in the 2000s. In May 2010, after surveying the websites of about one hundred U.S. think tanks, *The Bivings Report* placed Heritage.org in the top five, describing its site as "the best of the sites listed here."[34]

• • •

Heritage is successful at fund-raising because it is mission-led. The foundation's development people are trained to tell prospective and present members what Heritage is doing to limit government and keep America militarily strong and not to talk about money unless the other person does. "Money does not lead the mission," says John Von Kannon, who headed Heritage's development program for almost thirty years. "The mission comes first."[35]

Formerly publisher (and chief fund-raiser) of the feisty monthly *The American Spectator,* Von Kannon joined Heritage in March 1980 as assistant to the president and was named treasurer of the foundation in April 1981. Richard Larry, president of the Scaife Family Charitable Trusts, described Von Kannon as "the premier development guy" in the conservative movement.[36]

Because Heritage does not accept government grants or contracts, Von Kannon explains, it must compete in the marketplace for dollars that could be spent elsewhere. The foundation has been successful, he says, "because an ever increasing number of people see us as an effective spokesman for their views."[37]

Heritage's success can be measured in different ways, but the steady growth of income in its first seven years was remarkable, rising from $413,497 in 1974 (its first full year) to $5,329,998 in 1980—a thirteen-fold increase. Three decades later, in 2011, it raised more than $80 million and set a budget of $79 million for 2012. By contrast, Brookings's 2011 budget was $102 million, AEI's $32.1 million.

Donors explain, in often-emotional language, that they support Heritage because it champions conservative ideas in an increasingly hostile liberal environment. As one $10,000 donor put it, "We admire your commitment to preserving those principles and traditions that our founding fathers established more than 200 years ago." One President's Club member wrote, "We pray that people will be given ears to hear what you have to say, and then the courage to respond to the truth. We are grateful to be a small part of what you are doing."[38]

Like Heritage members, the Heritage development team believes deeply in the mission and will not compromise it. They will not trim the truth to gain a dollar. "Thou shalt not lie," says Von Kannon, "is a good commandment for fund-raising as well as for everyday life." And when he says it, the usual twinkle in his eye is replaced by a steely look.

It's important to understand the interests and needs of a donor, Von Kannon says. Some are interested in a specific policy or program. Some want to support the conservative cause. Some worry about what kind of country they will leave for their children and grandchildren. Some want to associate their name with a prestigious Washington institution. "We learn the specific interests and needs through research," says Von Kannon, "but more important by listening."

He tells the story of Dick Palmer of Fort Myers, Florida, who in

1992 increased his Heritage support from $1,000 to $10,000. Von Kannon telephoned to thank him and arranged to meet him at an upcoming Heritage event in Palm Beach. Afterward he asked Palmer how he had enjoyed the program. "It was terrible," said Palmer. "I couldn't hear a damned thing and I have perfectly good hearing." Trying not to stare at Palmer's hearing aids, Von Kannon apologized profusely.

Back in Washington, he reported the conversation to Phil Truluck, who suggested that the foundation start doing sound/audio checks before every event and always have two microphones at the podium. Von Kannon called Palmer to let him know about the changes.

After a number of years, and many more trips and donations, John Von Kannon was visiting Dick Palmer, who turned to him and said, "You know, John, I like the Boy Scouts and I like the Red Cross, but I love the Heritage Foundation."

"Why, Dick?" asked Von Kannon.

"You know."

"Tell me."

"Because you pay attention to me. You listen."[39]

Dick Palmer made several more gifts over the next ten years until his total giving almost reached $1 million. After he passed away, each of his four sons made memorial gifts of $25,000 each to the Heritage Foundation.

When Ed Feulner talks about Heritage members, he grows lyrical. "The backbone of our financial support is the $50 giver," he says. "His gift is the most meaningful because I know that it comes from a hard-working American who cannot easily afford the gift. He is making a real sacrifice when he writes a $50 check to us." It is his way of saying, suggests Feulner, that he cares about what kind of country he passes on to his children and grandchildren. "I feel a special responsibility to these smaller givers," Feulner says, "to ensure we spend their hard-earned money in the wisest, most effective way."[40]

But he also devotes careful attention to major donors. When the Samuel Roberts Noble Foundation approved a grant of $139,410 in early 1978—its donation the year before was only $5,000—Feulner asked every Heritage trustee to write a personal letter of thanks to all seven of the Noble trustees, explaining that Noble was "the first foundation other than the Scaife Family Charitable Trusts and the Coors Company to ever support us in six figures."[41]

It is these five principles of leadership—Mission, Management, Members, Media, and Money—that Ed Feulner applied when he took the reins of The Heritage Foundation in the spring of 1977 and began shaping a new kind of public policy institute, what *Time* would call an "advocacy tank."[42]

• • •

The first generation of policy research institutions in America emerged about a century ago, just before World War I, as an outgrowth of Progressivism and the "scientific management" movement. They operated in an era when the federal government was small, had limited intellectual resources, and welcomed outside knowledge and counsel. The Brookings Institution, founded in 1916, is the foremost example of this first generation of think tanks sustained for the most part by private philanthropy.[43]

The second generation—the first to be called "think tanks"—appeared in the years following World War II, when the federal government sought sophisticated technical expertise in waging the Cold War and then the war on poverty. Their work was mainly underwritten by federal funds. The RAND Corporation is the prototype of this kind of government-supported research institute.

The third generation of think tanks surfaced in the 1970s as a result of the philosophical debate between conservatives and liberals about the size and role of government that has characterized much of American politics for the past four decades. The Heritage Foundation is the exemplar of the new generation that spurns government money and is deliberately more aggressive in its marketing than previous research organizations.

The most recent development in the think tank world has been the emergence of the overtly political or "do" tank, exemplified by the liberal Center for American Progress (CAP), founded in 2003 and admittedly inspired by Heritage's success. Writing in the liberal *Nation*, Robert Dreyfuss said: "Heritage has won deserved envy and awe on the left for its ability not only to generate ideas but to place them squarely at the center of public attention—in the media, on Capitol Hill and among the capital's intelligentsia."[44] CAP's founding president, John Podesta, invites comparisons between his center and Heritage, but CAP is openly partisan. CAP has so linked itself to the Obama administration that it refrains from serious criticism of the president or his policies (in contrast to Heritage, which frequently criticized Reagan and both Bushes). In further contrast to Heritage, CAP rarely conducts original research, content to promote the work of other organizations.

The rank partisanship of the newer think tanks worries some. Their ideological thrust and their efforts to maintain a high media profile, wrote Hudson Institute fellow Tevi Troy, have undermined the credibility of *all* think tanks. Karlyn Bowman, a senior AEI fellow, has said that "politicization" limits the ability to provide new and innovative policy solutions and to get them implemented. Troy gloomily concluded that "it is not easy to see a way out of this problem. Every incentive—political, financial, and professional—points toward the further politicization of think tanks."

Heritage does not share Troy's gloom, confident that it can continue to maintain the right balance between research and marketing and to distinguish between electoral politics—the province of the do tanks—and policy politics, for which it is widely known.

• • •

Ed Feulner understood that his first year as Heritage president was critical. Even before he arrived at 513 C Street, N.E., he was making decisions. He memoed all employees that the central goal of the foundation was the public policy process and "our prime target audience, the Congress." He vetoed the suggested "Professors' Project" because Heritage was not an academic institution but a public policy organization. As he put it, "the assurance of funding is not a sufficient criteria for embarking on a new program" that does not advance the mission.[45] In the years to come, Feulner adhered strictly to the policy, turning down potential grants of as much as seven figures for projects that did not meet Heritage criteria.

Scanning the list of major donors, he suggested that the top twenty-five—those who had given at least $1,000—be put on a special category to receive "personalized attention" from himself and the foundation. Here was the genesis of a core development program—the President's Club. And he paid special attention to the three sources of revenue without which there would have been no Heritage Foundation—Coors, Scaife, and Noble.

He was taken aback at the general sloppiness of the researchers' desks and gave Phil Truluck three days to get things in good order, including his office. He was having a little fun with Truluck, whose office was so small it had room for only a narrow desk and one tiny chair. He softened his injunction by promising "to try and do the same thing" for his office.[46] But try as he might, Ed Feulner was never able, then or ever, to clear his desk of the colored folders, reports, publications, books, and other materials of a deeply involved think tank president.

No detail was too small for the new pipe-smoking, hands-on CEO. He queried Truluck about the distribution of Heritage materials on Capitol Hill, reporting that one congressional aide had told him he had received only the *Backgrounder* on Carter's energy plan and no others. This was critical because it went to the heart of the foundation's mission—get the right message to the right person at the right time.[47]

He reminded Truluck, Schuettinger, Newton, Tom Cantrell (a holdover from the Walton years), Willa Johnson, and Kathryn St. John that he expected a daily report about the activities of their departments. "This might be burdensome," he conceded, "but I assure you that it is necessary to keep each other informed."[48] Today, in the world of the Internet, everyone keeps everyone informed on an hourly if not a minute-by-minute basis by e-mail.

Because Heritage did not yet have a vice president for development or a department devoted to fund-raising, Feulner spent a major portion of his time—well over half—communicating with current or prospective major donors, a responsibility he carries out to the present day and enjoys.

He met with the vice president of Standard of Indiana, who said his company was "no longer as skittish about being involved" with Heritage, which should receive something from Standard in the not too distant future. He prepared a three-page memorandum for a possible donor who had expressed interest in supporting an expanded media program of Heritage. Among the initiatives was an 800 phone number that small-town radio affiliates could call for live actualities and a significant increase in radio and TV talk show interviews. This was a decade before the explosion of talk radio programs in the late 1980s and early 1990s.

Through the intercession of Bryce Harlow, former White House aide to President Eisenhower and the most respected corporate representative in Washington, Feulner, Truluck, Willa Johnson, and Schuettinger gave a briefing to Gerald Gendell of the Procter and Gamble Foundation. Feulner gave their presentation a B+, noting that Gendell was particularly interested in the Resource Bank and Heritage's quick-response capability. Gendell appreciated that Heritage and other think tanks like AEI were complementary in their research. As they left the meeting, Gendell told Feulner that Procter and Gamble would "certainly" support Heritage.[49]

In response to a letter of inquiry, Feulner informed the Council of Better Business Bureaus that Heritage had stepped up its direct-mail fund-raising, going from five thousand pieces of mail in 1976 to more than three million pieces in the first eight months of 1977. The preliminary results from the 1977 mailings were "very encouraging" and were obtained at a "reasonable" cost as the foundation built a house list. "Our overall fundraising expenditure to revenue of less than 3 percent," Feulner wrote, "is one of the best in the entire foundation world."[50]

"Ed was out there, selling Heritage," remembers Phil Truluck, "raising the money. That's what he did our first couple of years. If he hadn't done that, we would never have survived."[51]

Toward the end of the year, he sent the board of trustees a progress report about the foundation's fund-raising efforts. Amway had renewed its support of $5,000 (thanks in large measure to Jack Wilson). The Ford Motor Company Fund had donated $2,500, prompting Feulner to write: "Its board and policies are not at all like that of the Ford Foundation in New York!" The Olin Foundation, which contributed $21,000 in 1976, had indicated a willingness to increase its grant. He was in contact with the Irvine Foundation, William Brady, the Murdock Foundation, the Interlake Company, the Sun Company, Standard Oil, and other companies. Last but far from least, he would be visiting with Bob Walker of the Adolph Coors Company and Dick Larry of the Scaife Family Charitable Trusts to discuss their support of the foundation's ongoing programs.

While grateful for contributions, Ed Feulner had a greater goal in mind: to build an enduring relationship with major donors who would in time produce the million-dollar gifts that would enable Heritage to become a permanent Washington institution.

• • •

What could Heritage do, and not do, as it presented conservative research and analysis to members of Congress and their staffs? Feulner peppered William Lehrfeld, the foundation's legal counsel, with questions.

Can the foundation publish analyses of specific legislation? Can it draft or formulate legislation? Must every analysis present pro and con arguments? Can Heritage recruit witnesses to testify about proposed legislation? Can Heritage write a speech or testimony for a member of Congress about specific legislation? Can Heritage advocate a position on a public policy? In its forthcoming journal, must Heritage publish only articles that include pro and con arguments on a given public policy?

The answers would materially affect the operations of The Heritage Foundation, which was founded in order to influence legislative outcomes on Capitol Hill as much as it could legally. The new president was greatly relieved by Lehrfeld's detailed reply, based on the rules and regulations of the Internal Revenue Service regarding 501(c)(3) organizations.

- Heritage can prepare analyses of specific legislative proposals but must "juxtapose facts both pro and con without comment, leaving the reader to draw his own conclusions." The research material must be offered as a "resource tool" with balanced factual data.

- Heritage can prepare or formulate legislation providing public policy alternatives.

- Heritage can present "preferable approaches to issues" so long as it is analyzing general issues, not specific legislation.

- Heritage can provide witnesses to testify before congressional committees; it may pay their travel and living expenses but may not offer an honorarium. The foundation can secure a member of Congress to request a witness, but "this is not essential."

- Heritage can provide, at the request of a member of Congress, background material for a speech or testimony or prepare the speech or testimony.

- When it provides a speaker, Heritage is not responsible for the opinions of the expert, who is under no obligation to present both sides of an issue.

- All Heritage analyses of *specific* (emphasis added) legislation must present "a balance of ideas." (The "full and fair" test applies to any and all *Backgrounders, Issue Bulletins,* and other Heritage publications.)

- Regarding monographs, Heritage may "editorialize" because the monograph deals with public policies and not specific legislative proposals.

- The proposed quarterly journal can publish articles supporting a "given conclusion" so long as the author is not a Heritage employee. However, if the journal presented articles that consistently held a particular point of view on a specific bill, it might trigger a "reevaluation" of its tax status under the "full and fair" requirement.

The Lehrfeld memorandum on lobbying would serve as a general guideline for Heritage for more than thirty years until 2010, when the foundation decided as a result of a new lobbying disclosure act to create a sister 501(c)(4) organization—Heritage Action for America.

CHAPTER 8

"DR." FEULNER

Having launched what he thought of as a "new" Heritage, Feulner turned to a goal he had set aside for almost a decade—earning a PhD and demonstrating his personal commitment to scholarship. There were also professional reasons: he knew from his frequent trips to the Far East that Asian cultures frequently reserved a place of honor for those with advanced degrees.

At the suggestion of Stephen Haseler, the foundation's first distinguished scholar, he wrote to two British research universities—the University of Edinburgh and the University of Nottingham—that offered doctorate programs for foreign students. Aside from their excellent reputations, they did not require the extensive coursework most American schools did. Feulner explained that while he had sought a doctorate in economics at Georgetown University, he had decided it would be more practical to pursue a research degree in political science in Britain.

Because of his many contacts in Britain and frequent visits there, he was confident he could satisfy the university's residency requirements and meet on a regular basis with his adviser. He pointed out that he had been in residence at the University of Edinburgh in the summer of 1963 as part of the Scottish Universities Summer School and had been a student at the London School of Economics in 1965 studying under two distinguished British academics, Michael Beasley and Peter Bauer. "I hope," he wrote, "you will give this proposal serious consideration."

The chairman of the department of politics at the University of

Edinburgh responded favorably, and in early December, Feulner met with John Mackintosh, a professor of politics at Edinburgh as well as a Labour member of Parliament. Mackintosh was willing and "indeed eager" to pursue the possibility of Feulner doing a PhD under him.

He suggested that Feulner (1) do a detailed outline on his proposed study of the Republican Study Committee; (2) stress that his study would evaluate the usefulness and the impact of the RSC on congressional politics; and (3) commit to spending about one month at the university in September or October 1978 working on his study and giving lectures on the U.S. Congress and how it operates. Asked how long he thought it would take him to write the dissertation, Feulner estimated two to two and a half years, which suited Mackintosh's schedule. Feulner promised to stay in "close touch," and in return Mackintosh promised he would coach Feulner when it came time to defend his dissertation.[1]

Tragically, Mackintosh died in 1978 at the age of forty-eight, cutting short a promising political career and denying Edinburgh students one of the university's best lecturers. During the last year of his life, Mackintosh taught an introductory undergraduate course on political philosophy. At the end of the semester his students gave him a standing ovation. His successor at Edinburgh, Charles Raab, a longtime politics and international relations professor, honored Mackintosh's academic commitments, including the mentoring of an American in his late thirties seeking a PhD.

A determined Feulner began setting aside an hour or two early each morning to work on the dissertation before arriving at The Heritage Foundation by eight-thirty a.m. He also reserved time on the weekends and even during vacations. E.J. remembers that on a two-week family vacation at Nags Head, in North Carolina, his father would go up to the loft in the beach house and work for hours. "He spent time with us but not as much as we would have liked."[2]

The self-described "air mail student" met his deadline, submitting his dissertation in 1980 and defending it the following year. With Linda and both of their children (plus Fritz Rench) in attendance, he received his PhD in political science from the University of Edinburgh in November 1981. A prized family photograph is of a grinning bespectacled Ed Feulner in full university regalia and Scottish beret.

• • •

In mid-1977, Ed Feulner was invited as Heritage president to participate in a discussion of "Public Policy, Politics and Power" by representatives of AEI, Hoover, and other conservative think tanks. Feulner's inclusion was a recognition of Heritage's increasing importance by other research organizations.

Characteristically, Feulner got right to his main point: "Many people working for public policy research organizations have been overly cautious in deciding just how far they can opine. The result is that their impact has not been nearly as effective as it should be."

While readily conceding that long-range studies with in-depth analysis were necessary—he commended Hoover's Martin Anderson, among others—Feulner argued that just as needed was the timely delivery of information "geared to the political process" to congressmen, senators, and their key staff.

He reported that within fifteen hours of President Carter's energy message in April, Heritage hand-delivered to every member of Congress and senator a twenty-two-page critical analysis of the Carter plan. Such a quick-response system, Feulner said, provided the Congress with "reliable, easily digestible, well documented material" as it formed national policy and brought balance to the debate.

Such studies promoted limited government and a free competitive economic system and had, as John Maynard Keynes once said, "influence far beyond that which is immediately apparent." The key elements of public policy research in Washington, Feulner insisted, were "timing, delivery, and credibility."[3] They make the difference in whether a study will have immediate and possibly lasting impact or will be dismissed as dated and irrelevant. Feulner's three key elements of timing, delivery, and credibility formed Heritage's research paradigm from then on.

• • •

The Carter years from 1977 to 1980 were a time of economic misery for the American people and of Communist gains around the world, but they were golden days for conservatives. The president and his Georgia advisers offered almost daily targets for analysis and commentary.

GOP confidence was restored by the 1978 elections when, after just two years of Jimmy Carter, Republicans gained three seats in the Senate and fifteen seats in the House of Representatives. Half a dozen liberal senators were defeated, including Dick Clark of Iowa and Thomas McIntyre of New Hampshire.

By the end of 1979, the inflation rate stood at 13.3 percent—the highest since the Korean War and nearly double the rate Carter had inherited from Ford. Confronted by mounting economic woes, the self-righteous Carter faulted the American people who, he said, were deep in the throes of a "crisis of confidence." While the president was lecturing Americans and demanding they "snap out of it," the people were being slowly strangled by "stagflation"—a deadly combination of double-digit inflation and zero economic growth.[4]

There was a widespread feeling in much of America that our best days were behind us. We would have to learn to get along with less, and if we got into trouble, look to government to solve the problem. Carter had already established two new agencies—the Departments of Energy and Education—and spawned a myriad of new government regulations that inhibited business, large and small. The spirit of the age was reflected in books like *Limits to Growth* and *The Zero Sum Society*. As Carter's own *Global 2000 Report* predicted, "The world in 2000 will be more crowded, more polluted, less stable ecologically."[5]

Problems proliferated—the energy crisis, the plummeting dollar, soaring interest rates, the proposed giveaway of the Panama Canal, the fall of the shah of Iran and the rise of Islamic fundamentalism, the usurpation of power by the Sandinistas in Nicaragua, the unbalanced SALT II Treaty, the brutal Soviet invasion of Afghanistan, and the taking of sixty-six U.S. hostages in Teheran. The Panglossian nature of the Carter foreign policy was perhaps most obvious in Angola. After Congress passed the Clark Amendment barring all U.S. assistance to Jonas Savimbi's anti-Communist resistance movement, Andrew Young, Carter's ambassador to the United Nations, brightly said that the thirty thousand Cuban troops in Angola were a good thing for they brought "a certain stability and order" to the country.

Heritage set about offering practical solutions to some of the more critical problems, beginning with something that affected everyone—energy.

• • •

The foundation adamantly opposed Carter's proposed new Department of Energy, arguing that the way out of the energy crisis was through deregulation and an energy "mix" of oil, natural gas, hydroelectric, coal, and nuclear power. In February 1979 it cosponsored a three-day National Conference on Energy Advocacy along with other major national organizations. The meeting produced a four-hundred-page source book, *Energy Perspectives: An Advocate's Guide,* edited by Heritage's

Milton Copulos. As a result of Heritage's and other groups' efforts, the government began to lift controls on oil prices and reduce EPA regulations on oil exploration in the United States. When President Reagan swept away many more regulations in 1981, prices fell sharply, and in short order, as Heritage had predicted, the United States had an excess of oil.

Heritage's reputation in the energy field was strengthened by an early 1979 study, *The Iranian Oil Crisis,* by Middle East expert James Phillips, written before deregulation. He predicted that as a result of the political turmoil in Iran, there would soon be worldwide oil shortages and long gas lines in America. A month later the CIA publicly reached the same conclusion. Soon Phillips, who had come to Heritage from the Fletcher School of Law and Diplomacy at Tufts University, was briefing Washington's intelligence community on the politics of the region.[6] It was the beginning of a distinguished Heritage career for Phillips, who continues to stay ahead of developments in the always-turbulent Middle East.

In the late 1970s, as a result of Carter's neo-Keynesian policies and the continuing economic ripples from Nixon's command-and-control impulses, inflation in America hit double digits. Predictably, there was loud talk in the Carter administration of retrying the oft-failed tactic of wage and price controls. With the full encouragement of publisher Ed Feulner, *Policy Review* editor Robert Schuettinger determined to drive a sharp stake into the heart of the idea.

In *Forty Centuries of Wage and Price Controls: How Not to Fight Inflation,* coauthored by Eamonn Butler, Schuettinger showed that beginning with the Babylonians, government controls did only one thing well—produce inflation. The authors wrote:

> *The record of governmental attempts to control wages and prices is clear. Such efforts have been made in one form or another periodically in almost all times and all places since the very beginning of organized society. In all times and all places they have just as invariably failed to achieve their announced purposes.*[7]

Writing in *The Wall Street Journal,* Lindsay H. Clark, Jr., called the study "an admirable survey of controls' sorry history." The book also received a rave review from a future presidential hopeful, Republican Representative Ron Paul of Texas, who said: "If only everyone in this Congress would read . . . *Forty Centuries of Wage and Price Controls,* I do not believe there would ever be another attempt to institute compulsory controls."[8]

When President Carter announced his anti-inflation program in October 1978, he called for "voluntary" wage and price guidelines and was careful to say that he opposed mandatory controls and did not intend to ask Congress for the authority to impose them. Despite considerable pressure from inside and outside his administration, Carter never proposed wage and price controls—testimony to his good sense and the climate of public opinion created, in part, by Heritage.

In domestic policy, Heritage focused on (1) choice in education, (2) urban enterprise zones, (3) supply-side economics, (4) deregulation, and (5) significant reduction in the size of government. The foundation believed that these were achievable goals, not perhaps in a couple of years but in a decade or perhaps two, with the right legislation and the right leadership.

Education was a key component of the conservative strategy to reduce poverty. Giving poor families a tuition voucher would allow inner-city parents the option of removing their children from substandard and often dangerous public schools and placing them in better, secure schools. Vouchers, tuition tax credits, magnet schools, and other mechanisms to inject market competition into education, Heritage believed, would break the iron hold of the teachers' unions on public schools.

The seeds planted by Heritage took time to mature, but by the mid-1990s educational choice had become an accepted alternative in many school districts across the nation. Heritage analyst Lindsey Burke argues that school choice "means that more and more parents are able to send their children to safer, better schools." It means that low-income and special-needs children across the country are attending a public or private school of their parents' choice. It means that "students need not remain trapped in failing and dangerous schools—though too many students still are."[9]

Heritage continued to surprise Washington with its creative approaches to public policy when economist Stuart Butler published his paper "Enterprise Zones: A Unique Solution to Urban Decay." Butler urged the elimination of taxes and regulations on businesses operating in depressed inner-city areas, thus spurring commercial activity and creating the jobs people needed to pull themselves out of poverty.

Butler was building on a proposal made in 1967 by Senator Robert Kennedy (D-NY) that would have provided federal tax credits and other incentives for employers in urban poverty centers. The bill never passed Congress. In the mid-1970s the center-left British economist Peter Hall proposed the removal of government taxes and regulations in so-called "demonstration zones" in the most depressed parts of Britain. Shortly after coming into office in 1979, the conservative government of Prime Minister Margaret Thatcher established a number of enterprise zones, mostly in the inner cities, that set aside certain controls and provided local tax relief.

In a *New York Times* article, Butler pointed out that three years earlier President Carter had stood amid the rubble and burned-out tenements of the South Bronx and promised federal aid to rebuild the area "brick by brick and block by block." The pledge, Butler said, was symptomatic of the grandiose programs that were introduced with great fanfare but invariably produced disappointing results. In the words of one disillusioned senator, "All we have been doing is bulldozing great holes in our cities and throwing billions of federal dollars down them."[10]

Sensitive to the needs of the less advantaged, conservative Republican representative Jack Kemp from upstate New York and liberal Democratic representative Robert Garcia from New York City introduced legislation to establish enterprise zones in selected inner cities. The idea was adopted as a plank in the 1980 Republican platform and was introduced during the Reagan administration as the 1982 Enterprise Zone Act.

A less-than-satisfied Stuart Butler pointed out that the act emphasized tax credits rather than investor incentives and tended "to help those who are already on the ladder." He criticized the measure for requiring twenty-eight single-spaced pages of official explanation. "The administration's long-delayed plan," Butler said, "clearly has some serious flaws, but they are correctable."[11] Despite strong bipartisan congressional support as well as White House backing, the measure never passed both houses. The only legislation approved was a shell enterprise zone program that provided eligible areas with a few waivers from the Department of Housing and Urban Development.

However, urban enterprise zones became popular with state governments. Louisiana was the first state, in 1981, to adopt the approach, followed by Connecticut, Florida, Illinois, Texas, Virginia, and other states. Reliable statistics are scarce, but in their first five years, it is estimated that UEZs attracted $8.8 billion in private capital and created or saved about 180,000 jobs.[12]

In response to the states' initiative, the U.S. Congress in 1993 authorized the establishment of enterprise zones to "stimulate economic development" in selected distressed areas through tax incentives and direct government monies. It was a government-led program that disappointed conservatives, including Jack Kemp, who called the proposal a tragedy and "a hoax." Butler agreed with Kemp, saying that "the basic elements of their plan are upside down or just plain wrong."[13]

Butler and Kemp had envisioned hundreds of enterprise zones across the country from East Harlem to East Los Angeles. As an alternative, Heritage recommended passage of the 1995 Enhanced Enterprise Zone Act, sponsored by Senators Spencer Abraham (R-MI) and Joseph Lieberman (D-CT). The Abraham-Lieberman bill sought to make existing enterprise zones more attractive to private investors by eliminating the capital gains tax on investments in stock, business property, or a partnership in the zones as well as providing other tax incentives. The approach, Butler explained, recognized that "private investors are more likely than government officials" to identify the entrepreneurs that will function as "the engines of economic development" in depressed neighborhoods.[14] Congress never passed the legislation.

However, an undeterred Butler applied the lessons learned from the enterprise zone experience in his subsequent work on health care and welfare reform. In the course of seeking grassroots support for UEZs, he visited inner-city neighborhoods that had never before seen a white conservative, particularly with a British accent.

Butler struck up and maintained a close friendship with a remarkable African American, Robert L. Woodson, founder of the National Center for Neighborhood Enterprise and one of the most effective policy entrepreneurs in America. Through Woodson's leadership, residents of public housing projects were at last able to purchase their homes from the government. In addition, small minority-owned companies received tax incentives to help them set up shop in economically depressed urban areas—a direct application of the enterprise zone principle. "The end goal," says Butler, "is a welfare system that saves people not enslaves them."[15]

Stuart Butler's paper on enterprise zones was the first in a series of groundbreaking domestic studies that made him, by the mid-1980s, one of the most influential policy analysts in Washington, a position he holds to this day. Phil Truluck, who hired Butler, says, "Many people can analyze issues. Only a very few can predict what the major issues are going to be and stay out front on them."[16]

• • •

The ability of tax cuts to spur the economy and promote greater prosperity for everyone has been a core Heritage idea from the beginning. The foundation is opposed to raising taxes but is not against closing tax loopholes and eliminating bookkeeping gimmicks. In 1978 legislative analyst Donald J. Senese (who would hold important posts in the Reagan administration) authored a monograph, *Indexing the Inflationary Impact of Taxes,* based on a suggestion advocated by Milton Friedman.

Liberals had long used tax bracket creep to increase federal spending. Inflation pushed citizens automatically into ever-higher tax brackets, obviating the need for Congress to ask for politically unpopular tax increases. The conservative answer was to index tax rates—a central pillar of President Reagan's 1981 economic recovery program

Another Heritage study that helped establish the foundation as a credible source of analysis of domestic policy was published in August 1977—just two months after Feulner assumed the presidency of Heritage. President Carter introduced a much-ballyhooed "welfare reform" plan. Heritage policy analyst Samuel T. Francis concluded that instead of increasing the cost of welfare by $2.8 billion annually, as the administration claimed, the Carter welfare reform would cost taxpayers "at least" $17.8 billion more per year than the existing program. Francis said the Carter plan overstated present welfare costs by some $8.8 billion and underestimated the cost of the reform by about $9 billion.[17]

The administration and its congressional supporters immediately challenged the Heritage study and insisted that the Congressional Budget Office resolve the dispute over the true cost of the welfare reform program. After studying all the figures, CBO analysts reported that the Carter reform would increase the number of Americans who received some form of welfare assistance by almost 22 million. And they estimated that the additional annual cost would be about $20 billion, $2 billion *more* than Heritage's estimate.

The president and his allies were devastated. Furthermore, the CBO said, the reform plan would have a minimal effect on Americans living in poverty. Of the 22 million new people on welfare, 74 percent of them would come from families with incomes over $10,000 a year (in

1977 figures) and therefore above the official poverty line. As economist Martin Anderson wrote in *Policy Review,* the thrust of Carter's plan was not to reform welfare but "to further the idea of a guaranteed annual income."[18]

In June 1978 congressional leaders told President Carter that his proposed welfare reform was dead for that session of Congress. In the course of the welfare reform debate, the Francis study was often cited, and The Heritage Foundation emerged as a think tank to be listened to. Taking the long view, the foundation continued to push for genuine reform, with its efforts at last successful almost twenty years later, when a Republican Congress persuaded Democratic President Bill Clinton—after two of his vetoes had been overridden—to sign the Welfare Reform Act of 1996 (its official title: Personal Responsibility and Work Opportunity Reconciliation Act of 1996).

Policy Review contributed to Heritage's growing reputation by publishing articles by Senator Daniel Patrick Moynihan, former Hubert Humphrey aide Max Kampelman, and Eugene Rostow, undersecretary of state under President John F. Kennedy. Pulitzer Prize–winning journalist Paul Greenberg was moved to write that *"Policy Review* is the conservative's answer to the *New Republic.*"[19] The journal got an unexpected boost when mega-singer/actor/entertainer Frank Sinatra was so impressed by Kampelman's article on the "restrained power of the media" that he sent two thousand reprints to legislators and opinion leaders.

• • •

Heritage was similarly involved in the area of national security and foreign policy, taking seriously the constitutional injunction that the federal government shall "provide for the common defense" and "secure the blessings of liberty."

That meant, in the view of most conservatives, not a passive strategy of containment of Communism but a proactive strategy to roll back Communism. The main components of Heritage's plan were:

- Materially increase the cost of maintaining its empire to the Soviet Union.

- Build up U.S. defenses and maintain NATO's resolve to deter a Soviet attack, conventional or nuclear, on Western Europe.

- Protect America from the single greatest threat—an attack by Soviet long-range nuclear missiles (ICBMs).

- Contrast the prosperity produced by the free-market system with Communism's inability to provide more than subsistence living to its citizens except for its elites.

During the Carter years, Heritage used the monthly *National Security Record* and other publications to expose the flaws of the SALT II Treaty and the basing options for the MX missile; stress the importance of the neutron bomb to America's defense arsenal; and strongly criticize the Senate's abrogation of the U.S.-ROC defense treaty, an action that particularly angered conservatives, conscious that the Republic of China (Taiwan) had been a faithful U.S. ally since World War II.

The proposed SALT II Treaty—which sought to limit the manufacture of strategic nuclear weapons—was subjected to especially rigorous examination. In the summer of 1979 the foundation held a daylong seminar for editorial writers from *The Wall Street Journal, The Washington Post,* and other major newspapers on why it would be almost impossible to verify Soviet compliance with the treaty. The media were impressed. *The New York Times,* for example, credited Heritage with providing the "intellectual underpinnings" for the SALT II debate.[20]

Following the Soviet invasion of Afghanistan in December 1979, the Carter administration "delayed" Senate consideration of SALT II. Washington observers agreed that Heritage and other public policy institutes had raised so many substantive questions about the proposed treaty that approval by two-thirds of the Senate was no longer possible—if it had ever been.

The one study that established Heritage as a truly major player in the foreign policy debate was James Phillips's insightful *Backgrounder* "Afghanistan: The Soviet Quagmire," distributed on October 25, 1979, sixty-two days *before* the Soviet invasion of Afghanistan. Phillips pointed out that Afghanistan had been "convulsed" for over a year by a brutal civil war that showed no signs of abating. He described the broad spectrum of opposition to the Hafizollah Amin regime, the pervasive xenophobia of Afghans, and their strong resentment of the influence of "omnipresent Soviet advisers."

The Heritage analyst outlined the Soviet Union's options, ranging from military escalation to political compromise. He argued that Afghanistan was important to Moscow for regional as well as global political and strategic reasons. If the Soviets permitted Kabul to fall into the hands of religious/nationalist forces, he wrote, "they would be setting a dangerous precedent for Warsaw" and other Eastern European satellites.[21]

With remarkable foresight, Phillips concluded his analysis with these words:

> *The chronic turbulence in the Afghan political scene makes it more than likely that Amin will be (according to an old Afghan folk-expression) Barre Duzog Shah—"King for two days." If and when Amin falls prey to the same fate that befell his predecessors, it can be expected that Moscow will have other candidates for power waiting in the wings.*[22]

On December 27, 1979, a Soviet airborne brigade overthrew the government of Hafizollah, executed Amin for "crimes against the people," and installed the puppet Karmal regime. Within days, Soviet armored columns were fanning out across Afghanistan to occupy major population centers and begin waging a full-fledged counterinsurgency campaign against rebellious Muslim tribesmen.

Phillips could barely handle the flood of requests for media interviews; he was besieged by telephone calls from government officials wanting briefings. Speculation was widespread that Phillips must have gotten classified information from the CIA, even that he might be a CIA employee. The truth was that Phillips, like all good analysts, had used his knowledge of the region, his understanding of geopolitics, and a careful reading of the public record to conclude that the Soviets, at the end of a decade of ever-expanding global influence, would be willing to take decisive action to protect what they perceived as their vital interests in Afghanistan.

• • •

Another Heritage coup in these pre-Reagan years was its sponsorship of Growth Day, a conservative answer to Ralph Nader's "Big Business Day," which featured the most extreme antibusiness speakers and rhetoric (anticipating the radical Occupy Wall Streeters of 2011). The foundation sponsored Growth Day to celebrate the economic achievements of business, small, medium, and large, and to dismiss Nader's "zero growth" approach.

On April 17, 1980, Heritage held a well-attended news conference featuring Consumer Alert president Barbara Keating-Edh, Washington governor Dixy Lee Ray, a Democrat, and Georgetown University lecturer Walter Berns. Instead of automatically headlining Nader as they had in the past, the news media, including CBS News's Walter Cronkite, gave equal time to both sides. To the best of Heritage's knowledge, not a single major newspaper endorsed Ralph Nader's side, proving Herb Berkowitz's insistence that "it's a fatal mistake for conservatives to treat the media as the enemy."[23] This is a philosophy that Heritage follows to this day.

By early 1980, after three years of Feulner leadership, The Heritage Foundation had taken important steps toward becoming a consequential Washington think tank. Phil Truluck had put together a talented research team, mostly in their thirties, who could turn out a solid paper in a couple of days and, when necessary, in hours. In 1979 the foundation produced one hundred studies and monographs that were read and used by Democrats as well as Republicans. Democratic Representative Thomas A. Daschle of South Dakota (who would become Senate majority leader in 2001) remarked that Heritage's "SALT II Handbook [was] superbly written and a great deal of help to me and my staff."[24]

Heritage marketed its research aggressively and shrewdly to the policy-making community and the news media. United Auto Workers president Douglas Fraser complained that conservatives like Heritage "are out-lobbying, out-working, outspending and outhustling us and, unfortunately, at times they are out-thinking us." At the other end of the political spectrum, columnist Patrick J. Buchanan credited Heritage with "turning out, weekly, the timeliest, best-researched position papers floating around the Capitol."[25] Not satisfied to be just a Washington think tank, Heritage was reaching an estimated fourteen hundred daily and weekly newspapers with the syndicated Ed Feulner column.

The foundation also continued to broaden its financial base. In 1979 Heritage received gifts from eighty-seven U.S. corporations. Its budget for the year reached $3.7 million, a one-third increase over the previous year and four times what it had been in 1976 before Feulner became president.

The board of trustees was again expanded with the addition of such conservative heavyweights as Shelby Cullom Davis, former U.S. ambassador to Switzerland and head of one of the most successful investment firms on Wall Street; Frank Shakespeare, president of RKO General and former director of the U.S. Information Agency; Dr. Robert H. Krieble, board chairman of Loctite Corporation; and Dr. David R. Brown, a distinguished Oklahoma orthopedic surgeon and board member of the Samuel Roberts Noble Foundation, one of Heritage's earliest and most generous supporters.

Heritage trustees were more than men of means. They were men, and women, of deep experience and proven beliefs who shared both with the foundation's senior management. What Washington needed most, said Ambassador Davis, were "architects and engineers," not more politicians. Hayek, Kirk, and Friedman had convincingly explained "why totalitarianism is wrong and why freedom is right. But this doesn't tell us how to create policies and laws based on conservative principles. That's where Heritage comes in."

Dr. Brown took a long view of what needed to be done, saying that "the huge growth of government over the last several decades is impossible to roll back quickly." Priorities are important. He believed that conservatives should concentrate on economic and foreign policy issues and leave controversial moral questions to the "individual conscience."

Frank Shakespeare was convinced that through the force of their ideas, conservatives had "set the parameters" of the public policy debate. But he also said that conservative ideas, however popular, would not automatically produce victories at the polls. The right leaders would prove to be critical.[26]

All three men—Davis, Brown, and Shakespeare—would serve as chairmen of The Heritage Foundation in the years to come.

In 1979, John O'Sullivan, former assistant editor of the London *Daily Telegraph* (and later successor to William F. Buckley, Jr., as editor of *National Review*), replaced Robert Schuettinger as editor of *Policy Review*. O'Sullivan maintained the publication's reputation for lively discourse, although it did not always publish on time, a fault that irritated Heritage's prompt president. Among the highlights that year was a debate between Senators Barry Goldwater and Edward Kennedy of Massachusetts over President Carter's abrogation of America's Mutual Defense Treaty with the Republic of China (on Taiwan), with Goldwater vehemently opposed to Carter's unilateral action. Other articles included George Gilder's warning about "The Coming Welfare Crisis" and Midge Decter's analysis of affirmative action as "Benign Victimization."

Under Willa Johnson, the Resource Bank served as a clearinghouse for the latest conservative publications that often had an impact on public policy. Robert Huberty, Johnson's deputy, recalled the California research group that contacted Heritage about a projected book on health care.

"We knew that congressional hearings were soon to be held covering some of the issues raised in the book." So Heritage asked for photocopies of the pertinent chapters, which were then introduced at the committee hearings. The foundation arranged for the book's authors to testify before the committee. "Other research groups," said Huberty, "would have waited around until the book had been published before doing anything with it. But by that time the hearings would have been over." Heritage substantially increased the impact of the book by "intervening in the normally laid-back academic process."[27] Heritage showed once again that it was neither laid-back nor rigidly academic.

It began hosting a monthly luncheon of conservative public-interest law groups. (When he joined Heritage a decade later, Edwin Meese III would turn these meetings into a powerful national network.) Under the skillful guidance of Willa Johnson, the annual Resource Bank meeting attracted more and more participants. The Talent Bank placed twenty conservatives in Capitol Hill jobs in one year, while the Academic Bank now numbered more than a thousand scholars across the country.

In all these efforts, The Heritage Foundation functioned as the honest broker for the principal branches of American conservatism—the traditional right, the economic libertarians, the anti-Communist right, the New Right, and the neoconservatives. The role demanded tact, patience, and an understanding that, as Ed Feulner puts it, "successful politics is about addition and multiplication, not division and subtraction."[28]

In 1979, to foster the conservative intellectual renaissance in America, Heritage named Sovietologist Robert Conquest, historian Russell Kirk, economist Pedro Schwartz of Spain, and political scientist Patrick O'Brien of Australia as distinguished scholars.

In the spring of 1980, Heritage dedicated its expanded headquarters on C Street, N.E., facing Stanton Park—two buildings obtained through a gift from Joseph and Holly Coors and a $500,000 contribution from the Samuel Roberts Noble Foundation. A $270,000 donation by Jack Eckerd, founder of the drugstore chain, enabled the foundation to purchase a third building on C Street. To complete the expansion, a fourth row house was leased. Linking the buildings required some imaginative remodeling, but when it was completed, it was no longer necessary to exit one building and enter another to meet a colleague

At a dinner to celebrate the new headquarters William F. Buckley, Jr., remarked that "it seems incredible that we ever managed to do without the Heritage Foundation." Every American, he said, "live[s] off the fruits of its research which . . . fortifies the resolve to be free."[29]

Heritage had come a long way in a short while, but Ed Feulner and his colleagues were ever watchful for the opportunity to elevate the foundation to the front rank of Washington think tanks. That opportunity presented itself when Ronald Reagan, to the surprise of some but not the president of Heritage, announced his candidacy for the 1980 Republican presidential nomination.

CHAPTER 9

THE BIG GAMBLE

While some liberal observers dismissed the sixty-eight-year-old Ronald Reagan as too old—and too conservative—to try again for the Republican presidential nomination, many Americans were not bothered by his age and liked his limited-government philosophy. Their enthusiasm was fueled by the inept presidency of Jimmy Carter, who, confronted with double-digit inflation and interest rates, blamed the public, and who, when the Soviets invaded Afghanistan in December 1979, expressed amazement at their blatant disregard for the human rights of the Afghans.

A Harris poll revealed that the majority of voters liked Reagan's right-of-center philosophy, while nearly 60 percent felt that he would "inspire confidence as President." After all, he had proven himself, in the words of the *Los Angeles Times,* to be "an accomplished practitioner in the art of government" during his eight successful years as governor of California.[1]

In his formal announcement as a candidate in November 1979, Reagan pledged a 30 percent personal tax cut; an orderly transfer of federal programs with funding to state and local levels; a revitalized energy program based on increased production of oil, natural gas, and coal; a diplomatic and military strategy to meet the challenge of the Soviet Union; and a North American economic accord among the United States, Canada, and Mexico. He concluded with words that resonated with a people wondering whether their best days were behind them:

A troubled and afflicted mankind looks to us, pleading for us
to keep our rendezvous with destiny; that we will uphold the
principles of self-reliance, self-discipline, morality, and—above
all—responsible liberty for every individual; that we will become
that shining city on a hill.[2]

But first he had to best six of the GOP's most experienced leaders
in the primaries: Senate Republican leader Howard Baker of Tennessee; Senator Bob Dole of Kansas, the 1976 vice-presidential nominee;
former treasury secretary John Connally; Representative Philip Crane,
chairman of the American Conservative Union and cofounder of the
Republican Study Committee; liberal Representative John Anderson
of Illinois; and George H. W. Bush, former everything, including U.S.
envoy to China, CIA director, and chairman of the Republican National Committee.

Bush provided the most serious competition, but after Reagan won
a crucial New Hampshire debate and beat his Texas-based opponent in
the Texas, New York, and Oregon primaries, Bush conceded the nomination. Reagan spent the six weeks before the GOP national convention overseeing the writing of a conservative party platform and mulling
over his vice-presidential choice. He turned over the responsibility for
what he should do if elected to his longtime aide and adviser Edwin
Meese III. Meese was aware that Heritage was hard at work on a comprehensive plan for an incoming president to govern from the Right.

The idea of a manual for a conservative administration first surfaced at a meeting of the Heritage board of trustees in October 1979.
William Simon, who had been secretary of the treasury under Nixon,
and Jack Eckerd, who had headed the General Services Administration
under Ford, were talking about the challenges facing the new administration. Eckerd suggested that Heritage "should become involved in
some type of program which would study this problem [of government
size] and propose solutions."

Simon agreed it would be great if, instead of the theoretical book
that think tanks usually put out, there was a handbook that said,
"Here's what you should do if you really want to change the federal government once you come into office." Simon and Eckerd both recalled
that when they came to Washington, they spent so much time learning
how Washington works that months went by before they took a serious
look at policies and programs.

While no one could say with certainty in the fall of 1979 who the

Republican nominee would be—the trustees hoped and some prayed it would be Reagan—he was bound to be more conservative than Carter. And he stood an excellent chance of being elected given the state of the union. Ed Feulner suggested that Heritage "undertake a project which would suggest ways to cut government size, manage it more effectively, and promote free enterprise." It was up to Heritage to produce such a handbook because the new administration, preoccupied with electoral politics, would have given comparatively little thought to governing. Trustee Robert Krieble formally moved that "provided funding can be found for such a project, the President be authorized to undertake the production of a manual which would assist public policymakers in this regard."[3]

"Our strong feeling," explained Ed Feulner, "was that the people of the new and hopefully conservative administration should have some source of information and guidance other than what you get from the incumbents whom you replace." In the 1968–69 Nixon transition, he pointed out, "Republicans were briefed by Democrats, the very people whose jobs were at stake and who had a vested interest in maintaining the status quo."[4] The status quo was the last thing The Heritage Foundation wanted to preserve. It was eager to return the federal government to the limited-government philosophy of the Founders.

"It was a huge gamble," says Phil Truluck. "Really, we had no right to do it. We were a very small organization, probably thirty people, and our research department was less than ten. To take on something like [Mandate] required some innovative thinking. We didn't have anyone internally that could do it, so we had to look outside."[5]

Knowing they needed a top-flight editorial director for the "manual," Feulner telephoned Charles Heatherly, whom he had met when he was a field director of the ISI and who was now with the National Federation of Independent Business (NFIB) in California. Heatherly recalls that Feulner talked about the need for "our own agenda—a detailed blueprint" for, hopefully, an incoming conservative administration. Heatherly had already decided to leave the NFIB and move to Washington. He agreed to undertake the overall direction of the Heritage study, beginning November 15, 1979—one year before the voters would go the polls to elect a president.[6]

Heatherly and Willa Johnson began drawing up a list of key conservatives to talk to about possible writers and issues, starting with Paul Weyrich and the highly respected Senate staffer Margo Carlisle (who later joined Heritage as vice president and director of government relations). They also listed people in the Nixon administration, like William Simon and Caspar Weinberger, who had been secretary of health, education, and welfare, from whom they could draw suggestions.

"Willa was my partner and my mentor," says Heatherly. While Heatherly concentrated on the policy blueprint, Johnson was tasked with "organizing a Talent Bank for the new administration." They agreed from the beginning that policy and personnel had to fit together.[7]

At a trustees' meeting in December 1979, Feulner submitted a general plan for the study based on the idea that conservatives had to be prepared to answer the question "What is the conservative agenda, particularly for the First Hundred Days?" As Feulner later explained in the foreword to *Mandate for Leadership*, the recommendations were not offered as "cure-alls" for the nation's problems or as a catalog of every concept in the "conservative warehouse of ideas." They were, rather, concrete proposals that if implemented would help "revitalize our economy, strengthen our national security and halt the centralization of power in the federal government."[8] Feulner was trying to lower expectations, but it did not take a PhD in political science to recognize that *Mandate for Leadership* was intended to be a radical document that directly challenged the philosophy of the New Deal and modern American liberalism.

In the final days of 1979, while Reagan was preparing himself for several weeks of day-and-night campaigning in New Hampshire, Heatherly and his colleagues were still trying to figure out how to do something that had never been done before. Which cabinet departments should be analyzed? What agencies? How should the writers and editors be organized? Where should they meet? When should they meet? Heritage was too small to accommodate a dozen or more groups. Progress on the study stalled for several weeks until late January 1980 (only ten months to Election Day!), when Chuck Heatherly wrote a five-page outline titled *Mandate for Leadership*.

He proposed a team approach that would "scope out" every key department and agency of the government, from State, Defense, and Treasury to the EPA and the Legal Services Corporation. Each team—there were twenty in all—would have a chairman and a cochairman and would include congressional staff, conservatives who had been Nixon and Ford appointees, and academics. Each chair would be responsible for recruiting the members of his team. Heatherly set a deadline of June 1 for the first draft. "I insisted," he says, "that every draft had to have continuity and conformity" to conservative principles.[9] They would need a final draft by September to have a study in hand by November 1 to give to the transition-team leaders. Heatherly was reminded of Churchill's comment: So much to do and so little time in which to do it.

Ed Feulner approved the Heatherly memorandum, although almost from a hospital bed. In mid-January he had a coronary "event" that put him in intensive care for a few days and necessitated tests to determine what had happened. He was advised that he was trying to do too much, eating too much, and smoking more than was good for him. He promised to be more careful and plunged back into work.

The choice of some team chairs was obvious—the economist Norman Ture for Treasury, Sven Kramer and Tidal McCoy for Defense, Jeffrey Gayner for State. Some chairmen did not work out; others made false starts. For some agencies, there were not many knowledgeable or experienced conservatives. "Commerce was a nightmare for us," recalls Heatherly, and "transportation was difficult." There were "endless, endless meetings of teams, inside and outside" Heritage, during which many pizzas and six-packs of Coors beer were consumed.[10]

Yet Heritage seemed to know where to find the right analyst for a department or agency. There was unanimous agreement that the best man to head the team on regulatory agencies was James E. Hinish, Jr. Not one American in a thousand had heard of Hinish, but Heritage knew that he was counsel for the Senate Republican Policy Committee and one of the chief architects of the Republican National Convention's regulatory proposals. Hinish "recruited an outstanding team and did yeoman's work in coordinating the regulatory reform study."[11]

Here is a sample of the Hinish chapter: "Deregulation is working well in the airlines industry and it should work well in other forms of transportation. Communications seems a likely target for deregulation, although radio is an easier target then television."[12] It would take several years, but in 1987 the FCC's elimination of the Fairness Doctrine led to a new and politically powerful form of mass communication—talk radio.

Another team cochairman—of the section on the National Endowments for the Humanities and the Arts—was a young man named William Bennett, unknown to almost everyone in Washington. He was recommended by Michael Joyce of the Bradley Foundation. "We took Mike's word that Bennett was a good guy," recalls Phil Truluck, "and besides who else in the conservative movement knew about the arts?"[13]

Ultimately, more than 250 experts served on twenty teams, while dozens more contributed ideas and read drafts. To maintain Heritage's nonpartisan status, Heatherly wrote to both the Reagan-Bush and Carter-Mondale campaigns, offering to meet with them about the Heritage project. No one from Carter-Mondale headquarters ever responded, while Reagan-Bush quickly set up a meeting.

Every contributor from outside Heritage volunteered their time and expertise, cognizant of the historic nature of the project. Nevertheless, the cost of the luncheons and late-night snacks was considerable, sometimes reaching $6,000 in a single month. The total cost of producing *Mandate for Leadership: Policy Management in a Conservative Administration* was approximately $250,000, a major sum for any think tank, let alone a middle-sized organization like Heritage. The typesetting and printing costs of the book version, in the days before personal computers and desktop publishing, were about $100,000. The salaries of three full-time people were $100,000. Beer, pizza, and other incidentals totaled $50,000. Combined with the hundreds of hours expended and the inevitable diversion of staff and space, *Mandate* represented an enormous investment for the seven-year-old institute. But it was a calculated investment.

"It was something I will never forget," says Truluck, "the way people came together to do *Mandate*. Almost universally when we would ask people to help, they'd say, 'Yeah, let's do that—it'd be fun.' "[14]

Ed Meese was "totally supportive, absolutely delighted we were undertaking the project," Truluck remembers. "But like everybody else I think he was wondering, 'How can these guys pull it off? They have a really small organization.' " His questioning attitude changed when he learned that Heritage was recruiting dozens of people whom he knew and respected.[15]

In the spring Ed Meese visited Heritage and was briefed on *Mandate*. On another occasion campaign manager William Casey dropped by and was told about the study. In July—after all the first drafts had been submitted—the foundation decided to hold a dinner for the team chairmen and cochairmen at the University Club on 16th Street, N.W., four blocks from the White House. A smiling Meese attended and gave *Mandate* his blessing, ensuring the study would be warmly received by a Reagan administration.[16]

Feulner bombarded Heatherly with memoranda about the project. Make time for Bill Rusher when you are in New York, he directed, and be sure to "sit down and talk to [New Right leader] Howie Phillips." Don Devine "knows very well what the civil service situation is" and can be a valuable resource. (Reagan concurred, appointing Devine as the director of the Office of Personnel Management—the U.S. government's civil service.)[17]

In June, Feulner sent Heatherly a detailed memorandum that asked: How are you monitoring the work of the task forces? How can Heritage's other departments be more helpful? What is "a realistic schedule" for completion? How can Heritage's management be kept better informed? What are your main problems? He asked the foundation's other senior managers to detail how their department was assisting Heatherly.[18]

Ever prudent, he cautioned his staff about overt political activity in support of the man they devoutly hoped would win the presidency. Noting that Jeff Gayner has been listed as a foreign policy adviser to the Reagan campaign, Feulner reminded him that "any activities which you perform in this capacity must be done on your own time, that is, after hours or on the weekends." If Gayner did anything for Reagan during normal working hours, "you will please report [you are on] annual leave without pay in order to insure that the Foundation is not adversely affected in terms of our tax exempt status."[19]

Everyone associated with *Mandate* realized they were working on a historic document unprecedented in national policy making. Carefully tracing its progress throughout the year, Feulner became concerned about its ever-increasing length and asked Heatherly, "Can you cut it in half?" "Sure," responded the laconic editor, "if you can postpone Election Day. We don't have time for the editing that would be necessary."[20]

• • •

In his July acceptance speech at the Republican National Convention in Detroit, Ronald Reagan sought to bind together all the elements of the GOP while reaching out to independents and disillusioned Democrats. He articulated the traditional sources of American thought from the Mayflower Compact and the Founding Fathers to the Gettysburg Address and a quotation from Franklin D. Roosevelt attacking excessive government spending. He ended with a silent moment of prayer for the American hostages in Iran.

His theme was summed up in five words—"family, work, neighborhood, peace, freedom"—that would serve as guideposts for his administration. Although some in the national news media were puzzled by the FDR references, Reagan was deliberately reaching out to Americans, especially Democrats, who had lost confidence in President Carter and remembered the days when the White House was "the source of effective national leadership." Reagan believed that most Americans wanted that kind of leadership again.[21]

Although all the national polls placed Reagan well ahead of Carter after the Republican convention, the president got a sizable bump from the Democratic convention. By Labor Day, the two candidates were about even, but as Reagan biographer Lou Cannon neatly put it, Carter was dogged by the captivity of hostages he could not free, an economy he could not improve, and an opponent he could not shake.[22]

Reagan stayed on the offensive, delivering specialized messages to key constituencies he visited. In Miami he denounced Fidel Castro and promised that America would remain a refuge for those fleeing tyranny. In Springfield, Missouri, he criticized Carter for hesitating to declare the state a disaster area following a severe drought. In Tyler, Texas, he charged that Carter was afraid to debate energy policy with him. And in Grand Junction, Colorado, he declared that westerners knew how to manage their water resources better than the federal bureaucracy did.

The content of his speeches was traditional Republican—cut taxes, limit government—but his style was traditional Democrat, with constant references to family, neighborhood, work, and peace.

With two weeks left in the campaign, Reagan held a narrow lead of about seven points in the popular vote and a comfortable margin in the electoral vote. Reagan and most of his advisers concluded they could not sit on a safe but slim lead and played their last card—a televised debate with Jimmy Carter. Although some of his aides were nervous, Reagan was confident he could hold his own with the president.

On Tuesday, October 28, one week before Election Day—and sixteen years to the day when Reagan made his historic TV speech for Barry Goldwater—the two candidates stood behind specially constructed rostrums on the stage of Cleveland's Music Hall for the one and only debate of the 1980 presidential campaign. The viewership was estimated at 105 million Americans, one of the largest political audiences in history. Both men wore dark suits and muted ties, but the similarities ended there.

Carter was tight-lipped and rigid, rarely looking at his opponent. He immediately went on the attack and stayed there for ninety minutes, constantly describing Reagan's ideas and positions as "dangerous," "disturbing," and "radical."[23]

Reagan was calm and smiling. He spent much of his time patiently explaining where Carter had misquoted or misrepresented him, much like a professor gently correcting an overzealous student. The climax of the debate—and the effective end of the campaign—came when Carter tried to link Reagan with making Social Security voluntary and opposing Medicare. That familiar crooked smile appeared on Reagan's face, and with a rueful shake of his head, he looked at Carter and said, "There you go again."[24] The Carter campaign of fear collapsed in an instant. Reagan ensured Carter's defeat and his victory with his closing remarks when he looked straight into the camera and asked: "Are you better off than you were four years ago?"[25]

The man who was supposedly too conservative and too old to be president won by an electoral landslide and more than eight million popular votes. He carried forty-four states (the same number as Lyndon Johnson in his runaway 1964 victory over Barry Goldwater), with a total of 489 electoral votes. His coattails helped the GOP pick up twelve seats in the Senate, giving it majority control for the first time in a quarter-century. In the House, Republicans registered a gain of thirty-three, almost all of them conservative.

Former Senator George McGovern, the 1972 Democratic presidential nominee, said that the voters "had abandoned American liberalism." In an editorial titled "Tidal Wave," *The Washington Post* acknowledged that 1980 was no ordinary election year: "Nothing of that size and force and sweep could have been created over a weekend or even a week or two by the assorted mullahs and miseries of our times."[26]

Official Washington and the nation settled back to see what the president-elect would do with the mandate he had been handed. Very few knew that Reagan and his people had a 1,093-page manual to guide them.

· · ·

Ed Meese confirmed publicly that the Reagan administration would "rely heavily" on *Mandate for Leadership.* "Leaders in both the new administration and the Congress," said OMB director-designate David Stockman, "will find in this work all the tools they need to hit the ground running." Representative Trent Lott, the House minority whip, described *Mandate* as "unparalleled in scope" and "a useful guide, not only for the administration but also for many of us on Capitol Hill." Pendleton James, soon to be director of White House personnel, called the study "valuable because it's all concrete recommendations rather than generalities . . . we can get our teeth into it."[27]

There were notes of congratulation to Feulner from David Abshire, his old boss at the Center for Strategic Studies, who was a prominent member of the Reagan transition—"a very well done document"—and from former President Richard Nixon: "Your 'Mandate for Leadership' has stirred controversy. Consider this a plus."[28]

The news media were also impressed. *The Washington Post* called *Mandate* "an action plan for turning the government toward the right as fast as possible." "Unabashedly conservative," said the Gannett News Service, "the Heritage recommendations employ a candor and plain language absent from most Washington writing." In its article about the study, the *St. Louis Globe-Democrat* described Heritage as "one of the nation's most respected private research organizations."[29]

Unlike most transition studies of the past, *Mandate for Leadership* was not a work of political rhetoric but a public policy document. It was specific and realistic.

Addressing the question of submarines—a critical part of America's triad defense—the defense chapter recommended that Trident submarine construction be increased from the current one boat a year to three boats a year through fiscal year 1985 and then two boats every year thereafter. "While the Trident submarine is not an inexpensive program, the addition of 24 missiles tubes with each additional submarine can substantially improve the U.S. strategic posture in the early to mid-1980s."[30]

Some Heritage proposals reflected the differences within the Right. The interior chapter called for a return of control over most mining, reclamation, and water rights to the states but did not recommend legal action to transfer land to the states—a goal of the "Sagebrush Revolution" that Reagan supported.[31]

One of the study's timelier passages dealt with the possibility that PATCO, the air traffic controllers' union, might initiate an illegal strike, shutting down the U.S. air transport system. *Mandate* warned that such a strike would "far overshadow all other short-term [domestic] problems of a new administration." Therefore the administration could not afford to take "a weak and wishy-washy stance."[32]

When the controllers did go out on strike in the spring of 1981, President Reagan followed Heritage's advice: he quickly replaced the striking controllers and kept the nation's planes flying, serving notice to everyone at home and abroad (Moscow took special note of his firm action) that he would be a decisive chief executive.

Every page of *Mandate* reflected Heritage's mission—to change the way Washington worked. "We aimed to slash income tax rates," Ed Feulner later said, "ultimately moving toward a flat tax. We wanted to eliminate capital gains taxes and other corporate taxes. We were (and still are) convinced that we should tax consumption, not production. We believed that you should reward enterprise, work, savings, and investment. Norman Ture presented this vision in his Treasury chapter."[33]

But the authors of *Mandate* and Heritage itself recognized that political reality dictated that a pure "supply-side" tax code could not be achieved overnight. Ture outlined some initial steps. "In the short run," he wrote, "we suggest a relatively simple tax package to be presented in the next Budget Message in January." It had three pieces: (1) an across-the-board reduction in marginal personal income tax rates in each bracket of about 10 percent a year; (2) accelerated depreciation allowances for business; and (3) a reduction in corporate income tax rates.[34] These recommendations were adopted by the Reagan administration and became the center of the Economic Recovery Tax Act of 1981.

In the chapter on the Office of Management and Budget, author Joe Rogers proposed several dozen changes in the budget process to bring federal spending under control. Some were relatively minor, dealing with paper flow and office reorganization. Others were more substantive, such as urging the new president to push hard for line-item veto authority.

Presidents had the authority to delay or not spend appropriated funds before Congress passed the Congressional Budget and Impoundment Control Act of 1974. This post-Watergate law required congressional approval of any presidential decision not to spend money approved by Congress. Rogers suggested modifying the law to permit the president not to spend money unless vetoed by a simple majority vote in one house of Congress. Such a procedure would give the president greater ability to control unnecessary spending while providing enough congressional oversight to ensure that the president could not subvert the will of Congress.[35]

President Reagan lobbied Congress hard but was never able to persuade members to grant him line-item veto authority. However, in March 1992, President George H. W. Bush announced he would refuse to spend taxpayer monies earmarked for special interest pork-barrel projects unless Congress voted to pass the projects individually, not collectively. This was a variation of the line-item veto contained in *Mandate for Leadership*.

The premise of the chapter on national defense was straightforward:

"The past 15 years have witnessed history's most dramatic shift in the world's military balance of power. The United States has moved from a position of overwhelming military superiority over the USSR in the mid-1960s to second place in military power and is rapidly moving toward a state of military inferiority because of [President] Carter's no-growth defense budgets."[36]

Actions that would enable the United States to regain military superiority included the development of a new strategic bomber (which became the B-2 Stealth aircraft); reviving development and deployment of the cruise missile (canceled by Carter); speeding up deployment of the MX missile; and beginning development of a comprehensive space-based antimissile system that could protect the United States from an intercontinental nuclear missile attack (later introduced by Reagan as the Strategic Defense Initiative).

Feulner considered the defense chapter one of the most important parts of *Mandate for Leadership,* consistent with the foundation's mission of supporting a strong national defense in a perilous world.

The defense section urged increasing the budget for research and development of new weapons; invigorating our rapid deployment forces; vastly increasing salaries and benefits for America's volunteer army (morale in the armed forces had dropped precipitously); and laying out plans for a six-hundred-ship navy by the end of the decade. Secretary of Defense Caspar Weinberger and Pentagon officials adopted over half of Heritage's proposals.

One of *Mandate*'s most arresting chapters was "What the President Can Do by Executive Order," written by Danny Boggs, later a senior domestic policy adviser and then chief judge of the Sixth Circuit of the U.S. Court of Appeals, and his colleagues. They pointed out that the president could, if he so chose, do much to push the government in a conservative direction.

He could impose a federal hiring freeze (which Reagan did as soon as he took office). He could eliminate government regulations not mandated by congressional statute. He could repeal affirmative action guidelines and racial quotas in federal hiring and the awarding of government contracts.

Short of terminating government agencies and programs, he could refocus their mission to pursue conservative rather than liberal objectives. He could immediately complete the decontrol of energy prices and free up public lands for oil exploration. (Reagan did the former before he and Nancy finished unpacking.) He could end all wage and price guidelines, eliminate restrictions on foreign companies' ability to invest in America, and end government funding for politically motivated "public interest" organizations not mandated by statute. In his first year, Reagan issued executive orders that carried out almost all of the above recommendations.

CHAPTER 10

PEOPLE ARE POLICY

Mandate for Leadership also served as a prime recruiting tool. The White House, led by personnel chief Pendleton James, assumed that anyone smart enough to write a chapter on how to run a department was qualified to run the department. "There were many qualified conservatives in Washington capable of heading a federal agency or department," Feulner says. "There was no need to rely on political retreads from the Nixon and Ford administration who might not understand what the Reagan Revolution was all about."[1]

Of the 250 analysts and scholars who worked on *Mandate,* the new administration immediately selected more than fifteen for high-level executive branch positions. Norman Ture, for example, was tapped to be the Treasury's undersecretary for tax and economic affairs, a new office specifically mentioned in the Heritage study. Economist Manuel Johnson also went to Treasury and was later named vice chairman of the powerful board of governors of the Federal Reserve.

Fourteen Heritage people served on the Reagan transition team. Among those who went into the administration were Willa Johnson, who did a six-month stint in the White House personnel office; and analyst Eugene McAllister, who moved to the OMB under David Stockman. Charles Heatherly, majordomo of the *Mandate* project, became special assistant to the education secretary before returning to Heritage in the late 1980s as vice president of academic relations.

Of Heatherly's *Mandate* role, Phil Truluck says flatly, "it was one of the biggest tasks anyone's ever undertaken in this town. He got it organized, and kept it running. Without Chuck, it would have been extremely difficult to pull off, maybe impossible."[2]

Even with Ronald Reagan coming to town, engendering widespread anticipation among conservatives, Heritage did not ignore Capitol Hill. "We still saw Congress, not the administration, as our primary audience," says Feulner. "And there were lots of new conservative faces—twelve senators and thirty-three Congressmen." In December 1980, Heritage held its largest congressional staff training seminar ever, with more than two hundred job seekers in attendance.

For Ed Feulner, the direction of the new administration depended in large part on the mindset of those around the president. Were they solid conservatives—Reaganauts, to use Richard Allen's evocative term—committed to limited government and First Principles, or soft moderates with no fixed set of beliefs ready to compromise and give in if they encountered resistance?

Also critical to success was that the administration get off to a fast start, making as many dramatic changes as soon as possible to show the people that this was a new day. "The honeymoon is so short," Feulner pointed out to a reporter. "After you've been here for more than 60 or 90 days, people start looking on you as part of the problem rather than part of the solution."[3]

Reagan must have been listening. At his first news conference in late January, the president denounced the Soviet leadership as still dedicated to "world revolution and a one-world Socialist-Communist state," removed price controls on oil and gasoline, and repeated his intention to abolish the Departments of Energy and Education. *The New York Times* did not endorse his anti-Communist rhetoric but said he was "right" to end oil controls "eight months ahead of schedule."[4]

A week later Reagan delivered his first televised "fireside chat" from the Oval Office, saying Americans must accept cuts in almost every government program if the nation was to avoid an "economic calamity." He pledged a 30 percent personal income tax cut over the next three years—the Kemp-Roth bill—but promised to retain a "social safety net" for the truly needy. *Newsweek* called Reagan's plan to cut spending *and* income taxes a "second New Deal potentially as profound in its impact as the first was a half century ago."[5]

At the same time, the president increased the 1981 and 1982 defense budgets by $32.6 billion, infuriating the disarmament lobby. *The New*

York Times termed Reagan's military budget "a reversal of national priorities as basic and significant as the Great Society programs of President Johnson in the mid-1960s." But after a decade of military decline, Reagan was determined that the United States would once again achieve military superiority over the Soviet Union—not to wage war but to seek peace through strength.[6]

In late March, speaking at the Conservative Political Action Conference (CPAC) in Washington, Reagan outlined his goals and issued a challenge:

> *Fellow conservatives—our time is now, our moment has arrived.*
>
> *Because ours is a consistent philosophy of government, we can be very clear: we do not have a separate social agenda, a separate economic agenda, and a separate foreign agenda. We have one agenda.*
>
> *Just as surely as we seek to put our financial house in order and rebuild our nation's defenses, so too we seek to protect the unborn, to end the manipulation of school children by utopian planners, and permit the acknowledgement of a supreme being in our classrooms.*
>
> *If we carry the day and turn the tide we can hope that as long as men speak of freedom and those who have protected it they will remember us and they will say, "Here were the brave and here their place of honor."*[7]

The CPAC audience rose as one and roared their approval, vowing to carry out the marching orders they had just received.

• • •

The single most important domestic achievement of the Reagan presidency was the passage of the Economic Recovery Tax Act of 1981, in which Heritage played a critical role. The act would put $749 billion into the hands of individual taxpayers and businesses over the next five years. In approving Reagan's tax-cut bill—he reluctantly agreed to a tax cut of 25 rather than 30 percent—Congress veered sharply away from the tax-and-spend Keynesian philosophy that had guided liberal Congresses since the New Deal.

Passage did not come easily. The Republican Senate was expected to approve the measure easily, but the Democratic House under Speaker Thomas P. (Tip) O'Neill and Ways and Means chairman Dan Rostenkowski was another matter. House liberals crafted an alternative to the Reagan proposal, giving two-thirds of the tax cuts to Americans earning $20,000 to $50,000 a year and pitting the middle class against the wealthy (an approach similar to that of the Democratic Congresses of 2009 and 2010).

O'Neill and Rostenkowski hoped that their tax-cut package would prevent defection by conservative Southern Democrats—the so-called Boll Weevils—many of whom appeared ready to support the Reagan plan. Today such conservative Democrats are called Blue Dog Democrats and are a vanishing breed, numbering perhaps two dozen, according to Heritage vice president Mike Franc.

The president did his part, inviting Boll Weevil Democrats to the White House, telephoning them frequently, recalling his days as a Democrat, encouraging them to join a bipartisan effort to get the economy moving again by cutting everyone's taxes.

Responding to the liberal proposal, Heritage published *An Analysis of the Reagan Tax Cuts and the Democratic Alternative* by analyst Thomas M. Humbert, who conceded that the Democratic bill had some good provisions but said the Reagan plan was superior because (1) its tax cut was bigger—25 percent to the Democrats' 15 percent; (2) it would be enacted over three years instead of the Democrats' two years; and (3) it cut marginal tax rates across the board, while the Democrats aimed two-thirds of their cuts at low- and middle-income taxpayers.

The underlying Hayekian assumption of the Reagan approach, Humbert wrote, is that when individuals are left to pursue their self-interest "unhindered by government," they will generate enormous productive activity to the benefit of the entire nation.[8]

Here was Heritage at its best, providing detailed analysis of a major issue in the middle of a national debate. The Humbert paper served as the basis for dozens of speeches by members of Congress and newspaper editorials backing the Reagan bill. Humbert's analysis established him as an acknowledged expert on tax legislation and later earned him a position as a senior economic adviser to Jack Kemp.

Reagan's economic recovery program was assured congressional approval in late July, when the Democratic-controlled house acceded to enormous public pressure—generated by a strong TV appeal by President Reagan—and adopted his plan rather than the O'Neill-Rostenkowski alternative. Forty-eight Democrats defected as the House voted 238–195 to adopt the bill introduced by Republican Barber Conable and Democrat Kent Hance of Texas. Hance, a leader of the Boll Weevils, publicly praised Heritage research as "one of the most valuable tools that Congress can use."

Would Reagan's economic plan have passed Congress without Humbert's analysis and Heritage's pinpoint delivery to the right congressmen and their staffs? Probably. But Hance's open acknowledgment suggests that without Humbert and the work of other Heritage analysts, victory would have been much more difficult and prolonged.

President Reagan acknowledged as much in a warm "Dear Ed" letter that thanked Feulner for his "hard work" and his role in a "superb team effort." "Thanks to you," he wrote, "we have begun our historic journey toward national renewal. . . . We have achieved a great deal together already. I would like to continue our partnership for the American people."[9]

The epic battle over the Reagan tax-cut bill reinforced the importance of coalition building. Liberals had converted their proposals into laws for decades by giving taxpayer money to constituent groups—such as organized labor and the poor—that grew accustomed to the largesse of the welfare state. "With the Reagan economic recovery plan," says Feulner, "we set out to build a counter-coalition that gave people a vested financial interest in an alternative to the welfare state—the free enterprise system."[10]

The coalition included ordinary working Americans and businesses—in other words, taxpayers. Within these constituencies were groups that had traditionally voted Democratic, like rank-and-file union members, conservative Southern Democrats, and black and Hispanic entrepreneurs. Instead of taking people's money and then giving it away, with a large part siphoned off by government bureaucrats, the conservative coalition would ensure that Americans would be allowed to keep more of their hard-earned money and spend it or save it or invest it as they wished.

"We also needed American business to get fully behind the program," Feulner says. That meant giving business a "tax cut" of 40 percent in accelerated depreciation on capital investments. This was good economics and good politics. "If the tax cuts worked," Feulner explains, "they would provide the cornerstone of a coalition favoring free enterprise that would be as powerful and enduring as the one that supported FDR's New Deal for four decades."[11]

Feulner, Jack Kemp, Arthur Laffer, and editor Robert Bartley of *The Wall Street Journal* were supply-side conservatives committed to tax cuts because they put people's money in their pockets. There was another reason: "We believed that cutting taxes would have an automatic restraining effect on government spending," Feulner says, "by depriving Congress of the money it wanted and would spend if they got their hands on it."[12]

And they were right. Government spending did grow under President Reagan—about 2 percent a year—but far less than under the two presidents who bracketed him: about 5 percent a year under Carter and 10 percent a year under George H. W. Bush. Spending increased under Reagan in constant dollars due to unprecedented economic growth that had been spurred by tax cuts, as Feulner and other supply-siders predicted.

Heritage did not neglect the budget debate, publishing in early 1981 another blockbuster—the 378-page *Agenda for Progress: Examining Federal Spending.* Written by a twenty-member panel of university scholars and economists and edited by Eugene McAllister, the Walker fellow in economics, the study named dozens of programs, such as the space shuttle and FHA-insured loans, that could be shifted to the private sector, for savings of $58.6 billion in 1982 alone. At the heart of the study was the principle that the time had come to give private-sector institutions and individuals a larger role in implementing public policy.

The Reagan administration again expressed its public appreciation as OMB director David Stockman said: "The ideas that we received from the Heritage Foundation were used, were implemented, and have now become the law of the land." Summing up the foundation's contribution, Stockman said: "What has become known as the 'Reagan Revolution' in federal tax and spending policy would have literally been impossible without the invaluable . . . work done by the Heritage Foundation."[13]

• • •

Always mindful of the importance of national defense, Heritage in 1981 released *Reforming the Military,* edited by Jeffrey G. Barlow, which outlined how military planners could greatly increase the effectiveness of military spending. A five-member panel of defense analysts and military scholars recommended sweeping changes in manpower and procurement policies as well as shifts in combat strategy.

The main criterion in making military decisions, said the experts, should be that "of combat effectiveness—improving our ability to defeat the enemy rather than economic efficiency." Surprising some conservatives, the study argued that "dollars alone" would not "bridge the chasm between American and Soviet capabilities." The Maginot Line would not have been "any more useful" to France in World War II had it cost less to build. What was needed, said Edward Luttwak of Georgetown University, was a comprehensive, coordinated strategy, "not bureaucratically-preferred procedures."[14]

Recommendations included replacing America's "attrition/firepower" style of warfare with one emphasizing maneuverability, scratching plans to reactivate mothballed World War II battleships, and moving away from procuring additional large, expensive, avionics-laden aircraft in favor of less expensive, highly maneuverable fighters.

Even during the hectic summer of 1981, Heritage did not neglect ongoing issues, producing *Backgrounders* and *Issue Bulletins* on "The Illusive Mitterand and French Foreign Policy," "Social Security Reform," and "The Soviet Military Role in Cuba." And it responded quickly when necessary.

Just before Jamaica's prime minister visited the United States and met with President Reagan, the foundation issued a report on Jamaica's economy—a central topic between the two leaders. The day after Secretary of State Alexander Haig declared that combating terrorism would be one of his top priorities, Heritage released a major monograph titled *The Soviet Strategy of Terror,* showing the Soviet Union was one of the world's chief sponsors of international terrorism. In the middle of congressional debate on whether to maintain the U.S. grain embargo against the Soviet Union, Heritage published a study urging the embargo be strengthened—a position that put it at odds with the White House.

• • •

In September 1981, Heritage made a lasting personnel decision when it hired Burton Yale Pines as its vice president of research. Pines came to the foundation from *Time* magazine where, during his fifteen-year career, he served in its Bonn, Vienna, Chicago, and Saigon bureaus. He had solid academic credentials, having completed his coursework for a PhD in modern European history at the University of Wisconsin. From 1980 to 1981, Pines was at the American Enterprise Institute writing *Back to Basics,* an examination of what he called "traditional America."

During his ten years at Heritage, Pines multiplied the foundation's research output five-fold, from about one paper a week to 250 papers a year. His goal: when any major topic came up at the White House or a congressional office, someone would remark, "Let's see what Heritage has to say." Pines made Heritage researchers think more like journalists and less like academics.

He insisted that every Heritage study read quickly, like a *Time* article. Determined to enforce editorial discipline, he personally edited every Heritage study (totaling about 2.5 million words a year) and often sent a paper back for a second or third rewrite.

He launched new publications such as the two-page *Executive Memo,* which enabled Heritage to comment on an event or issue within hours. In early 1984, for example, the Marxist Sandinista government of Nicaragua filed a suit in the World Court seeking to stop U.S. funding for the contras, the anti-Communist resistance movement. When the White House chose to ignore the World Court's demand that the United States appear before the tribunal, liberals accused the Reagan administration of ignoring international law.

Drawing on his foreign policy experience, Pines wrote an *Executive Memo* defending the White House decision as legally and politically justified. "It would be foolish," he wrote, to engage in a legal dispute with "a regime that routinely disregards international laws and norms, violates its citizens' human rights, suppresses dissent, imposes censorship, and refuses to hold free elections."[15] Conservative members of Congress extensively cited the memo, and Pines appeared on several network television programs. Public opinion shifted in favor of the administration, and a potential embarrassment for the Reagan administration was turned into a setback for the Sandinista regime.

The Heritage Foundation "is like no think tank you've ever seen," reported *The Washington Post.* "If America is weaving unsteadily back toward the right-hand side of the road, The Heritage Foundation, while not at the steering wheel exactly, is filling the gas tank, tuning the engine and shoving a road map under the driver's nose."[16]

Pines expanded the Heritage lecture series from about one formal address a month to more than one hundred talks, panels, and other events a year. "By 2012, the foundation held two hundred public events annually." He hired Ben Hart, a former editor of the combative *Dartmouth Review,* as director of lectures and seminars. Pines said he didn't care how large the audience was—"all those who turned up at Heritage were participants in the Reagan revolution."[17]

Someone who remembers Burt Pines well is social scientist Charles Murray, author of *Losing Ground,* the seminal work about the failure of the American welfare system. In the fall of 1981, Murray decided to leave his position as chief scientist for the American Institutes of Research in Washington to make a living as an independent researcher and author. He wrote to several think tanks inquiring about possible fellowships. The only response came from Burt Pines, who invited Murray to drop by Heritage.

At the time liberals were charging that Reagan's budget cuts would "shred" the safety net that protected needy Americans. Murray said that such criticism was silly. Trained to follow the money trail, Pines told Murray that he wanted to know what had happened to the billions of dollars spent fighting the War on Poverty, which clearly had not been won—millions of Americans remained below the poverty line.

He suggested that Murray write a monograph on whether Lyndon B. Johnson's welfare programs had been a success or a failure. The result was a 1982 Heritage study (edited and approved by Stuart Butler) that made history—*Safety Nets and the Truly Needy: Rethinking the Social Welfare System.*

Murray showed that the percentage of Americans in poverty had been dropping since World War II but slowed in the 1960s and then stopped in the mid-1970s—just as government spending on poverty programs rose sharply. Murray declared that welfare programs, which were supposed to lift people out of poverty, undermined the work ethic and created a culture of dependency and a permanent dependent underclass.

Furthermore, the combination of public assistance and nonwork time contributed to the breakdown of the family and the community, especially in the inner cities. "The poor are living in worse conditions now than they were twenty years ago," Murray summed up. "The social ills that a progressive social welfare policy proposed to eradicate have accelerated under its aegis."[18]

Murray proposed four reforms: (1) assistance should be provided for those unable to hold work; (2) holding a full-time job is preferable to "any combination of work and welfare"; (3) a stigma should be attached to anyone who is able-bodied and on welfare; and (4) rewards for those who "achieve" should be greater than rewards for those who do not. These commonsense ideas would guide much of the discussion of the next decade that resulted in the Welfare Reform Act of 1996, based in large part on Heritage research and analysis, especially by the formidable Robert Rector, who joined Heritage in 1984.

In the spring of 1981, Feulner and Truluck sketched out a major restructure of Heritage management on a plane ride to Chicago to attend the annual meeting of the Philadelphia Society.

"Ed, I want to show you something," Truluck said, holding up a little chart. "We now have about seventy people at Heritage."

"Oh, really?" Feulner responded, somewhat surprised.

"Yes," said Truluck, "and the best I can tell, five report to you, and that leaves sixty-five for me. Which explains why I can't get much done."

"We'll have to do something about that," Feulner agreed.

And so they did, right then and there on the plane, drawing up a classic organizational chart based on their business school training, with a CEO, a COO, and half a dozen vice presidents, including Burt Pines. "Almost all of the new vice presidents were already there," explains Truluck. "We just moved them up, gave them management authority for their budget and their department. The structure is still what we have today. We have a lot more boxes now, a lot more lines, a lot more depth, but we haven't really changed."[19]

Phil Truluck became executive vice president and chief operating officer of the foundation with direct responsibility for daily operations. Ed Feulner no longer had to worry about who was minding the store when he was on the road, meeting major donors and developing relationships with public officials, donors, and scholars around the world.

"We created a management structure that remained in place for thirty-five years," says Truluck.[20] In effect, Phil Truluck became Mr. Inside (the coordinator and implementer) while Ed Feulner became Mr. Outside (the visionary and supersalesman), although when he is in the building, Feulner is a hands-on president. It is a sign of Feulner's inner confidence and managerial acumen that he welcomed as his number-two man a strong but low-key individual like Truluck. Their decades-long partnership is based on mutual respect and trust, a commitment to the foundation and the conservative movement, and a belief that conservatism contains the best answers for the nation's problems. It has evolved over the years into a trusting friendship.

At the same time John Von Kannon, former publisher of *The American Spectator,* was named vice president and treasurer, taking over the financial affairs of the foundation, especially fund-raising. The ever-smiling Von Kannon is widely acknowledged to be one of the most effective fund-raisers in America.

Nothing is more important to Heritage than its financial independence. Von Kannon recalls one year when five steel companies and a prominent textile manufacturer stopped giving (their donations were in the six figures) because of the foundation's free-trade stance. One steel executive became so angry that he tore up a $10,000 check in front of Feulner. With Ronald Reagan in the White House and Ed Feulner on the road, Heritage's income rose more than a third, from $5.3 million in 1980 to almost $7.1 million in 1981, its staff increased to eighty-seven full-time employees.

There was also a change in the leadership of the board of trustees when Frank Shakespeare succeeded Ben Blackburn as chairman and Shelby Cullom Davis became vice chairman. Shakespeare brought thirty years of broadcasting and political experience to the board. President Reagan would later appoint Shakespeare U.S. ambassador, first to Portugal and then to the Vatican (where he helped facilitate assistance to freedom fighters in Poland and other Soviet satellites). Davis combined a highly successful business and financial career in New York with diplomacy as U.S. ambassador to Switzerland. He succeeded Shakespeare as Heritage chairman when the latter went to Lisbon. Under their leadership, Heritage experienced what Phil Truluck calls "the glory days."[21]

Someone who experienced those glorious days firsthand was the Italian economist and politician Antonio Martino, who was at Heritage from 1980 to 1981 as a visiting distinguished scholar. Martino would serve as Italy's minister of foreign affairs in the 1990s and minister of defense in the 2000s. He first met Ed Feulner in 1975 at a regional meeting of the Mont Pelerin Society at Hillsdale College in Michigan. The two young conservative intellectuals—both in their thirties—became fast friends.

"I saw the [1980] campaign, the election, and how Heritage cooperated with the incoming administration," Martino recalls. "It was one of the most exciting years in my life. I remember my first lecture at Heritage. I gave it sitting on a carton of books in the basement. Heritage had only about twenty-two employees at the time."

Of Heritage's president, he says, "Ed is a workaholic, dedicated to the cause of liberty, freedom, and prosperity in the world. He does not spare himself. He is a conservative in civil matters and a revolutionary in economics—a Friedman liberal."

Martino speaks with awe of Feulner's ability to read—"he's the most avid and rapid reader I know. And he reads everything. He knows more about things in Italy than I do."

Of Heritage, he says, "It has performed a small miracle—it has grown and grown without losing effectiveness or efficiency. And it is because of the two pillars—Ed and Phil."

Asked how much he values his friendship with Ed Feulner, Antonio Martino smiles and tells a story. "In the 1990s when I was defense minister of Italy, Tony Lake, President Clinton's national security adviser, arranged a meeting for me with Clinton. When I arrived at the White House, I was told that the president was a little delayed and would I mind waiting for a few minutes? I replied that I was very sorry, but I have an appointment with another president, President Ed Feulner of the Heritage Foundation, and cannot keep him waiting."[22]

CHAPTER II

THE MOST IMPORTANT INITIATIVE

Of Heritage's many projects, none was more critical to America's national defense and the outcome of the Cold War than its sponsorship of a new space strategy called High Frontier. At a March 1982 news conference, Ed Feulner and retired Lt. Gen. Daniel O. Graham, former director of the Pentagon's Defense Intelligence Agency, outlined the results of a months-long, $50,000 study that urged the Reagan administration and the Congress to adopt an all-out effort to develop both military and peaceful uses of space. The study's most dramatic recommendation was for the development of a multisatellite ballistic missile defense system capable of knocking out enemy nuclear missiles aimed at the United States.

High Frontier, explained General Graham, constituted a change of U.S. strategy "from the bankrupt and basically immoral precepts of Mutually Assured Destruction (MAD) to a stable and morally defensible strategy of Assured Survival." He asserted that a layered strategic defense, including a "capacity to intercept" Soviet missiles midcourse, could be accomplished in a remarkably short time if there was "a national commitment to do so."[1]

Graham had been a military adviser to Reagan during the 1980 presidential campaign and the leader of a group that advocated a fundamental change in U.S. strategy by making a technological end run around the Soviets in space. The Reagan administration initially focused on plugging up the yawning gaps between American and Soviet military capabilities.

While not denying that weapons like the MX missile and the B-1 bomber were needed—Heritage had recommended both weapons in *Mandate for Leadership*—Feulner said that a High Frontier strategy would enable the administration and the nation to make greater use of "the industrialized and peaceful applications of space as well as the tapping of its military potential."[2] The Heritage study found a receptive audience in the Oval Office. Since the mid-1960s, Reagan had been unhappy with America's reliance on the policy of MAD and had often pressed scientific and military experts to come up with alternatives.

In the early fall of 1981, Reagan kitchen cabinet member Jacquelin Hume and defense specialist Karl Bendetsen talked to presidential counselor Ed Meese about the possibility of a missile defense system. Meese, who was aware of Heritage's work with General Graham on such a system, was receptive. Subsequently, Meese, domestic policy assistant Martin Anderson, and national security adviser Richard Allen decided to bring together a select group to discuss missile defense. On September 14, 1981, Meese chaired the first White House discussion of what would become the Strategic Defense Initiative.

Present, in addition to Meese and Anderson, were Bendetsen, General Graham, George Keyworth, the president's science adviser, famed nuclear physicist Edward Teller, and Edwin Thomas, Meese's assistant. "Not only did everyone feel we should pursue the idea of missile defense," Anderson recalled, "they also deeply believed that it could be done." There was general agreement that a major part of the missile defense effort would "probably" be based in space, and that such a system "could defend not only our population and cities, but also our offensive nuclear missiles."[3]

A smaller follow-up meeting took place a month later, and included Meese, Thomas, Anderson, General Graham, and Bendetsen. The latter two reported growing support and interest in the idea from members of Congress, the National Aeronautics and Space Administration, the CIA, the Air Force, and the Department of Defense.

Meese decided it was time to go directly to the president, and on January 8, 1982, the informal missile defense group met with Reagan in the Roosevelt Room. The outside advisers included Teller, Bendetsen, and kitchen cabinet members Jacquelin Hume, William Wilson, and Joseph Coors. Representing the White House were Meese, Anderson, Keyworth, and William Clark, who had been serving as deputy secretary of state and had just been named national security adviser, succeeding Richard Allen, who had resigned.

Originally scheduled for fifteen minutes, the meeting lasted for almost an hour. Coors later told Ed Feulner that Reagan's eyes lit up during the presentation. Meese remembers the tenor of the discussion as "highly favorable," so much so that Reagan directed the National Security Council staff to develop a proposal for a strategic defense initiative.[4]

A critical turning point in the creation of SDI was a meeting between the president and the Joint Chiefs of Staff in December 1982 at which Reagan asked his top military advisers, "What if . . . we began to move away from our total reliance on offense to deter a nuclear attack and moved toward a relatively greater reliance on defense?" As the president continued to press the issue, "small lights and bells" began to go off in the minds of the Joint Chiefs. One of them later telephoned Bill Clark, "Did we just get instructions to take a hard look at missile defense?" "Yes," replied Clark, confirming that the Joint Chiefs had been given their marching orders.[5]

There were more meetings inside and outside the White House, including a Keyworth visit to The Heritage Foundation. Keyworth's support of SDI was critical. By his own admission, the science adviser had been skeptical about strategic defense since his days at Los Alamos in the 1960s. But he was brought around by long conversations with his mentor Ed Teller, his own reading and research, and interactions with advocates like Graham and others at Heritage.

Notwithstanding the president's enthusiasm, there was strong opposition to SDI within the administration. Secretary of State George Shultz once called Keyworth "a lunatic" in front of the president for his advocacy of SDI, arguing that it would "destroy" NATO. But Reagan did not budge, causing an admiring Keyworth to remark that the president "has this marvelous ability to work the whole while everybody else is working the parts."[6]

Finally, on March 23, 1983, President Reagan, in a nationally televised address (drafted by deputy national security adviser Robert McFarlane), announced that the development and deployment of a comprehensive antiballistic missile system would be his top defense priority—his "ultimate goal." "I call upon the scientific community in our country," he said, "those who gave us nuclear weapons, to turn their great talents now to the cause of mankind and world peace, to give us the means of rendering these nuclear weapons impotent and obsolete." He called the system the Strategic Defense Initiative although it was derided as "Star Wars" by detractors. *The New York Times* called the initiative "a pipe dream, a projection of fantasy into policy."[7]

Feulner suggests that the "Star Wars" epithet backfired because *Star Wars* was among the most popular movies ever produced and reflected the American penchant for amazing technological feats. He says most Americans reasoned: "If we can put a man on the moon in a decade, why can't we put an anti-missile defense in space in the same time?"[8]

The vehement protest of Soviet leader Yuri Andropov suggested that Soviet scientists regarded SDI not as a fantasy but as a technological feat they could not match. Gen. Vladimir Slipchenko, a leading military scientist who served on the Soviet General Staff, recalled that SDI put the Soviet military "in a state of fear and shock." A decade later Gen. Makhmut Gareev, who headed the department of strategic analysis in the Soviet Ministry of Defense, revealed what he had told the Soviet General Staff and the Politburo in 1983: "Not only could we not defeat SDI, SDI defeated all our possible countermeasures."[9]

The Kremlin tried desperately to contain the Strategic Defense Initiative. At the Reykjavik summit in October 1986, Mikhail Gorbachev went so far as to suggest the elimination of all U.S. and Soviet offensive ballistic missiles if the United States would limit missile defense to research and testing in so-called "strategic laboratories." That translated into a ban on serious testing and deployment. Forced to choose between a seemingly "historic deal" eliminating nuclear weapons in ten years and keeping SDI, a resolute Reagan refused to surrender what he considered an essential element of a world without nuclear weapons—SDI.

Reagan's top advisers at Reykjavik—like Secretary of State George Shultz—were distraught and almost speechless. But Charles Wick, an old Hollywood friend of the president who had headed the U.S. Information Agency in the first term, offered a different reading on the flight back to Washington in Air Force One. "Ronnie," he said, "you just won the Cold War. They admitted they can't compete."[10]

Wick was right. Only nine months later, in July 1987, Gorbachev announced his acceptance of the zero-zero option on INF (Intermediate-Range Nuclear Forces) missiles. In October, Reagan announced that Gorbachev would be visiting Washington in early

December to sign the treaty eliminating INF missiles worldwide. More than any other strategic action he took, Reagan's unflinching commitment to SDI—especially at Reykjavik—convinced the Kremlin it could not win an accelerated arms race and led Gorbachev and his Kremlin colleagues to end the Cold War at the bargaining table and not on the battlefield.

In October 1991, at a Washington dinner hosted by Heritage trustee Robert Krieble, Moscow mayor Gavriil Popov said that SDI convinced Soviet leaders they had to gamble on radical economic reform or be left behind the United States. In the end, said Popov, Gorbachev lost control of the reform, and Communism died. Yeltsin adviser Ilya Zaslavsky added that it was Reagan not Gorbachev who was the real "initiator of perestroika."[11]

Reagan's SDI established a missile defense program that has been continued by every succeeding president. Following his 1983 speech, the Strategic Defense Initiative Organization (SDIO) was created to coordinate research and development. In the 1990s the name was changed to the Ballistic Missile Defense Organization (BMDO). Early in the George W. Bush administration, the BMDO became the Missile Defense Agency. Reagan also initiated the all-important appropriations process, requesting about $20 billion in current dollars for the initiative from 1985 through 1989.

More broadly, SDI buried Mutual Assured Destruction forever. Although a MAD proponent in the past, President Clinton signed into law the National Missile Defense Act of 1999, making it the official policy of the United States to defend itself against limited ballistic missile attacks as soon as technology permitted—a long-sought objective of The Heritage Foundation.

One other SDI accomplishment was to break the stranglehold of arms control on missile defense. It took many *Backgrounders* by Heritage senior analyst Baker Spring and a different political climate, but in 2001, President George W. Bush announced that the United States was withdrawing from the 1972 Anti-Ballistic Missile (ABM) Treaty with the Soviet Union for the obvious reason that the Soviet Union no longer existed.

The following year the United States and Russia signed a strategic nuclear arms reduction treaty, reducing the weapons to between 1,700 and 2,200 on each side. Reagan's argument has been proven correct: As the United States has moved forward with missile defenses, the number of deployed missile weapons in both the United States and the Soviet Union and later in Russia has come down dramatically.

• • •

Feulner's appointment-packed travels to Europe and especially Asia in the 1980s produced high dividends in prestige and financial support for Heritage. He has loved to travel since his first European visit as a Regis College undergraduate. Richard Allen, who accompanied him on many overseas trips, says, "Ed never met an airplane ticket he didn't like."

In 1982 the foundation established its first and still one of its most influential centers—the Asian Studies Center (ASC), initially chaired by Dick Allen, who had recently resigned as President Reagan's national security adviser and been named Heritage's first distinguished fellow. The center reflected Ed Feulner's conviction that Asia, not Europe, would become the more consequential region for America, strategically as well as economically. Feulner and Allen assured the Heritage board of trustees that the center would be funded through its own endowment and not out of the foundation's operating budget. They were as good as their word, raising more than $13 million over the next decade and a half, most of it from South Korean, Taiwanese, and other Asian foundations, corporations, and individuals.

"Dick and I were agreed that Asia was really the land of the future," Feulner recalls. "The relationship of the United States with these sovereign entities across the Pacific Ocean was what was going to matter in the long haul. At the time the economic relationship with Europe was much more than it was with Asia. Today the Asian relationship is more than twice what it is with Europe. The United States has become even more of a Pacific-centered power."[12]

Initially, the Asian Studies Center focused much of its attention on the lessons to be learned from the economic "miracles" of South Korea, Taiwan, Hong Kong, and Singapore. The number-one lesson was that freedom, particularly economic freedom, and prosperity were inseparable. Over the years ASC analysts often discussed the People's Republic of China, taking a hard line on its flagrant violations of human rights—of which the vast network of forced labor camps, the *laogai*, is the most conspicuous example—but following a realistic line on U.S.-PRC trade.

"It's very important," says Feulner, "that the United States and China keep talking to each other and whenever possible to come closer and closer to the same set of rules. So when The Heritage Foundation

supports China's admission to the World Trade Organization, it's because we want them to abide by the same set of rules that we abide by."[13]

At the same time the Asian Studies Center has supported the Taiwan Relations Act, which pledges the U.S. government to preserve
and promote "extensive, close and friendly commercial and cultural
contacts" with Taiwan. Washington is also required to make available
weapons to enable Taiwan to "maintain a sufficient self-defense capability." Although unstated, mainland China is the obvious threat. Furthermore, the president is obligated to promptly inform Congress "of
any threat to the security or the social or economic system" of Taiwan
and, should that happen, to take "appropriate action" in response to
any such danger.[14] In effect, the Taiwan Relations Act established an
informal two-China policy for the United States, a policy that remains
in place after more than three decades.

Ed Feulner is proud of the role that the Asian Studies Center has
played in furthering U.S. understanding of the region and Asian understanding of the United States. "It's exciting," he says, "to go to Seoul
and see former Heritage fellows sitting in cabinet-level positions. And
to be able to say that Ban Ki-moon, the secretary general of the United
Nations—arguably the number-one civil servant in the world—is somebody I knew back when he was the deputy foreign minister of South
Korea." He adds, firmly, "The U.S-Asia relationship is going to be the
predominant one in this new century."[15]

Among all the Asian nations, it is South Korea—the Republic of
Korea—with which Heritage and Ed Feulner have the closest relationship. During some 120 visits to Asia in the last four decades, Feulner has
met with and discussed U.S.-South Korean issues with the last six South
Korean presidents:

"When I go over there and meet or talk to a prominent South Korean, we're not after something. It's because these are good honorable
people—some to the left, some to the right—who might be doing good
things for the U.S.- Korean relationship in the future, and it's important
to keep the lines open."[16]

That relationship is publicly acknowledged with two handsomely
decorated meeting rooms at Heritage headquarters—the B. C. Lee
Room and the Chung Ju Yung Room. Feulner and Lee Kun Hee, the
chairman of Samsung, began discussing in 1985 the idea of a meeting
room and an annual lecture in the name of B. C. Lee, the fabled founder
of Samsung, one of the most successful corporations (or *chaebols*) in

South Korea. The room was dedicated in 1994 and has been in continuous use ever since; the lecture series was inaugurated in 1995 with a talk by former secretary of state Henry Kissinger.

Dedicated in 1999, the Chung Ju Yung Room is named for Chung Ju Yung, the entrepreneurial founder of the Hyundai Group, who built the largest shipyard in the world and led Hyundai into becoming one of the largest auto manufacturers globally. In 1999 former senator Malcolm Wallop of Wyoming was named Heritage's Chung Ju Yung Fellow in Policy Studies, the first named fellowship in the Asian Studies Center.

Ed Feulner speaks warmly of "my friend" Kim Dae Jung, whom he knew long before he won the Nobel Peace Prize in 2000. In the early 1980s, when Kim was living in exile in the United States, Heritage hosted him in a number of seminars and conferences. "He taught us a great deal about the need for structural, political, and economic reform in Korea," says Feulner, and "articulated his views favoring a free and open market system to produce long-term economic vitality for Korea."

After Kim was elected president of South Korea and before he was sworn in, he asked Feulner, who was in Seoul for the ceremony, for a favor: would he talk to the pop music icon Michael Jackson, who was also in town, and ask him not to give a contemplated concert in Pyongyang in North Korea because, in his words, "It would not be helpful at this time"? Although doubtful how much influence a conservative think tank president could have, Ed Feulner called on Michael Jackson in his hotel and gave him D.J.'s message. (There is a framed photo of Jackson and Feulner, both looking a little puzzled, hanging in Feulner's Heritage office.)

Whatever the reason, Jackson did not go north, and when Feulner returned to Korea in a couple of weeks, he was invited to the president's home for a private dinner prepared and served by the president's wife. After dinner and cigars, President Kim walked Ed Feulner to the front door, where they were greeted by a gaggle of Korean reporters.

One of them shouted, "Hey, D.J., what are you doing meeting with the head of the right-wing Heritage Foundation?"

Without missing a beat, the president put his hand on Feulner's shoulder and replied, "In Washington I have friends from Ted Kennedy to Ted Feulner."[17]

This is one of "Ted" Feulner's favorite Asian stories.

A few years later, during the Clinton administration, President Kim Dae Jung was in New York City to address the annual meeting of the

UN General Assembly about his "sunshine" initiative to improve relations with North Korea. He hosted a small dinner at the Waldorf Astoria that included Ed Feulner. When everyone else, including the deputy secretary of state, had left after a rather long evening, Feulner was asked to stay.

Speaking in English, President Kim said to Feulner: "I want to tell you and I want you to tell your friends that I am not going into this with any illusions. I view my recent visit to Pyongyang as one small starting step on a very long road. Things are not going to change there soon. It's going to take a very long time. Don't think that I've been sucked in or I'm being delusional."[18]

The Heritage president was pleased to pass along this application of realpolitik to conservative friends as well as aides of President Clinton.

• • •

In the spring of 1981, Feulner kept faith with the foundation's practice of representing the different branches of conservatism, by inviting Midge Decter, author, social critic, and a leading neoconservative, to join the foundation's board of trustees. At the time traditional conservatives and neoconservatives were still getting used to each other. Some paleoconservatives have never accepted what they regard as a neoconservative invasion of the conservative movement. Feulner and Decter first met when she and her husband, Norman Podhoretz, the feisty editor of *Commentary* magazine, were invited by *Policy Review* editor John O'Sullivan to spend a day at Heritage giving talks and meeting people.

Always an advocate of inclusion rather than exclusion, Feulner, with the approval of the board, extended an invitation to Decter. "It's just crazy to try to drive out the neoconservatives," he explained later. "They bring new intellectual vigor to conservative debate. . . . They're manning the ramparts in the liberals' greatest bastion—New York City. . . . And the contribution of neocons such as Irving Kristol and Midge Decter has never been limited to foreign policy. They have made significant contributions to social and cultural policy as well."[19]

Decter happily accepted the invitation, explaining that far from finding Feulner to be the scary right-wing radical depicted by many liberals, she found him to be "the most innocent, uncynical, open-hearted big important person I've ever run into."[20]

She also recalls an event in the 1980s in New York City where for the first time she met Paul Weyrich and Phyllis Schlafly, the organizing genius of the Eagle Forum, which defeated the Equal Rights

Amendment against all odds. To the surprise of many, Decter and Schlafly "got along instantly" because both realized they were allies in the battle against the counterculture. When someone asked Decter how she could be so friendly with a "right-winger" like Schlafly, she replied, "It's easy—she's been doing my dirty work for years."[21]

It was Ed Feulner's special pleasure in the fall of 1983 to invite Nobel laureate Friedrich A. Hayek, whose lectures he had attended at the London School of Economics, to visit the foundation as a distinguished scholar. On the whole, Hayek said in a public lecture, he approved of the Reagan administration's economic policy.

Regarding Reagan's tax policy, Hayek offered that the idea of cutting taxes to produce higher revenues was right "in principle" but that he was a little apprehensive about the scale of the tax cuts. "I'm all for reduction of government expenditures," he explained, "but to anticipate it by reducing the rate of taxation before you have reduced expenditures is a very risky thing to do."[22]

Reagan was aware of the risks but was convinced that the U.S. economy needed a jump start that only tax cuts across the board could provide. He turned out to be right: his economic plan produced the longest economic expansion in peacetime in the twentieth century, continuing for some twenty years with only one dip, in 1990–91.

Hayek surprised the libertarians in the Heritage audience when he suggested that the enormous framework of human cooperation rests on the institutions of private property, on the idea of honesty, and on the family—not the individual. Furthermore, he said, traditional morality "is vital to human survival."[23]

The similarity between the moral heritage outlined by the classical liberal Hayek and the custom and tradition often cited by traditional conservative Russell Kirk is striking and suggests that conservatism is a far larger philosophical tent than some libertarians care to admit. Ed Feulner was in the front row of the auditorium enthusiastically applauding Hayek's remarks. In November 1983 he had the opportunity to bring together for the first time two of his heroes—Hayek and President Ronald Reagan.

When Hayek and Feulner walked into the Oval Office of the White House that fall day, the smiling president said, according to the official White House transcript and clearly referring to *The Road to Serfdom:*

"I have read one Friedrich von Hayek book for many years—you have influenced my thinking on economics."

"Well, I am very pleased," said Hayek.

"Just encourage me," said the president, "and tell me once again that I shouldn't raise taxes until we are out of this recession."

"Well, I don't know," said Hayek cautiously, "you have military problems that may be more important."

"Yes, I know that. We are not going to let up on that," responded the president. "Well, it's been wonderful meeting you."

"I shall remember it for a long time," Hayek said. "Thank you for this opportunity."

"Well, it was nice to meet you. I am an avid reader of yours."

As they prepared to leave, Feulner mentioned Calvin Coolidge, which prompted Reagan to say: "When I moved in here, they told me I could choose the presidents whose portraits would be on the wall of the Cabinet room. One of the first I chose was Calvin Coolidge. I think he has been probably one of the most misunderstood and least appreciated presidents."

"Yes," said Hayek, "but he is being rediscovered."

"Incidently," said the president, "my only BA degree was in economics."

"Oh really?" said Hayek.

"So I continued my studies by reading you. Thank you."

"Thank you, Mr. President," said Feulner.[24]

* * *

The relationship between President Reagan and Ed Feulner reinforced the special bond between the president and the foundation. Through the efforts of Analysis and Research Associates, Heritage's predecessor, Reagan was invited by the Senate Finance Committee in 1972 to explain why he opposed President Nixon's Family Assistance Plan.

The major nexus of the Reagan-Heritage connection was *Mandate for Leadership,* which the administration constantly turned to for guidance and inspiration. Shortly after taking office, the president publicly acknowledged the administration's and his personal debt to the foundation:

> *It seems like just yesterday that our transition team set up shop in Washington to prepare for our administration. From the outset we were swamped with offers of assistance from groups and individuals supporting our basic goals: restoring America's defenses and her leadership abroad while rebuilding her economy and restricting runaway government at home.*

But there was one group which gave us special substantive help
we'll never forget. I'm talking, of course, about that feisty new kid
on the conservative block, The Heritage Foundation.

Led by its able president, Edwin J. Feulner, The Heritage Founda-
tion provided us with copies of the remarkable 1,093-page work,
Mandate for Leadership. The material combined mastery of the
federal bureaucracy with a no-nonsense plan to cut it down to size.

We've been using it to our and the country's advantage ever since,
and by remaining so thorough, to the point, and up to date, The
Heritage Foundation's research continues to be useful to us and to
our policy-making process. As a matter of fact, one of the people it's
been most useful to and used by is me.[25]

When the president referred to Heritage research as "thorough, to
the point, and up to date," he brought smiles of satisfaction to foundation researchers who prided themselves on being all those things.
However, while Heritage did help shape the Reagan administration in
policy and personnel, it was not an appendage of the White House. The
foundation did not hesitate to criticize the president when it felt it was
warranted.

In *The First Year* the foundation noted approvingly that the Reagan administration had implemented or initiated nearly 700 of the 1,270
"short-term" recommendations in *Mandate for Leadership* in its first
year. That was 55 percent, a good average in any league.

But, said the study, the administration "should and could have accomplished more" since coming into office, and it explained why and
where it had failed. The primary cause was the appointment of people
"who fail to understand and accept the President's goals and policies."
Many qualified appointees naïvely thought they could make major
changes "simply through the force of their will," when in fact policy
changes must be institutionalized through revised regulations, executive orders, and in many cases legislation.[26]

The first-year study, edited by Heritage vice president Richard N.
Holwill, acknowledged it had set the bar high for the Reagan administration but had done so because of what was at stake—"to reestablish the principles of personal liberty and responsibility, an economy
freed from undue regulation, and a strengthened national defense." It
praised Reagan for his personal leadership on the issues of tax cuts and
foreign policy and for sticking to "an admirable set of principles." His

administration had made a good start, declared the editors, particularly in the area of economic policy —"the key to the long-term success of all other programs." But the foundation promised to keep assessing "what has been done and what remains to be accomplished."[27]

Reagan reacted with characteristic grace, writing Feulner that he appreciated that Heritage had maintained "a responsible tone." He was reminded "how much our friends expect of us. I . . . look forward to working with you and the members of [our] team in pursuit of our common goals for a better America."[28]

Feulner could claim some personal credit for the administration's success in its first year because Ed Meese asked him to accept a ninety-day appointment as a consultant and help organize his White House office. Feulner agreed to assist Meese on the following conditions: the appointment would be part-time and temporary, and he would accept no compensation for his advice and counsel. No Heritage employee had ever accepted government funds for his work, and no one ever would.

In Reagan's first term, the White House was run by a talented troika of James Baker, chief of staff; Michael Deaver, deputy chief of staff; and Meese, counselor to the president. Meese was the true conservative of the three men, dedicated to the president and the implementation of his conservative agenda. Baker was a moderate conservative Republican inclined to seek a deal in the face of resistance, while Deaver was a nonideological expert in communications who enjoyed the first lady's implicit trust—a considerable asset in the Reagan White House.

Feulner observed that Meese was happiest making speeches outside the White House to assorted citizens' groups and broadening the base of support for the administration. Baker and Deaver were at their best consolidating their positions of power and excluding all competitors, including Ed Meese. Feulner tried to alert Meese to the machinations going on around him, but Meese, who always believed the best about everybody, chose not to respond—it was just not in his character.

"He would go on *Meet the Press* on Sunday morning," says Feulner, "and it would never cross his mind to ever say anything negative or even questioning about his two distinguished colleagues because all he wanted to do was advance the cause."[29]

At the end of ninety days, in June, Feulner explained he could not extend the White House assignment "indefinitely on this intensive basis" for two reasons: (1) the role could be filled better by someone who could devote full time to it, and (2) he had commitments to Heritage, including substantial travel. He said he would be willing to be available for consultation on "specific projects at advanced stages." "I would only be a phone call away (when in the city) if you wanted me to review/analyze/comment" on a project.

Meese accepted Feulner's resignation but continued to call on him informally.

· · ·

Another opportunity to serve the Reagan administration appeared in early 1982, one that combined two of Ed Feulner's favorite things—foreign policy and foreign travel.

Organized in 1948 at the start of the Cold War, the U.S. Advisory Commission on Public Diplomacy (ACPD), under the U.S. Information Agency, was "charged with appraising [overseas] U.S. government activities" that informed and influenced foreign publics about American foreign policy. It played a useful supporting role early on, but by 1980 the ACPD was a shadow of its early self, routinely ignored by the State Department and reluctantly funded by the Congress, which had created it.

However, in *Mandate for Leadership,* Heritage looked closely at the contribution of advisory boards in areas like public diplomacy or "soft power." Heritage board chairman Frank Shakespeare, who had directed the U.S. Information Agency under Nixon, suggested that the ACPD and Feulner would make a good fit. Feulner had turned down an invitation from Secretary of State Al Haig to be undersecretary of state for administration and then to be counselor to the secretary. There was little doubt in his mind that Heritage needed him more than the Department of State did. As he told an interviewer, "Heritage is not just my job, it's my life."[30]

But he saw the potential of the ACPD and accepted an appointment as its part-time unsalaried chairman. As with every other institution he joined—the Republican Study Committee, The Heritage Foundation, the Mont Pelerin Society, the ISI, and the Philadelphia Society—Feulner set about reorganizing and revitalizing the agency. "Ed took that sleepy little agency by the throat," recalls Tom Korologos, the veteran political operative who became vice chairman, "not unlike how he took Heritage by the throat. He grew the Commission into a policy-setting place that had ideas, that put out annual reports, that took public diplomacy from the depths and made it an important issue."[31]

With President Reagan seeking an end to the Cold War, Feulner and Korologos went on fact-finding trips to China, East Berlin, and the Soviet Union, where, says Korologos, they urged Soviet officials to "let us bring in our books and our libraries, although we knew that everybody who went into the American library got his picture taken, so it was kind of tense."

There were light moments. On the trip to Moscow, Linda Feulner and Joy Korologos accompanied their husbands. After visiting Red Square and being turned back by guards because they were walking too close to the Kremlin, they returned to their hotel. Wanting to wash up, Linda picked up a towel the size of a washcloth and said to Ed, "How can I take a shower with these flimsy little things?" Ten minutes later there was a knock on the door, and a maid handed them an armful of large bath towels.[32]

Feulner's interest in public diplomacy has not waned with the years. Helle Dale, Heritage's senior fellow for public diplomacy, recalls that Defense Secretary Donald Rumsfeld asked Feulner and his colleagues "to produce a proposal for improving public diplomacy in the early days of Iraq and Afghanistan." Along with Feulner, Dale later published a *WebMemo* on the idea of "a semi-governmental research institute on foreign opinion." Although the institute has not yet been created, both the State Department and the Department of Defense "have since engaged more systemically and seriously in foreign opinion research."

In 2008, Feulner hosted a conference on "Public Diplomacy: Reinvigorating America's Strategic Communications Policy" and also hired the late editor and columnist Tony Blankley as a visiting fellow on public diplomacy. Many on the Right, says Dale, tend to regard public diplomacy as either "a waste of money or a positively un-American activity because it focuses on winning over foreign audiences. Feulner knows better." As a result, she points out, "Heritage often gets credit on both sides of the aisle for engaging in the global war of ideas."[33]

CHAPTER 12

"STUNNING" IMPACT

In 1974, Heritage's first full year, the fallout from the Watergate scandal affected everything in Washington, bringing Nixon's resignation, the widespread defeat of conservative candidates for the U.S. House and Senate, and the arrival of an aggressive freshman class of liberal legislators on Capitol Hill. Some apprehensive conservatives, notably *National Review* publisher William A. Rusher, spoke of starting a third party. Others said the Grand Old Party was headed for the junkyard.

Heritage could fit all its employees into a couple of rented rooms and operated on a minuscule budget, much of it provided by one man, Joseph Coors. *USA Today* later commented, "Many of Washington's liberals derided [Heritage] as an inconsequential band of right-wingers."[1]

A decade later Washington was a very different city and America a different nation. Ronald Reagan sat in the White House, radiating confidence and optimism. Republicans enjoyed a majority in the Senate and challenged the Democratic leadership in the House at every opportunity. Conservative ideas like supply-side economics and the need to challenge the Soviet "evil empire" dominated the political debate. The U.S. economy grew 6 percent in 1983, and Americans began recovering their confidence in themselves and the future.

Heritage now had a staff of more than one hundred analysts, communications experts, development officers, and support personnel and an annual budget of over $10.5 million. It received support from 140,000 individual members and dozens of corporations and foundations.

Remarked *The Washington Post,* with perhaps more than a little disbelief, "The impact of Heritage has been stunning."[2]

It was pleasant for Feulner and his colleagues to read in the *National Journal* that the foundation was "the marvel of the political establishment and the intellectual community," and it was gratifying to
have *The New Republic* cite Heritage as a model that the liberal establishment would do well to emulate. (More than twenty years would
pass before liberals took the magazine's advice and started the Center
for American Progress, headed by former Clinton aide John Podesta.)

Seeking ideas for a forthcoming speech on "Marketing the Product," Feulner spent several days in the fall of 1984 talking to communications aides, researchers, and other Heritage people. He passed along
"some of their very good ideas" in a memo to senior management.

- *Don't assume who is your enemy.* The liberal black columnist William Raspberry wrote a column about how a subminimum wage
  would negatively affect black youth after he read a column by the
  black conservative economist Walter Williams. Heritage had made
  sure that Raspberry saw the column.

- *Work with media, not on it.* "It does you no good to gratuitously
  slam them." Feulner described how Richard Threlkeld of ABC
  News did a favorable five-minute special report about privatization.
  His primary source was Steve Hanke, then a Heritage senior fellow
  and now a senior fellow at the Manhattan Institute.

- *Develop contacts with the speechwriters of national and local policy makers.* When the president begins to talk about a particular
  subject in his speeches, said Feulner, "he moves an idea into the
  public debate, he helps to form the public opinion, and in a [real]
  sense he frames the debate."

- *Use* Policy Review *"to get out our ideas."* Feulner gave several examples. George Gilder's "Triumph of the American Mind" was
  excerpted in *The Washington Times* and highlighted in a lead editorial in *The Detroit News.* As a result, Gilder appeared on PBS's
  MacNeil/Lehrer NewsHour and the financial news network. Editor Adam Meyerson's article about Elliott Abrams and the cause of
  human rights was distributed by Representative Jack Kemp to every
  Republican congressman. The article was widely discussed—just

how widely was revealed at a reception in Managua, Nicaragua. Abrams met the director of the North American desk of the Marxist Sandinista Party, who said, "Mr. Abrams, I am so happy to meet you. I was just reading about you in *Policy Review*."

- *Think internationally.* The White House came to Heritage and asked for the foundation's help in getting conservative groups to participate in the third UN Women's Conference, to be held in Nairobi. One obstacle was that participating groups had to have official NGO (nongovernmental organization) status. "This is really no problem," Feulner wrote. "Heritage has had NGO status since early 1982." Those who wanted to attend the Nairobi conference had only to talk to Bob Huberty, who would detail how to get on the White House list.

All these examples, Feulner wrote—Bill Raspberry, George Gilder, Elliott Abrams, the UN—"all illustrate the key hypotheses upon which THF was founded and rests":

1. Ideas have consequences.

2. Mobilizing data in support of ideas changes minds and helps set the public policy agenda.

3. Marketing ideas is as important as producing the research.

4. Public policy decisions are influenced most effectively by parallel outside-inside operations, with THF functioning on the outside.

5. It is essential to address a great number of ideas simultaneously to be prepared to exploit circumstances (almost always triggered by events beyond our control) that become ripe for influencing policy.

6. Mainstream America and mainstream policy makers are receptive to conservative ideas and policies when properly exposed to them.[3]

Despite the foundation's visibly increasing influence, acknowledged by many in Washington, Feulner could not put it out of his mind that

Heritage was headquartered in a string of townhouses facing a public park with a playground while Brookings had an imposing eight-story building on Massachusetts Avenue just off Dupont Circle in the center of the city, a striking symbol of power and prestige. There were practical problems as well for Heritage.

With the election of Ronald Reagan, the conservative movement had come of age, and the Heritage Foundation was experiencing severe growing pains. The townhouses on Stanton Park were small and unconnected, contributing to a "silo" mentality among the departments.

Communications was in one building, domestic studies in another, and the executive offices in still another. Heritage had turned into an institutional gerrymander. The foundation was unable to host a luncheon, a lecture by a distinguished scholar, and a private meeting with policy makers at the same time.

Feulner and Truluck were agreed: Heritage had to move. But where to, and could they afford it? In late 1981, while Feulner was debating whether to present a proposal for a multimillion-dollar building to the board of trustees, he breakfasted with Republican Senator John Warner of Virginia, a veteran Washingtonian. Warner listened to Feulner outline the pros and cons of the move and responded: "Ed, the buildings you have now are nice, but you need a major physical presence, like Brookings. Otherwise, you're just one more Washington think tank."[4]

Warner's counsel and the reference to Brookings (the organization Feulner was determined to surpass one day) decided the Heritage president. At the next board meeting he and Truluck explained that an eight-story building at 214 Massachusetts Avenue, N.E., just three blocks from the U.S. Capitol, was available. It had been the annex of the Library of Congress but had been unoccupied since the 1980 opening of the library's Madison building.

The trustees' first reaction, Phil Truluck recalls, was "You guys are policy experts—what do you know about real estate?" They directed Feulner and Truluck to come back with a specific plan, including purchase price, renovation cost, means of financing, and how they intended to use the expanded space.

At the next board meeting Truluck, who would oversee the purchase and renovation of the new headquarters, pointed out that a building with 65,000 square feet and a prime location on Capitol Hill would not come on the market very often. Since the building had double the space Heritage needed at the time, the foundation could rent extra space and generate income. The estimated total cost was a little more than $9 million, a jaw-dropping sum almost equal to the foundation's annual budget.

It was a gamble, but given the improving economy and the expanding conservative movement under the Reagan presidency, it was a reasonable gamble. In a leap of conservative faith, the board of trustees approved the plan. A limited partnership was formed, consisting of six trustees who put up $250,000 each toward the purchase. The partners leased the building with the expectation that they would later donate it to the foundation—which they did in a couple of years. Ironically, Reagan's 1986 tax reform bill prevented such purchase-gift arrangements in the future.

It was, Truluck says, "a very bold decision" by an institution not yet a decade old. It was made possible because Joseph Coors, Richard Scaife, Thomas A. Roe, Arthur Spitzer, Lewis Lehrman, and Robert Krieble (and his wife Nancy) had confidence in what Heritage was doing—and would yet do. Over the next twelve months Truluck and foundation controller Peter Pover oversaw the multiple contractors and workers, who transformed an aging, long-neglected library annex into a modern, up-to-date research and conference center. Heritage moved into its new headquarters on schedule and on budget in the summer of 1983. Official Washington, in the person of both the president and the vice president, acknowledged the significance of the move—on the same day. At the October ribbon-cutting ceremony, Vice President George H. W. Bush said: "To paraphrase Archimedes, give me a place to stand and a lever strong enough and I can move the world. Well, The Heritage Foundation has been that place, and their lever has been the truth. And so far, you have been real world movers."

There followed a formal lecture by UN ambassador Jeane Kirkpatrick and a roundtable discussion of the future of conservatism by four speakers representing the major branches of the conservative movement: *Wall Street Journal* editor Robert Bartley, historian Russell Kirk, Representative (and future House Speaker) Newt Gingrich of Georgia, and neoconservative founder Irving Kristol. Their consensus was that conservatism had yet to reach its peak. The discussion was another demonstration of Heritage's role as the disinterested broker of conservative ideas.

That evening at a black-tie banquet, President Reagan told thirteen hundred Heritage guests that the gathering marked "an extraordinary moment, not only in the history of The Heritage Foundation, but

I firmly believe in the intellectual history of the West." The president said the age of "overwhelming government power" was coming to an end. "There is no better evidence that the time of the conservative idea has come than the [astonishing] growth of The Heritage Foundation." He acknowledged the foundation's enormous influence "on Capitol Hill and—believe me, I know—at the White House." And then he offered a prediction:

When historians of the future seek the real meaning of the latter part of the twentieth century, Reagan said, they will have to look at "gatherings like this. They will find among your number the leaders of an intellectual revolution that recaptured and renewed the great lessons of Western culture." Echoing his 1982 remarks before the British Parliament at Westminster, the president said the revolution in defense of Western culture and human freedom "is also writing the last sad pages in a bizarre chapter in human history known as Communism."[5]

Linda Feulner remembers the evening well. As the military honor guard removed the colors, following the singing of the national anthem, President Reagan whispered to Linda who was standing next to him, "That's always so moving, I just want to clap, but you're not supposed to." Linda whispered back, "Mr. President, I bet if you did, everybody else would right away." And when he did, within two nanoseconds the whole room was applauding.[6]

A younger Feulner also had a special experience with the president. Two years later Reagan again agreed to attend a Heritage function—a luncheon at a downtown Washington hotel. The head table included Ed and Linda Feulner, their children E.J. and Emily, Clare Boothe Luce, Shelby and Kathryn Davis, and the president. Fourteen-year-old E.J. had come back from his boarding school to be present.

The entrée had barely been served when Ed Feulner looked across at his sturdy six-foot son, who had apparently eaten his steak in about two bites. "The president was seated next to me," Feulner recalls, "and saw me look in a kind of horror at the speed with which E.J. had finished." The president, who had barely touched his meal, said, "Hey, E.J., are you still hungry?' and switched plates with him. "It had to be one of the most special steaks E.J. has ever consumed," says Feulner.[7]

• • •

During its tenth-anniversary festivities, the foundation launched its first major fund-raising campaign, "Heritage 10—Funding the Conservative Decade," under the chairmanship of New York businessman and trustee Lewis Lehrman. Assisting Lehrman were foundation treasurer John Von Kannon and development consultant Robert Russell. The goal was $27.5 million, to be used for 1984 operations, to help pay for the new headquarters, and to contribute to the endowment for the Asian Studies Center. It was an ambitious move, seeking to raise ten times the amount of its annual operating budget a few years earlier, and it turned out—too ambitious.

The campaign did not meet its goal, falling some $8 million short. It was the first major fund-raising failure in Heritage's history. Undaunted, the foundation set a new goal of $35.3 million (adding 1985's needs) and extended the deadline by a year. A determined Feulner led the way, traveling from city to city and major donor to major donor. And in early 1986 Heritage proudly announced it had raised $37 million, topping its goal by nearly $2 million.

Speaking at the April dinner celebrating the successful conclusion of the campaign, President Reagan said, "I can't help reflecting tonight on the fact that Heritage 10 actually exceeded its fundraising goal by $2 million. Ed Feulner says he's thinking of using the extra money to set up a first aid station for Washington liberals. Which just goes to show the conservative movement has come of age. We've gone from hope to charity."[8]

On a more serious note, the president saluted the foundation and its president, whom he described as "intellectual, administrator, politician, diplomat, but most of all, dreamer and darer." Feulner understood, Reagan said, that "the best way to ride the tide of history is to make a few waves of our own."[9]

Inspired by the campaign's success, chairman Lew Lehrman envisioned the 1980s as the "conservative decade," a time when conservative ideas and ideals would triumph in Washington. It was necessary, he argued, to persuade those who decide policy in Washington and the country that the conservative way "is the right way, the American way."[10]

President Reagan did his part, winning reelection in 1984 in a landslide, carrying forty-nine states and receiving 525 electoral votes against the Democratic nominee, former vice president Walter Mondale, who insisted on calling himself a liberal. Reagan's lopsided victory confirmed how much the political debate had changed since Heritage was founded a little over a decade earlier.

Washington policy makers no longer talked about containing the Soviet Union but about liberating the Soviet Empire. They no longer proposed new welfare programs but new ways to free the underclass from welfare dependency. They no longer suggested new government regulations but new methods to unleash American enterprise.

The air was full of liberating ideas such as enterprise zones in the inner cities, privatizing government services, choice in education, health care vouchers, private-sector alternatives to Social Security, free-trade zones, missile defense, and a six-hundred-ship navy.

Every one of these ideas had been born at or nurtured by Heritage. By the mid-1980s the foundation was being described by *Forbes* as "eclipsing much older, more established fixtures such as the Brookings Institution" and by *Time* as "the foremost of the new breed of advocacy tanks."[11]

• • •

Sometimes Heritage punctures an old, unworkable idea, like a national industrial policy. In February 1984 it published *A Blueprint for Jobs and Industrial Growth,* edited by senior fellow Richard McKenzie, professor of economics at Clemson University. McKenzie's plan offered forty-three specific proposals for stimulating economic and industrial growth and employment without additional government spending. They included reducing corporate income tax rates by 50 percent over the next ten years and indexing and eventually eliminating capital gains taxes. Following the publication of *Blueprint,* industrial policy became a nonissue in the nation's capital until Labor Secretary Robert Reich unearthed it in the early Clinton years. However, it soon faded in the face of the aggressive free-market philosophy of the Gingrich Congress.

Obama, the would-be transformational president, sought to resuscitate the concept with an emphasis on government support of "new technologies" like robotics, nanotech advanced materials, biotechnology, solar panels, and "high-speed rail" (which would strike only a visitor from the Amazon as new). But in an era of trillion-dollar deficits, the Jobs Council's *Road Map to Renewal* received little attention on Capitol Hill or elsewhere.[12]

Committed to the long view, Heritage does not hesitate to take on the most contentious issues—like the third rail of American politics, Social Security.

When President Reagan was sworn in in January 1981, Congress was still congratulating itself for having "solved" the Social Security crisis of the mid-1970s. In December 1977, Heritage analyst Peter J.

Ferrara wrote, Congress enacted "the largest peacetime tax increase in U.S. history," designed to guarantee the financial soundness of the system for the rest of the century and well into the next one.[13] Yet the 1981 annual report of the Social Security Board of Trustees concluded that, by late 1982 or early 1983, the system would be unable to pay promised benefits.

The Reagan administration attempted to deal rationally with the problem by proposing a one-time, three-month delay in cost-of-living increases and a reduction in benefits for those who chose early retirement before sixty-five. There was an immediate outcry by the Social Security lobby. Reagan was accused of trying to "smash" the financial security of American retirees, and panicky congressional Republicans backed away quickly from the administration's proposals.[14]

In turn, the Reagan administration appointed a national commission to devise a bailout scheme for Social Security and defuse the political crisis. Released in January 1983, the commission's proposals were predictable, dependent upon tax increases, and they were swiftly adopted. They included an acceleration of payroll tax increases, an increase in payroll taxes on self-employed workers, federal taxation of formerly tax-exempt Social Security benefits, and termination of the right of state and local government employees to opt out of the system. Congress also added a gradual increase in the retirement age from sixty-five to sixty-seven. It was not conservatism's finest hour.

As Ferrara wrote, the package only "tinkered with the basic structure of Social Security." Nearly everyone was hurt by the reforms, from the elderly, whose benefits were now taxed, to workers, whose FICA taxes were increased and whose promised benefits were reduced.[15]

Heritage concluded that a new compact between generations regarding Social Security and other entitlements was needed. Thus began a reform campaign that continues to this day.

Starting in mid-1983, the foundation published a series of studies about a private-sector retirement system that would supplement and then partially replace the existing Social Security program. Developed largely by former White House analyst Ferrara, the "privatized" Social Security system, built around expanded Individual Retirement Accounts (Super IRAs), would be gradually eased in. Wage earners would have the option of remaining in the Social Security system or enrolling in a private plan. But everyone without exception—and this requirement was a sticking point with conservatives of a libertarian persuasion— would have to have either private or public coverage. Those electing to stay in Social Security would be guaranteed benefits through a Social Security bond.

When Barry Goldwater ran for president in 1964, he said that Social Security was in actuarial trouble and that a voluntary option ought to be considered. Republicans as well as Democrats immediately accused him of seeking to "destroy" Social Security. Twenty years later, Heritage's suggestion of a partially privatized system was coolly received but not dismissed out of hand.

By the mid-1990s, leaders of both political parties were willing to concede that Social Security required more fundamental reform than one more tax hike or another extension of the retirement age. In 2005, following his reelection, President George W. Bush called for a gradual transition of Social Security to a combination of a government-funded program and Personal Retirement Accounts (PRAs). He sought public support with a series of town hall meetings and public addresses in selected parts of the country.

However, Bush was unable to galvanize sufficient public support for his proposal, and once again Congress declined to take action. The Heritage Foundation continues to press for basic reform of Social Security and entitlements such as Medicare and Medicaid because they will collectively cause federal spending to jump from a historical average of 20 percent of the economy to an alarming 30 percent by the year 2033, only twenty years away. The estimated long-term liability of Social Security and Medicare is now $40 trillion, over $200,000 for every man, woman, and child in America.

The lesson from the attempted reform of Social Security was clear to Ed Feulner: when dealing with radioactive issues like Social Security, persistence and prudence are required. Policy makers have to be specific about how they intend to downsize government, shift power from Washington to the states, and encourage individual and local community responsibility.

• • •

One of Stuart Butler's favorite sayings is "We sweat the details." In early 1984 the foundation released a major budget-cutting plan by analyst John M. Palffy. His proposals could have reduced the federal deficit by $119 billion in FY1985 without affecting services to the poor or weakening national defense. OMB director David Stockman credited the report with providing many of the ideas in the administration's 1986 budget. Representative William Dannemeyer of California, chairman of the Republican Study Committee, termed the report "must reading."[16]

Recommendations included increasing fees to all vessels that use inland waterways and deep-draft ports (at the time, user fees covered about 8 percent of federal expenditures) and improving military procurement (then running at about $3.2 billion annually) through second sourcing competition—the use of more than one contractor to make a particular weapon.[17]

Nor was that all. Butler's 1985 book, *Privatizing Federal Spending: A Strategy to Eliminate the Deficit,* was widely reviewed and drew the attention of the new OMB director, James C. Miller, who invited Butler to brief high-level White House and budget officials on the potential of privatization. As a result, the administration's FY1987 budget plan contained several proposals to privatize government programs.

When Conrail was "privatized" in early 1987 through a public stock offering, the stock-sale plan closely resembled the one proposed by Heritage analyst James Gattuso. Stephen Moore, who had put together an extensive privatization blueprint for the foundation, took a leave of absence from Heritage in 1987 to serve as coordinator of research for President Reagan's Commission on Privatization. "Conservative thinking," commented *The Atlantic Monthly,* "has liberal thinking outgunned. . . . In vigor, freshness, and appeal, market-oriented theories have surpassed government-oriented theories at nearly every turn."[18]

• • •

On the foreign affairs front, despite a new and allegedly more liberal Soviet leader, Mikhail Gorbachev, the Cold War was still being waged in many different lands, including Nicaragua, Afghanistan, Angola, and Cambodia. According to W. Bruce Weinrod, Heritage's director of foreign policy and defense studies, the Soviet Union and its proxies were "clearly the source of much of the turmoil which threatens freedom and democratic government around the world."[19]

Between 1969 and 1980 the Soviets and their surrogates took over the Congo, South Yemen, Benin, South Vietnam, Laos, Mozambique, Angola, Ethiopia, the Seychelles, Cambodia, Nicaragua, Grenada, Afghanistan, and Suriname. Some fourteen countries fell to Communism, while none broke free of its grip. Here was the incarnation of the Brezhnev Doctrine—once a country goes Communist, it stays Communist.

A new rollback strategy was urgently needed, and President Reagan provided one. By 1982 seven major anti-Communist resistance movements were operating inside the Soviet empire. There were guerrilla forces in Afghanistan, Nicaragua, Angola, Mozambique, Ethiopia, Cambodia, and Laos. Solidarity was gaining strength in Poland. There was nationalist unrest within the Soviet Union, in Ukraine, and among the Muslim republics in Soviet Central Asia.

Heritage counseled Reagan to deal with all these uprisings and reactions as part of a continuing global trend toward decolonization. Writing in the *National Security Record*, Jack Wheeler described the phenomenon this way: "Just as the Third World rejected Western colonialism in the 1950s and 1960s, so it is now rejecting Soviet colonialism in the 1980s. And it is using the Soviets' own strategy of armed guerrilla resistance—wars of liberation—to do so."[20]

When President Reagan traveled to Geneva in November 1985 for a get-acquainted summit with Gorbachev, Heritage made certain that the president benefited from its foreign policy analysts' best thinking. Ed Feulner personally handed a fifty-four-page briefing book to Reagan at a White House meeting of conservative leaders, two weeks before the summit.

At Geneva the president called on the Soviets to abandon their occupation of Afghanistan, stop subsidizing and training terrorists, rein in the Cubans and the Sandinistas in Nicaragua, and obey all existing treaties, including the ABM Treaty and the Helsinki Accords governing human rights in Eastern and Central Europe. He said flatly that the United States intended to move forward with research and development of strategic missile defense: SDI was not negotiable. All of these points followed recommendations contained in Heritage's briefing book.

The Soviets were upset and angry. No American president had talked to them like this since Harry Truman at the start of the Cold War. In the first ten minutes of the summit, Gorbachev cited the Heritage study as evidence of "right-wing pressure" on their talks. The president admitted calmly that yes, he did have the Heritage study and that he liked it.[21]

A still-fuming Gorbachev returned to Moscow, where he told the Supreme Soviet that Reagan had stood fast on SDI because of "the 'mandate' given to the U.S. president by the forces of the American extreme right wing, represented by their ideological headquarters, The Heritage Foundation."[22] Heritage made sure that its members learned of Gorbachev's ire about the foundation's influential role in international affairs.

Some Heritage critics went to extremes. In April 1986 the Middle East terrorist organization Abu Nidal announced—through CBS News—that it had singled out The Heritage Foundation and three prominent antiterrorists as targets. The Abu Nidal threat came two weeks after President Reagan ordered U.S. air strikes on Libya in retaliation for the bombing of a Berlin discotheque that killed two people, including a U.S. soldier. The foundation quickly responded: "While it is certainly unnerving to be singled out as an alleged U.S. target, we don't intend to be silenced."

Feulner kept his cool, although he admitted years later that the threat "scared my wife and kids" because the primary target would have been the president of The Heritage Foundation. He did not take the warning lightly. He had seen what terrorists could do with the bombing of the Marine barracks in Beirut. The Abu Nidal threat served to strengthen Feulner's resolve to maintain a full-scale national security research operation.[23]

• • •

As President Reagan continued to seek peace through strength in his foreign policy, he made it a point to stand by old friends while trying to make new ones. A case in point was Taiwan. Before his first trip to China in April 1984, he reassured conservatives that he would not sacrifice Taiwan, with some 20 million citizens, to curry favor with China, the most populous nation in the world, with 1.1 billion people. One of the conservative leaders he made sure he talked to was the president of The Heritage Foundation.

Ed Feulner and his son E.J. were skiing at Hunter Mountain in upstate New York. It was Saturday afternoon, and they were thinking about dinner, when suddenly the owner of the modest motel where they were staying was pounding on the door and shouting, "Mr. Feulner, Mr. Feulner, you've got to come down to the lobby. I've got the president of the United States on the telephone. He wants to talk to you in my hotel!" It wasn't the president, of course, but the famed White House telephone operators who had tracked Feulner down. He went downstairs to the lobby because there was no phone in their room.

"Ed," the president began, "I know that you and my good conservative friends at The Heritage Foundation are worried about what's going to happen when I go over to China. I don't want you to worry about it. I know our friends are in Taiwan. I know what China represents, I know the problems that we've had with China and that we will continue to have with them in terms of human rights, in terms of how the individual is treated by the government, and how there is no representative form of government. I understand all of that. I'm not going over there hoping that some new set of miracles is going to occur. I'm going over there very realistically and I just want you to know that."

The phone call did not last more than a minute and a half, but it meant a great deal to Ed Feulner and every other conservative because "he was giving all of us a message that he was very realistic in terms of what the U.S.-Chinese relationship would be in the future."[24] The phone call also meant much to the owner of the motel, who spent the rest of the day in bed recovering from the excitement of talking to somebody who had talked to the president of the United States.

• • •

A Heritage strength is its ability to identify targets of opportunity for conservative analysis. Early on, the foundation targeted the United Nations and discovered to its surprise that almost no one in Washington was monitoring the UN very closely. With Feulner's approval, Heritage set up a research group to study the organization and start a serious debate of the pluses and minuses of the UN.

For most of its history, the United States had paid about 40 percent of the annual budget—the figure later dropped to 20 percent—while the Soviet Union paid only 13 percent. Yet in vote after vote a majority of UN members sided with Moscow and branded the United States as an "imperialist aggressor." The persistent anti-American bias of the UN "shocked even some Congressional liberals," recalls Feulner.[25]

The foundation's UN Assessment Project saturated Washington with studies documenting the abuses of the UN. "We pointed out, for example," Feulner said, "that the UN had become a major base for Soviet spies, that KGB agents were in charge of personnel at the UN's Geneva headquarters, that the KGB was using UN information agencies to disseminate anti-American and anti-Western propaganda around the world."[26]

Heritage supplied the Reagan administration with research on why the United States should not ratify the UN-sponsored Law of the Sea Treaty, pointing out that the treaty would put U.S. commercial ships at the mercy of an international organization hostile to the United States and private enterprise. The Reagan administration rejected the treaty, which had been strongly backed by the Carter administration. For a quarter-century, Heritage has not wavered in its opposition to the Law of the Sea Treaty, which was once again pushed by the Obama administration.

"While the treaty purports to protect the world's oceans," Ed Feulner wrote on Townhall.com, it would "make the high seas even more dangerous" through a new UN bureaucracy, the International Seabed Authority Secretariat. One of the treaty's most restrictive conditions is that American submarines would be required to travel on the surface and show their flags while sailing within another country's waters. "Pirates could confidently evade our Navy," Feulner said, "by simply ducking into any country's territorial waters." The world, he wrote, "needs an empowered American military, not a U.N. bureaucracy, to protect commerce at sea."[27]

When the United States withdrew in December 1984 from the UN Educational, Scientific, and Cultural Organization (UNESCO), Heritage took satisfaction that its recommendation of withdrawal had prevailed with the Reagan administration. The foundation documented a persistent pattern of waste, corruption, cronyism, anti-Americanism, and anticapitalism in most UNESCO programs. The director general, for example, had six official limousines at his disposal in Paris and New York City. Millions of dollars had evaporated on needless projects like a study of the epistemological foundation of economic theory.

The same year Heritage published two book-length studies—*A World Without a U.N.* and *The U.S. and the U.N.: A Balance Sheet.* The foreword of the former work was written by Ambassador Charles M. Lichenstein, who had joined Heritage as a senior fellow after serving as UN ambassador Jeane Kirkpatrick's deputy.

Like his boss, Lichenstein could call on a large and when necessary pointed vocabulary. After a prolonged and acrimonious public exchange with the Soviet representative, Ambassador Lichenstein informed the Soviet Union and other critics of America that if they were dissatisfied with things, they were free to move the UN headquarters to some other country.

In a memorable sentence quoted around the world, Lichenstein said: "We will put no impediment in your way, and we will be at dockside bidding you a farewell as you set off into the sunset."[28]

Over a period of two years, leading up to the U.S. withdrawal from UNESCO, Heritage released thirty-seven studies of the United Nations (six of them specifically about UNESCO). U.S. officials acknowledged that Heritage had contributed significantly to "the changed American mood toward that body."

When UNESCO began pressing for a New World Information Order, including the licensing of journalists by UNESCO, Heritage objected strenuously and found itself in league with *The Washington Post* and *The New York Times,* rare allies indeed.

A key individual in the battle was the articulate and highly productive Owen Harries, the former Australian ambassador to UNESCO and Heritage's John M. Olin Distinguished Fellow. So persuasive were the arguments tendered by Heritage as well as other groups that in one of the Democratic primary debates in 1984, Vice President Walter Mondale agreed with the Reagan administration that America should withdraw from UNESCO.[29]

Ed Feulner often cited the UN project when asked to describe how Heritage worked. It was a prime example of what he called "the three I's of think tanks—ideas, individuals, and institutions."

Ideas do have consequences, he said in 1985 to a group of grassroots leaders in Maryland; ideas matter. They filter into the system through *individuals* who expound, explain, and proclaim ideas, like Milton Friedman on tax limitation. "*Institutions* provide a base of support and a sense of continuity for *individuals* along with an operational center to popularize an idea, target an audience, and market the product." Because Heritage studies meet these three operating principles, Feulner explained, the foundation is able to fill "an information void in Washington."

• • •

Heritage's tenth year had been extraordinary for the foundation, capped by the dedication of its new eight-story beige-brick building on Capitol Hill and congratulatory messages from British prime minister Margaret Thatcher and West German chancellor Helmut Kohl; the publication of *Agenda '83,* the third installment of the *Mandate for Leadership* series; a gala banquet with President Reagan as guest of honor and keynote speaker; and the formation of the Asian Studies Center with Richard V. Allen as chairman, among major events.

"The rapid rise of Heritage from modest beginnings is something of a Washington Cinderella story," wrote *The New York Times,* but Heritage was no fairy tale. It was the story of the right idea at the right time, with the right leadership imbued with an optimistic entrepreneurial spirit. The foundation's leaders could be forgiven for being a little boastful, proclaiming that "in less than ten years, The Heritage Foundation has become *the* nerve center of a conservative intellectual renaissance sweeping the Free World."[30]

That remained to be proven, but in the meantime Heritage was preparing for a non-Orwellian 1984 and discussing what could be done to keep the Reagan Revolution alive and well.

CHAPTER 13

CONTINUING THE REVOLUTION

Heritage had proven, with *Mandate for Leadership,* that the right study could significantly affect the course of policy making. Feulner wondered: Should the foundation attempt to repeat its *Mandate* success in 1984? He and his colleagues surveyed the state of the union and the world. Government was still too big, and the Soviets and their satraps were still active in Afghanistan, Nicaragua, and elsewhere. Who better than Heritage to show how conservative ideas could be transformed into conservative policies? As a matter of fact, most policy makers in Washington expected Heritage to produce another *Mandate.*

In December 1984, following President Reagan's landslide reelection, the foundation published *Mandate for Leadership II: Continuing the Conservative Revolution.* Like its predecessor, it was a big book—comprising twenty-six chapters and 568 pages, featuring 150 contributors, and offering thirteen hundred recommendations calculated to reform the federal government and strengthen U.S. defenses. The editors were Stuart Butler, Bruce Weinrod, and Michael Sanera, an assistant professor of political science at Northern Arizona University.

In his introduction to domestic issues, Butler proposed (1) the restructuring of incentives, such as linking federal assistance to students to academic performance; (2) putting control of federal programs into the hands of those helped through housing and other social service vouchers; (3) creating competitive open markets by eliminating trade barriers; (4) reforming decision making by targeting food assistance to those in genuine need; and (5) privatizing federal programs like Social Security.

Butler challenged the president and his administration to take full advantage of his overwhelming victory. If the White House is content, he warned sternly, merely "to bask in the glow of the good feeling generated by Ronald Reagan," the administration will be no more than "an interesting footnote in the growth of federal government."[1]

In his introduction to defense and foreign policy issues, Heritage foreign policy director Bruce Weinrod proposed that the administration: (1) raise SDI's priority, expand modern conventional forces, and treat terrorism as "a form of warfare rather than as isolated violence"; (2) strengthen alliances like NATO and assist friends like Israel; (3) promote democratic pluralism through the "full observance of human rights" and the channeling of National Endowment for Democracy funds into democratic institutions; and (4) take into account that the USSR "is an empire with many weaknesses and vulnerabilities, internally and on its periphery." Seventeen years later in the wake of the 9/11 terrorist attacks, President George W. Bush adopted the recommendation that terrorism be treated as "a form of warfare."

Because people are policy, Weinrod said, the president must assemble in his second term a foreign policy and national security team that shares his worldview and will promote his vision of a world "where tyranny of the left and the right is fading" and "democratic pluralism and self-determination flourish."[2]

USA Today called *Mandate for Leadership II* "a new battle cry for recasting the U.S. government in a conservative image." *Saturday Review* wrote that "if ideas really do have consequences, this may well be one of the most important books published in 1984."[3]

The most gratifying compliment to the Heritage study came in February 1985 when President Reagan delivered his State of the Union address to Congress and the nation. While it may be a little bit of an exaggeration, remarked *The New York Times,* to suggest that the president used *Mandate for Leadership II* as a model, many of the proposals in the president's speech and in the foundation's document "were strikingly familiar."[4]

Reagan's reliance on the limited-government ideas of the Heritage study reflected the measurable shift in the American public's attitude toward government. By the second Nixon administration in the early

1970s, Ed Feulner told a Washington journal, "a very healthy skepticism" had developed about government's capabilities. In 1980 candidate Reagan was able to appeal to "a critical mass of public opinion" with his smaller-government message. But, the Heritage president said, "we are still at the start of the power curve insofar as conservative ideas taking over. We've got a long way to go."[5]

. . .

Whenever he was given the chance to explain the relationship between ideas, think tanks, and governments, Feulner went a long way to provide his answer, even as far as Australia. Delivering the prestigious Latham Memorial Lecture in Sydney, he explained that ideas like supply-side economics, privatization, and the flat tax begin with individuals like Milton Friedman and are then popularized by institutions like Heritage. He offered the example of *Essays in Supply Side Economics,* a book coproduced by Heritage and the Washington-based Institute for Research on the Economics of Taxation.

The two organizations hosted a conference to introduce the book and discuss its major theme: reducing government barriers like taxes leads inevitably to a stronger, healthier economy. Some four hundred congressional aides, members of Congress, administration officials, professors, and journalists attended—an impressive turnout. Heritage and the institute distributed copies to selected editors and columnists and crafted op-ed articles based on chapters. "We emphasized not only a scholarly work but the marketing of the finished product to our target audiences."[6]

Feulner described how Heritage had worked with Representative Jack Kemp of New York on the privatization of public housing and with other congressmen on Individual Retirement Accounts in Social Security and on privatizing Amtrak and the Postal Service. "The fact is we are now working from our agenda instead of the traditional Left-liberal agenda . . . [but] it took 30 years for these 'conservative' ideas to move into the mainstream."

In the field of foreign policy and national security, Feulner mentioned strategic defense and U.S. membership in UNESCO as issues that Heritage focused on. In the case of UNESCO, "we have brought to light the abuses in a program which was previously thought sacrosanct." Rather than reacting to the other side, Heritage was advocating change—"a change in the power structure away from the central government back to the people."

The American people have called for more responsibility and greater freedom, Feulner said. "They have called for change. As conservatives we must continue to be innovative. We must build on our ideas, popularize them, and make them available to the people."[7]

Heritage stepped up its research and marketing, relying on a staff of 106. About half of the staff were professionals, either policy analysts, communicators, or administrators. While other think tanks featured superstars like Jeane Kirkpatrick, Arthur Burns, and Alice Rivlin, the typical Heritage analyst, Feulner told a C-SPAN interviewer, was "a young PhD, maybe twenty-nine or thirty, probably on his or her first job, but with an ability to write clearly and succinctly and a commitment to the fundamental values that Heritage holds dear."

These analysts would normally stay with Heritage for about three years, when someone would often come along and offer a much higher salary than the foundation could match. "We're sorry to see them go," said Feulner, "but pleased at the same time. We're proud of the fact that we have an elaborate alumni system with Heritage 'graduates' at the White House, half a dozen government agencies, and I suppose the offices of twenty-five senators and congressmen."[8]

In more recent years, Heritage has accumulated a group of seasoned analysts such as Robert Rector, James Phillips, Baker Spring, Robert Moffit, Ariel Cohen, J. D. Foster, and James Gattuso, who can be depended upon to produce carefully reasoned and widely accepted papers on front-line issues.

When rumors—on which Washington thrives—circulated widely about Ed Feulner taking a post in the second Reagan term, he wrote a soothing letter to Heritage founder Joseph Coors, saying, "I have no plans, intentions or even wild anticipation of leaving Heritage." He revealed that only two government jobs interested him—White House chief of staff and secretary of state—and both were well occupied. In 1996, Feulner hedged, "Who knows? Maybe one of them might be possible." But in the meantime, he said, he wanted to stay where he was, "and if the Board agrees, I hope to continue doing so for the foreseeable future."[9]

• • •

"Expect the unexpected" is a good rule in politics, and certainly Heritage did not expect the Iran-contra affair. It might have brought down the Reagan administration if the president had tried to cover it up, as Richard Nixon had attempted to conceal Watergate.

It was not global strategy or high politics but a desire to rescue Americans held captive that led the president to approve the sale of arms to Iran. As Reagan biographer Lou Cannon put it, "Reagan was determined to get the hostages out, by whatever means possible." Indeed, the president "became so stubbornly committed to the trade of arms for hostages" that he could not be dissuaded from the policy even when new hostages were taken.[10]

Conservatives did their best to defend their favorite president. Heritage senior vice president Burt Pines argued that the Reagan administration's goal of encouraging and developing influence with "moderate elements in Iran" was sensible and necessary. He conceded that the president's policy required that "we close an eye to our embargo on arms for Iran," but it was justified, he insisted, "by the necessities of realpolitik."[11]

But realpolitik demands that a policy be successful.

In his memoir, Edwin Meese III—then Reagan's attorney general—asserts that when it became clear that the U.S. initiative to build ties with Iranian moderates was not succeeding, "it should have been dropped and Congress should have been notified of what had happened." Meese did not defend "the protracted failure to disclose" but argued that it was "a policy error, not a crime."[12]

Nicaragua was not a peripheral issue for either Reagan or his critics. For the president, Nicaragua was another Cuba; for the Democratic leadership in Congress, it was another Vietnam. Believing that the vital interests of the nation were at stake, each side dug in hard and prepared for political war.

U.S. funding of the contras continued until December 1984, when Congress strengthened the Boland Amendment, denying any U.S. support "directly or indirectly" to the contras. Administration lawyers decided that although the Boland Amendment prohibited American agencies "engaged in intelligence activities" (i.e., the CIA) from operating in Nicaragua, the National Security Council was not an intelligence agency. The pro-contra campaign was shifted to the NSC under the direction of national security adviser John Poindexter and NSC staffer Oliver North.

With Poindexter's approval, North illegally diverted about $4 million in profits from the Iranian arms sales to the contras. Ed Meese called the funds diversion "a tremendous error that should never have been allowed to happen. That it did happen was a failure of the administration—for which it paid dearly."[13] In December 1986 a national poll recorded a drop in Reagan's approval rating from 67 percent to 46 percent, the sharpest one-month fall in presidential surveys since such polling began in 1936.

However mistaken, Iran-contra centered on public policy, while Watergate had been about electoral politics. Reagan approved the arms-for-hostages deal to save American lives, while Nixon had tried to contain the Watergate scandal to save himself.

The Tower-Muskie Commission report found that the president had not known about the diversion of funds. The Democratic majority of the House-Senate select committee concluded that the president had been unaware of the funds diversion. The Republican minority said that the mistakes of Iran-contra were just that—"mistakes in judgment and nothing more. There was no constitutional crisis; no systematic disrespect for the 'internal rule of law,' no grand conspiracy."[14]

Iran-contra faded from the public's consciousness as most Americans, remembering the president's courage after the 1981 attempted assassination and conscious of the impressive accomplishments of his presidency, decided that Iran-contra was an exception rather than the rule of the administration.

"We considered Iran-contra to be marginal," recalls Feulner, "no big deal. Our attitude was, Let Ed Meese handle it and let's move on to other things of greater concern," like rolling back the welfare state.[15]

One personnel outcome of Iran-contra was the firing of White House chief of staff Donald Regan and the naming of former senator Howard A. Baker as his successor. One of Baker's first moves was to appoint Ed Feulner as an unpaid part-time consultant to work with the cabinet and the White House staff on the administration's domestic agenda in its last eighteen months. The appointment suited all sides: Baker demonstrated that he was open to conservative ideas, and Feulner was pleased to work directly with his longtime friend Kenneth Cribb (just named domestic adviser to the president) to advance conservative ideas.

· · ·

From its beginning, Heritage was not just a Washington think tank but a builder of the conservative movement. Ed Feulner was not just the president of The Heritage Foundation but a prime maker of a national movement. Bringing Willa Johnson on board as head of the Resource Bank was one of the four key appointments he made when he assumed the presidency of Heritage. He constantly pressed Johnson to expand

and deepen the bank's activities and allotted the necessary funds for such a goal. By the mid-1980s the foundation was in constant communication with some twelve hundred scholars and more than 250 think tanks, public-interest law groups, educational institutions, and other policy organizations across the country.

Its annual spring meeting remains a key event for the conservative movement. In April 1988, 130 representatives of over ninety public policy groups, including twenty-five state think tanks, attended the Resource Bank's eleventh annual meeting in Chicago. Every one of the state organizations had received tangible and often significant assistance from Heritage, including the names and addresses of the foundation's major donors in their states.

John Andrews, founder of the Independence Institute in Denver, says that his organization "nursed at Heritage's breast." The institute combed the pages of the *Annual Guide to Public Policy Experts* for the names of local professors to build "a board of leading Coloradans." Heritage provided a printout of its major donors in Colorado. Byron Lamm, an early director of the State Policy Network, describes Heritage as "an invaluable agent of coordination."[16]

A key supporter of the State Policy Network was Heritage trustee Thomas Roe, who explained, "I'm a grassroots person." He recalled that at a trustees' meeting in the mid-1980s, Robert Krieble said, "The evil empire can be dissolved—I'm going to go out and help do it." To which Roe responded, "You capture the Soviet Union—I'm going to capture the states."[17]

While Krieble underwrote the training of hundreds of dissidents and would-be democrats from behind the Iron Curtain on the techniques of electoral politics—Paul Weyrich and Leadership Institute founder Morton Blackwell led the instructors—Roe encouraged the formation of think tanks in his native South Carolina and other states. "Heritage is a nurturer," explains Terrence Scanlon, president of the Capital Research Center and a former Heritage vice president, "especially of state think tanks, which will become more important as Americans work to downsize the federal government and shift government power to the states."[18]

No other Washington think tank attempts, let alone succeeds, in carrying out such a nurturing role, a primary example of Heritage's consistent commitment to building the American conservative movement.

Heritage people from top to bottom take this responsibility seriously. In September 1984, Ed Feulner flew to Chicago to talk to "students" of the Catholic Center for Free Enterprise Graduate Program. He discussed what he called his "Ten Commandments" in dealing with policy makers in Washington or anywhere else.

The research product "must be credible and concise," able to pass the briefcase test. That is, can it fit into the congressman's briefcase and be read in no more than thirty minutes?

The research must be timely.

An effective delivery system must be developed for the research.

The research will be more effective if its impact is translated "into jobs rather than [dollars]."

Use the media and the grass roots to achieve credibility for the research.

Adhere to your principles. "But do not concern yourself with absolute purity."

Work with the smallest number of possible persons (a congressional subcommittee) rather than larger groups.

"Do not worry about who gets the credit for doing the job."

Do not hesitate to restate old, but true, arguments, time after time.

"Loan to and borrow from each other to advance the free society."[19]

Feulner would give the same advice to countless conservative groups throughout his tenure as Heritage president.

Another example of the foundation's movement building was the launching in 1987 of the Bradley Resident Scholars, who spent up to one year at Heritage working on a major research project and familiarizing themselves with Congress and other parts of the Washington policy-making community. The program was made possible through a $510,000 gift from the Lynde and Harry Bradley Foundation, one of the more creative grant-giving institutions in America.

Among the prominent conservative intellectuals who came to Washington under the Bradley program were Robert P. George, Princeton University; Hadley Arkes, Amherst College; Thomas West, University of Dallas (now at Hillsdale College); William Donohue, now head of the Catholic Civil Rights League; Steven W. Mosher, Human Life International; Eugene Hickok, who went on to become undersecretary of education; and Marvin Olasky, University of Texas at Austin, who would write a bestselling book about an unlikely subject—compassion.

Olasky had long been curious about the contemporary understanding of compassion, the desire to help those in need. The failures of the welfare state (as outlined by Charles Murray and others) were obvious, but what were the alternatives? How had Americans dealt with poverty, sickness, and other social problems in the eighteenth and nineteenth centuries? Had Americans been indifferent to the poor and disadvantaged until the New Deal?

Accepted as a Bradley scholar, Olasky spent a year from August 1989 to July 1990 plowing through the stacks at the Library of Congress and working with editor Adam Meyerson on a *Policy Review* article. "Adam is the best editor I've ever had," says Olasky. "He deserves special laud and honor." It was because Meyerson pushed him that "I came up with seven principles of effective compassion." The role of faith-based (church) help was critical.[20]

"Beyond the Stingy Welfare State: What We Can Learn from the Compassion of the 19th Century" was reprinted all over America and led to the 1992 publication of *The Tragedy of American Compassion* (which Olasky wrote in one month with Rocky Balboa's theme song "Eye of the Tiger" playing in the background). The book sold only a few thousand copies until former secretary of education William J. Bennett read it and recommended it to Representative Newt Gingrich nearly two years later.

Gingrich got around to reading *The Tragedy of American Compassion* over Christmas 1994 after leading Republicans to the capture of the House of Representatives for the first time in forty years. He loved it. In his inaugural address as Speaker of the House, Gingrich kept talking about the book until he turned it into a bestseller. "No one would have paid much attention to Newt in 1992," says Olasky, "but in 1994 they did. It all worked out very providentially."[21]

But that is not the end of the story. Texas governor George W. Bush also read the book and was so impressed that he described himself as a "compassionate conservative" when he ran for president in 2000. Once in the White House, he approved a faith-based initiative inspired by *The Tragedy of American Compassion*. All of which demonstrated yet again the impact of the right idea at the right time.

• • •

For today's liberals a black conservative is as much an oxymoron as Russell Kirk's idea of a conservative mind was to the liberals of fifty years ago. But in June 1987, Clarence Thomas, then chairman of the Equal Employment Opportunity Commission and now an associate justice of the Supreme Court, lectured at Heritage on "Why Black Americans Should Look to Conservative Policies."

Thomas said that black Americans would move naturally toward conservatism when conservatives treated them as "a diverse group with differing interests" and stopped treating them with condescension and timidity. "There need be no ideological concessions," he said, "just a major attitudinal change."

Thomas went on to discuss the emphasis of the Founders on the connection between natural law and constitutional government. The thesis of natural law, he said, is that human nature provides the key to how men ought to live their lives. He quoted John Quincy Adams that "our political way of life is by the laws of nature [and] of nature's God, and of course presupposes the existence of God and . . . a rule of right and wrong, of just and unjust, binding upon man, preceding all institutions of human society and of government."

This approach, Thomas said, "allows us to reassert the primacy of the individual and establishes our inherent equality as a God-given right." This principled approach would make it clear to blacks, he said, that "conservatives are not hostile to their interests but aggressively supportive."[22] In the years to come, Thomas would depend on his understanding of natural law and its binding on man for his decisions as a Supreme Court justice.

• • •

Heritage's board of trustees has had its share of conservative stars—former treasury secretary William E. Simon, Pittsburgh publisher and philanthropist Richard Scaife, beer baron Joseph Coors, publisher and presidential candidate Steve Forbes, Amway chairman Jay Van Andel. But when Clare Boothe Luce became a Heritage trustee in 1985, the board and the foundation took on a special luster.

Luce had brilliantly played a wide variety of public roles—ambassador, playwright, editor, essayist, war correspondent, congresswoman, presidential adviser. She was beautiful, charismatic, and witty. Among her bons mots: "No good deed goes unpunished" and "Conservatives are liberals with children." She was also wise, saying: "Courage is the ladder on which all the other virtues mount" and "There are no hopeless situations: There are only people who have grown hopeless about them."[23]

Asked to join many organizations when she moved to Washington in 1981 after Ronald Reagan was elected president, Luce turned down everyone but The Heritage Foundation, explaining, "Many things give me concern today, but Heritage gives me hope." When she died in

October 1987 (at the age of eighty-four), Feulner felt her loss personally and deeply.

"Among the women I've admired most," he says, "is Clare Boothe Luce, who broke through so many barriers in her life."[24] During her final weeks, after Feulner learned she was seriously ill, he sent her flowers, tape cassettes of Gregorian chants, and a postcard from London of two purple-haired punkers (with the suggestion she could do with a new hairdo). "Clare's life," Feulner says, "was a refutation of the stereotype of conservatives as 'stuffed shirts'—a phrase, by the way, that she coined."[25]

Reflecting their profound admiration for Luce's life and example, Heritage trustees named the foundation's highest public award after her. The first Clare Boothe Luce Award was given jointly in September 1991 to Ambassador Shelby Cullom Davis and his remarkable scholar wife Dr. Kathryn Davis (still active and traveling at the age of 105). The first Clare Boothe Luce Lecture was delivered by the Right Honorable Margaret Thatcher of the United Kingdom, who took advantage of the occasion to utter a memorable line about her old friend and colleague, "Ronald Reagan won the Cold War without firing a shot."[26]

· · ·

Remembering the letters his father had written to him as a young man, Ed Feulner wrote in October 1987 a series of fatherly letters to E.J. on his sixteenth birthday, which he called a rite of passage "from childhood to becoming a young adult." He must have typed the letters himself because they are so personal and because they contain typographical errors that Kathy Rowan or Missy Stephens would have caught.

He explained that he wanted to write down his thoughts and suggestions because when they were together "it seems we are always wrapped up in *doing* things instead of *talking about* things." He recalled that he had written to E.J. when he was in the third grade about making choices in life.

Back then "it was a question of [choosing either] a fishing pole or an electronic baseball game for your birthday present." Now "your choices are do you spend the extra hour in the afternoon studying, or do you talk with your friends, listen to music and have a good time? In other words, do you work hard on your studies, or do you goof off and enjoy yourself. I know that sounds like an unfair way of putting it, but isn't that what the choice really becomes?"

The decision facing E.J., said his father, "is what economists call a 'consumption vs. saving' decision." Consumption means "immediate gratification." Saving means "buying something for the future" where "deep in your heart you know the long-term payoff is going to be very important and will help you the whole rest of your life."

For Ed Feulner, the decision was simple: "What America needs—and what you need—is more saving and less consumption!"

In his second letter, he began by explaining that studying was important not just because it would improve E.J.'s grades and help get him into college but because it would enable him to learn about "the ideas and the work of many generations of great men before our time." He quoted Russell Kirk: "The reason the current generation seems like giants is because we stand on the shoulders of our ancestors." That was why when they were on trips, he wrote, "I insist on the family going to some museums, cathedrals and other important places where [we can see] the accomplishments of past generations" and be inspired by them.

He said he had recently been in St. George's Chapel at Windsor Castle outside London and had looked up at the Gothic roof. "It is about 140 feet up (the same as a 14 story building) with buttresses on the outside to hold the roof in place, all built 700 years ago when there were not any steam engines to lift the stones up one on top of the other. . . . They did it the hard way and we learned from them."

"Please think about this as you work ahead in the next weeks and months."

In his final letter, Feulner talked about Clare Boothe Luce, who had just died. He reminded E.J. that they had ridden with Mrs. Luce on a visit to the Basilica of the Shrine of the Immaculate Conception in northeast Washington, D.C.

He recalled that Clare had once mentioned why she had become a Catholic. She said "she wanted to go with a religion that 'had been around for a long time, and [she] figured that 2,000 years was long enough.'" That was why she used the Chase Manhattan Bank—it too had been around for a long time. And that was why she was so enthusiastic about Heritage and helping it—"because she wanted Heritage to be around for a long time."

He asked his son if he had thought about young people in other countries and what would happen to them when they became young adults.

If you are sixteen in China, he wrote, and have "an average or mediocre academic record, your career is already decided. . . . If you are lucky, you may have one or two more years of school after which time you will be a mechanic or a farmer or whatever for the rest of your life."

If you are sixteen in the Soviet Union, "you will be spending many hours a week in a Young Pioneer camp learning about Marx and Lenin and their ideas about how to control the world."

If you are sixteen in Afghanistan, "you would have a choice of either being drafted into the army of the communist-controlled government, or hopefully working with the Mujahadin to try and overthrow the communists and probably living from hand to mouth with a rifle, a few rounds of ammunition, and a little bit of rice."

A similar fate would be yours "if you lived in Nicaragua: either be drafted into the army of the communist Sandinista regime . . . or you could be fighting with the Contras or Freedom Fighters to try and gain back the basic rights which the Sandinistas took away—and which we here in United States take for granted.

"Son," he wrote, "these are hard choices in the big cruel world that you are getting closer to entering. The older you get, the harder the choices are."

He praised E.J. for the choices he had made so far—including the maturity he had shown the past summer while working at the Bicycle Exchange. He urged him to keep on making choices "that are the best for you in the long run." I hope, he wrote, "you are investing (saving) and not just consuming." In so doing, he said, you are building a base for the years ahead.

The last sentence of the last letter to his sixteen-year-old son E.J. read: "The choices we make today really will affect what we are able to do in the future."[27]

It was good advice both for a sixteen-year-old boy on the edge of adulthood and for members of Congress confronting the issues of life, liberty, and the pursuit of happiness.

CHAPTER 14

BEYOND REAGAN

Change comes slowly in Washington, where bureaucrats, members of Congress, lobbyists, and even public policy analysts are comfortable with the status quo. But The Heritage Foundation has always been committed to changing Washington.

In 1987 two of Heritage's most influential analysts published books that challenged conventional thinking. Stuart Butler, along with Anna Kondratas, released *Out of the Poverty Trap: A Conservative Strategy for Welfare Reform,* a landmark study on welfare reform. Robert Rector and visiting fellow Michael Sanera published *Steering the Elephant: How Washington Works.*

For several years, the foundation had been building a body of scholarship on alternative approaches to poverty problems. Heritage's research team spent many hours with the welfare poor in the inner cities, obtaining a better understanding of their problems and learning of community-based solutions unknown to policy makers and generally ignored by antipoverty bureaucrats. Their work was supported by grants from both conservative and nonconservative institutions.

In mid-1985 the foundation received special funding from the New Jersey–based Schultz Foundation, which had a long-term interest in health and social welfare issues. That same year Butler and Kondratas presented a paper on "The Future of the Welfare State: Beyond Welfarism" at a Ford Foundation conference. The paper drew together for the first time the data and analysis that provided the framework for *Out of the Poverty Trap*. A subsequent gift from Tom and Shirley Roe endowed the Thomas A. Roe Institute for Economic Policy Studies, which supported the writing and final research of the Butler-Kondratas book.

The book attracted widespread attention because it presented a comprehensive strategy for rebuilding the family based on: (1) reforming the tax code so that it does not hurt those who leave the welfare rolls; (2) eliminating or streamlining regulations that make it impossible for parents to work at home; (3) requiring parents on welfare to be responsible for the actions, including the sexual behavior, of their children; (4) adding a work component to every welfare program; and (5) making Aid to Families with Dependent Children (AFDC) a temporary and no longer a permanent program. The authors appeared on dozens of television and radio interview programs including the ultimate—*The Oprah Winfrey Show*.

A decade later Congress passed welfare reform, justifying what Butler and Kondratas had predicted in *Out of the Poverty Trap:* Washington would one day awaken to the fact that it had badly erred when it decided that "decentralization, competition and pluralism were good for everything except fighting poverty, and that uniformity and central planning were bad for everyone except the poor."[1]

In *Steering the Elephant,* Rector and Sanera offered a blunt assessment of the successes and failures of the Reagan administration in implementing public policy with an emphasis on the failures. Contrary to conservative hopes, President Reagan had not been able to cut government spending. In fact, it had risen from 22 percent to 24 percent of GNP in his first six years in office. However, Rector and Sanera said, the change in priorities was significant because defense spending increased from 5 percent to 6.5 percent of GNP, enabling the president to deal with the Soviet Union from a position of strength and bring about a peaceful resolution of the Cold War.

Successful presidencies, wrote the authors, set the stage for "long-term change by altering public perceptions." They gave Reagan a passing grade but no higher. Although "the great communicator" made a good case for a stronger military in a hostile world, he failed to stress that reducing government was not just an "unpleasant necessity" but "a positive investment" that would make all Americans more prosperous in the future. They singled out public education as a particular disappointment, stating that "there is no middle ground between offense and defense" in education and that the Reagan administration had too often been on the defensive.[2] In fact, federal spending on state education increased 20 percent or almost $35 billion during the Reagan presidency.

A fundamental political transformation, stated the authors, could not be effected in six or eight years. Both incremental and cumulative change had to last for two decades or longer. The importance of the Reagan administration, therefore, "will be determined as much by its impact on the attitudes that the American public carry into the 21st century as by its impact on budget, legislation, regulation and administration in the 1980s." Then and only then, said Rector and Santera, would it would be possible to say whether there had been a real "Reagan Revolution."[3]

There was no doubt in Ed Feulner's mind that Reagan had led a revolution. Writing in *The New York Times,* he and Heritage chairman Shelby Cullom Davis said that the Reagan presidency would be compared with that of Franklin D. Roosevelt for the groundwork laid for future administrations.

"Presidents leave lasting legacies by creating new frameworks for public policy debates," they wrote. "Franklin Roosevelt's policies culminated in Lyndon Johnson's Great Society programs twenty-one years after FDR's death. The new framework Mr. Reagan created has spawned a generation of new institutions staffed by young people shorn of the delusions of their 1960s counterparts. . . . The full flower of the Reagan era will come in the next century."[4]

Their 1988 prediction was fulfilled in Newt Gingrich's revolutionary 1994 Contract with America, Democratic President Bill Clinton's 1996 statement that "the era of big government is over," George W. Bush's "compassionate conservatism" of the 2000s, and the eagerness with which every Republican candidate seeking the presidential nomination in 2012 described himself or herself as a devoted follower of Ronald Reagan.

Reagan's legacy as CEO of the economy, commander in chief of the armed forces, American statesman and national symbol, and political leader is almost without precedent in modern U.S. history.

At the core of Reaganomics was lower income taxes so that people could spend, save, or invest as they wished. Economic growth rose steadily from late 1982 for the next ninety months—the longest peacetime economic expansion in the twentieth century.

Seeking peace through strength, Reagan nearly doubled defense spending, expending $1.7 trillion, and he inaugurated the Reagan

Doctrine, which put the Soviet Union on the defensive for the first time in the Cold War. A clear and present danger that had preoccupied the world for forty years was no more as Communism collapsed in Eastern and Central Europe and the evil empire disappeared.

Building on his legacy, Republicans in 1994 captured the House of Representatives for the first time in forty years and extended the reach of the party from the White House to the statehouse. If there had been no Ronald Reagan, there would have been no Speaker Newt Gingrich, no Bush 41 or Bush 43, and no conservative alternative like the Tea Party to a more aggressive and progressive Democratic Party.

Ronald Reagan was important to Heritage for two reasons. "Because we were so simpatico with each other on the issues," says Feulner, "he knew that he could rely on us, whether it was costing out a tax bill or how to move ahead with a antiballistic missile system that could lead to a reduction in nuclear weapons around the world or how to keep Americans proud while not undercutting or pulling apart the social safety network."

The other reason was that "Ronald Reagan's embrace of our ideas was making Heritage into a respectable Washington institution. That was huge," admits Feulner. "When Heritage started less than ten years before Reagan came into office, the notion that there would be a serious and outspokenly conservative competitor to the liberal Brookings Institution or the establishment American Enterprise Institute was beyond understanding."[5]

* * *

In one of his last official acts, President Reagan bestowed the Presidential Citizens Medal on Ed Feulner at a simple White House ceremony. The citation read:

> *As President of The Heritage Foundation, Edwin J. Feulner Jr. has been a leader of the conservative movement. By building an organization dedicated to ideas and their consequences, he has helped to shape the policy of our Government. His has been a voice of reason and values in service to his country and the cause of freedom around the world.*

Feulner was moved because the medal honored the two most important things in his professional life—The Heritage Foundation and the conservative movement—and because it acknowledged the power of ideas to shape policy in "the cause of freedom" everywhere. The medal meant all the more because it was conferred by the president whom he admired most. "It was," he says, "the proudest moment of my life."[6]

• • •

As grateful as they were for the glorious Reagan years, Ed Feulner and his colleagues appreciated Senator Bob Dole's comment at a President's Club meeting in the fall of 1987: "We don't know who's going to be in the Oval Office in January 1989 [but] we know it's not going to be Ronald Reagan."[7]

A year earlier Feulner had addressed the issue of presidential succession and future public policy in a talk at the annual meeting of the American Political Science Association titled "Conservatism After Reagan: Ideas." He was confident that conservatism would not falter, fade, or expire because of the enduring strength of its ideas.

He quoted prominent Democrats to prove his point. Senator Daniel Patrick Moynihan of New York, arguably the most intellectual member of the U.S. Senate, confessed that the Republicans had left the Democrats behind because the Republicans "became the party of ideas, and the Democrats were, in John Stuart Mill's phrase, 'the Stupid Party.' " Who wound up running the country? asked Moynihan. The politicians who knew how to use ideas. "The end product of government is laws—and laws emerge from ideas."[8]

Building on Moynihan's comment, Feulner described how Heritage research in the person of Charles Murray had changed the debate on welfare and the welfare state. Murray's classic *Losing Ground* had its genesis in a *Critical Issues* booklet published by The Heritage Foundation. Even Democrats like former Virginia governor (and future U.S. Senator) Charles Robb admitted that the welfare system "clearly isn't working and . . . seems to be subsidizing the spread of self-destructive behavior in our poor communities."

Since 1977, when he became Heritage president, said Feulner, the foundation had published more than thirty studies, monographs, and magazine articles on "the benefits of tax cuts and indexation." Now "Congress is debating whether our top tax bracket should be 27 or 28 percent when only five years ago the top rate was 70 percent!"

What will conservatives be talking about after the Reagan presidency? He listed the following: a balanced federal budget, privatization of government services, health care Individual Retirement Accounts (IRAs), free-trade agreements with other nations, and a peace-through-strength foreign policy, including supporting anti-Communist/pro-democratic forces.

Far from worrying about the future, Feulner looked forward to it, determined to "build the pressure in Congress to force the politicians to make hard choices" based on "the ideas that helped to elect Ronald Reagan in 1980 and that have been the standard rallying cry for conservatives."[9]

Washington insider Tom Korologos remembers that many of his friends predicted that Heritage would recede in importance and influence with the passing of the conservative Reagan administration, "but it didn't work out that way, absolutely not."[10] The foundation's senior management dismissed the mostly liberal prediction as wishful thinking—they were confident that conservative ideas and applications would be favorably received by the administration of George H. W. Bush, who had, after all, been Ronald Reagan's vice president for eight years. Bush seemed a likely winner over the proudly liberal Governor Michael Dukakis of Massachusetts.

Even so, Heritage decided it would be prudent to return to its congressional roots and seek to move policy in a conservative direction through the people's branch of government. Experienced Hill people were added to the congressional liaison office, including the redoubtable Kate O'Beirne, who had run the office of Senator James Buckley (C-NY) and become a leader of the network of conservative staffers on Capitol Hill. While continuing to publish *Backgrounders* on the issues of the day, the foundation elected to emphasize welfare reform and free trade, two overriding issues of the 1990s.

And there were more big books, starting with the copublication (along with Paul Weyrich's Free Congress Foundation) of *Issues '88: A Conservative Platform for America*, a 633-page policy outline for candidates seeking federal office. The Platform Committee at the 1988 Republican National Committee relied upon *Issues '88* to write an estimated forty foreign and domestic policy planks.

With the Claremont Institute, Heritage published *The Imperial Congress: Crisis in the Separation of Powers*, edited by Gordon S. Jones and John A. Marini. The crisis had resulted from a decades-long dominance of Congress by liberals in love with pork-barrel politics. The book's essays recalled the original purposes of the Constitution and the separation of powers, said Ed Feulner in a brief preface, showed how the Constitution had been undermined, and suggested ways to its restoration. Among the recommendations: a Balanced Budget Amendment, term limits for congressional leaders, and no exemptions for Congress from laws it passes such as working conditions and wages (all of which were included in the historic 1994 Contract with America).

In December 1988, Heritage released its third policy manual for an incoming administration, *Mandate for Leadership III: Policy Strategies for the 1990s,* edited by Charles Heatherly (who had returned to Heritage as its vice president for academic affairs) and Burt Pines. Like its predecessors, *Mandate III* was big (953 pages, four hundred contributors) and unambiguously conservative. It asserted that the federal government should be the last not the first resort to solve America's problems and that the United States was duty-bound to resist Communism and expand freedom around the world.

But its emphasis was different. As Ed Feulner said in the foreword, "The first two *Mandates* diagnosed the federal government's afflictions, obesity and arthritis, and prescribed the right therapies, deregulation and reduced spending." *Mandate III* outlined how to administer the therapies and "retrain the patient" by managing the federal bureaucracy. *The Christian Science Monitor* said the study was "as comprehensive as the Yellow Pages." Representative Tom DeLay of Texas, who would serve as House Majority Whip in the historic 104th Congress, called *Mandate III* "cover-to-cover good government."[11]

In the first chapter, Heatherly asked a haunting political question: "If Ronald Reagan and his 'Reaganauts' could only *slow down* the growth of federal spending, not reverse it or eliminate wasteful programs, what hope is there for any other conservative president who wants to challenge the entrenched orthodoxies of the modern liberal welfare state?"[12]

The challenging answer was that conservatives should pursue a "politics of governance that would seek control of the policy apparatus at both ends of Pennsylvania Avenue"—the White House and Congress. The strategy would require a commitment to "party government" as distinct from "government by personality." It would mean uniting a political party around principles that would constrain "the economic interests and passions" that motivate most human endeavor. Each major party would vie for control of the White House *and* Congress. The result would be a renewed public interest in politics as citizens realized that the elections would make a lasting difference in their lives.[13]

How quixotic, said Washington liberals, to suggest that Republicans compete for control of Congress. Had the author forgotten that Democrats had ruled the House of Representatives since 1955? The

Republican majority in the Senate between 1981 and 1986 was simply a deviation from the liberal norm, made possible by the personal appeal of President Reagan. Political realignment was an impossible dream, despite the consecutive presidential victories of Reagan and George H. W. Bush in 1980, 1984, and 1988. The Democratic majority in Congress was here to stay, liberals proclaimed.

Heritage was quick to respond that the conservative victories of the 1980s were *not* simply the personal triumphs of a popular president but were made possible by increasing public acceptance of conservative ideas. As Ed Feulner pointed out in the *Mandate III* foreword:

> *What history will find remarkable about the 1980s is how far and fast we've advanced. In many ways, the dreadful 1970s have been repealed. We've taken what, ten years ago, was called unthinkable and shown that it's workable—when given a chance. Just as the New Deal revolution of the 1930s laid the foundation for the Great Society of the 1960s, the intellectual battles we've won over the last decade have established the premises for formulating public policy well into the next century.*[14]

CHAPTER 15

THE YEAR OF MIRACLES

The collapse of Communism in Eastern and Central Europe in 1989 was produced by decades of political tyranny and economic failure. While the West enjoyed prosperity and freedom, the East fell into an economic and political morass. With no incentives to compete or modernize, the Soviet satellites became a museum of the early industrial age.

Singapore, an Asian city-state of two million people, exported 20 percent more machinery to the West in 1987 than all of Eastern Europe. Life expectancy declined dramatically in the Soviet bloc, and infant mortality rose. The only people exempted from economic and social hardship were Communist Party leaders, upper-echelon military officers, and the managerial elite.

All the while the once-impenetrable Iron Curtain was being breached by modern communications and technology, allowing the inhabitants of Eastern Europe to see how the other half of Europe lived. Increasingly, Poles, Hungarians, Czechs, and East Germans demanded change and reform, not only in the marketplace but in the realm of human rights and liberties.

For nearly forty years, the Communist governments of Eastern Europe depended on the Soviets to perpetuate their power, but by the mid-1980s, when Mikhail Gorbachev became secretary-general of the

Communist Party, the Soviet Union could no longer afford the empire it had so carefully and expensively built.

But no one anticipated how quickly Marxism-Leninism would collapse—in just one year, a year of miracles.

In February 1989, Václav Havel was jailed in Prague for participating in human rights protests; in December he was elected president of Czechoslovakia.

In March, 75,000 people demonstrated in Budapest demanding a withdrawal of Soviet troops and free elections.

In April, the once-outlawed Solidarity union and the Polish government agreed to the first open elections in Poland since World War II.

In May, the Hungarian Communist government began dismantling the Iron Curtain along the border with Austria.

In June, Solidarity won an overwhelming victory over Communist opponents in the Soviet bloc's first free elections in forty years.

In July, Gorbachev reminded the Council of Europe meeting in Strasbourg that he rejected the Brezhnev Doctrine of once a Communist state always a Communist state.

In September, Hungary opened its borders with Austria and allowed thousands of East Germans to cross into Austria.

In October, hundreds of thousands of people began demonstrating every Monday evening in the major cities of East Germany.

In November, a tidal wave of East Germans poured across the border into West Berlin and the Berlin Wall came tumbling down.

In December, proposals for free elections were made in Bulgaria and mass protests occurred in the Romanian cities of Timişoara and Bucharest. On Christmas Day the Romanian despot Nicolae Ceauşescu was executed.

Ed Feulner, who had gotten into politics in the early 1960s because of Barry Goldwater and his "Why Not Victory?" philosophy, was ecstatic. He proclaimed that "1989 was the most significant year in the most important decade since World War II." The victory over Communism belonged to American conservatives, especially Ronald Reagan, who had strengthened America's defenses and stopped "winking at Soviet adventurism."[1]

He celebrated the collapse of Communism in Eastern and Central Europe by traveling to Berlin the following year with members of the Heritage board of trustees and personally taking a hammer to the wall—once a divider of peoples, now a symbol of Communism's inability to contain man's innate desire for freedom.

• • •

A year later Linda Feulner accompanied Ed on a Heritage trip to Eastern Europe that included a stop in Albania, which had suffered for decades under one of the most repressive Communist leaders—Enver Hoxha. They were the first Americans to visit Albania since Secretary of State James Baker. The dictator Hoxha was gone, but there was abundant evidence of his brutal regime. As they drove into the capital, Linda noticed that many of the trees had been cut down and replaced by sharp stakes intended to impale paratroopers in the event of an invasion.

"We saw lovely villas that had almost been destroyed," she recalls, "and mice running over the beds. And we visited the university where all the windows were broken and the poor students were freezing in winter. They said that Secretary Baker had promised them blankets, but they never got any. That was all Ed had to hear."[2]

Once back in Washington, Feulner called in Larry Wortzel and a few other Heritage analysts who had good connections at the Pentagon. He explained the needs of the Albanian students and directed his colleagues to come up with a solution; they dubbed their effort "Operation Blanket." In less than three weeks, several hundred army blankets were shipped via military transport to Frankfurt, Germany, and then to Albania. Heritage literally delivered the goods, keeping a promise made by the U.S. government.

• • •

Heritage became deeply involved in the difficult transition that the former satellites of the Soviet Union faced while moving from a command economy and one-party politics to a market economy and democratic politics. Leaders of the Republic of Estonia, still under titular Soviet control, came to Heritage in November 1989, asking for guidance; the following month Heritage dispatched a delegation of free-market economists to Tallinn, the capital of Estonia. The foundation also sent a delegation to Poland and Hungary.

One of the emotional highlights of the year was the visit of Lech Walesa, founder of the Polish trade union Solidarity and future Nobel laureate. Walesa told Phil Truluck, "We are burying the Communist system, but we need help in creating a new system to replace it."[3] The foundation handed Walesa a nuts-and-bolts blueprint to privatize state-owned industries, decontrol prices, and create an economic climate to encourage foreign investors.

As part of his September 1990 trip to Eastern Europe, Feulner visited Ukraine, not yet independent of the Soviet Union. (It would declare its independence in August 1991.) Speaking from the pulpit of a Baptist church in Kiev, Feulner discussed briefly why the "evil empire" was crumbling. Some said it was a sign of *political* failure—that the politicians had failed to listen to the people. And "they are right of course." Others said that the empire's fall could be traced to *economic* failure—the Communist system had not given the people enough to live in comfort and dignity. "Those people are right also."

But the fundamental flaw of Communism was neither political nor economic but spiritual. "What is wrong with the system," he said, "is that it is Godless. . . . It is based on a denial of the Supreme Being." And yet throughout the Soviet Union, and especially in Ukraine, the people had the courage and were willing to make sacrifices for many, many years "to keep alive the word of Jesus Christ."

"Remember," said Feulner speaking for himself, the trustees sitting in the pews, and believers throughout America, "that we are always with you in our hearts and in our prayers."[4]

As a result of Communism's collapse, Ed Feulner argued, conservatives had "a chance like none other since the New Deal to reshape the political landscape." In the 1990s "our goal must be to translate [our] principles into policy." There must be no more adjusting to liberal initiatives but a more aggressive push for the adoption of conservative programs. Otherwise, he warned, what Ed Meese called the "tin-cup syndrome" would continue, turning America from "a nation of entrepreneurs into a nation of lobbyists" who poured into Washington to beg Congress for money.[5]

Conservatives were up to the task, a confident Feulner said. Four conservative economists—F. A. Hayek, Milton Friedman, George Stigler, and James Buchanan—had received Nobel Prizes. Younger intellectuals like Charles Murray, Stuart Butler, George Gilder, Daniel Pipes, Kim Holmes, and Richard McKenzie had helped reshape the way Washington thought. There was a growing conservative public-interest law movement, dozens of lively conservative journals on college campuses, a lengthening list of state think tanks, and an increasing interest among mainstream publishers in conservative books.

We have spent the last forty-five years, Feulner said, "preventing the Left from dismantling the barricades against Soviet Communism." Now we have to do battle on the domestic front, as many were already doing, like Stuart Butler, Anna Kondratas, and Jack Kemp, with their "conservative war on poverty." Feulner predicted that if conservatives put their principles into practice, the 1990s would be remembered as "a decade of freedom" and "unprecedented opportunity" for every American.[6]

To put it another way, it would be a decade in which the American Dream would become a reality for many more Americans. Many have offered their definition of that dream. Here is Ed Feulner's version, offered in September 1989 at a Lincoln Club meeting in Orange County, California:

> *We all share [an] idea. It's called the American Dream, in which:*
> *We can all own a home—even public housing tenants.*
> *We—as parents—can choose the best education for our children.*
> *We can work where we want, start our own businesses & provide for our own retirement.*
> *We can build communities & churches which help our neighbors in need (as we have for hundreds of years).*
> *We can do all this & more, if we are just given the opportunity.*[7]

For Heritage, said Feulner, that meant continuing to perfect the foundation's "quick-response capability" while keeping in mind the long-term goals of a more limited government, a strong defense, and greater individual freedom. "We look forward to working closely with President Bush and his cabinet to bring these goals about."[8]

• • •

There was good reason to expect that Heritage and Bush would be allies.

Then–Vice President Bush had spoken at the 1983 dedication of the Heritage headquarters. Bush and Feulner had exchanged cordial notes throughout the Reagan presidency. In January 1988, Feulner sent the vice president a memorandum, prepared by a colleague, suggesting how Bush might respond to Iran-contra questions by fellow Republican candidates. The thrust of the memo was that discussion ought to focus on an upcoming vote on a request by President Reagan to provide additional military and humanitarian assistance to "anti-Communist forces in Nicaragua"—not who did what and when in Iran.

In a handwritten note, Bush thanked "Ed" and his "senior colleague" for the memorandum, writing that "the libs bash me on Iran-Contra, and some short sighted GOP candidates think they'll sink me with it. They're wrong."[9]

After Bush secured the Republican presidential nomination, Feulner along with Paul Weyrich and other conservatives had breakfast in
August with the vice president at a meeting arranged by Senator James
McClure of Idaho. Among the topics was SDI. A few days later Bush
wrote Feulner emphasizing his strong support for the Strategic Defense
Initiative in contrast to his Democratic opponent, Governor Michael
Dukakis, who labeled it a "fantasy and a fraud." "I am on record," Bush
said, "supporting full funding of research, development *and deployment* of a comprehensive strategic defense system."[10]

In September of that year Feulner agreed to join Catholics for Bush
as a cochairman, along with such notable Catholics as Peter Grace, William Simon, William Bennett, and Michael Joyce. In early December,
following the elections, President-elect Bush met with Feulner and a
dozen other conservatives in the Executive Office Building to discuss
some of the issues that concerned the group, including Central America,
Supreme Court appointments, and tenant ownership of public housing.
Feulner and Phil Truluck presented Bush with a copy of *Mandate for
Leadership III*.

Not easily impressed and accustomed to meeting with heads of
state, Ed Feulner wrote a personal note of thanks in February 1989 to
President Bush for including him and Linda in a "memorable dinner" in
the private quarters of the White House. Never one to pass up an opportunity, Feulner included a new Heritage paper that he hoped would
"find its way into your briefing book."[11]

Early in 1989, when he faced political pressure to ban imported
assault rifles, President Bush called Ed Feulner for his opinion. When
the president was asked at a news conference what he was going to do
about assault rifles and drug-related crime, he suggested the reporter
read "that very intelligent, thoughtful paper from Ed Feulner's group
over at Heritage."[12]

Later that year, before President Bush went to Malta for his first
summit meeting with Soviet premier Gorbachev, he told members of
Heritage's President's Club that he was looking forward to seeing the
foundation's summit recommendations. At a private Camp David meeting, Ed Feulner personally handed the president Heritage's analysis,
written by Leon Aron and Jay Kosminsky, urging him to take a firm
line with the Soviet leader. (It was Feulner's first and only time at Camp
David.) At an earlier White House briefing—that was attended by the
president, Vice President Dan Quayle, Secretary of State James Baker,
national security adviser Brent Scowcroft, and several national security

aides, and lasted an unusually long two hours—Feulner urged "no conciliation to Gorbachev in terms of internal suppression" and that "if the Cold War was going to be over, [Gorbachev] would have to admit it."[13]

In pursuit of the good rather than the perfect, Heritage offered a comprehensive national health care plan that guaranteed affordable medical care to all Americans. The plan, developed by Stuart Butler and health care policy analyst Edmund Haislmaier, was detailed in a 127-page study, *A National Health System for America*. It proposed that the existing employer-provided health insurance system be replaced by a new system, based on tax credits, in which most Americans would pay directly for routine medical needs and buy their own health insurance to cover the cost of major illnesses. Included was the proviso that *every* American would have to participate (an early version of the controversial "individual mandate" directive of Obamacare).

John Goodman of the National Center for Policy Analysis and the Cato Institute quickly criticized the Heritage plan as statist and unconservative. Butler responded that his philosophy was that "if a proposal moves policy in a conservative direction, go for it." Regarding health care reform, he said that conservatives were steadily losing "a yard at a time. We could keep on losing ground or put forward a real alternative that contained real risk."[14] Heritage's senior management was in agreement.

Another Butler proposal—changing federal policy to allow tenants to own and manage public housing—became a reality for families for Washington, D.C., and St. Louis, Missouri. Butler had first suggested the idea in a 1984 Heritage *Backgrounder* and worked closely with the chief sponsor of the law allowing such conversions, Republican Representative Jack Kemp of New York.

Despite liberal predictions that it would fade from sight after Reagan, Heritage continued to influence Washington in ways large and small.

In its 1990 budget proposal, the Bush administration offered six of the ten budget reforms listed in *Mandate for Leadership III*. For the first time in decades, for example, the president submitted a federal budget without the "current services" baseline method of estimating spending. This was no mere matter of juggling figures. Under the old method, *projections* were used as the baseline for computing federal spending. Thus, if the administration in 1989 projected that the 1990 spending for a program would be at a certain level, the actual spending for that year would be called a "cut" unless it met or exceeded that amount—even

if the actual dollar amount exceeded the previous year's level. It was
through such Alice in Wonderland accounting devices, wherein an increase is called a decrease, that politicians and bureaucrats had been
able to keep raising government spending without admitting it or getting permission to do so.

In the area of child care, Heritage's Robert Rector continued to
have substantial impact on Capitol Hill and downtown. Four different
family tax-relief bills, based in large part on Rector's work, were introduced in the House of Representatives. A White House policy statement
on child care echoed the language of *Backgrounders* written by Rector.
A White House official told Rector at a White House meeting, "I've
read all your materials on families and child care. I can't tell you how
crucial your research has been on the issue, but then I guess everyone
tells you that."[15]

In the course of the child-care debate, Rector did things he had not
done before as a Heritage analyst so that Heritage could have a telling
legislative impact. He and other conservatives, not the liberals, framed
the debate. "Our theme was that the American family is over-taxed and
should be allowed to keep more of its income."

At the request of a member of Congress, he helped write legislation.
"After a while," says Rector, "I could rip out a draft amendment in a
couple of hours." In keeping with the Lehrfeld memorandum on lobbying, the congressman first asked for legislative help, and Rector then
responded.

He did a lot of original research, creating for example a database
about the American family. "It was the first time Heritage did that." A
decade later the foundation started the Center for Data Analysis (CDA),
which has created dozens of databases on a wide variety of issues.

Rector worked closely with conservative groups like the Family
Research Council, Eagle Forum, and Concerned Women of America.
"When Jim Dobson went on the air and talked about the child-care
bill," he recalls, "the congressional switchboards were frozen for days."
Talk radio has since become a critical part of the conservative network,
capable of spawning thousands and tens of thousands of telephone calls
and e-mails.

He constantly monitored the progress of the bill, watching for any
Republican defections. Since it was launched in early 2011, the foundation's 501(c)(4) companion organization, Heritage Action, has taken on
this responsibility. "The battle of public policy never stops," says Rector,
who is never happier than when he is fighting for the right legislation.

As a result of the child-care campaign, he says, conservatives were able to mainstream the voucher principle in public policy.[16]

When the Act for Better Childcare was introduced in 1987, recalled Kate O'Beirne, "it was a moving freight train." No one "dreamed that there wouldn't be a federal child-care scheme in place within a year." ABC was derailed, principally by Robert Rector, whose emphasis on original research and a close working relationship with congressional staffers became the model for a Heritage analyst.[17] However, as a result of the Honest Leadership and Open Government Act of 2007, which amended the Lobbying Disclosure Act of 1995, Heritage has instructed its analysts to be careful how directly they affect the course of legislation. The foundation now looks to its sister organization, Heritage Action for America, to carry the heavy load of monitoring and scoring congressional votes.

• • •

Committed to preserving the Reagan legacy, Heritage established in the spring of 1989 the Ronald Reagan Chair in Public Policy, the only Reagan chair formally approved by the former president. It was a fitting honor for the foundation so closely identified with the fortieth president. The chair was endowed with a $1 million grant from the Grover M. Hermann Foundation and $1.5 million raised by a committee chaired by Ambassador Holland H. (Holly) Coors.

The following year, former attorney general Edwin Meese III was named the Ronald Reagan Fellow in Public Policy, a position he holds to this day. President Reagan warmly endorsed the selection of his longtime friend and colleague and praised the foundation's many contributions to his administration. "You [were] an invaluable resource on key issues," Reagan said, "such as tax cuts, reducing government spending, SDI, supporting freedom in Grenada, Nicaragua, Eastern Europe—whenever I needed Heritage, you were there."

Conceding that he might sound "a little mystical," the seventy-nine-year-old statesman repeated one of his favorite themes: Americans "were pre-ordained to carry the torch of freedom for the whole world. One of the places that torch has burned most brightly has been at The Heritage Foundation, as it always will."[18]

Taking advantage of Meese's decades-long relationship with Reagan, his high standing in the conservative movement, and his proven analytical skills, Feulner immediately made the former attorney general a member of senior management and frequently calls on him for advice and counsel on questions far removed from the courtroom.

Phillip Truluck (left) and Ed Feulner with other senior managers in front of Heritage's town house office. Second row: Hugh Newton, Willa Johnson, Richard Holwill; third row: Herb Berkowitz, Burton Pines, John Von Kannon.

Founding fathers Paul Weyrich and Ed Feulner.

Joseph and Holly Coors welcome William F. Buckley, Jr.

Russell Kirk and Ed Feulner.

Senator Barry Goldwater and Clare Boothe Luce.

President Ronald Reagan briefs conservative leaders, including Ed Feulner, at the White House.

President Ronald Reagan with Ed and Linda Feulner at Heritage's tenth anniversary dinner.

Ed Feulner and President Reagan congratulate Milton and Rose Friedman on receiving the Clare Boothe Luce Award.

Ed Feulner helps tear down the Berlin Wall.

Midge Decter cuts the ribbon of Heritage's new headquarters (1983). Front row: Ed Feulner, Benjamin Blackburn, Robert Krieble, Senator John Warner, Frank Shakespeare; back row: Joseph Coors, Vice President George H. W. Bush, Lewis Lehrman, Jack Eckerd, Fritz Rench.

Ed Feulner with Jeane Kirkpatrick, former U.S. representative to the United Nations.

Heritage triumvirate Phil Truluck, John Von Kannon, and Ed Feulner.

Heritage's board of trustees in the 1990s. Front row: Frank Shakespeare, Richard M. Scaife, J. Frederic Rench, David R. Brown, Ed Feulner, Thomas (Dusty) Rhodes, Midge Decter; back row: Preston A. Wells, Jerry Hume, J. William Middendorf II, Grover Coors, Robert H. Krieble, and Thomas A. Roe.

Officers of the Mont Pelerin Society. Seated: Günter Schmölders, James Buchanan, George Stigler, Milton Friedman, Herbert Giersch; standing: C. J. Westholm, Max Thurn, Ralph Harris, Chiaki Nishiyama, Antonio Martino, Allen Wallis, and Ed Feulner.

Ed Feulner and Ann Brown along with Michael Cawley, David Brown, and Lloyd Noble burn the mortgage on the Heritage headquarters.

Ed Feulner applauds Shelby Cullom Davis and Kathryn Davis, winners of the Clare Boothe Luce Award.

House Speaker Newt Gingrich with Ed Feulner.

Ed Feulner with Senator
Mitch McConnell, Elaine
Chao, Kim Dae Jung, Jack
Kemp, Paul Wolfowitz, and
John Taylor.

Ed Feulner with Heritage
trustees Barb Van Andel-Gaby
and Jay Van Andel.

Heritage's senior management team in December 2012. First row: Mike Franc,
Genevieve Wood, David Addington, Ed Feulner, Jim DeMint, Phil Truluck, Becky
Norton Dunlop, Kim Holmes; second row: Stuart Butler, John Von Kannon,
Geoff Lysaught, Derrick Morgan, John Fogarty, Matthew Spalding, Michael
Spiller; third row: Mike Gonzalez, Edwin Meese III, James Carafano.

Left to right: 1) Talk-show host Sean Hannity; 2) President George W. Bush and Ed Feulner; 3) Representative Paul Ryan of Wisconsin, chairman of the House Budget Committee.

Ed Feulner releases the *2012 Index of Economic Freedom* along with Terry Miller, Heritage board of trustees chairman Thomas A. Saunders III, and Hugo Restall.

Ed Feulner welcomes a national television audience to the CNN Republican debate on foreign policy.

Heritage's eight-story headquarters on Capitol Hill.

Linda and Ed Feulner celebrate an anniversary.

The Feulner family in June 2012 on the evening Ed received the prestigious Bradley Prize. Back row: Wendy, E.J., Linda, Ed, Emily Lown, Christian Lown; front row: Sara Feulner, Betsy Feulner, William Lown.

In a formal 1990 address titled "The Reagan Legacy," Ed Meese said that "perhaps more than any other organization in Washington," The Heritage Foundation was instrumental in developing that legacy. Rather than talk about the Reagan administration's economic record or the "triumph of democracy" around the world, Meese stressed the former president's spiritual legacy, starting with how he "restored the confidence of a nation which had been badly shattered." Reagan restored Americans' faith "in the vital credos of personal, political, and economic liberty."

Meese defined the principles of the Reagan Revolution as "limited government, individual liberty, free enterprise, and peace through strength." It did not escape the audience that those same principles animated the mission of The Heritage Foundation.

Reagan provided a vision, said Meese, of "where America was going, where it should go, and how to get there." One part of that vision was a U.S. defense against intercontinental missiles—SDI. Another part was lower taxes so that "people could make more of their own choices about how to use their wealth." Still another part of the Reagan vision, offered in Westminster in 1982, was that "the march of freedom and democracy . . . will leave Marxism-Leninism on the ash heap of history."

Meese said that he understood the mounting concern about a possible recession and he heard the rising cry for a tax increase and more government spending. But he urged policy makers in Washington to abide by the tested Reagan principle that "tax cuts and decreased federal spending are the only way to cope with the problems of the budget." He concluded by assuring all those present that Heritage would lead the way in the effort "to preserve, protect, and perpetuate the Reagan Legacy."[19]

That meant that Heritage was prepared to challenge anyone who ignored or impaired the legacy, even a sitting president.

There was no denying the economy was sluggish, growing by barely 2 percent annually, and that the annual budget deficit was rising and estimated to hit $160 billion in 1990. For liberals, the solution was clear—raise taxes. Conservatives at first ignored the liberal chorus. A tax increase would be bad policy and worse politics, reversing Bush's famous campaign promise "Read my lips: No new taxes." The promise and his eight years as Reagan's loyal vice president had produced a solid 53–46 percent victory for him in 1988.

But progressives in and out of Congress persisted, and Heritage came to realize that President Bush was seriously considering a tax hike. The foundation quickly produced a number of studies showing that new taxes would slow economic growth and could lead to a recession. A Heritage panel of economists in May 1990 agreed that the budget deficit was being hyped to stampede voters into accepting an unnecessary tax increase. There was no *deficit* crisis, they asserted, only a *political* crisis for big spenders seeking more money for their programs.[20]

In a carefully reasoned letter devoid of rhetoric, Feulner urged President Bush to stand by his 1988 promise to reject any tax increase. "The case against higher taxes is stronger than it has ever been." Tax collections were at an all-time high. Taxes had climbed to 19.6 percent of GNP, the fourth-highest level in peacetime history. The only two times that taxes had exceeded 20 percent were in 1969 and 1981 and each time there was a recession the following year.

"We reject deficit-phobia," Feulner said. "The deficit as a percent of GNP is less than half the size it was five years ago." What was needed was a pro-growth deficit reduction package as proposed by Senators Phil Gramm (R-TX) and Warren Rudman (R-NH). "We at The Heritage Foundation," Feulner told the president, "will support a decision to choose a sequester [of spending] over higher taxes."[21]

Between late July, when policy makers began serious negotiations on the federal budget, and October, when the so-called "deficit-reduction" package was finalized, Heritage published fifteen *Backgrounders* and other studies on the budget. A Heritage paper, written by analyst Scott Hodge, proposed a "Four Percent Solution," showing that the federal budget could be balanced and a budget *surplus* produced by 1995 by limiting spending increases to 4 percent a year. (There were two balanced budgets in 1999 and 2000 because, basically, a Republican congress forced a Democratic president to limit federal spending to federal income.)

However, President Bush gave in to the pressure and agreed to a deal with the Democratic Congress that included "tax-revenue increases." A deeply disappointed Feulner said that Bush had "retreated" on one of conservatism's first principles—low taxes. A year later, as Bush began his reelection campaign, the Heritage president was still unhappy, stating that the United States was a "Ship of State without a helmsman" and Bush a "president without purpose."[22]

Two decades later, Ed Feulner was more generous in his assessment of the forty-first president, who he said always wanted to receive information from different people—"he was a good listener." He recalled his private White House dinner with the president and the first lady, and his Camp David visit when a young National Security Council staffer named Condoleezza Rice encouraged him to be candid in his advice to the president prior to his first summit meeting with Gorbachev in Malta.

"George H. W. Bush's record," says Feulner, "is mixed, but I think on balance probably the good outweighs the bad. After all it was on his watch that the Berlin Wall fell, although Ronald Reagan put all the building blocks in place. He saw the threat to the United States in the Middle East and was willing to make commitments in terms of Operation Desert Storm and in countering Iraq's invasion of Kuwait."

And the Supreme Court nomination of Clarence Thomas was "one of those decisions that has changed the course, really, of modern history . . . like George W. Bush with John Roberts and Sam Alito." But then there was his reversal of his speech at the Republican National Convention when he said, "They will come at me and say, 'Raise taxes,' and I will say, 'Read my lips: no new taxes.' "[23]

Heritage has always been outspoken, says Feulner, committed to the conservative principle that new taxes are not the way to solve a financial crisis. "It was very clear to us then and now that the problem is not that there's not enough income coming from the people to the federal government [but] that the federal government is spending too much.

"We were very very disappointed [in the president]. We made that disappointment well known. That did not make us great friends in the White House. In fact we were shunned for some months thereafter. But it showed, I think, that Heritage had matured in our ability to work with administrations that we could be sympathetic and supportive of, but at the same time we could take a principled stand that no, this is not the way we as conservatives should be going."[24]

In its dealings with the Bush 41 administration, The Heritage Foundation demonstrated yet again that it was not a Republican think tank fueled by partisan politics but a conservative think tank grounded in First Principles.

Even when things got hot and tempers flared, says Feulner, "we managed to act with a certain civility. We didn't do it by knocking people over the head. We said, 'This is our perspective, this is the way we think you should be going, let's have a reasonable discussion.' This is something I'm very proud of over the years at Heritage."[25]

• • •

In his look at the state of conservatism in 1992, Feulner conceded that the Washington power elite were still dictating much of the public policy agenda. But he insisted that liberalism was "a dying creed with little popular support." The problem was that conservatism lacked a national leader because of President Bush's unwillingness or inability to articulate a conservative vision. The answer was to renew and redouble efforts to build "an effective counter-establishment to replace the existing order," one grounded in "solid, traditional American principles."[26] Here was an early expression of an idea—First Principles—that would animate the foundation and its Leadership for America initiative in the 2000s and beyond.

Due in large measure to Heritage, the conservative counterestablishment was becoming more and more visible in Washington and in the states where think tanks offered conservative alternatives to the tax-spend-regulate policies that had produced a recession. These organizations strengthened the federalism that Alexis de Tocqueville praised in *Democracy in America* and that Russell Kirk saw as the most effective counterweight to what he called "the behemoth state."[27]

Conservative voices were increasingly heard in the mass media. Columnists like Cal Thomas, William F. Buckley, Patrick J. Buchanan, George Will, and Thomas Sowell dominated much of the newspaper commentary. Talk radio was nearly the exclusive domain of voluble conservatives such as Rush Limbaugh and Sean Hannity.

There were more than a dozen conservative policy journals, including *National Review, Policy Review, The American Spectator, Chronicles, Commentary, The American Enterprise,* and *The National Interest.* The most important journal of all, according to Feulner, was the magazine that "the intellectual establishment most loves to hate: *Reader's Digest,* which has done more to popularize conservative ideas than any other publication in the world."[28] It was the *Digest,* for example, that in April 1945 had published a condensation of *The Road to Serfdom* that had sparked one million reprints.

The family values coalition, led by Focus on the Family and the Family Research Council, was displaying muscle power in Washington and at the grass roots. There were signs that conservatives were loosening the grip of the Left on minority communities with the emergence of J. A. Parker's Lincoln Institute and Robert Woodson's National Center for Neighborhood Enterprise. A hopeful Feulner noted the growth of "a centrist faction within the Democratic Party, which for three decades has been hostile to conservative ideas."[29]

However, components of a true counterestablishment were missing, chief among them a conservative Congress. There were many conservatives but "too little conservative leadership." The task of conservatives was to work even harder to build the institutional base "with or without the president and the Republican Party."[30]

Feulner was stating a simple truth: individuals like himself and institutions like Heritage were committed to ideas rather than to any political party. They were conservative first and Republican or Democratic second, depending upon the issue and the policy. Heritage fellow Scott Hodge believes that with Bush's budget "deal," The Heritage Foundation truly "matured as a leader in the conservative movement. We became the loyal opposition, looking for ways to redefine the conservative agenda."[31]

But Heritage did not have to define conservative principles that rested securely on the Declaration of Independence and the Constitution and on the classic works of Western civilization. In a talk at the 1990 Conservative Political Action Conference (CPAC), Ed Feulner listed seven basic ideas. The philosophical tone of his remarks probably surprised some in the audience, who thought of the Heritage president as an eminently successful manager and fund-raiser, not an intellectual familiar with the works of Hayek, Kirk, Friedman, Minogue, Roepke, and Von Mises, to name a few. Feulner said that conservatives believe in:

- The integrity of man as God's creation.

- The fallibility of man, tainted by original sin and limited by imperfect judgment.

- The inequality of man, meaning that "those who are more fortunate have a responsibility for those who are less fortunate."

- The stewardship of leadership, requiring us to preserve what is valuable for future generations.

- The creation of wealth only by human beings, meaning "we need an economic system that unleashes the creativity and mobilizes the efforts of individuals."

- The specialness of America—a Shining City on the Hill, a Zion in the wilderness.

- The hostility of the world, meaning we must take the necessary measures to arm and defend ourselves against our enemies.

The challenges that conservatives and Americans faced in the 1990s, Feulner said, demanded a "continued commitment to these basic principles." That meant ensuring that any "peace dividend" that resulted from winning the Cold War was used to make the nation "economically stronger, *not* to increase the size of the federal government."[32]

The foundation readied itself for the challenges with two significant organizational changes. Shelby Cullom Davis, who had served as a trustee since 1979 and as chairman since 1985, stepped down and was succeeded by David R. Brown, M.D., a well-known orthopedic surgeon and Noble Foundation trustee. Robert H. Krieble, who had been vice chairman since 1985, was succeeded by one of Heritage's earliest and most generous supporters—Richard M. Scaife, philanthropist and publisher of the Greensburg, Pennsylvania, *Tribune-Review.*

After a decade of brilliant but often tempestuous service, senior vice president Burton Yale Pines resigned, and the board of trustees rewarded two senior managers, electing Stuart Butler as vice president and director of domestic and economic studies and Kim Holmes vice president and director of foreign and defense policy studies.

• • •

At a private twentieth-anniversary party at the Metropolitan Club in downtown Washington, Ed Feulner, Phil Truluck, Hugh Newton, Herb Berkowitz, and other old-timers toasted Heritage and razzed each other and themselves.

Truluck recalled that his wife Ann had asked him in 1977 why he wanted to leave a high-prestige job on Capitol Hill for "a so-called think tank that no one had ever heard of." Among other things, he thought the foundation's red, white, and blue letterhead "slightly tacky" and that keeping the front door locked during office hours "didn't quite set the proper tone for a research institution." And then there was the morning prayer service. But "Ed assured me there would be a new day at Heritage and I took the plunge and in all seriousness it was the best decision I have made in my life—in my professional life, that is."

Newton offered a brief history of the early headquarters on Stanton Park and its interesting roots: the first building had been "a porno theater that showed X-rated movies," the second building a Korean deli, and the third building a halfway house for recovering addicts. In a city where many forget where they came from, he recalled a February conference in the early 1980s when it was snowing so badly that Irving Kristol, the featured speaker, called from New York to say he could not make it. "Ed called Jack Kemp who was at home in his pajamas, and an hour later he was at the hotel and gave the featured speech. Some people don't forget their roots."

In response, Kemp held up a copy of the 1977 Heritage *Annual Report* and read the headlines. " 'Model Cities Program Test Case Fails,' and they were right. 'Reforms Will Add to Welfare Rolls.' They were right. 'Energy Plan Is a Big Tax Hike.' You were right about that. 'Human Rights Definition: A Key to Foreign Policy.' You were right about the Carter Administration's so-called human rights programs. 'Spendthrift Congress.' And listen to this 1977 Heritage Foundation article: 'SALT Withdrawal would be good for the United States of America.'

"When the history of the twentieth century is written," Kemp said, "they will in my view say that there were four major elements in the defeat of Communism and socialism in our lifetime. Ronald Reagan, to be sure. The Pope, and I say that as a good practicing Presbyterian. Margaret Thatcher. And the Heritage Foundation, whose brand of optimistic, enthusiastic, positive, constructive alternatives to liberal spending and redistribute-the-wealth programs has been a source of strength to conservatives in the Congress, to conservatives in the administration, to conservatives everywhere."

Don Lipsett, who had known Ed Feulner longer than anyone else present, including his wife Linda, quoted several of Feulner's Laws: "Number 1: Don't bring me your problems unless they are unsolvable at a lower level." Number 2: "People are policy." Number 52: "I don't like surprises." Number 60 (borrowed from Margaret Thatcher): "I don't mind how much my ministers talk as long as they do what I say."

Stuart Butler, whose first Heritage study—on health care—was published in June 1976 and for which he was paid five hundred dollars, remembered his first visit to Heritage when it was located on Stanton Park. Escorted by Barbara Smith, he had turned the corner to enter the building when "there was someone with his hands against the wall with one policeman frisking him and another with a shotgun. Barbara said: 'Welcome to the Unites States of America.' " There were better days to come, but there must have been something about the British-born Butler that attracted lawbreakers. Several years later, when writing his book on free-enterprise zones, he had just finished the chapter on crime in the inner cities and was walking to his car when he was mugged on the way.

Chuck Heatherly reminisced about the first *Mandate for Leadership* and how it grew and grew like a tropical forest in the rainy season.

By the late summer of 1980, all twenty of the chairmen had handed in their chapters, and "I started to get an idea of how it was going to shape up." Heatherly set about delivering *Mandate* on schedule and "dumped the 20 manuscript volumes on the top Reagan advisers a week after the election." He added: "I still claim to this day that no one in Washington other than me has ever read all 1,100 pages of *Mandate*."

John Von Kannon told stories about the steadfastness of Heritage donors, such as Wayne Holman, a wealthy physicist who once met Andrei Sakharov at a physics conference. They didn't talk much, Holman admitted, because "I didn't know much Russian, but I saw him three months later and by then I had learned Russian so we could talk about physics and politics." "He's a very bright man," explained Von Kannon. At a dinner in Chicago, Von Kannon asked Holman for his continued support, and he replied, "I will stop eating before I stop supporting The Heritage Foundation."

Kim Holmes recalled, with barely concealed emotion, a Heritage banquet for a visiting Russian delegation. A Russian parliamentary deputy who had been silent throughout the conference stood to make a toast. He explained that he had been a prisoner of conscience who had spent nearly a decade in the Gulag in Siberia. While in prison, he had looked to one person and one American institution to give him hope that someday his country would be free.

He said how important it was to him and other prisoners to know they were not forgotten, that there was someone outside the Soviet Union who believed that this vast Soviet Empire could come to an end. "As he ended his toast," said Holmes, "he said that the person who gave him hope was Ronald Reagan and the institution which gave him hope was The Heritage Foundation. That was probably the proudest moment I have ever had as an employee of The Heritage Foundation."[33]

CHAPTER 16

A PERMANENT PLACE

In its twentieth year, Heritage was pushing the speed limit, popularizing conservative ideas that helped change the way many Washington policy makers looked at government. Here was a typical Monday of its CEO in 1993:

At 7:45 a.m., Ed Feulner is in his eighth-floor office overlooking the U.S. Capitol, having a cup of coffee. He goes over the day's schedule with his chief of staff—he has a meeting scheduled every fifteen or thirty minutes, usually with Heritage people. He gives one and a half tapes of notes and letters that he dictated the previous evening to Missy Stephens. Since it is Monday, there is a management meeting in the Van Andel Room on the first floor. In white shirtsleeves and wearing a muted Heritage tie, he begins the meeting promptly at eight-thirty. Some thirty people outline the coming week's activities in the House, in the Senate, and in the White House, upcoming publications in domestic, foreign, and national security policy, lectures and talks by visiting members of Congress, and seminars and conferences at the foundation and outside Washington. At the end of the meeting, which never runs longer than one hour, he goes around the table calling each person by first name and inviting him or her to comment "for the good of the order." He never misses a name.

"There's no doubt who's in charge," says Michael Needham, who heads Heritage Action after serving as research assistant and chief of staff for Feulner and then head of the Asian Studies Center. "At our monthly senior management meetings, he lays the groundwork for the meeting, talks through issues he's grappling with. It's important for everyone to know what he's hearing, what he's thinking about, even if it's not on the agenda. As we go through the meeting, he'll ask penetrating questions. And there's no detail that's too small for Ed Feulner to deal with—which is both a benefit and a form of micromanagement."[1]

Feulner spends the rest of Monday morning meeting with Heritage people and taking calls from a senator or congressman who feels that Heritage should be more (or less) outspoken about a particular bill, usually *his* bill. He confers with Phil Truluck about a new hire, a sudden dip or rise in revenues, or perhaps a building they are thinking about buying. He goes over an upcoming visit with a major donor with John Von Kannon. He talks to Linda about E.J.'s or Emily's latest accomplishment or that of their grandchildren or about the beach house they are building at Bethany Beach in Delaware. Often he will bring up a Heritage initiative seeking her reaction. "She's built the institution as well," comments former chief of staff Tim Chapman. "They are a team."[2] He lunches with a prominent visitor from South Korea or Britain or another friendly country in the Krieble Board Room, a handsome wood-paneled room dominated by an enormous cherrywood conference table that would impress any Fortune 500 CEO.

After lunch there are more meetings with Heritage staffers and perhaps a conservative movement leader seeking advice and often something more substantial. "People think he's tough," reveals Chapman. "He's really soft. He will always help those who come to him, always."[3] There are more telephone calls and e-mails as he keeps abreast of issues, friends, and colleagues inside and outside the building, all the while swigging Frescas.

He keeps the door open if he has no visitors and in a booming baritone directs Kathy or Missy to get this memo or that letter. He sifts through the stacks of paper on his desk for something, quickly making decisions if it is a minor matter and collaborating with Truluck on the major ones. It's a roller-coaster life on which he thrives, but if he didn't have Linda—and his faith—he could not survive.

The walls of his oriental-carpeted office are crowded with photos of him with the men and women with whom he has worked—Phil Crane, Mel Laird, Ronald Reagan, George and Barbara Bush, Margaret Thatcher, Bill Buckley, Rush Limbaugh, Bill Bennett, Irving Kristol,

Dan Quayle, Jack Kemp, Jeane Kirkpatrick, and F. A. Hayek with Reagan and Feulner. In the early 1990s—when he is not yet weaned from tobacco—there are sixty-three pipes on various mantels, tables, and other surfaces nestling among citations, proclamations, awards, and honorary degrees from the United States of America, the Republic of China on Taiwan, the Republic of Korea, Grove City College, Regis University, Francisco Marroquín University in Guatemala, Pepperdine University, Hillsdale College, Gonzaga University, Thomas More College, George Mason University, and other institutions. In a special place of honor is the PhD in political science from the University of Edinburgh, in Latin, and the honorary degree it conferred on him.

And there are books, dozens of books, hundreds of books, filling shelves from the ceiling to the floor, books of economics and politics and history, bestselling books, obscure books, books by friends and colleagues and even enemies, books with titles like *The Quest for Community* by Robert Nisbet, *The Solzhenitsyn Reader, Statecraft* by Margaret Thatcher, *The Essential Russell Kirk, My Grandfather's Son* by Clarence Thomas, *The Churchill War Papers, A Nation Like No Other* by Newt Gingrich, *Studies in Philosophy, Politics and Economics* by F. A. Hayek, *Surrender in Panama* by Philip Crane, and *Catholic Intellectuals and Conservative Politics in America 1950–1985.*

At day's end, around six-thirty p.m., if there is no reception or dinner to attend, he packs all he can into one and sometimes two bulging legal briefcases and walks out the back door into the waiting car, greets Kevin Germany, his driver for over twenty years, settles into the backseat, and takes out his cell phone to tell Linda he is on the way home while scanning a draft letter to the Speaker of the House.

He has dinner and a glass of wine with Linda. In their first year of marriage, Ed often cooked but found it more and more difficult to find the time. No follower of Julia Child, Linda limits herself to baking Ed's birthday banana cake. After dinner he retires, not to bed but to his study to go over papers and dictate memos. "He's a doer every minute," explains Linda.[4] He gets into bed around midnight, satisfied that he has put in a good day and looking forward to the morrow as the CEO of the most important think tank in the most important city in the most powerful country in the world.

"He is the true definition of a leader," says Phil Truluck, who has worked with Ed Feulner for some forty years. "You walk into the room, it doesn't matter if he's sitting at the head of the table or the middle of the table, you know who's in charge.

"He's an incredible optimist. Sometimes he can be gruff and tough, but underneath all that he is optimistic, and that comes through very clear to everyone here.

"He's been a great salesman for Heritage all over the world. Ed is so respected in Asia, he has a greater status than most senators and cabinet officers. Early in the eighties he was at the forefront of seeing the emerging relationship between Asia and the United States. If you travel with him overseas, you can see in an instant the respect that he's held in in all the capitals of Asia. The importance of Asia was a truly absolute Ed Feulner idea from start to finish."[5]

Feulner is never too busy to pay his respects when a well-known—and often an unknown—conservative dies. When Bill Buckley's sister Priscilla passed away in the spring of 2012, Ed Feulner and Linda Bridges of *National Review* exchanged a number of e-mails about the circumstances of her death and the burial arrangements, capped by his very Catholic comment to Linda, who had worked with Priscilla for years, "The Feulner family spent our weekend not praying *for* her but praying *to* her"—an acknowledgment that she was already in Heaven and among the saints.[6]

He is renowned for his loyalty to friends and fellow true believers. He provided a Heritage platform for Russell Kirk when that eminent author was ignored by liberals and neglected by conservatives. From 1978 until his death in 1994, Kirk delivered more than forty lectures before foundation audiences. Remembering the impact of *The Conservative Mind* on him as an undergraduate, Feulner found it easy to refer to Kirk as the "paterfamilias" of the conservative movement.

In 1981 when Dick Allen was railroaded out of his position as national security adviser to President Reagan and the media sharks were circling him, Feulner organized a standing-room-only luncheon at the Mayflower Hotel under "Friends of Dick Allen." Shortly thereafter he and Allen started the Asian Studies Center at Heritage.

Belden Bell and Feulner first met on Capitol Hill in the late 1960s, when Bell was administrative assistant to Representative Roger Zion (R-IN). When Zion retired in 1976, Bell ran to succeed him but lost by just 0.04 percent. The next morning, while going over what he could or should have done to win, he got a telephone call from Feulner, inviting him to come to work for the Republican Study Committee as deputy director. Bell accepted and went on to serve in the Reagan administration in a number of pivotal positions, including U.S. ambassador to the Federation of St. Kitts and Nevis. He is today a member of Heritage's board of trustees—all because of a telephone call that brought him back to Washington.

Feulner's oldest friend in the conservative movement, going back to the early 1960s, was Don Lipsett, who found himself in his early fifties without a job. Knowing that Lipsett had been an investment counselor before "enlisting" in the movement, Feulner arranged for him to advise Heritage on its investments, a relationship that continued until Lipsett's death. The small meeting room next to his office is the Lipsett Room.

The Intercollegiate Studies Institute (ISI) faced a testing time in the late 1980s, when its longtime president E. Victor Milione announced that after a quarter-century of service he would be stepping down. After a brief experiment with the multitalented Robert Reilly (an ISI alumnus and former national director), the board of trustees turned in 1989 to T. Kenneth Cribb, Jr., who had been the first choice of several trustees but had declined because of his promise to remain in the Reagan administration. (Cribb was head of domestic policy during Reagan's last two years.)

Cribb said he would accept the ISI presidency "if Ed Feulner agreed to be chairman at the same time." Despite the fact that Heritage was also being tested, politically and financially, in the post-Reagan era, Feulner did not hesitate but stipulated he would serve as chair for only three years. It was long enough: under his chairmanship, the ISI raised over $1 million annually for the first time in its history. "He was invaluable," says Cribb, "pointing me in the right direction for possible donors."[7] When ISI chairman Richard Wells resigned for health reasons in 2003, on the occasion of the ISI's fiftieth anniversary, an ever-obliging Feulner stepped in once again as chairman of what he called "an extraordinary organization whose salutary influence on young minds is crucial to the future of the conservative movement and America."[8]

To help both the National Center for Neighborhood Enterprise, headed by Robert Woodson, and Daniel Graham's High Frontier get started, and with legal approval, he permitted donors to contribute to Heritage while they were waiting for formal tax-exempt status for the two groups.

One of the many young conservatives whom Ed Feulner found room for at Heritage was Steve Moore, today an editorial board member and senior economics writer of *The Wall Street Journal*. "He launched my career [at twenty-three] and literally hundreds like me who have infiltrated every nook and cranny of the conservative movement." Moore has kidded Feulner that the foundation should be called "Heritage

University because it has helped train so many influential scholars and policy leaders."[9]

Another conservative leader who got his start at Heritage is the ISI's new president Christopher Long. After graduating from George Mason University in Virginia in 1989, Long was seeking his first full-time job and went calling on Heritage. They were looking for a young conservative to fill a paid internship at the Bush White House, "and I was thrilled when they offered me the position." And he was dejected when he was told the White House counsel had "nixed" the internship. "While he had no obligation to do so," Long recalls, "Ed created a place for me as deputy director of special projects and put me in charge of the recently launched New Majority Project, Heritage's outreach to blacks, Hispanics, and Asian Americans." No matter how large it has grown, says Long, "Heritage has never forgotten that it is of the movement" and is always helping "smaller sister organizations within the broad American conservative movement."[10]

That Feulner never seems to stop working has been attested by many, including Brent Bozell, the head of the Media Research Council, scourge of the mainstream media. "Several years ago," recalls Bozell, "I ran into Ed at some conference in New York City. It was a very long, very tiring day-long event." That evening Bozell and Feulner took the same air shuttle from LaGuardia Airport to Reagan National Airport and sat across the aisle from each other. Before the plane had left the ground, Bozell had dozed off.

"I awoke halfway through the trip," says Bozell, "and looked over at Ed. He had his tray down and was furiously going through a stack of cards, handwriting messages to people he had met at the conference. Only when that was done with a few minutes left in the flight did he allow himself to close his eyes. 'That,' I thought to myself, 'is why he's where he's at.' "[11]

• • •

In late 1990, before Bush 41 went south on no new taxes, Heritage was concerned with cutting taxes to stimulate economic growth, controlling federal spending, building a strategic missile defense shield, pushing parental choice in education, privatizing government programs, and urging an antipoverty program based on less government intervention and more individual empowerment.

Heritage believed—and still does—that the great majority of Americans want a destiny based on the "ideals of freedom and democracy and a belief in the remarkable potential of the individual"—words uttered by Ronald Reagan at the foundation's annual board meeting in 1990.[12]

When Iraq invaded Kuwait in January 1991, Heritage's government relations staff, headed by Kate O'Beirne, provided Congress with policy guidance written by Jim Phillips and other analysts. On the House floor, Representatives Duncan Hunter and Wally Herger of California distributed copies of the foundation's initial paper dealing with the invasion, "How to Stop Iraq's Saddam Hussein." Such studies, according to the head of *The Baltimore Sun*'s Washington bureau, "laid much of the groundwork for Bush administration thinking" about what constituted American interests in a world where the Soviet Union was no longer able to project its military strength in conflicts around the world.[13] In a *New York Times* essay, Christopher Gacek, Heritage's Jay Kingham Fellow, warned that the United States and its allies should not stop short of removing Saddam from power, a recommendation that would haunt America in the years to come.

At home the foundation's health care reform plan became one of the three options seriously considered by Washington. Under the Heritage plan, consumers would shop for health coverage as they do for other goods and services, making providers like hospitals and physicians compete for business. The foundation proposal would have had limited impact without Heritage-style marketing. "Heritage is unique among think tanks," wrote Hoover fellow Thomas Sowell. "As fast as various organizations and movements on the Left can create hysteria over some issue, Heritage can shoot it down in flames with facts and figures. They must work through the night."[14]

"By getting individuals to pay medical bills themselves," *National Review* wrote of Heritage's health care plan, "we might just end the insane overuse that has brought the system to its knees." Critics pointed to what they called significant flaws, beginning with the assumption that Americans were sophisticated enough to compete in the marketplace for the best insurance. Millions of Americans have been the victims of scams and swindles in the life insurance business, *The Los Angeles Times* pointed out, and a free market might not lead to major savings. As long as insurance covered the cost of serious illness, patients and physicians would have an incentive "to use the newest—and most expensive—medical technology." Only government regulations, argued the critics of the Heritage plan, could restrain the growth of such high-priced technology.[15] Led by Stuart Butler and senior policy analyst Robert Moffit, Heritage would rebut such criticism, particularly when the new Clinton administration proposed its radical health care plan.

• • •

In the fall of 1991, at the urging of Richard Larry of the Sarah Scaife Foundation and Michael Joyce of the Lynde and Harry Bradley Foundation, Heritage formally entered America's culture wars and named former Secretary of Education William J. Bennett as its distinguished fellow in cultural policy studies.

At a private New York City meeting, Larry had sharply questioned the foundation's downplaying of cultural issues. "Don't you understand everything is deteriorating," he asked Heritage senior management, "and the rest of your stuff doesn't mean anything if the culture deteriorates?" Larry was especially worried about the disintegration of the family. Feulner and his colleagues responded not simply because Dick Larry was the head of a major foundation but because upon examination, they concluded he was right—Heritage should examine governmental policy for its impact on the culture and not leave that examination to other groups as it previously had.

In his first Heritage lecture, Bennett quoted commentator (and Heritage trustee) Midge Decter that "a culture war is a war to the death . . . [because] it is a battle about matters of the spirit."[16] The next year Heritage published eight major cultural studies on topics ranging from the fraud of multiculturalism to America's ailing families.

The foundation hit the cultural jackpot in March 1993 with the release, along with Empower America and the Free Congress Foundation, of one of the most popular studies in its history—*The Index of Leading Cultural Indicators,* edited by William Bennett. In just twenty-two graph-filled pages, the index documented how crime, illegitimacy, divorce, teenage suicide, drug use, and fourteen other social indicators had become measurably worse over the last thirty years. Bennett argued that many things could be done to "encourage cultural renewal," starting with a government that heeded the old injunction "Do no harm."

He urged lawmakers to ask themselves such questions as "Will this legislation support or undermine families?" and "Will it encourage individual responsibility or dependency?" He proposed a legislative social agenda that included "a reversal of the destructive incentives of the welfare system, a substantial increase in the personal dependent exemption from $2,300 to $7,000, removal of major obstacles to adoption, and enforcement of laws requiring fathers to take responsibility for their children."[17]

So hungry were Americans for explanations about what was happening to their families that forty-eight hours after Bill Bennett aired his findings on Rush Limbaugh's radio talk program, 73,000 people contacted Heritage to request copies of the Bennett study. The following year, the index was published as a book by Simon & Schuster and wound up a bestseller. In the acknowledgments, Bennett thanked Heritage and "especially its president, Edwin J. Feulner, Jr., for their encouragement, assistance, and cooperation." The extraordinary impact of the study led to Bill Bennett's bestselling *The Book of Virtues* and its offspring, including the PBS animated series *Adventures in the Book of Virtues*.

Heritage's societal efforts did not end there. Presidential candidate Bill Clinton campaigned on a pledge to "end welfare as we know it" and promised to make welfare reform a top priority. Heritage analyst Robert Rector was ready and waiting.

Throughout 1993 Rector made clear in *Backgrounders* and other studies that many of the social pathologies laying waste to America's cities—as set forth in *The Index of Leading Cultural Indicators*—could be traced to the flight from personal responsibility and the destruction of families brought about by the welfare state. Called on to testify before Congress on subjects ranging from the Census Bureau to poverty statistics to child nutrition, Rector offered specific welfare reform ideas, such as requiring welfare recipients to work for their benefits and placing a cap on the annual growth of welfare spending.

To help bypass the welfare bureaucracy and help inner-city residents build stable families and create safer neighborhoods, Stuart Butler spoke at neighborhood meetings in Washington, D.C., and other cities. In a reversal of the usual policy conference, the meetings featured successful community activists with the researchers and politicians placed in the audience.

Besides their practical purpose, such meetings were intended to show that conservatives had a heart as well as a head. Conservatives must demonstrate, Feulner says, "that there are more compassionate ways of helping the poor, more enlightened ways of protecting the environment, more effective ways of educating our children, healing our sick, and tending our elderly than the cut-and-paste solutions offered by a distant governmental bureaucracy."[18]

• • •

In the wake of the dissolution of the Soviet Union and Saddam Hussein's failed attempt to seize Kuwait (successfully thwarted by a U.S.-led coalition), Heritage determined to draw up a blueprint for a new U.S. foreign policy, described by one national columnist as "a strategy to guide America safely into the twenty-first century." While other think tanks reduced their international studies in the wake of the end of the Cold War, Heritage—at the insistence of its chief executive Ed Feulner—rejected any trace of neoisolationism and maintained its commitment to in-depth foreign policy and national security analysis.

In a major study, vice president Kim Holmes and Thomas G. Moore, deputy director of foreign policy and defense studies, wrote that the only prudent course for America was to use all possible components of national power and influence "to shape a world friendly to America's interests and values." The central thesis of *Making the World Safe for America* and its successor study *A Safe and Prosperous America* was that the United States should intervene abroad but only when its vital interests were at stake. They were defined as:

Protecting American territory, sea lanes, and airspace.

Preventing a major power from controlling Europe, East Asia, or the Persian Gulf.

Ensuring U.S. access to world resources.

Expanding free trade throughout the world.

Protecting Americans against threats to their lives and well-being.[19]

As Russell Kirk put it in a Heritage lecture, a conservative foreign policy should be neither interventionist nor isolationist but prudent. Its objective should be not the triumph everywhere of "America's name and manners" but the preservation of "the true national interest and acceptance of the diversity of economic and political institutions throughout the world."[20]

Heritage identified several leading threats to U.S. interests, including nuclear weapons development in North Korea and a breakdown of democracy in post-Communist Russia, both of which have come to pass.

The study emphasized that the United States should not allow its armed forces to be used as proxies for every conflict the United Nations favored, should not condition its decision to take military action on UN approval, and should not, under any circumstances, place U.S. forces under UN command. In its first year the Clinton administration violated all three prohibitions.

In the foreword, Ed Feulner stated that promoting American national interests was not amoral or selfish but rather "a moral act required by the Constitution" (a copy of which Feulner always carries in his inside coat pocket). American freedom and democracy "are beacons to the rest of the world," he wrote, serving as models for other countries. America's survival depends upon the advancement of "the cause of freedom and democracy around the world" but not by the force of arms.

America can and should take "moral stands" on foreign policy issues, Feulner said, but without becoming "the world's policeman." Supporting humanitarian causes should be an "act of charity," not the fulfillment of a fundamental goal of U.S. strategy or purpose. A humanitarian act "is something Americans may choose to do, not something they must do."[21]

Ed Feulner's commonsense approach made all the more sense after the debacle in Somalia, where an ill-defined mission turned a once-thankful populace against the United States and resulted in the unnecessary deaths of eighteen American servicemen and the ugly spectacle of a dead American soldier being dragged through the dusty streets of Mogadishu.

Several years later, speaking overseas to prodemocracy activists and policy makers in Poland, Feulner congratulated them for carrying on "the glorious, disheartening, frustrating, God-inspired battle for human freedom." Some of their hopes, after the collapse of Communism in 1989, had been fulfilled; others had brought heartache. But he urged them to remember that "the practice of democracy is an *imperfect* art . . . democracy is like a raft—it doesn't sink, but your feet are always in the water."[22]

He shared his frustrations about the direction of U.S. foreign policy with his audience. There are, he said, "a scraggly band of conservative isolationists on the fringe" who want America to withdraw from the world while "a suddenly-macho band of liberal interventionists" seeks to remake Haiti, Rwanda, Somalia, and the rest of the world "in its own preening self-image."

The isolationist Right hides behind protectionism, "having no confidence that the U.S. can compete in the international trade arena," while the interventionist Left hides behind multilateralism, "having no confidence that the U.S. can compete in values and in the integrity of its interests." Neither group, said Feulner, has any conception of America's *true* national interests.

The biggest threat to the United States, he said, remains long-range missiles armed with nuclear weapons. Our response should include an antimissile defense and a broad nonproliferation policy.

The greatest danger to U.S. trade comes not from outside U.S. borders but from inside "by those who fear America can't compete." That is why Heritage supported the Clinton administration on the North American Free Trade Agreement (NAFTA) and on GATT (the General Agreement on Tariffs and Trade).

Anticipating a danger that would profoundly affect the nation, after September 11, 2001, Feulner said that the United States "has an obligation whenever possible to protect American citizens from terrorist activity." Such forward thinking enabled Heritage analysts to provide answers about the why and the who of the 9/11 terrorist attacks.

A threat to our oil supply is a threat to our national interest, Feulner said bluntly, and we cannot depend on "assertive multilateralism" to protect that interest. "I believe," he said, that "multilateralism is the abandonment of America's leadership in the world"—a "leadership which the world need not fear."[23]

• • •

"The Clinton administration does take national interests into account when formulating foreign policy," remarked Heritage defense analyst Lawrence Di Rita. "The trouble is they are frequently the interests of other nations."[24] Another problem with the administration was its propensity to underfund the nation's defense needs.

Heritage found the Clinton administration's "Bottom-Up Review" of military requirements in the 1990s haphazard, its downsizing plans damaging to America's defense industrial base, and its frequent use of U.S. forces for noncombat missions ill-considered. In March 1994 senior defense analyst Baker Spring revealed that the administration had underfunded its own defense plan by a five-year total of $100 billion. Spring quoted the army chief of staff as saying, "Smaller is not better. Better is better."[25]

Both the White House and the Pentagon dismissed the foundation's findings (just as the Carter administration had dismissed Heritage's charge that the administration had badly underestimated the cost of its welfare reform). But to the embarrassment of President Clinton—just as President Carter had been embarrassed— an examination by the General Accounting Office (GAO), Congress's auditing arm, found that Heritage had been too conservative in its estimate: the shortfall of Clinton's welfare reform was closer to $150 billion.

To help the president find the money to close the gap, Heritage identified billions of dollars in "nondefense pork" that had been buried in the defense budget, such as $161 million for small business "innovative research," $40 million for the Civilian Community Corps, and $9 million for World Cup USA. Analyst John Luddy pointed out that one disturbing result of the misguided spending was that the first army brigade sent to Kuwait in October 1993 had platoon leaders who had never trained with their troops in the field, and tank crews that had not completed vital crew drills.[26]

Close to home, Heritage played a crucial role in the debate on the North American Free Trade Agreement (NAFTA), signed by President George H. W. Bush, Mexican president Carlos Salinas de Gortari, and Canadian prime minister Brian Mulroney on December 17, 1992. Consistent with its belief in free trade and with Ed Feulner personally involved, the foundation supported NAFTA from beginning to end; Heritage's support came naturally inasmuch as the idea of such an agreement had first been broached by Richard Allen, Ed Feulner's longtime colleague, before Reagan was elected president.

One of Heritage's most influential papers was a state-by-state survey compiled by analyst Doug Seay (before the creation of the Center for Data Analysis and its megacomputer). The survey showed that forty-two governors, Democratic and Republican, liberal and conservative, strongly favored the agreement because it would create thousands of new jobs and improve the economy of their states.

The foundation followed up by inviting Governors Tommy Thompson of Wisconsin and Kirk Fordice of Mississippi to Washington to explain to policy makers how global economic development would promote employment within the states. President Clinton and international trade representative Mickey Kantor both cited Heritage in their hard-fought campaign to persuade Congress to approve NAFTA, which it did in November 1993. "President Clinton said the governors' support was key," recalls vice president Kim Holmes.[27] Ed Feulner invariably describes the passage of NAFTA as one of Heritage's most important "scalps" or victories.

Throughout the 1980s the Kremlin had frequently and sharply

criticized Heritage. One Soviet publication charged that the foundation was the "ideological headquarters" of American "reactionary circles." Another described Heritage as the "brain center" of "U.S. ultra right-wing circles." Hardliners in Politboro meetings routinely cited the foundation's policy recommendations and argued that Moscow should do the opposite.[28]

With the collapse of Soviet Communism, Russian reformers turned to Heritage for advice and assistance. While liberals in America continued to extol the leadership of Mikhail Gorbachev, Heritage analysts focused on Boris Yeltsin, the ex-Communist turned reform populist. The foundation invited Yeltsin's economic advisers to attend a privatization workshop in June 1991. Yeltsin, in Washington at the same time to meet with President George H. W. Bush, told Heritage trustee J. William Middendorf II that the Heritage seminar was the most important part of his delegation's visit and remarked, "The Russian republic is in good hands with Heritage."[29]

Heritage formalized its efforts to help Russia stay on a democratic and capitalist course by opening an office in Moscow in November 1991 and putting Jeffrey Gayner, its veteran counselor for international affairs, in charge. Reform leaders in Russia and the NIS (Newly Independent States) constantly asked Heritage for research and advice on how to make the transition to a market economy. During a Washington visit, former deputy prime minister Yegor Gaidar summarized Heritage's leading role: "We remember that Heritage supported us long before it was fashionable to do so in the West." Dimitri Karaulov, cochairman of the Russian Republican Party, said flatly, "Heritage's ideas are the guiding light" for Russian reformers.[30]

Russian analyst Yevgeny Volk succeeded Gayner as coordinator of the Moscow office in 1994 and produced a number of studies widely cited in Russia until the increasingly restrictive regulations of President/Prime Minister Vladimir Putin made operations so difficult for Volk that Heritage reluctantly closed its Moscow office in 2010.

But the foundation had made a difference. "Probably the most important achievement," says Volk, was "our advice and expertise on the introduction of the 13 percent flat income tax in 2001." Heritage also established the Reform Forum, an informal political discussion club that became a popular Moscow venue for politicians, analysts, businessmen, and media people who shared a belief in individual freedom, free enterprise, and limited government.[31]

Delivering the first Clare Boothe Luce Lecture in September 1991, former British prime minister Margaret Thatcher expressed the hope that the twenty-first century would be the "American Century," a time when people everywhere would turn to what have become American ideas—"ideas of liberty, democracy, free markets, free trade, and limited government."[32]

Heritage was prepared to do its part in the war of ideas but would soon be challenged by a new occupant of the White House who had a different view of what the government should and shouldn't do.

CHAPTER 17

NEW DEMOCRATS AND NEWT REPUBLICANS

Rarely before in modern politics has a sitting president seeking re-election gone more quickly from sure thing to long shot. A disbelieving President George H. W. Bush watched his approval ratings plummet nearly 60 points, from just over 90 percent in early 1991 following the successful end of the Persian Gulf War to the mid-30s just before the Republican National Convention in July 1992.

The central reason was the faltering economy. Median household income in 1991 fell 3.5 percent. Only one million new jobs had been created since Bush entered office. Unemployment hit 7.7 percent, the highest since the 1982 recession.

Facing a charismatic candidate in Bill Clinton, a united Democratic Party, and a third-party nominee, billionaire Ross Perot, whose balance-the-budget message resonated with the public, Bush was decisively defeated, winning only 37.4 percent of the popular vote, less than Barry Goldwater did in his humiliating loss in 1964.

Clinton campaigned as a "different kind of Democrat," a founder of the moderate Democratic Leadership Council, not as the liberal successor to George McGovern. Often sounding like a conservative

Republican, Clinton endorsed a balanced budget amendment, federal deregulation, free trade with Mexico, the line-item veto, the death penalty, getting tough with China over its violations of human rights, and intervening in the war in former Yugoslavia. He even quoted Heritage studies, including the critical one that reported the Bush administration had "increased regulation on the private sector more than anyone in the last 20 years." These were the kind of issues, remarked one conservative congressman, "Ronald Reagan would probably have been running on if he ran in 1992."[1]

President Clinton had a choice, Ed Feulner explained in his annual report on the conservative movement: to embrace the conservative ideas he had advanced during the campaign, or give in to the liberal demands of the special interests that had dominated the Democratic Party—and the Congress—for so long. An administration bent on "real change," he said, would undertake to:

- Tackle the budget deficit by restraining government spending.

- Empower poor and middle-income families by, among other things, giving them school choice vouchers.

- Champion tax relief, not tax increases. In 1948 the typical American family of four paid the federal government 2 to 3 percent of its income in taxes. In 1992 it paid 24 percent, plus another 8 to 10 percent to state and local governments.

- Reduce "the regulatory burden" on American business and society. The *Federal Register*, the encyclopedia of federal rules and regulations, was an elephantine 67,716 pages.

- Solve the national health care problem in a way that "won't make matters worse."[2]

Turning to the conservative movement, Feulner reported that its philosophy remained "prescient, clear, and unchanged." The major enemy at home was the bureaucratic state with its "insatiable appetite for our money and our obedience." The conservative alternative was, is, and ever will be "free men, free minds, and free markets." Abroad, conservatives rejected both isolationism and "crusaderism" but accepted prudent internationalism. America, Feulner insisted, "must remain engaged in the world."[3]

The movement needed a set of practical realistic objectives to roll back the Leviathan state, he said. It was not enough, as Bill Buckley did when launching *National Review,* to stand athwart history yelling "Stop!" We must remember, said Feulner, "the bottom line in everything we say and do is people." Rather than condemning welfare dependency, for example, conservatives had to make the case for "the strategy we call empowerment." "If we are wise enough, well-organized enough, and persistent enough—as big government liberals were during the Reagan and Bush years—we can advance the conservative agenda even during the Clinton presidency."[4]

Many conservatives were worried, wondering whether conservatism was fated to fade away as other idea-based movements in American politics had.

The always-optimistic Feulner rejected the suggestion that conservatism was headed for a crack-up or collapse. He mentioned a new generation of conservatives like Governor John Engler of Michigan, Governor Tommy Thompson of Wisconsin, Senator Phil Gramm of Texas, and former education secretary William Bennett who were providing leadership. Looking back over the last decade, the Heritage president listed the important lessons that had been learned:

One, "there are no permanent victories in Washington." Two, "there are no permanent defeats in Washington either." Three, "most Americans remain committed to the low-taxes, pro-growth, limited-government message of contemporary conservatism."[5] Gallup confirmed this commitment, reporting that just over 40 percent of Americans identified themselves as conservative. (Conservatives have been the largest ideological group in America for nearly two decades, double the number of self-identified liberals.) [6]

Ed Feulner's positive attitude was buttressed by Heritage's constant growth. Its 1993 income was $22.9 million, more than double the 1983 income of $10.6 million. The staff, including analysts, media and development experts, and support personnel, now topped 160. In 1993, its twentieth year, the foundation held more than 120 lectures, seminars, and debates, published more than 250 monographs and policy studies, and circulated 2.3 million paperback copies of *The Ruling Class,* its popular new book on congressional reform. Its analysts appeared on nearly eight hundred major radio programs and almost three hundred TV news and public affairs shows (excluding Fox News, which did not begin operations until 1995). Long the most broadly based public policy institute in America, Heritage in 1993 passed the 200,000 mark in individual supporters. One donor wrote: "If it were possible to abolish Congress and put Heritage in charge of managing our country I feel it would be the wisest thing to do."[7]

Following a series of planning sessions by Stuart Butler and his team, Heritage adopted the following domestic strategy for Clinton: first, attack directly the welfare system, pointing out its many weaknesses and failures; and second, address a concern of almost every American, the breakdown of the family.

Analyst Robert Rector was set to work. He found that the federal government had spent $5.1 trillion since the War on Poverty was started in the mid-1960s with little impact on the level of poverty in America. The percentage of Americans who lived below the poverty line seemed to be frozen at about 30 million or 12 percent of the population. And just how "poor" were they?

Forty percent of them owned their homes. Sixty-four percent owned a car, 15 percent owned two or more cars, 60 percent had air conditioning, a third owned microwave ovens.

The Census Bureau counted as "poor" any household with a cash income less than the official poverty threshold, $14,343 for a family of four in 1992. But according to Rector, the bureau did not include all assets and omitted nearly all government welfare benefits that poor families received.[8]

Regarding family, Heritage proposed a number of measures calculated to strengthen and rebuild the institution broadly acknowledged to be the cornerstone of every society. In "Putting Families First," the foundation suggested a $500-per-child tax credit, fulfilling the president's campaign promise of a middle-class tax cut.

The Heritage strategy suggested moving the locus of the welfare debate to the right, but before change could be affected, there came a gargantuan issue absorbing one-seventh of the nation's economy.

• • •

During the presidential campaign, Bill Clinton often mentioned the need for health care reform, but he waited until taking office to declare his support for a comprehensive top-to-bottom overhaul of the nation's health care system. He promised to submit a proposal to Congress within ninety days.

To meet his hubristic deadline, President Clinton announced that his wife, Hillary Rodham Clinton, would chair a health care task force of cabinet officials and White House aides to draft the historic measure.

The task force was instructed to produce a system that expanded health care to include all Americans—about 38 million were uninsured—and reduce the rapidly rising rate of health care spending. Liberals were ecstatic. This would be the culmination of a decades-long campaign to produce government-run and -financed health care for everyone in America.

Everyone agreed the health care system was in serious trouble. Costs had rocketed, reaching $832 billion in 1992, one-seventh of the national economy. The total annual cost of health care was projected to approach an alarming $1.6 trillion by 2000. Most Americans felt an overhaul was needed, but there were sharp differences about the kind and cost of the cure. Some called for a single-payer plan like Canada's, under which the federal government would pay the health care bills of all Americans. Others, like Heritage, recommended using tax credits to encourage consumers to buy their own health insurance from among competing plans and on the open market.

In September 1993, President Clinton delivered a national television address to Congress, in which he asked Congress and the people to work with him to give "every American health security—health care that's always there, health care that can never be taken away." The core provision required every employer to provide health insurance coverage to all his employees through closely regulated HMOs (health maintenance organizations) that would be included in a "health alliance." An alliance would have the power to negotiate doctors' fees, limit the plans consumers could subscribe to (that is, limit health care services), and monitor the plans' performance.[9]

The very title of Clinton's proposal, "Health Security," recalled the Social Security Act of 1935. The president's reference to a "health security card" that every American would receive if his reforms were enacted was an obvious variation on the Social Security card in every citizen's pocket. As one Harvard social scientist put it, Clinton's invocation of Social Security "symbolized a faith that problems shared by a majority of Americans could be effectively addressed through a comprehensive initiative of the federal government."[10]

One year later, in September 1994, Senate majority leader George Mitchell reluctantly abandoned his efforts to pass Clinton health care, blaming Republicans and special interests for blocking the bill—which was never voted on by either house, both of which had Democratic majorities.

How could a timely and seemingly widely supported idea die so ignominious a death? Clinton's proposal suffered from being too sweeping and too difficult to explain to the public and to lawmakers: the text of the legislation ran more than thirteen hundred pages. Big business initially pushed for reform but concluded later that the Clinton plan would mean new taxes and more regulations and declared its opposition. Small business was concerned from the beginning that the costs of providing health insurance for employees would eliminate jobs and cut into profits needed to survive and grow.

The Clinton administration and the Democratic leadership in Congress did little to build bipartisan support until it was too late. The White House kept insisting that the one principle it would not surrender was universal coverage but never explained satisfactorily how it would be paid for.

The health alliances at the core of the Clinton plan were attacked as bureaucratic, restrictive, and susceptible to federal control. A bumper sticker captured the public's skepticism:

NATIONAL HEALTH CARE?

THE COMPASSION OF THE IRS!

THE EFFICIENCY OF THE POST OFFICE!

ALL AT PENTAGON PRICES![11]

• • •

For years, Stuart Butler, Robert Moffit, Edmund Haislmaier, and other Heritage people had been crosscrossing the country talking about health care reform and promoting the Heritage Consumer Choice Health Plan.

The Heritage plan would allow workers to purchase their own health insurance policies or pay directly for their health care, using the money their employers currently spent on premiums as a supplement to their own resources. In addition, employees would receive federal tax credits to ease family health expenses in place of the tax benefits now available for employer-sponsored coverage. The credits could also be used for contributions to a medical savings account (a concept first developed by John Goodman of the National Center for Policy Analysis). Employees would "shop wisely for health benefits," Ed Feulner said, "since they would be paying for them."[12]

The Heritage plan did require everyone to participate—in other words, it contained an "individual mandate," although those words were not used. It was a requirement that would come back to haunt Heritage two decades later, when President Barack Obama introduced his health care plan that included an individual mandate. The president pointedly and frequently referred to Heritage's endorsement of such a provision.

But in 1993 the liberal establishment dismissed the Heritage proposal for its consumer choice emphasis. *The New York Times* argued that consumer choice relied on "individuals to buy their own coverage. But complexity of insurance plans makes comparison shopping virtually impossible by anyone other than an experienced professional."[13] Heritage responded to the elitist criticism by citing a consumer-oriented system that already existed and worked for more than nine million people—the thirty-two-year-old Federal Employees Health Benefits Program.

What was available for federal employees, Heritage said, should be made available to every American family. The foundation admitted that its consumer-choice plan did include some government regulation and was not 100 percent market-oriented. Consumers could choose, but from among government-approved insurance plans. Ed Haislmaier explained that the Heritage proposal was constructed to achieve as much market-oriented reform as possible and to be adopted by Congress and the public. The foundation was abiding by Feulner's adage "Do not let the perfect be the enemy of the good."

Conservative columnist James J. Kilpatrick described Heritage's health care recommendations as "conservatively radical." Noting the key element was the marketplace, Kilpatrick wrote that both insurance carriers and health care providers would be obliged to compete for the business of consumers. At the other end of the political spectrum, liberal commentator Michael Kinsley wrote that "Washington's leading right-wing think tank has produced the simplest, most promising, and, in important ways, most progressive idea for health care reform."[14]

Even before Kinsley described the Heritage plan as "beyond socialism," John Goodman of the National Center for Policy Analysis and Ed Crane of the Cato Institute questioned the foundation's approach. Goodman said that ordinary Americans were capable of shopping around in the medical marketplace without any guidance from Washington and that government policy should encourage self-insurance through Medical Savings Accounts (MSAs). Nobody under the Goodman plan would be required to obtain insurance coverage—a key demand of Obamacare proponents in 2011–12.

"The liberals [defending managed competition]," Goodman argued, "can point to their plan and say that 'even the conservative Heritage Foundation says government must intervene' in many areas."[15] Which is what Barack Obama later did.

Cato president Ed Crane remarked: "Our friends at The Heritage Foundation have endorsed a mandated, compulsory, universal 'national health plan' which flies in the face of the American heritage of individual liberty and individual responsibility." Health expert Grace-Marie Turner of the Galen Institute later insisted that "most conservatives" including herself never supported an individual mandate. "We knew from the beginning," she said, that such a mandate would lead to "government determining what kind of health insurance we must buy . . . and a slew of mandates and regulations."[16]

Curiously, no one—not Goodman, not Cato, not Galen, and not anyone at Heritage—raised any constitutional objection to the Heritage plan with its individual mandate or to the Clinton proposal with its explicit governmental control of health care. The Constitution would not be invoked until the great debate over Obamacare. Heritage had an excuse for its silence: it did not create the Center on Legal and Judicial Studies until 2000, seven years after Hillarycare. The center was adamantly and constitutionally opposed to Obamacare, filing its first-ever amicus curiae brief against the Affordable Care Act, first in the Eleventh Circuit Court of Appeals and then with the Supreme Court.

Whatever the differences among conservatives in 1993 about the right way to reform health care, they were agreed about the wrong way—the Clinton plan, which Heritage called the largest power grab by the federal government since the New Deal.

The Heritage analyst who provided the details about the administration's bid to control one-seventh of the economy was Robert E. Moffit, deputy director of domestic studies. Moffit was one of the few people in America who read every word of the 1,342-page Clinton health care plan. Working out of his home, he got up at six a.m., had his first cup of black coffee, and made notes on yellow pads until midnight. His wife brought him sandwiches when he was hungry. "At the end of six days," he remembers, "I called Stuart and said, 'This will never pass.' "[17]

Aware of how much was at stake—the future of health care, the nation's economy, the Clinton presidency—Moffit was scrupulous in his thirty-seven-page analysis, "A Guide to the Clinton Health Plan." His critique was never challenged as misrepresenting the president's proposal in any way. The guide was especially critical of the National

Health Board, whose cost-containment decisions—including the pricing of insurance premiums and the enforcement of public and private spending limits—would not be subject to judicial or administrative review.

"Whatever may have been the intentions of its framers," Moffit wrote, "the Clinton plan will eventually herd every aspect of private-sector medicine under the government's umbrella, and punish those who resist."[18]

Heritage undertook a multiple-front campaign against Clintoncare. Its experts testified before congressional committees and conducted dozens of TV-radio interviews. The foundation ran ads in selected publications and told its members through mailed alerts what Clinton "health security" would do. One report began:

> We all know socialism when we see it: The Berlin Wall. The
> Kremlin. Castro's Cuba. Red China. But what does it sound like?
> Try these: Standard Benefits Package. National Health Board.
> Regional Alliances. Managed Competition. Gatekeepers. Price
> Controls. These are the sounds of the Clinton health plan—and of
> socialized medicine.[19]

• • •

In the Carter years, Heritage had been a young and sometimes brash member of the loyal opposition, consigned to the outer circle by the Establishment. In the Clinton years, Heritage stood at the very center of the national political debate, a respected and effective champion of conservative ideas and policies. *The Economist* identified a major reason for the foundation's transformation: the think tank had replaced the university as the primary producer of new and relevant ideas.

"In the 1960s," wrote the British journal, "it looked as if universities would establish a monopoly over the life of the mind, providing policies for politicians, sinecures for writers, ideas for journalists, and breakthroughs for industrialists. The 1980s changed all that. Governments in search of advice looked to think tanks such as the Institute of Economic Affairs in Britain and the Heritage Foundation in the United States, rather than to Oxford or Harvard."[20] The IEA—Ed Feulner's first employer in the think tank world—was Margaret Thatcher's favorite think tank just as Heritage was Ronald Reagan's.

Heritage was not Bill Clinton's favorite think tank, but he was obliged to accept some of its prescriptions.

In the spring of 1994, as the president had done little to redeem his campaign pledge on welfare, senior analyst Robert Rector proposed a comprehensive reform of the system that would end government subsidization of "self-destructive behavior" and reinforce "moral and cultural renewal." The Heritage paper was the culmination of years of thought and study by the veteran expert on welfare and family issues.

Rector pointed out that more than ten thousand days—dating back to the mid-1960s—had passed since President Lyndon B. Johnson told the nation that "the days of the dole are numbered." Nearly thirty years later, the vaunted War on Poverty had cost American taxpayers some $5 trillion. But instead of eliminating poverty, the welfare system had actually "bribe[d] individuals into behavior—such as not marrying and having children out of wedlock—which is self-defeating to the individual, a tragic handicap for children, and . . . increasingly a threat to society."[21]

What was needed, Rector said, was a complete reversal of existing policies. A true welfare reform strategy would be based on three principles: promoting individual responsibility by requiring welfare recipients to give something in return for benefits; controlling welfare costs; and dramatically reducing the illegitimate birth rate by increasing the marriage rate. Conservative Republicans liked these principles so much, they were embodied in pledge number three of the 1994 Contract with America.

Specific changes included establishing "serious workfare," denying additional payments to mothers who had more children while on welfare, and putting a 3.5 percent cap on welfare spending growth. All these ideas were included in the welfare reform legislation of 1996, which won Rector's praise as "historic."[22]

Stuart Butler recalls that at a critical point in the debate, Gingrich telephoned Ed Feulner and asked Heritage to "back off" or else it might wreck a deal in the making that would significantly advance welfare reform. However, Butler had explained to Feulner that any deal at that point was premature. "Ed was absolutely solid and held the line. It was a very good example of how, once he has made up his mind, he stands firm behind his people."[23]

• • •

Heritage was no longer, in Hayek's language, "a second-hand dealer in ideas," but engaged in serious and often original research. A good example is the annual *Index of Economic Freedom*.

It was Milton Friedman who first suggested in the 1980s—to

Canada's Fraser Institute—that a country's economic freedom and growth ought to be measured. A few years later Heritage trustee J. William Middendorf II urged the foundation to undertake the monitoring of economic freedom around the world. In the late 1980s, Edward L. Hudgins, then director of Heritage's Center for International Economic Growth, devised a set of criteria for members of Congress to judge how economically free different countries were and how they had prospered as a result of their freedom.

In the developing world, Heritage research showed, the key to economic prosperity was not foreign aid but economic freedom. It was an idea that Ed Feulner had heard Peter Bauer discuss at length at the London School of Economics in the 1960s. Feulner and Kim Holmes agreed that a comparative study of economic freedom around the world—among developed as well as developing nations—could "lay to rest once and for all doubts about whether economic freedom is integral to economic development."[24]

The first *Index of Economic Freedom,* published in 1995, was hailed by former treasury secretary and Heritage trustee William Simon as "the most important publication" ever issued by the foundation, even surpassing the *Mandate for Leadership* reports that had helped guide the Reagan administration during the 1980s.[25]

For the first time in economic analysis, the *Index* examined the economies of 101 countries in ten areas, ranging from tax policy and foreign investment to property rights and regulation. Each country was given a numerical score from 1 to 5 in each area; the lower the total score, the freer the economy. The method of measurement was changed in 1997 after *The Wall Street Journal* became a copublisher and was refined at various times since then. Now each of ten economic freedoms is graded on a scale from 0 to 100, with the highest score being the best. The ten scores are equally weighted and averaged to get an overall economic freedom score for each economy.

In 1995, Hong Kong—still under British rule—and Singapore tied for first place, with the United States in fourth place. Only forty-three countries were found to have "free" or "mostly free" economies while fifty had "mostly unfree" and eight "repressed" economies.

Seventeen years later in the 2012 *Index,* the eighteenth edition, Hong Kong remained number one as it had been in every previous survey. Singapore was second, but the United States had slipped to tenth place and was now ranked among the "mostly free" economies. Restoring the U.S. economy to the status of "free," the *Index* said, "will require significant policy changes to reduce the size of government, overhaul the tax system, and transform costly entitlement programs." Such pro-freedom policies "are the best hope for bringing down high unemployment rates and reducing public debt to manageable levels."[26]

The news was no better outside America's borders. While the scores of seventy-five economies improved (led by Chile and Mauritius, which made the top ten), ninety-nine countries lost economic freedom, and fourteen showed no change. Government spending, the *Index* said, has not only failed to arrest the very real global economic crisis but in many countries "seems to be prolonging it." A big-government approach "has led to bloated public debt, turning an economic slowdown into a fiscal crisis with economic stagnation fueling long-term unemployment."[27]

Despite the discouraging results, Ed Feulner argued that the findings of the *Index* confirmed "the strong interplay between economic freedom and prosperity in countries around the world." The Index revealed that it was "the dreadful policies" put in place that held back economic growth. Greater prosperity for individuals and societies, he said, depend on "our commitment to preserving and enhancing freedom."[28]

• • •

American-style democracy had its say in 1994, when the electorate chose Reagan's limited-government policies of the 1980s over Clinton's expanded government policies of the 1990s. The election is one of Feulner's most vivid political memories.

"As I sat contemplating the 'tsunami' or shock wave that the national elections had unleashed on official Washington," he recalled, "I noted a copy of *The Imperial Congress* in my bookcase, a book that Heritage published in 1988.

"In the foreword to that book, a young Georgia congressman wrote, 'Every citizen should be concerned about the arrogance and corruption of the present day Congress. At stake is the liberty of the American public. We must reform Congress to make it truly representative once again.' "

Newt Gingrich had judged public concern correctly, Feulner said, and on November 8, 1994, millions of Americans sent to Washington and the statehouses and state legislatures "an army of lawmakers dedicated to reforming Congress and finishing the conservative revolution Ronald Reagan began in 1980."[29] Seventy-three of the eighty-six new members of Congress were "terminally conservative," according to Heritage analysis.

A week later, at the largest President's Club meeting in Heritage history, House Speaker-presumptive Gingrich lauded the foundation, saying, "Heritage is without question the most far-reaching conservative organization in the country in the war of ideas, and one which has had a tremendous impact not just in Washington, but literally across the planet."[30]

The foundation had been feeding conservative ideas to present and future members of Congress throughout the year, beginning in May with a first-of-its-kind briefing book for congressional candidates. Conceived by Heritage vice president Kate O'Beirne, cleared by the foundation's legal counsel, and edited by Peter J. Ferrara, *Issues '94* analyzed key national issues from federal spending and taxes to foreign policy and congressional reform. Postelection interviews proved that dozens of candidates constantly used the 296-page book. Fred Thompson, elected to the U.S. Senate from Tennessee that year, would open *Issues '94* and read from it to reporters.

The effects of the political tsunami were felt outside Washington. Harvard University's School of Government canceled its usual orientation program for newly elected members of Congress for "lack of interest." Instead, most members of Congress's Class of 1994 chose to attend the Heritage/Empower America orientation conference, which had been first suggested by Kate O'Beirne. Remarked the liberal *Boston Globe,* "In the capricious business of supplying politicians with academic expertise and advice, if Harvard's star is fading, The Heritage Foundation's is surely on the ascent."[31]

The year 1994 was in fact the single most productive year in Heritage's twenty-one-year history by any reasonable measurement.

The foundation developed *The Index of Economic Freedom;* produced a comprehensive tax-relief and deficit-reduction plan, "Putting Families First"; provided much of the documentation that led to the demise of Clinton health care reform; played a major role in the GATT debate; exposed the crime bill as little more than another pork-laden social spending bill; crafted a welfare reform plan that would truly "end welfare as we know it"; began work on a major study of agriculture policy; and launched the American Trader Initiative, calling for a liberalized trade policy that would increase international business opportunities.

That was not all. A study by military analysts found that the Clinton administration had underfunded its own defense plan by more than

$100 billion over five years. Senior policy analyst Patrick Fagan chronicled the terrible consequences to children and society of out-of-wedlock births, adding new urgency to the welfare reform debate.

In response, foundation income topped $25 million for the first time, donated by some 200,000 individuals, foundations, and businesses. Amid all the good news, Feulner noted the passing of three conservative giants: author-historian Russell Kirk, a longtime Heritage distinguished scholar; Dr. Walter Judd, former congressman, medical missionary, recipient of the Presidential Medal of Freedom, and a dedicated member of the President's Club; and Shelby Cullom Davis, the New York investment banker and former ambassador to Switzerland who had served as chairman of the board of trustees.

Commenting on the conservative agenda that would be taken up by the new Congress, the very liberal *Village Voice* wrote that the driving force behind it was "the Heritage Foundation, which over the last decade has occupied center stage as the preeminent think tank in Washington."[32]

No one played a more central role in the ongoing drama of Washington policy making than senior policy analyst Robert Rector, who in August 1994 began his remarks before a congressional hearing on welfare reform this way:

"The 'War on Poverty' has been an incredibly costly failure."

Rector went on to say that the "welfare state" was made up of some seventy-five programs targeted to low-income and poor Americans, with a total annual cost exceeding $324 billion. All told, he said, pausing for effect, the nation has spent $5.3 trillion since the War on Poverty began in 1965.[33]

"What are the names of these programs? Do you have a listing of these programs?" interrupted Representative Harold Ford (D-TN), the chairman of the House Human Relations Subcommittee.

"They're listed in my testimony," Rector replied calmly, and went on to explain that the average tax-paying household in America spent $3,400 in 1993 to combat poverty. By 1999, he estimated, the nation could be spending $550 billion a year on welfare.

"I'm going to correct you now," Representative Ford interrupted again. "You're not going to come here to this committee and give us these numbers. . . . You're not going to leave the public perception that we are spending all these billions and billions of dollars on welfare."[34]

But we were. The reliable Congressional Research Service included some eighty programs in its inventory of "means-tested" federal welfare programs, and neither Representative Ford nor any other congressman successfully refuted Robert Rector's arithmetic.

• • •

Keeping faith with the promises made in the Contract with America, the House of Representatives of the 104th Congress stayed in continuous session for fourteen and a half hours on its first day of business. When the final gavel sounded, the House had adopted a far-ranging series of new rules calculated to produce a more efficient and open national legislature. Of fifteen reforms, thirteen had been recommended by Heritage, going back as far as *The Imperial Congress* in 1988.

Heritage kept the ball moving in April 1995 when it published *Rolling Back Government: A Budget Plan to Rebuild America,* which proposed the elimination of nine cabinet departments, an overhaul of Medicare, a tax cut of $152 billion, and a shift of many federal responsibilities to the states and the private sector. In all, the proposals would save nearly $800 billion and balance the federal budget by 2000—two years earlier than the deadline later designated by Congress and President Clinton in their agreement to balance the budget.

Commenting on the Heritage analysis, the management guru Peter Drucker wrote that " 'really re-inventing government' will remain the central and urgent political 'hot button' in the United States—and in all developed countries—for years to come."[35]

A lifelong reader and follower of Drucker, Feulner quoted his words over and over again in memos to and conversations with Heritage senior managers.

But he also felt it was necessary to go beyond the numbers and consider a fundamental question: what are the moral principles that guide the federal government, particularly in its entitlement programs? In remarks delivered at an Acton Institute program, Ed Feulner reported "a growing recognition in Washington that the human condition is influenced by elements beyond the flow of tax dollars." He quoted a liberal columnist who said he was struck by the discovery that "the most successful social programs are those that are driven—even if only tacitly—by moral or religious values."[36]

In the eighteenth century, Feulner noted, America experienced a religious revival known as the Great Awakening—a reaction against the secularization of life in the colonies. He believed that "an awakening is underway inside the [Washington] Beltway." It was a reaction against our secular society and "the abandonment of moral standards by its institutions and its people."

He closed by quoting an architect of the Great Society, John Gardner, President Johnson's secretary of health, education, and welfare, who wrote: "A nation is never finished. You can't build it and leave it standing as the pharaohs did the pyramids. It has to be recreated for each new generation."

Feulner agreed, saying that he believed "we can recreate our nation" to meet the changing world but that "we must remain grounded in our founding values and in their abiding morality," as laid down by the laws of nature and nature's God in the Declaration of Independence and the Constitution. A decade later the First Principles of America's founding would become the foundation of Heritage's Leadership for America program, and "First Principles" would be widely adopted by the conservative movement as a guiding idea.

•••

For decades, the federal government and the institutes and consultants it funded had enjoyed a monopoly on the official data used to make public policy decisions. This was not acceptable to Heritage, which launched the Center for Data Analysis (CDA) to provide alternative analysis of policy proposals based on free-market principles. With start-up funding from the Jaquelin Hume Foundation, CDA became an alternative to the Congressional Budget Office (CBO) and the Office of Management and Budget (OMB) and was recognized by members of Congress as able to furnish reliable, sophisticated analysis of legislation and deliver the results often before a federal agency warmed up its computers.

For example, President Clinton appointed an advisory council to examine the economic condition of Social Security and advise how to reform the system. The council asked the Social Security Administration (SSA) for data on the system's "rates of return"—that is, how much Americans earn over time on the taxes they pay into the system. SSA was asked to adjust the rates for various income levels and demographic groups, since low-income Americans have shorter life expectancies than high-wage earners and will therefore receive fewer Social Security benefits.

The SSA failed to deliver the estimates, and the advisory council was forced to base its recommendations on incomplete information. CDA, headed by senior economist William Beach, stepped forward to fill the gap, providing a wide range of demographic variables and using the government's own data and software. One critical CDA finding was that Social Security "provides poor rates of return for virtually all Americans," especially those who rely most on Social Security for their retirement income—citizens with the lowest income.[37] The finding was emphasized by Heritage, which insisted that Individual Retirement Accounts (IRAs) must be included in any reform of Social Security.

"Our ultimate aim," explains Bill Beach, "is to provide the data not only to the public policy community in Washington but to every American—through the Internet—to help them make informed decisions about Social Security and other important things in their lives."[38]

That aim is being realized: Heritage's Social Security Calculator—allowing an individual worker to estimate the total benefits he is likely to collect from Social Security during his lifetime—is one of the most popular private-sector models on the Internet. CDA's use of the Internet reflects Heritage's ability to adapt quickly to cutting-edge technology. The calculator also projects the total amount of Social Security taxes paid over the course of a working lifetime and then calculates the personalized rate of return workers can expect from the taxes paid into Social Security. Such information, Beach explains, will help workers understand how much better their lives—and those of their children and grandchildren—would be if they had the option of personal retirement accounts.

CHAPTER 18

TURNING SPLENDID

While liberals offered only nominal alterations of the complex mix of almost eighty overlapping federal programs dealing with welfare, Heritage recommended sweeping change. Many were developed by the foundation's welfare expert Robert Rector and his social scientist colleague Patrick Fagan. They pointed out that despite the estimated $5.3 trillion that had poured out of Washington since 1965 and the birth of the Great Society, low-income families had disintegrated, illegitimacy had soared, and crime in the inner city had multiplied.

Heritage recommendations included limiting the length of time a family can be on welfare; requiring young teenage mothers to live with their families rather than setting up government-subsidized households of their own; returning primary responsibility for public assistance to state and local governments through block grants; and ending the entitlement Aid to Families with Dependent Children (AFDC), the government's largest and most unregulated welfare program. Congress and President Clinton accepted the last proposal in their compromise welfare reform legislation of August 1996.

The positive role of religion in society was thoroughly documented by Fagan's widely quoted study, "Why Religion Matters: The Impact of Religious Practice on Social Stability." The studiously secular *Washington Post* devoted a full page of coverage to the study. Pointing to almost one hundred social science studies, some going back more than twenty years, Fagan stated that "the time is ripe for a deeper dialogue on the contributions of religion to the welfare of the nation." These studies, said Fagan, were in agreement that regular religious practice produced healthier, happier, more stable individuals and families. "Congress and the courts," he concluded, "have crowded religion out of the public square. It is time to bring it back."[1]

George W. Bush took Fagan's advice and instituted a faith-based office in the White House at the beginning of his presidency. In fact, his first executive order directed the office to lead the "Federal Government's comprehensive effort to enlist, equip, enable, empower, and expand the work of faith-based and other community organizations." Although controversy surrounded the office, Bush declared, on more than one occasion, that America's Judeo-Christian tradition had a proper place in governance. In his second inaugural address, he said that "every man and woman on this earth has rights, and dignity, and matchless value, because they bear the image of the Maker of Heaven and earth."[2]

Today Jennifer Marshall and her colleagues in the Richard and Helen DeVos Center for Religion and Civil Society build on the work of Pat Fagan and other earlier analysts as they expose the negative impact of divorce and broken families on our society.

• • •

Following President Clinton's dramatic declaration in his 1996 State of the Union message that "the era of big government is over," Ed Feulner surprised many conservatives by not echoing *The Weekly Standard,* which trumpeted, "WE WIN." Normally first to stress the positive, Feulner described Clinton's admission as a "victory" but not a surrender in the ongoing war of ideas. He pointed out, for example, that Clinton's first request to the returning Congress was for $8 billion in new federal spending in the current fiscal year.[3]

However, Feulner disagreed with conservatives who complained that the 104th Republican Congress had so far failed to pass term limits, a balanced budget amendment, and entitlement reform, and to close down the Department of Commerce, the Legal Services Corporation, and the National Endowment for the Arts. "We have made real progress," he insisted. "The American people and the tide of history remain on our side." But inasmuch as it took sixty years to build "the liberal dynasty in this country, it cannot be undone in a year."[4]

Feulner admitted that the congressional leadership had made mistakes. Too much had been attempted, and the message had become "too unfocused and thus susceptible to redefinition by the special interests and the media."[5] He was referring to the government shutdowns that had occurred in late 1995 and early 1996, when Gingrich and other GOP leaders underestimated Clinton's determination to stand firm in the battle over the budget. Furthermore, Republicans did not respond to the AFL-CIO's multimillion-dollar advertising campaign that misled many Americans, especially senior citizens, into believing that Republicans wanted to "cut" Medicare.

Conservatism's slow progress notwithstanding, Feulner said, its future was far brighter than that of liberalism, which he dismissed as "increasingly irrelevant." Conservatism would prevail because it was grounded in "sound economic principles and a realistic understanding of human nature, not wishful thinking." Plumbing deep into Western civilization, he quoted the Greek dramatist Sophocles: "One must wait until the evening to see how splendid the day has been." For all the mistakes and lost chances, Feulner said, the hour was early, and the day, for conservatism, would "turn splendid."[6]

· · ·

But first the day turned splendid for Bill Clinton, who won an easy re-election victory over the Republican challenger, Senator Bob Dole, in November 1996. Widely dismissed as a one-term president following the national triumph of the GOP in the 1994 elections, the president engineered another comeback in his roller-coaster political career.

In the lowest turnout of eligible voters in seventy years, Clinton received 45.6 million votes to Dole's 37.9 million, a solid 49 percent to 41 percent advantage in the popular vote. The president's electoral margin was more decisive—379 to 159, with 270 electoral votes needed to win. Reform Party candidate Ross Perot received 7.9 million votes, less than half his 1992 total, and won no electoral votes.

While campaigning as a champion of the "vital center," Clinton actually ran to the right of center—promising a balanced budget, focusing on family values, adopting a get-tough attitude toward crime, declaring an end to big government, and pledging honest welfare reform. The nation was locked, according to *The New York Times,* on a "Rightward Path, Leaving Liberals Beside [the] Road."[7]

Ed Feulner saw the election up close, for he took a three-month leave of absence as Heritage president to serve as staff director and counselor to Jack Kemp, the Republican vice-presidential nominee and a longtime friend and colleague. (Kemp had been a distinguished fellow at Heritage.)

"It was a fascinating and frustrating experience," he reported at a President's Club meeting, "that I neither regret nor desire to repeat."

He shared some of the lessons he had learned, beginning on a light note.

- *Politics is truly a science.* Feulner discovered from firsthand observation that if you have an outdoor rally with red, white, and blue balloons, the white balloons will always go up while the red and blue ones will rise, hover, and then fall to the ground "where everyone stomps on them." The reason is that heat affects colors differently.

- *Heritage has the people who have the answers to almost any public policy question.* Two days before the election, Kemp was scheduled to speak at the naval shipyard in Long Beach, California. To give the speech more substance, Feulner called Baker Spring, a senior Heritage analyst, to get facts and figures on the navy's capabilities and the official rationale for Long Beach Dry Dock No. 1. Spring had the information "on the tip of his tongue"—including the fact that the navy had declined from 600 ships under Reagan to 360 ships under Clinton—"and his arguments became the basis of Jack's speech later that day."

- *The vice-presidential candidate is rarely in charge of his agenda, his itinerary, or his speeches.* These things, Feulner reported, are "headquarters-driven and consultant driven, which usually means poll-driven." (Privately he told friends that he had scant respect for the campaign consultants with their astronomical fees, who protected the candidate like grim Secret Service agents.)

- *The news media and the campaigns are too poll-driven.* He quoted the head of the Roper Center for Public Opinion Research as saying that the process of election polling had become so flawed, it should be reviewed by a blue-ribbon panel. He cited the last pre-election CBS/*New York Times* poll that predicted that Clinton would win in a landslide defeating Dole by 18 percent. The actual result was an 8 percent victory for Clinton.

- *Ideas are critical to political victory.* "I have no doubt that the Republican ticket would have done better if we had focused on an overarching, compelling idea and then stuck with it. If you asked most voters where a Dole White House wanted to take the country, they could not have told you. The closest thing they *might* have said is a 15 percent tax cut." He then quoted David Letterman, who gave his list of the top ten reasons Bob Dole lost the election. One was: "Should have promised a SIXTEEN percent tax cut."[8]

"Campaigns have a choice," Feulner said, "they can *follow* polls or they can *lead* through ideas. I ask you—which is a stronger foundation?"

- *There are people in Hollywood who are sensible and who share our views.* He came to this conclusion after having actress Bo Derek of *10* fame as his seatmate on the campaign plane for three days. He also learned "how incredibly hard it is to hold your stomach in for three days straight."

- *A democracy must be ever vigilant to recognize lies, which must be addressed immediately.* The public's attention span is such that once a perception becomes lodged in its mind, it is very hard to reverse that perception.

- *A [vice] presidential candidate is a man on roller skates being pushed along by consultants, media, polls, random events of history, and his own vulnerabilities.* The only stability he has is his own integrity and principles.

- *Conservatism, not the centrist tide the networks are proclaiming, won this election.* Even though millions of voters may not have focused on the campaign, their outlook remains conservative. "They want the government out of their pocket and off their backs." The president—rhetorically at least—accepted conservative principles. Exit polls showed that many people thought Bill Clinton stood to the right of Bob Dole. *The New Republic* pointed out that fourteen of the accomplishments that Clinton bragged about in his acceptance speech at the Democratic National Convention were actually GOP measures.[9]

In other words, in reelecting Clinton and retaining a Republican majority in the House—and slightly increasing the Republican margin in the Senate—the voters were voting not for divided government but for conservative government.

• • •

Although he had not hesitated to help his good friend Jack Kemp in his vice-presidential campaign, Ed Feulner was happy to return to his first love—The Heritage Foundation. But it was not an exclusive love. The one organization that meant almost as much to him as Heritage was the Mont Pelerin Society, the global organization of classical liberals that met every other year in a national capital to discuss the condition of freedom around the world.

The society was founded in 1947, when the world seemed to be turning left. It was a time when Eastern and Central Europe had been seized by Soviet Communism. When the future course of Western Europe seemed likely to be determined by socialist ideas, like those proposed by the Labour government of Great Britain. When Mao Zedong and his "agrarian reformers" were pressing a civil war that would secure their control of China. When President Harry Truman was carrying forward Franklin D. Roosevelt's New Deal, including an economic bill of rights for all citizens.

The American historian Mortimer Smith asserted at the time that the "central fact" of the last seventy-five years had been the march to collectivism and that one theme had dominated the "progressive" proposals of the postwar planners: "The individual must surrender more and more of his rights to the state which will in return guarantee him what is euphemistically called security."[10]

Not everyone was willing to surrender. In April 1947 a small group of European and American intellectuals gathered in the Hotel du Parc in Mont Pèlerin sur Vevey, Switzerland, to discuss the possibility of a "liberal" (i.e., classical liberal) revival and the formation of an association of individuals committed to the principles of a free society. The principal organizer and first president of the society was F. A. Hayek. The majority of the thirty-nine attendees were economists (including future Nobel laureates Milton Friedman and George Stigler), along with representatives of other academic disciplines and three journalists.

In a note to those invited to the founding conference, Hayek said that "an intense intellectual effort is needed. We must kindle an interest in—and an understanding of—the great principles of Social organization and of the conditions of individual liberty as we have not known it in our lifetime." And then came this arresting phrase that would inspire Ed Feulner when he read it: "We must raise and train an army of fighters for freedom."[11]

Hayek stressed the critical importance of shaping public opinion and therefore public policy: "Public opinion on these matters is the work of men like ourselves, the economists and political philosophers of the last few generations, who have created the political climate in which the politicians of our time must move."

Nineteen ninety-seven was a special year because it was the fiftieth anniversary of the society, and the gathering would be in Mont Pèlerin, where the founders first met. Not by coincidence, the president of the Mont Pelerin Society in its anniversary year was Ed Feulner, who, members were confident, would ensure a meeting worthy of the society. He had proven that while serving as treasurer without compensation from 1978 to 1996 (and he would take up the responsibility again after his two-year term as president).

In his presidential address, Feulner described the group as "the most distinguished assembly of minds on the face of the planet." He pointed out that seven society members had been awarded the Nobel Prize for Economics—Hayek, Milton Friedman, George Stigler, James Buchanan, Maurice Allais, Ronald Coase, and Gary Becker. Throughout his remarks, he used the word *liberal* when referring to the society—that is, a believer in liberty.

The society is not really a society, Feulner said, because it does not have a permanent address, it shuns publicity (all meetings are off the record and closed to the news media), and it does not have a fixed point of view on issues but welcomes diversity. "Our permanent preoccupation," said Feulner, "is to work out, in so far as we can, a durable philosophy of freedom."

Ed Feulner first attended a general meeting of the Mont Pelerin Society in 1968 as a guest of Hayek and under the sponsorship of the Earhart Foundation, one of the most quietly effective conservative foundations in the country. He became a member in 1972 at the age of thirty-one, one of the youngest members ever. He vividly remembered that year's meeting because Milton Friedman rose to argue that "the battle of economics had been won, our work was done, and we should dissolve the society." Given that President Nixon had just imposed wage and price controls and the Soviet Union was busily using détente to expand its empire, Feulner asked himself: "If this is Milton's idea of victory, I wonder how he'd define defeat?"

Upon reflection, he realized that Friedman was referring to the battle of ideas, that in Ronald Reagan's words, the statists "had had their turn at bat in the 1960s and had struck out." Feulner listed a score of impressive victories for classical "liberalism" since then, including:

Margaret Thatcher's 1979 election as prime minister and her pledge to dismantle socialism; Reagan's decisive 1980 presidential victory and his historic tax cuts; John Paul II's 1984 condemnation of the Marxist aspects of liberation philosophy; China's 1984 public assertion that some Marxist ideas were "no longer suited" to China's problems; the 1986 election of Jacques Chirac, who lowered taxes and denationalized several state-owned enterprises.

A decisive influence in many of these cases was the thought of such Mont Pelerin members as Wilhelm Roepke, Arthur Seldon, Peter Bauer, Milton Friedman, and Václav Klaus of the Czech Republic, the society's first member in Eastern Europe, who as prime minister and president has presided over "his country's transition from communism to capitalism."[12]

Can it therefore be said, Feulner asked, "We are all liberals now?" No, for as James Buchanan has said, "Socialism is dead, but Leviathan lives on." Why? Because "going from a Western welfare state to a truly free, deregulated society is a transformation almost as great and far-reaching as the transition from communism to capitalism."

We must set about, he said, to translate the ideas of freedom into laws "that not only block the road to serfdom" but clear a path to liberty. We must reach beyond the economic realm to the historians and political philosophers who Hayek thought were underrepresented at the first Mont Pelerin meeting and to businessmen, artists, and the religious to build the "critical intellectual mass" that will articulate a philosophy of freedom.

He ended by quoting John Paul II from his 1995 address to the United Nations, "We must not be afraid of the future. . . . We have within us the capacities for wisdom and virtue. . . . We can build in the next century and the next millennium a civilization worthy of the human person, a true culture of freedom."[13]

Prior to the "gathering," Milton Friedman wrote to Ed that he and Rose, his wife and close collaborator on all his writing, "are very much looking forward to the event. In your capable hands, we know it will be outstanding." Indeed, it was so successful that the society decided to hold a "Golden Anniversary" meeting the following year in Washington, D.C. The honorary chairman of the organizing committee was Nobel laureate James M. Buchanan; the chair was MPS president Edwin J. Feulner.

More than four hundred "liberals" from around the world gathered in America's capital city to discuss "Free Markets and Free People—the

Barriers Remaining" and how to remove the barriers. The major speakers included House majority leader Dick Armey (R-TX); *Wall Street Journal* editor Robert Bartley; University of Chicago law professor Richard Epstein; professor Viktor Vanberg, chairman of economic policy at the University of Freiberg; and Angelo Petroni, philosophy of science professor at the University of Bologna.

Ed Feulner's presidential address focused on the practical philosophy of the founding fathers of the American Revolution, who had "an abiding faith in the capacities of private man, working with his friends, his neighbors, and his community, to build a just, decent and free society." He singled out one of the largest barriers to freedom in American society—Social Security—and suggested how it could be breached through privatization.

Privatization, he insisted, was not "some harebrained scheme devised by ivory-tower economists" but a tried and tested solution in twenty-six countries, large and small, like Mexico and Denmark. "They make it clear—not just in theory but in actual practice," Feulner said, "that we don't need Big Brother to look after us in our old age."

The vision of the American Founders and their faith in the private man, he concluded, is the same vision that gave birth to the Mont Pelerin Society five decades ago, "animates our discussions today," and will "inspire the future generations of our Society."[14]

That the society has a future, in the opinion of Kenneth Minogue, a past president and arguably the leading "liberal" intellectual in Great Britain, is due to the leadership of one man, Ed Feulner. Minogue sees a direct line from F. A. Hayek, who became somewhat discouraged when "the obvious truth of the free market" was not accepted by the people, to Milton Friedman, who picked up the baton, to Feulner, who "believes in the same principles as Hayek and Friedman" but in neither an obtrusive nor a dogmatic way. "He keeps the Society going."[15]

• • •

Mandate for Leadership I had materially shaped the Reagan administration. *Mandate II* was called "one of the most important books of 1984" because it detailed how the administration could continue the Reagan Revolution. Published in 1989, *Mandate III* described minutely how to manage the federal bureaucracy in the post-Reagan era.

Mandate for Leadership IV: Turning Ideas into Actions was different, reflecting the changed character of American politics and The Heritage Foundation in the year 1997. It could not be a blueprint for a conservative administration because the White House was held by an opportunistic Democrat who was a "counterfeit" conservative. Therefore the 760-page *Mandate IV* was a closely reasoned political strategy by which Congress could carry out the conservative platform endorsed by the American electorate in 1994 and 1996, a strategy first outlined in 1980.[16]

Among the specific reforms proposed were (1) the funds allotted for Department of Education programs should be transferred to the states as block grants with few strings attached; (2) the Department of Housing and Urban Development should be closed down, with all low-income housing assistance to be consolidated into a single welfare block grant to be used in accordance with the new welfare reform law; (3) sponsors of congressional bills should be required to cite the constitutional authority for their legislative initiative; (4) functions of the Department of Transportation such as Amtrak should be privatized; (5) the American Bar Association should be removed from its special role in the judicial selection process; (6) seventeen separate strategies should be used for building support for missile defense.[17]

In the entitlements chapter, Stuart Butler and coauthor John S. Barry argued that Congress must convince Americans, particularly the elderly, that the entitlements crisis "is real and needs decisive action *before* a detailed [reform] proposal is unveiled." The American people must be informed, for example, that Social Security is not "a real account with their own money in it, like savings in a bank," but "a program in which the government spends every penny paid into the system and in which benefits have little to do with contributions made." Because public apprehension about the future of Social Security is so intense, change should not be presented as "Social Security reform," but as part of a comprehensive plan for "improving the retirement options of all Americans."[18]

Mandate IV was a prime subject of discussion at an orientation conference for twenty-three freshman congressmen—sixteen Republicans and seven Democrats—held by Heritage and Empower America. GOP senators at an agenda-setting session at the Library of Congress pored over the Heritage study, leading a veteran reporter to say that *Mandate IV* was "must reading" on Capitol Hill.[19]

But the mid-1990s were a far different time from the late 1970s, when the nation was mired in economic stagflation and Soviet Communism was on the march in Afghanistan and still regnant in Eastern and Central Europe.

The nation was in the midst of undeniable prosperity. Unemployment was the lowest in a quarter-century, inflation was under 3 percent, and the gross domestic product (GDP) was growing at more than 3 percent a year.

And America was at peace. U.S. forces had been dispatched to Bosnia and Haiti during Clinton's watch, but not a single American had died in a combat-related incident in the past five years—although forty-four Americans had died in Clinton's poorly conceived "nation-building" mission in Somalia.

Most Americans did not seem to care much about the questions raised concerning the Clinton campaign's fund-raising practices (Chinese agents tried to direct contributions to the Democratic National Committee in violation of U.S. law), and the allegations of sexual misconduct between the president and a young White House intern named Monica Lewinsky had not yet turned into a public scandal.

The president challenged critics in January 1998 with an optimistic State of the Union address and the most expensive domestic agenda since Republicans gained control of Congress in 1995. A week later he pulled another rabbit out of his hat—the first balanced budget in thirty years. House Speaker Gingrich retorted that the $1.7 trillion budget was a "far cry from the 'leaner, more flexible' government touted in the State of the Union address." Clinton ignored the finding by the columnist James K. Glassman that federal spending had increased 21 percent since Clinton took office.[20] Ed Feulner's skepticism about the conservative "victory" over big government was confirmed.

The burgeoning Clinton-Lewinsky scandal and the accompanying allegations of perjury and obstruction of justice eclipsed the 1998 legislative agenda. In September independent counsel Kenneth W. Starr sent his report to Congress, detailing a host of possibly impeachable offenses. A month later the House of Representatives authorized an impeachment inquiry.

As the House Judiciary Committee prepared to hold hearings, an aggressive Speaker Gingrich decided to use the Clinton scandal to galvanize Republican support in some thirty congressional races, most of them in the South. Gingrich believed that Republicans could run a series of local TV ads attacking the president, at a cost of $25 million, without attracting national notice. He was proven wrong, in short order.

The anti-Clinton commercials were used by the Democrats, first, to expose the "secret" Republican plan and, second, to turn out their core constituencies, particularly Southern blacks. Republicans went down to defeat in congressional districts once considered safe for the GOP and barely maintained their majority. There was no Republican gain in the Senate, making the GOP the first party since before the Civil War to lose seats to the party of a president in his second term.

Angry Republicans pilloried Gingrich for failing to deliver the twenty to thirty House seats he had predicted. Challenged for the speakership, Gingrich announced that rather than precipitate a bitter and divisive fight—which he believed he could win—he was stepping down as Speaker and resigning his seat in the House as well. Given the circumstances, it was an act of prudence and statesmanship.

Despite the unplanned exit, Newt Gingrich's place in modern political history is secure. The Contract with America was brilliant politics and produced the Republican capture of the House of Representatives (after a gap of forty years) and a Republican majority in the House for another decade. A string of balanced federal budgets and substantive welfare reform occurred under his leadership.

But from his first to his last days in Congress, Gingrich attempted too much and—at the same time—he was known as the Man with a Thousand Ideas. As Speaker, he tried to govern the nation from Congress, an impossibility given the political and communication skills of the modern president. David Keene, then chairman of the American Conservative Union and now president of the National Rifle Association, compared Gingrich to Samuel Adams, the fiery Boston radical who led the Boston Tea Party, rather than John Adams, the Harvard lawyer and constitutional expert who served as America's second president. Revolutionary? Yes. Chief executive? No.

Meanwhile the House of Representatives and much of the conservative movement focused in an almost lascivious way on President Clinton's personal misbehavior and impeachment. When the Senate in February 1999 failed to convict Clinton of high crimes and misdemeanors, many conservatives were outraged. How could the Senate let him get away with it?

National Review editor Rich Lowry, a worthy successor to Bill Buckley, argued there were two overriding factors that ultimately saved Clinton in the Lewinsky affair: "His wife [Hillary] and a broad cultural shift in the American public that predisposed it to go easy on him."[21]

• • •

Long before Washington became embroiled in impeachment and off-year election politics, Heritage decided to concentrate on the longer-term policy challenges facing America and to "retool" the foundation to be a more effective conservative champion in the twenty-first century.

It launched the Leadership for America campaign, running from December 1997 through December 1999, to build a sound financial base in the new millennium. The goal was $85 million, the most ambitious fund-raising goal in Heritage's twenty-five-year history.

It made significant organizational changes, starting with an expansion of the Center for Data Analysis so that it could better compete in "numbers-crunching" with the Congressional Budget Office and the Office of Management and Budget. The foundation broadened its commitment to the examination of faith-based programs and social issues with the creation of the Project on Religion in a Civil Society—made possible through substantial grants from the Richard and Helen DeVos Foundation and Heritage trustee William E. Simon.

It launched the B. Kenneth Simon Center for American Studies—under the multitalented Matthew Spalding, a widely respected George Washington scholar—to promote the wisdom of the Founding Fathers and the genius of the Constitution. "It's too easy for our political leaders," explains Spalding, "to get caught up in the process of governing and neglect the principles—the First Principles—on which this country was founded." The center's mission "is to explain how America's founding principles apply to today's politics." To that end, the center produced an impressive list of publications large and small, including the magisterial *The Heritage Guide to the Constitution* and Spalding's own bestselling volume, *We Still Hold These Truths* (which was the theme of the 2012 Conservative Political Action Conference in Washington).

It opened a Center for Media and Public Policy that offered workshops and coaching sessions for conservatives on how to improve their writing and speaking skills. The center, in cooperation with the Center for Data Analysis, also developed databases for reporters left and right who were writing on issues that required in-depth calculations and complex statistical analysis. "Growing numbers of reporters are using computer-assisted reporting," said the Media Center's Mark Tapscott, "because that's where they can get 'the story behind the story.' "[22] Heritage was the first Washington think tank to offer such a service, long before the Internet came to dominate media research as it does today.

Every day Congress is in session (and even when it is not), Heritage provides a steady flow of information to congressional offices about leading issues. All Washington think tanks do the same. What is different about Heritage is its personal approach. "We cultivate close relationships with members of Congress and their staff," explains Mike Franc, the foundation's vice president for government studies and one of Washington's most knowledgeable experts on Congress. "We constantly look for opportunities to advise our friends on the Hill about the specifics of the legislative proposals before them."[23] The opportunities are still there for the foundation despite the advent of Heritage's lobbying arm Heritage Action for America, because Franc and his associates, like the Hill veteran Dani Doane, focus on the issues while Mike Needham and Tim Chapman of Heritage Action apply serious political pressure with their legislative scorecard.

• • •

Heritage's reach beyond the Washington beltway is led by Vice President Becky Norton Dunlop, a former high-ranking state government official and a White House assistant in the Reagan administration. "Our outreach informs and motivates leading conservatives across America who in turn communicate with policy makers on Capitol Hill."[24] Dunlop's department, including the indefatigable Bridgett Wagner, distributes Heritage material at dozens of national, regional, and state meetings of conservative groups.

Careful not to pick favorites among the Heritage staff, Ed Feulner could not resist talking about Wagner in a monthly letter to President's Club members. He said: "She's a dynamo. She has brains, energy and ingenuity . . . she knows the conservative movement the way you know your own back porch." He praised her ability to unite conservatives around a common cause, saying that she was born for the job.

"If she encounters a stranger waiting for an elevator in our lobby, she'll be in animated conversation with him before the doors open. By the time they reach their floor, the visitor will have a new friend, a business card, a lunch date for next week, invitations to several Heritage events, and a whole new outlook on the conservative movement."

Because of Wagner and her colleagues, said Feulner, the Resource Bank meeting in Philadelphia that year (2001) was the largest ever, with 453 attendees (including 108 CEOs) representing 251 conservative organizations from seventeen countries. After the meeting, one CEO remarked, "I really do think this meeting is becoming the mother church of the conservative movement."[25]

From its founding, Heritage emphasized the importance of legal and constitutional issues in policy making—since 1989 this research was under the general direction of former attorney general Edwin

Meese III. In November 2000 the foundation expanded its commitment to legal analysis by creating the Center for Legal and Judicial Studies. Meese became chairman of the center, while constitutional expert Todd Gaziano was named a senior fellow in legal studies and would later become director of the Center for Legal and Judicial Studies.

"Much of the talk about the Constitution being a 'living document,'" said Meese, "is little more than code-speak to cover a wide range of activities that are constitutionally suspect. This is wrong, and the Center for Legal and Judicial Studies aims to correct that trend."[26] The center has grown into a six-lawyer operation that issues Supreme Court "alerts" on its decisions, holds moot court sessions for Supreme Court cases, brings together public-interest law groups monthly, and analyzes a wide variety of legal issues like overcriminalization and vote fraud.

Toward the end of Leadership for America, the foundation added several analysts to the Kathryn and Shelby Cullom Davis Institute for International Studies. They were not big names but seasoned experts in critical areas like international trade and U.S.-China relations. Daniel Fisk, an expert on Latin America and a former senior aide to Senator Jesse Helms (R-NC), became deputy director of the institute, while Gerald O'Driscoll, formerly the director of policy analysis for Citigroup, was named director of Heritage's new Center for International Trade and Economics. Larry Wortzel, former director of the Strategic Studies Institute at the U.S. Army War College and a leading expert on the Chinese military, was appointed director of the Asian Studies Center.

In the 1990s, Heritage kept its eye on an issue that had been a central concern of the foundation for nearly two decades—missile defense. In January 1999, Defense Secretary William Cohen announced plans to spend $6.6 billion on missile defenses—the first time the Clinton administration admitted the need for a strategic defense program. But even as Cohen was speaking, President Clinton was assuring Russian president Boris Yeltsin that no decision had been made to *deploy* such defenses. Clearly there was work to be done, particularly on the 1972 ABM Treaty.

Senior analyst Baker Spring pointed out that the ABM Treaty was no longer legally binding because the other nation that had signed the treaty—the Soviet Union—no longer existed. Many policy makers agreed with Heritage, including Senate majority leader Trent Lott and Senate Foreign Relations Committee chairman Jesse Helms. Even former secretary of state Henry Kissinger, an architect of the original treaty, said at a Heritage conference that he "wouldn't let the ABM Treaty stand in the way [of missile defense development]. It is an entity that no longer exists."[27]

Beijing's belligerence and Washington's uncertain response made the U.S.-Taiwan relationship another key policy issue in 1999. While the Clinton administration practiced "strategic ambiguity," Heritage cosponsored with the American Enterprise Institute a symposium on the 1979 Taiwan Relations Act that sets forth America's commitments to Taiwan, including the sale of "defensive" arms to offset any threat from the mainland. Later that year, twenty-two prominent conservatives, including Ed Feulner, called on the United States to "declare unambiguously that it will come to Taiwan's defense" if China attacked or blockaded the island nation.[28]

A decade earlier, speaking in Taiwan in the wake of the Tiananmen Square massacre in Beijing, Feulner had praised the wisdom of the Taiwan Relations Act, saying that the United States "did not make the mistake of improving relations with [Beijing] at any cost." Feulner explained that the foundation supported the Republic of China on Taiwan for strategic as well as economic reasons, saying that Taiwan "can demonstrate to [Beijing] and the world how economic dynamism is complemented by political pluralism and a free society."[29] In the years since, China has moved significantly closer to a market economy but has firmly suppressed any serious discussion of political pluralism, let alone political freedom.

Confirmation of Heritage's leading role in public policy in the 1990s came from the Left as well as the Right. Kristin Luker of the University of California at Berkeley said that "the most effective in terms of shaping public discourse" were the "right-wing think tanks" like Heritage because they shared "passion, energy, commitment, and overarching vision of society." A survey by Andrew Rich, professor of politics at Wake Forest University and a former fellow at the Brookings Institution, ranked Heritage as the "most influential" of twenty-seven prominent think tanks. One reason for the influence, as offered by a leading daily newspaper, was that Heritage's policy analysts were "warriors with Ph.D.s."[30]

When they considered the intellectual half of the Leadership for America campaign, Ed Feulner and the other senior managers decided it would not be the usual talks by the usual over-the-hill speakers in a Washington setting. Instead, Heritage invited sixteen distinguished men and women of ideas to discuss the basic values of a free society, each in a different city, over two years. Their combined remarks equaled a university course in modern political science. No other think tank would have undertaken such an ambitious program—both in its intellectual scope and in its logistical demands.

The lead-off speaker was former prime minister Margaret Thatcher, speaking on courage, followed by Supreme Court associate justice Clarence Thomas (character); publisher Steve Forbes (enterprise); polymath William F. Buckley, Jr. (heritage); economist and Nobel laureate Gary Becker (competition); former UN ambassador and Georgetown University professor Jeane Kirkpatrick (strength); former attorney general Edwin Meese III (freedom); former House Speaker Newt Gingrich (responsibility); Rev. Richard John Neuhaus (faith); political scientist James Q. Wilson (human nature); former education secretary William Bennett (truth); *Wall Street Journal* columnist Peggy Noonan (patriotism); neoconservative turned conservative social critic Midge Decter (family); Czech Republic president Václav Klaus (liberty and the rule of law); Bradley Foundation president Michael Joyce (self-government); and award-winning columnist and TV commentator George Will (leadership).

Here are some of the things they said:

"We are the beneficiaries of [Adam] Smith's understanding of how human nature could lead, through market economies, to personal and national wealth, and have inherited from the American Founders a written Constitution that leaves power divided and people empowered."

—JAMES Q. WILSON

"Whether there will be another Great Awakening, God only knows. We can know some things, and in knowing them embrace the obligations that attend them. . . . We know, first, that we must continue to make the public argument for the Judeo-Christian tradition, recognizing that, uniquely in America, Jews and Christians can cooperate in giving political and legal expression to moral truth."

—RICHARD JOHN NEUHAUS

"Competition is, indeed, the lifeblood of any dynamic economic system, but it is also much more than that. Competition is the

*foundation of the good life and the most precious parts of human
existence: educational, civil, religious, and cultural as well as
economic."*

—GARY BECKER

*"President Ronald Reagan closed his second inaugural address by
asking that we recall 'the American sound.' It is, he said, . . . 'hopeful, big-hearted, idealistic—daring, decent and fair. We sing it still,'
he said. 'We raise our voices to the God who is the author of this
most tender music.' "*

—WILLIAM F. BUCKLEY, JR.[31]

When the Leadership for America campaign ended in December
1999, Heritage had raised $104,868,342, some 20 percent more than its
announced goal of $85 million. There had been very large gifts—$10
million from the Shelby Cullom Davis Foundation of New York City and
$10 million from Timothy Mellon of Lyme, Connecticut, eighteen other
gifts of $1 million or more—and many small donations of $100, $50,
$25 from among the 200,000 members of Heritage. All donors, large
and small, apparently shared the view of one President's Club member
who wrote, "There is little doubt in our minds if there were no Heritage
Foundation, the void [in] innovative policy would be immense."[32]

For their extraordinary contributions during the Leadership campaign and dating back to Heritage's founding (totaling tens of millions
of dollars), Joseph Coors, Edward E. Noble, and Richard M. Scaife received special recognition. The redesigned foundation lobby was named
Founders' Hall, and a special wall plaque was erected in their honor.

But Leadership for America was not just about money. It hired a
team of specialists to work full-time on Social Security reform. As a
result, it was possible to talk about a free-market alternative to Social
Security without being pilloried.

In the field of education, it put special emphasis on promoting school
choice. Florida established the first statewide school choice program.

It created a permanent program to help restore religion to its proper
place in civil society.

It commissioned a legal study that led to a congressional consensus
that America must build a missile defense system.

All this allowed Ed Feulner to affirm that Heritage "remains the
most effective conservative organization in America."[33]

• • •

Innovative. Creative. Entrepreneurial. These are the words that members constantly invoke when describing Heritage. And not just supporters.

The liberal National Committee for Responsive Philanthropy, in a comprehensive 1999 report on conservative think tanks, conceded that "it is now beyond dispute that left-of-center funders have made a calamitous strategic blunder by underfunding public intellectuals and policy thinkers. This mistake is profoundly ironic," the committee lamented. "Who would have ever thought, thirty or forty years ago, that the right would come to believe more deeply in the power of ideas than the left."[34]

It is a backhanded and incorrect compliment. The Right has always believed in ideas. The profound difference was that there were now organizations like The Heritage Foundation that could turn ideas into policies and policies into legislation and legislation into laws that advanced ideas like missile defense, welfare reform, school choice, and tax reform.

At the closing banquet of Leadership for America, Ed Feulner spoke of the past twenty-five years and the next twenty-five years for Heritage, conceding that as an eternal optimist, he liked to dream great dreams and try "whatever it takes to make them come true." That was why the foundation had chosen "Leadership for America" as the theme for its twenty-fifth anniversary. That was why the foundation had adopted a vision for America that was audacious even for Heritage:

The Heritage Foundation is committed to building an America where freedom, opportunity, prosperity, and civil society flourish.[35]

It seemed, on that December evening in 1999, that almost anything was possible. Heritage was financially stronger, more broad-based, more media aware, more alert to the myriad issues of the day than ever before—it had even been able to "burn" its mortgage, thanks to a gift from the Samuel Roberts Noble Foundation. When he became president of the foundation in 1977, Ed Feulner said that a prime goal was to make Heritage a permanent Washington institution like Brookings. And he, with more than a little help from Phil Truluck and John Von Kannon and the board of trustees and dozens of research analysts and the development team and the communications experts and 200,000 members, had succeeded.

The one constant amid the conservative ups and downs, the victories and the defeats, the celebrations and the disappointments of the past quarter-century was The Heritage Foundation. No matter the lasting impact of Ronald Reagan, the rise and fall of George H. W. Bush, the resilience of Bill Clinton, the hubris of Newt Gingrich, the disappointment of Bob Dole, the vagaries of the stock market, the fall of the Soviet Union and the rise of Communist China, Heritage was always there—a rock-solid foundation on which the conservative movement rested secure. Little wonder that Heritage grew and grew and grew.

What Ed Feulner did not reveal to the happy celebrants that evening was that he was not certain whether he would be able to see the end of the Leadership for America campaign. The best doctors in America had told him he was going blind in the left eye, and there was little they could do about it.

"I had been through all kinds of examinations at the Wilmer Center at Johns Hopkins," remembers Feulner. "Nobody could diagnose the problem." Retina specialists conducted a series of sensitive measurements while keeping him overnight: "It was very very unpleasant." But they failed to come up with an explanation for the deterioration. Feulner had had severe vision problems from his childhood because of his "egg-shaped" eyeballs, which necessitated heavy correction in his eyeglasses, but he had never experienced anything so life-altering as this.

It was suggested he talk to someone at Columbia University Medical Center in New York City. The specialist there, one of the most respected in the country, had no better luck in his diagnosis. What would he do, Feulner asked himself, if he became blind in the left eye and then the right eye began to go? How could he function as Heritage president? Have someone read documents to him? Learn Braille?

At a trustees' meeting, he mentioned to William E. Simon, whose eyeglasses were as thick as Feulner's, what he faced.

"You're coming out to California, and you're going to Doheny," Simon immediately said.

"Who's Doheny?" asked Feulner.

"It's not who's Doheny," Simon replied. "It's what's Doheny." The famed Doheny Eye Institute is at the University of Southern California.

"I've been to the best," Feulner said. "I've been to Wilmer at Johns Hopkins. They don't know what it is."

"You're going to Doheny," Simon insisted.

Two weeks later, after checking out the Doheny Eye Institute on a new information source called the Internet, Feulner was in Los Angeles at Doheny. After talking to a couple of senior associates, he was turned over to a young Asian female M.D. who "took a couple of looks at my left eye and gave what turned out to be absolutely the correct diagnosis." An oil droplet cataract had developed but had not been spotted because such a cataract is clear rather than yellow like most cataracts.

"Everybody else had been looking through the cataract at the retina," Feulner says, "when the problem wasn't the retina at all—the problem was the thing on the outside, a clear cataract." A senior colleague confirmed the finding of "this wonderful young Asian doctor."

Back at Hopkins, the cataract was removed and a lens was inserted in his left eye. Three years later Feulner developed a cataract in his right eye that was removed and a lens inserted. A couple of weeks later a piggyback lens was placed on top of the first lens in his left eye. "My vision," he says, "from being on the edge of blindness is now better than it has been since I was in first or second grade."

Ed Feulner does not like to talk about it, and to this day few people besides Linda know how close the president of Heritage came to going blind. Even Phil Truluck, his closest colleague, was not aware of the severity of the problem. "He doesn't wear something like that on his sleeve," says Truluck.[36]

CHAPTER 19

9/11

Because 2000 was a presidential election year, nearly everyone in Washington expected Heritage to produce another mammoth *Mandate* study, as it had done since 1980. Instead the foundation did the unexpected: it held a series of seminars on "The Keys to a Successful Presidency" and published the results in a series of four slim paperback books. The public forums were scrupulously nonpartisan and nonideological, examining how past presidents and their administrations had implemented their policy agendas from their first day in office.

They took up such topics as "Running the White House," "Working with Congress to Enact an Agenda," and "The Media." Participants included Leon Panetta, former chief of staff to President Clinton (and later President Barack Obama's secretary of defense); Martin Anderson, President Reagan's first domestic policy adviser; and Zbigniew Brzezinski, President Carter's national security adviser. Among the journalists were conservative columnist Robert Novak and liberal television correspondent Sander Vanocur. The presidential historians were led by Harvard's award-wining Richard Neustadt. Panelist Barry Toiv, former deputy press secretary to President Clinton, said that the Heritage seminars made "an extraordinary contribution to the national dialogue."[1]

"The Keys to a Successful Presidency" was one part of *Mandate for Leadership 2000.* The other parts were *Issues 2000,* a guide to election topics for presidential and congressional candidates; *Priorities for the*

President, which set forth the essential elements of a responsible—that is, conservative—agenda for the next administration; and *A Budget for America.* The director and editor in chief of *Mandate for Leadership 2000* was historian and former congressional aide Alvin S. Felzenberg, who explained that it was the presidential candidates who were prepared to govern "who met with success as president."[2] The incoming Bush administration got off to a quick start, despite the protracted resolution of who won the presidency, because it drew upon the recommendations of *Mandate 2000.* "All indications," reported the *Austin American-Statesman,* "are that the Bush team has been following the [Heritage] advice."[3]

Like his presidential father, President George W. Bush experienced great swings in public approval but in reverse. His father had plummeted from historic heights to near depths, some 60 points, as the country slipped into a recession. In contrast, no modern president was as coolly welcomed and then warmly praised as George W. in his first year. His beginning was overshadowed by the fiercely disputed nature of his victory—narrowly losing the popular vote to Democrat Al Gore but winning the Electoral College by just one vote more than the needed 270.

Ed Feulner liked Bush's inaugural address so much that he devoted his monthly letter to members of the President's Club to it, describing it as "a magnificent statement of principles without a wasted word." He said it emphasized all the elements of Heritage's vision statement—freedom, opportunity, prosperity, and civil society. He liked Bush's cabinet choices. He reported that Robert Rector had been invited to advise the administration about the next phase of welfare reform.

He noted the sharp media criticism of the president for pushing "an ideological agenda," to which he responded: "President Bush has committed the cardinal sin of being a principled conservative." Therefore, said Feulner, "all of us at Heritage are determined to make an extraordinary effort to seize the opportunity now before us."[4]

Widely described—and not only by partisan Democrats—as the man who "stole" the 2000 election, Bush began his presidency by focusing on taxes and education as a reflection of his "compassionate conservatism." Although the president seemed detached and sometimes even uncomfortable in the job, he was receiving favorable public approval ratings in the mid-50s (and higher marks from conservatives) by mid-July. His major accomplishment was a monumental tax cut of $1.6 trillion, although most of the reductions were scheduled for later in the decade.

Heritage backed Bush's tax cuts by building a special tax calculator that allowed users to compare the taxes that would be paid with and without the proposed reductions. The calculator was up and running the same evening of February 27 when Bush addressed Congress about his tax plan.

The foundation also opened a Tax Briefing room on its website to answer frequently asked questions (FAQs) about the tax cut and to "debunk the latest liberal fictions about it," in Feulner's words. When the White House National Economic Council needed a breakdown of the number of people in various income brackets, the Treasury Department couldn't meet its deadline. "The White House called us," said Feulner, "and we delivered the goods in two hours flat."[5]

Heritage's timely contributions in the tax battle were noted by liberals like Ken Baer, Al Gore's senior speechwriter, who woefully wrote: "Advocacy think tanks—the foremost being the conservative Heritage Foundation—work so well because they bring policy, political and communications people together all under one roof. . . . What's left for Democrats? Think tanks without the firepower to match their conservative opponents."[6]

However, by early fall, there were signs—unemployment up, sales down, stagnant economic growth—that the country was close to a recession. But no major politician was ready as yet to use the r-word. After all, America was the strongest, most prosperous nation in the world and probably in human history. If the occupant of the White House did not seem to be destined for greatness, what difference did it make?

• • •

And then on the morning of September 11, 2001, Islamic terrorists hijacked three jet airliners that they smashed into the twin towers of the World Trade Center in New York City and the mammoth Pentagon building in Washington, D.C., killing nearly three thousand Americans. A fourth jet, probably intended for the U.S. Capitol, was diverted by brave passengers, all of whom died when the plane crashed in the Pennsylvania countryside.

In an instant, the political and social detritus of the previous ten months was swept away. Signs of a New America abounded. There was an overnight surge in military enlistments by teens and young adults previously dismissed as spoiled and self-absorbed. Thousands lined up to give blood. Tens of millions of dollars flowed to the Salvation Army and other faith-based organizations. There was a runaway sale of American flags—one store in Chicago sold 25,000 in one day, more than it had in all the past year.

The nation was no longer divided into red and blue (as depicted in a much-reproduced electoral map) but united in red, white, and blue.

President Bush led the way. The day following the attacks, he met with congressional leaders in the White House. As elected leaders, he said, "we [have] a responsibility to stay focused on the threat and fight the war until we . . . prevailed." Later that same day he visited the still-smoldering Pentagon with Defense Secretary Rumsfeld and nodded approvingly when a team of workers atop the building unfurled a giant American flag. "It was a sign of defiance and resolve," he later wrote, "exactly what the nation needed to see."[7]

He set aside September 14 as a National Day of Prayer and Remembrance and delivered a moving yet firm talk at the National Cathedral, saying, "Our responsibility to history is already clear: to answer these attacks and rid the world of evil." In the afternoon he flew to New York City to visit what had once been the Twin Towers.

There he descended into a pit at Ground Zero, where soot-covered rescue workers were searching for survivors. They were exhausted and angry, and many had been crying. One man yelled as the president surveyed the devastation, "Do whatever it takes!"

Standing on a mound of metal that had been a fire truck and speaking into a bullhorn, the president began speaking softly and consolingly. Someone shouted, "We can't hear you." Bush shot back, "I can hear you." There was a cheer, and the president responded with words that echoed down the months and years of his presidency: "I can hear you. The rest of the world hears you. And the people who knocked these buildings down will hear all of us soon!" "The crowd exploded," Bush recalled. "It was a release of energy I had never felt before. They struck up a chant of 'USA, USA, USA.' "[8]

A resolute Bush moved to rally Congress, our overseas allies, and the American public. Congress overwhelmingly authorized an initial $40 billion for a war on terrorism. NATO invoked Article 5 of its charter for the first time ever, declaring that an attack on one member was an attack on all. A tidal wave of patriotism swept America. Bush's approval ratings skyrocketed until they topped 90 percent.

Although not in the rhetorical league of Ronald Reagan or Bill

Clinton, President Bush was able to bring members of Congress to their feet repeatedly in an address to a joint session of Congress eight days after the terrorist attacks. He promised—and would soon deliver on his promise—to oust the radical Taliban government of Afghanistan and put terrorist leader Osama bin Laden on the run.

Unique among Washington think tanks, Heritage was ready for the terrorist attacks. While other research organizations had focused almost exclusively on domestic policy during the 1990s, Heritage continued to emphasize the critical importance of foreign policy and national security in a still-hazardous world, depending on the insights of analysts like senior research fellow James Phillips. In July 2000, fourteen months *before* the terrorist attacks, Phillips warned U.S. policy makers that Osama bin Laden and his Taliban-supported terrorist network had the United States in their sights. "The United States," he wrote, "should focus on uprooting the Taliban regime that sustains [Osama] and others like him."[9] This was the strategy President Bush would adopt.

In the days following 9/11, federal officials, members of Congress and their aides, journalists, state officeholders, and ordinary citizens besieged Heritage with questions: What is the Taliban? Who is Osama bin Laden? Could the attacks have been prevented? What measures should the United States now take to defend itself against Islamic terrorism? A team of specialists provided a unified Heritage response. In the first month after the attacks, analysts delivered twenty research papers, twelve op-ed articles, 250 newspaper and magazine interviews, and 185 radio and television interviews. There were also eight public events on the nature of Islam, the structure of the al-Qaeda network, the political situation in Afghanistan, and military strategies for the war on terrorism. "Heritage's role," Feulner explains, "is not just to get on top of an issue but to take the longer view and think beyond the headlines of the day."[10]

Here is some of what Heritage said:

> *"The President should ask Congress for a declaration of war against any international group and/or state that participated in yesterday's attack.*
>
> *"We need to root out the networks that support terrorists, and not just retaliate against individuals.*
>
> *"If a regime is found to have harbored or supported these terrorists, it should be the goal of U.S. policy to remove that regime from power with any means necessary.*

"We must end our complacency about the missile threat and start building a defense against ballistic missiles, **which inevitably will be the next weapon of choice for terrorist states**" (emphasis in the original).

—KIM R. HOLMES, VICE PRESIDENT OF
FOREIGN AND DEFENSE POLICY STUDIES

"[The United States] must be relentless in hunting down bin Laden and eradicating his terrorist infrastructure in Afghanistan.

"Bin Laden, who has gone into hiding, will be extremely difficult to target with cruise missiles or air strikes. The Pentagon must wage a protracted, unconventional war against such an unconventional enemy.

"The United States should coordinate its efforts to oust the Taliban with states threatened by the Taliban's jihad. . . . It is particularly important to pressure Pakistan, which initially sponsored the Taliban but lost influence over it, to join the effort."

—JAMES PHILLIPS, SENIOR RESEARCH FELLOW
FOR MIDDLE EASTERN AFFAIRS

"The United States is not legally bound to consult the U.N. before responding to these attacks. While it should thank the Secretary General and the Security Council for their condolences for the brutal attacks . . . the United States does not require moral, material, or legal permission to respond to an act of war and should not feel obligated to seek the U.N.'s approval before acting."

—BRETT D. SCHAEFER, JAY KINGHAM FELLOW,
CENTER FOR INTERNATIONAL TRADE AND ECONOMICS,
AND MICHAEL SCARDAVILLE, FOREIGN POLICY ANALYST

"[Heritage's] war against terrorism began way before last week's attacks.

"In 1992, we wrote a Backgrounder Update on the importance of supporting the moderate Afghans against the Islamic radicals, who were bound to export international terrorism, Islamic revolution and drugs if they came to power.

"In 1994, we wrote a Backgrounder analyzing the security threats posed by the rise of transnational pan-Islamic terrorist groups which anticipated the rise of bin Laden.

"In July 2000, we published a lecture by Amb. L. Paul Bremer, *chairman of the National Commission on Terrorism, who discussed the unconventional threats posed by terrorists such as bin Laden.*

"In September 2001, we called for a systematic strategy to up-root terrorist groups from sanctuaries and uproot regimes that give state support for terrorism."

—HERITAGE FOUNDATION *WebMemo* NO. 40

"The U.S. air strikes against targets inside Afghanistan are the be-ginning of the military phase of the campaign against global terror-ism. . . . We need to look beyond Afghanistan and to the next phase of the war. . . . As has been said repeatedly by the President and his team, the war cannot be won by merely destroying bin Laden or the Taliban regime. . . . Our next steps should be:

- *A pledge of humanitarian aid and other material and diplo-matic support to any regime in Afghanistan that forswears ter-rorism, respects the human rights of its people, and agrees to live in peace with its neighbors.*
- *Couple the issue of international terrorism and rogue states ac-quiring weapons of mass destruction.*
- *Begin the diplomatic preparations for a campaign to remove Saddam Hussein from power.*

"The goal of U.S. policy should be to show countries like Iran, Syria, Sudan and Libya that support for terrorism is not only unproduc-tive and unprofitable, but even potentially dangerous."

—KIM R. HOLMES[11]

• • •

There were many milestones in Heritage's first twenty-five years—the coming of Ed Feulner and his unflappable colleague Phil Truluck, Ron-ald Reagan's election and *Mandate for Leadership,* High Frontier and the Strategic Defense Initiative, the dedication of the imposing new headquarters at 214 Massachusetts Avenue, N.E., the fall of the Berlin Wall and working with Boris Yeltsin toward a new Russia, squelching Hillarycare, advising Newt Gingrich and his congressional colleagues on the Contract with America, welfare reform and a North American Free Trade Agreement, launching the *Index of Economic Freedom,* Leadership for America and the first $10 million gift, lifting the board of trustees to a new level with the addition of Clare Boothe Luce, Jeb Bush, Steve Forbes, and Jay Van Andel, the adoption by every other

Washington think tank of Heritage's "rapid response" research, the steady growth of the annual Resource Bank meeting confirming the conservative movement as a major player in policy making from Augusta, Maine, to Sacramento, California.

And then came the terrorist attacks of September 11, 2001. Led by George W. Bush, who saw himself as a wartime president, the nation went on a wartime footing, and Heritage under its president Ed Feulner enlisted for the duration. The foundation calmly, professionally, and comprehensively analyzed the events of 9/11 and recommended what should be done next, verifying it as the go-to think tank in a crisis. Other research organizations stressed long-distance research, but in an emergency, especially in foreign policy and national security, policy makers from the White House to Capitol Hill turned to Heritage. "Heritage has the mind of a think tank and the reflexes of an emergency room," remarked one political observer.[12]

Always careful to let the analysts take the lead, Feulner limited himself to two statements, significant for their content. Three days after the attacks, he counseled the president and the Congress to declare "war on terrorism," arguing that those who planned and carried out the attacks saw themselves not as criminals but "as warriors against the United States, and it would be irresponsible for us not to treat them as such."

The declaration of war and the resulting policy, he said, "should allow for the use of all necessary means, including the use of military force, to destroy the organization(s) responsible for these attacks" and to "remove from power any foreign government that likewise aided and abetted these attacks."

"The world changed on Sept. 11," said Feulner, "and our response should be a sustained, aggressive response to international terrorism, its organizers, proponents, financiers, and supporters. The thousands of Americans who were killed deserve nothing less."[13]

A week later the Heritage president released another strong statement declaring that "now more than ever" the United States should move forward with a missile defense system. He pointed out that regimes like Iraq and North Korea that sponsor and support terrorism "have aggressive ballistic missile programs. Do we wait until the next tragedy to move aggressively against this threat as well?

"We no longer can underestimate the capabilities . . . of those who wish us harm," Feulner said. "We now have learned the hard way that defending America means closing down avenues of attack that once would have seemed the stuff of science fiction."[14]

In a September 17 letter to the foundation's friends and supporters, Ed Feulner reported that the spirit of Heritage was firm and resolute. "You can be certain," he wrote, "that all of our resources are now trained on promoting the only honorable American response to these attacks. . . . I cannot think of another time in my life," said the sixty-year-old Feulner, "when I felt more saddened by an attack against my country, more infuriated by those responsible for it, more proud of my countrymen's patriotic response, nor more determined to stand with them and see this trial through to a noble victory."[15]

· · ·

Ed Feulner and every other person in Washington, perhaps even in the entire United States, remembers where he was that sunny September morning when Islamic terrorists slammed jet planes into the World Trade Center and then the Pentagon, just across the Potomac River from the U.S. Capitol and the Heritage headquarters.

Feulner had flown in from Frankfurt, Germany, the night before, after attending a meeting of the Mont Pelerin Society in Bratislava, the Slovak Republic capital. He was in his eighth-floor office preparing for a nine a.m. meeting when his daughter Emily called from New York City to say that an airplane had just hit one of the Trade Center towers in lower Manhattan.

"I thought it might be an accident," recalls Feulner, and then an assistant came running in to report that a second plane had smashed into the other Trade Center tower. "I turned on the television and quickly realized this was no accident but a deliberate act." Phil Truluck joined him, and they were discussing what to do when Feulner looked out the window and saw a giant plume of black smoke rising behind the U.S. Capitol: the Pentagon had been hit. He could see people streaming out of the Senate Office Buildings a block away. Who knew what the next target might be—perhaps the Capitol? At eleven a.m. they closed down Heritage.

But Feulner and Truluck decided to reopen the next day, Wednesday. "We felt it was important to be here," remembers Truluck. And it was important to consider what to do in the wake of the attacks. There had been discussion about homeland defense at the April board of trustees' meeting, and now Feulner and Truluck turned to Kim Holmes, the man in charge of the foundation's national security studies, and gave him the go-ahead. Feulner and Truluck conferred with Dr.

David Brown, the board chairman, and several other trustees, who said, "Don't worry about the budget. Get on top of this emergency."

The next morning, at eight-thirty a.m., Holmes met in his office with Larry Wortzel, Dan Fisk, and Jim Phillips, all of them with extensive knowledge about terrorism. He had mapped out the idea of a Homeland Defense Task Force months before, and he now set about refashioning it to include the 9/11 attacks and their meaning for America.

Heritage was able to handle the tidal wave of requests for information and produce a 101-page paper about homeland security in just three months because, Holmes explains, "everybody in their different departments rose to the occasion." Second, because "there was no bureaucratic structure we had the freedom to act and quickly. Ed and Phil trusted us." Third, we had "multitalented people like John Hulsman, a talking head of the first order," who knew the issue. "We brought all these forces together and pushed where the need was." "Any other think tank," says Holmes, "would have gone off in all directions. But coordination is natural at Heritage."[16]

Jim Phillips was driving into work and heard the terrible news on the radio. "I was ninety percent sure it was al-Qaeda. They like to do simultaneous operations. They had missed bringing down the Trade Center earlier, and they were back again. Why? It was not just our policies but our values they saw as a threat to their idea of Islam." The rest of the week was a blur of media activity for Phillips, who had never before done so many interviews.

He wrote a paper on the support of al-Qaeda by the Taliban government in Afghanistan, predicting that when the Taliban collapsed, it would happen very quickly. Even he was surprised when Kabul fell before the Twin Towers in New York City stopped smoldering. "It was an incredible feat for the U.S. military. No American died until after the fall of Kabul."[17]

• • •

The Homeland Security Task Force put together by Kim Holmes and his colleagues included three dozen local and state officials, counterterrorism specialists, and former high-ranking military officers. Chaired by Ed Meese and L. Paul Bremer, President Reagan's ambassador-at-large for counterterrorism, the task force published "Defending the American Homeland" in early January 2002. The paper focused on protecting national infrastructure, defending against weapons of mass destruction, strengthening intelligence and law enforcement, and improving military operations.

Among the specific recommendations: (1) enhance the intelligence-gathering and surveillance activities of the nation's seventeen thousand state and local police departments; (2) expand the training offered by the Office of Domestic Preparedness, whose graduates could then help train local police, firefighters, and other "first responders"; (3) relieve the National Guard of some of its overseas duties so it could assume more responsibility for homeland defense; (4) strengthen the visa-approval process; (5) give U.S. air defenses higher priority; and (6) move ahead with deployment of missile defenses.

The task force stressed that homeland defense demanded the coordinated cooperative efforts of a broad range of public institutions—the Border Patrol, Customs Service, Coast Guard, state and local police, fire departments, EMS personnel, the military, hospitals, water authorities—as well as private sector institutions.

"We're talking about transportation. We're talking about water facilities. We're talking about food production," Ed Meese explained in a cable TV interview. "Obviously most of these are in the hands of private-sector organizations. So what we need to do is to have the private sector assist local governments in making an inventory of possible targets as well as working with governments to improve the security of these facilities."[18]

The report outlined which federal agencies should be incorporated into the Department of Homeland Security and which should not be—such as most Defense Department operations, the FBI, the CIA, state and local police, medical personnel, and private businesses. Its central recommendation, obvious and difficult, was that information sharing must be improved. Heritage's solution was the creation of an intelligence "fusion center" that would collect and share information among federal, state, and local agencies.

Almost three-fourths of the Heritage task force's recommendations were ultimately adopted and implemented by the Bush and Obama administrations. Two examples: the U.S. Customs Service for the first time deployed a team of inspectors outside North America to target and screen cargo bound for the United States; and the Transportation Department implemented an action plan to "secure" the Global Positioning System (GPS) of navigational satellites, including working with the Defense Department to apply antijamming technology.

But so large and encompassing a governmental agency as the

Department of Homeland Security called for constant monitoring. In their papers and appearances, Heritage analysts, led by Larry Wortzel and James Carafano, a new senior research fellow, insisted that what was needed was "smarter" homeland security funding rather than ever-increasing appropriations and additional federal mandates.

Critical as it was, terrorism was not Heritage's only priority in 2001. The Bush tax cuts were approved and signed into law by Congress—now divided into a Democrat-controlled Senate and a Republican-led House—with the help of considerable numbers crunching by the Center for Data Analysis. House majority leader Richard Armey (R-TX) told CDA director William Beach that its analysis was "invaluable for its accuracy and timeliness." Representative Patrick Toomey (R-PA), a member of the House Budget Committee (and future U.S. senator), said that "Heritage's voice was particularly credible in the tax debate because of the empirical evidence provided by its Center for Data Analysis."[19]

The president appointed a bipartisan commission to recommend ways to overhaul Social Security, emphasizing personal investment options, a long-held Heritage proposal. As in the past, the foundation's Social Security calculator helped demonstrate the need for change. After entering age, wage history, and other relevant information, the calculator showed how much an individual could expect to receive from Social Security on retirement and compared that with the amount he would get from alternative market investments. Peter Ferrara of George Mason University praised the foundation's work on the rate of return for African Americans as "ground-breaking."[20]

Bush recruited churches and other members of the faith-based community to participate in the war on poverty—a partnership advanced by Stuart Butler years before and later by Joseph Laconte, the William E. Simon Fellow in Religion and a Free Society. Laconte pointed out that after 9/11, many religious charities quickly provided help to those affected by the attacks. "Rarely in the nation's history," he wrote, "have religious communities mobilized with such unity of purpose to help their needy neighbors. And even more rarely have America's political leaders shown such good judgment in promoting their civic influence."[21]

In a move advocated by Heritage and detailed by senior analyst Baker Spring for more than a decade, President Bush announced in December that the United States would withdraw from the 1972 ABM Treaty, effective June 1, 2002. Explained the president: "For the good of peace, we're moving forward with an active program to determine what works and what does not work. In order to do so, we must move beyond the [ABM Treaty], a treaty that was written in a different time, [for] a different enemy."[22]

Responding to a Feulner letter of congratulations about the withdrawal decision, Bush spoke of "a range of threats fundamentally different from those of the Cold War. We are committed to defending against these new threats, including weapons of mass destruction in the hands of terrorists and rogue states." At the same time, he said, we must keep in mind that "Russia is not the Soviet Union, nor is Russia an enemy or a threat." By "forging new relationships with new friends like Russia," he wrote, we would make the world "a safer place for generations to come."[23]

Heritage appreciated the president's positive attitude but was more skeptical than he about forging a "new" relationship with a nation that was led by a former KGB colonel and whose people still lamented a loss of superpower status.

The president confirmed the foundation's special expertise on missile defense. While traveling on Air Force One, Senator Mary Landrieu (D-LA) told the president she wanted to know more about missile defense. His response: call Heritage. Within hours, Landrieu's Washington office had done exactly that.[24]

As it had for more than a quarter-century, Heritage maintained daily personal contact with members of Congress, executive department officials, and other Washington policy makers. In early January, Vice President Mike Franc and his government relations team hosted the regular bipartisan orientation seminar for new members of Congress. They were also careful to seek out the top aides to the new members, to offer their help, and to get their direct telephone numbers.

When President Bush asked the Treasury Department to analyze the impact of his tax cut plan, he was told it would take weeks to get the data. The National Economic Council asked Heritage for help, and the Center for Data Analysis produced the necessary information in a couple of days. A CDA study showed the number of couples and children in each congressional district who would benefit from the bill's proposed $500-per-child tax credit and marriage penalty relief. The data were cited frequently during the debate.

Heritage helped shape an early draft of the Bush administration's education reform proposal—the No Child Left Behind Act—which included vouchers for children in failing schools, regular testing to determine achievement, and removing support for schools unable to improve themselves. Although the final legislation sent to the president was significantly watered down, it established the principle, as Ed Feulner said, that "schools should be held accountable."[25]

Cognizant of Heritage's help in his first year, President Bush took Ed Feulner aside at the White House Christmas party to thank him and the foundation's "great team" for their papers, articles, and other assistance "on the war, on the economic package, and on TPA [Trade Promotion Authority]. We really appreciate it."[26]

• • •

As a firm advocate of federalism, Heritage knows that the best and the brightest are to be found not only in Washington but in the states and cities and towns and neighborhoods of America. Under Vice President Becky Norton Dunlop and her external relations colleagues, the foundation partnered with conservative groups like the Beacon Hill Institute of Boston to create econometric models of the fifty state economies. The models are used to show how state and federal policy changes will affect state growth, employment, capital spending, tax revenues, and other economic variables.

When Colorado governor Bill Owens sought Heritage's help on education, transportation, and "smart growth" issues, the foundation sent senior research fellow Ron Utt to Colorado to meet with the governor's staff and fifty state legislators. In 2001 the state relations staff hosted or participated in thirty-five conferences and briefings in seventeen states.

Heritage has never been about just the immediate policy agenda but has emphasized the enduring principles that buttress the agenda. And so in late 2001, only a few days after 9/11, it published Matthew Spalding's latest book, *The Founder's Almanac: A Practical Guide to the Notable Events, Greatest Leaders and Most Eloquent Words of the American Founding*. There were essays on George Washington, John Adams, Thomas Jefferson, Alexander Hamilton, James Madison, and Benjamin Franklin. A special target of the book was young people. "You have to teach every generation what liberty means," Spalding says.

In the first month, Heritage distributed more than nine thousand copies of what Feulner called a "rich source of information about America's fundamental goodness." He reported that a state leader was using the book for a history course he was designing for high school students and that the National Center for Public Policy Research was sending copies to African American leaders who write op-eds for black-owned newspapers.[27]

Two Heritage programs in particular advanced the objective of teaching young people: the Young Leadership Network, composed of one thousand young professionals in the Washington area, and its year-round intern program, which accepts approximately two hundred college students from the country's best public and private schools. "They're a key component in fulfilling Heritage's mission to build a better America," explains Spalding. "We can't do that without identifying and preparing the next generation of leaders. That's what these programs are all about, creating the team that will lead the Heritage Foundation, the conservative movement, and our country in the decades ahead."[28]

Heritage members liked the sound of that as well as the other things the foundation was doing to preserve and protect liberty. In 2001 they donated $28.4 million, an increase of about half a million dollars over the previous year. Heritage also announced that its headquarters was nearly doubling in size, thanks to the late Thomas Johnson of Pittsburgh, who with several family members owned the sixty-thousand-square-foot apartment building adjacent to the foundation's present quarters. Shortly before Johnson's death in 2000, the family offered to donate 208 Massachusetts Avenue, N.E., valued at $8.5 million, and Heritage gratefully accepted.

The Johnson family's generosity inspired Heritage trustee Douglas Allison and his wife Sarah to make a $2 million gift to convert the top two floors of the new building into a state-of-the-art two-hundred-seat auditorium. "It's like the Louisiana Purchase for us," said Ed Feulner.[29] With renovations costing $9.5 million, the new companion building, including intern housing, additional conference and office space, and the spacious auditorium, was opened in September 2003.

The foundation had long been aware that House members and their staffs found it difficult to come to Heritage—located as it was on the Senate side of the Capitol—when they were in session. Breakfast meetings at the private Capitol Hill Club behind the Longworth House Office Buiding often cost $1,000. Reserving rooms in House office buildings for briefings and seminars often proved difficult and then became almost impossible during the years of House Speaker Nancy Pelosi.

With donations from some 23,500 Heritage members—including

major gifts from Henry Haller, Thomas Colbert, Bernice and William Grewcock, Tony Saliba, Michael Jude, Betty Anderlik, and Bob Zinser—Heritage bought a two-story row house at 227 Pennsylvania Avenue, S.E., only two blocks from the Cannon House Office Building, and added a third floor. The purchase cost plus renovation and upkeep totaled $10.25 million.

Heritage named the second floor for Kim Seung Youn, the chairman and CEO of Hanwha, one of South Korea's largest conglomerates, who made a multimillion-dollar pledge toward the operations of 227. With 9,600 square feet and two large conference rooms, the Pennsylvania Building opened in June 2010 and has become "a conservative hub on the House side," as hoped.[30]

In May 2012 the foundation acquired the Congressional House, a large commercial office building with 36,000 square feet, located at 236 Massachusetts Avenue, N.E., two doors down from Heritage headquarters. The purchase price was $10.5 million. Heritage will honor all existing lease agreements—including the ground-floor Bagels and Baguettes and a Subway—as it considers how best to integrate 236 Massachusetts Avenue into its Building for the Future Project.

"To succeed in the business of marketing ideas," Ed Feulner explains, "you need an idea factory to generate your products. As time has passed, Heritage has repeatedly outgrown its factory." Each new building Heritage acquires, he says, sends a strong signal "to our primary audience on Capitol Hill—the Congress—that we aren't going anywhere. We are here to stay."[31]

• • •

The foundation is always alert to the possibility of promoting its ideas. June 26, 2002, was a slow news day—until a news alert got media manager Khristine Bershers's attention. The federal appeals court in San Francisco had just ruled that school kids in nine states could no longer recite the Pledge of Allegiance, because it contains the phrase "Under God."

Bershers picked up the phone, and ten minutes later Paul Rosenzweig, a senior legal research fellow, was on the Fox News Channel explaining how liberal judges were overruling the Founding Fathers' views on religion. Ten minutes later he was live on CNN. Over the next two weeks, Heritage booked Rosenzweig and other experts on twenty-seven radio programs to critique the Pledge ruling.

In October, Rebecca Hagelin, with seventeen years of experience in managing public affairs and marketing strategies, replaced Herb Berkowitz, who retired after twenty-five exemplary years as Heritage's vice president for communications. Hagelin took the foundation into new fields, such as buying time on the Rush Limbaugh and Sean Hannity national radio programs and going into the documentary film business. "This is why Heritage is a leader among think tanks in mass media," says Feulner. "We treat news as a business—our business."[32]

CHAPTER 20

GETTING AMERICA RIGHT

As Heritage celebrated its thirtieth anniversary and set its 2003 agenda, it focused on tax reform and reduction, health care, and homeland security; at year's end Heritage had made real gains in two of the three areas.

"Reality-based scoring" instead of static scoring was adopted for all tax bills. CDA director Bill Beach explains that "static" scoring assumes the economy will not change in response to tax hikes or cuts. For example, Congress approves a 50 percent increase in the federal gas tax. That means, say proponents of static scoring, that gas tax revenue will be boosted by 50 percent. Here is the simple (but misleading) formula: Gas tax revenue + 50 percent tax increase = 50 percent more gas tax revenue.

But economics isn't just arithmetic, says Beach. People react to change. "If you had to pay 50 percent more in gas taxes," he asks, "would you use as much gas as you do now?" Businesses and people often change their behavior in response to tax hikes and cuts and do so in predictable ways. Tax cuts can spur investment, which spurs hiring, which spurs additional payroll taxes, which leads to economic growth and more money for the government. "It's this dynamic that static scoring misses," says Beach, "and 'reality-based scoring' captures."[1]

"It is a 'wonkish' achievement," Ed Feulner conceded, "but one that can keep real money in taxpayers' pockets for years to come."[2]

• • •

Congressional passage of the new drug benefit program for seniors—Medicare Part D—was an enormous disappointment for Heritage and a triumph of electoral politics over sound public policy. It was the largest expansion of federal entitlements in forty years, and it was approved by a conservative Republican Congress and signed into law by a conservative Republican president.

Stuart Butler sees the Medicare Part D debate as a prime example of Ed Feulner not buckling under the most extreme political pressure and standing firm on a key issue.

Two days before the final House vote on the Medicare prescription drug bill, members of the Republican Study Committee asked Butler and health policy expert Robert Moffit for a closed-door briefing. The congressmen were skeptical about the program with its estimated $400 billion price tag, but they were under relentless pressure from the Republican leadership and the White House to support it. As they had in the past, they turned to Heritage for an objective assessment.

Some fifty members of Congress jammed themselves into the meeting room in the U.S. Capitol, filling every seat. "You could feel the tension," recalls Heritage vice president Mike Franc. The meeting turned into a tense confrontation between House majority leader Tom (The Hammer) DeLay and Heritage. Butler had begun his presentation when a grim-faced DeLay entered. He dismissed Heritage's analysis as wrong and its research as inaccurate. Moffit, who had written the report, flushed red but remained silent. He had checked and rechecked every line of the five-page *WebMemo*, whose reference to "huge unfunded liabilities" would later be validated by the director of the Congressional Budget Office.[3]

DeLay plowed ahead, saying that think tanks like Heritage didn't understand the politics of the issue—Medicare Part D would enable Republicans to get the support of senior citizens in the 2004 elections, perhaps even that of AARP, and allow Republicans to take up Social Security reform. He castigated Heritage for not understanding that "this was the best we can get" regarding Medicare reform. Among the reasons for passage, he said, was that the program would pay for itself—a gross misstatement. He spoke for about ten minutes, and then without acknowledging the presence of the Heritage people or waiting for a response, he stalked out of the room.

In the charged atmosphere, the imperturbable Butler precisely outlined the bill's critical flaws—its enormous unfunded liability and the radical extension of federal authority. "We are not telling you how to vote," he said, "but we believe this is one of the most important votes of your career." "Ask yourself," he said to the congressmen: "Did you come to Washington to approve the greatest expansion of the Great Society since Lyndon Johnson?"

Butler was able to speak with such authority because he had Heritage's and Ed Feulner's unqualified backing. "Ed was rock solid," recalls Butler, despite urgent calls from Karl Rove and other Bush aides. After Butler finished speaking, Moffit answered a few specific questions, summarizing the legislation in one word—*disaster*. "Not only will it subsidize high-income people who don't need the help," he said, "it will displace existing private coverage and bankrupt the children and grandchildren of this country."

Feulner later revealed that Heritage, like the congressmen, had been under extraordinary pressure from the congressional leadership and the White House to endorse the legislation. But, he said, "our role is to provide policy analysis, not political cover."[4]

The Heritage briefing reinforced the resolve of several conservative members to oppose the measure, which infuriated the leadership. When the House first voted, the Medicare bill was defeated 218–216, but only temporarily. Its resurrection began when House Republican leaders, led by Tom DeLay, held the vote open for an unprecedented three hours of nonstop political arm twisting and bullying, including three a.m. telephone calls from President Bush to vacillating lawmakers. In the small hours of Saturday morning, the House leaders finally got enough votes to pass the measure, barely, by 220–215. It was a significant political victory for the administration but was obtained at a significant price.

Conservatives in and out of Washington wondered when and if Leviathan would ever be contained. But true to Feulner's belief that there are no permanent defeats in politics, Heritage continued to seek ways to limit government's growth. The foundation took some comfort from the comments of one congressman, present at the RSC briefing, who said to Moffit, "I just want you to know that we think the world of you guys."[5]

• • •

On November 2, 2002, the Department of Homeland Security was born—a gigantic cabinet-level department that incorporated twenty-two agencies and 180,000 employees ranging from Secret Service agents to airline baggage inspectors. Now what? Washington policy makers asked.

Heritage had been ready with the answer even before 9/11. Since the terrorist attacks, it had produced sixty-five research papers and studies. Just before Christmas 2002, Homeland Security secretary Tom Ridge had a two-hour meeting with Heritage analyst Michael Scardaville and nineteen other think tank experts. Ridge took copious notes and stayed thirty minutes after the meeting's designated end. He asked participants to send him a short summary of their research. Scardaville immediately responded, explaining, "When Tom Ridge asks you for a memo about your work, you start typing."[6]

Following the lead of the Heritage homeland security team, the Bush administration did the following:

- The CIA established the Terrorist Threat Integration Center, an intelligence fusion center first advocated in the foundation's *Defending the American Homeland* and highlighted in the president's 2003 State of the Union address.

- The Department of Homeland Security launched the U.S. VISIT program to better monitor the entries and exits of foreign nationals.

- Homeland Security began integrating the various border security agencies within the department.

Heritage's contributions past and present were acknowledged by a grateful President Bush, who on the foundation's thirtieth anniversary said: "I want to thank you for your decades of leadership in the conservative movement. . . . My administration has benefited from your good work, and so has our country."[7]

But the foundation forcefully opposed what it considered bad legislation like the prescription drug benefit and the bloated farm subsidy bill, prompting David Broder of *The Washington Post*, the dean of political correspondents, to write about Heritage and the Cato Institute:

Their usefulness in Washington stems from their intellectual honesty and their willingness to question conventional wisdom, even

when their friends are in power. A case in point is the bipartisan but
outlandishly expensive farm subsidy bill which . . . Heritage's Stuart
Butler denounced last week as a "shameless example of corporate
pork-barrel spending.". . . In this city, noted for the narrowness of
its intellectual range, it is sometimes wildly unpopular—but abso-
lutely vital—to have institutions that question the fundamental as-
sumptions and occasionally declare that the emperor of the moment
has no clothes.[8]

• • •

Despite disappointments like the above, Heritage liked on balance the
major decisions of the Bush administration, especially in the realm of
foreign policy. The foundation firmly supported the U.S. action against
the radical Taliban regime in Afghanistan. In his September 2002 remarks to a joint session of Congress, the president asked Americans to
prepare for a war against terrorism, "a lengthy campaign unlike any
other we have ever seen." He demanded that the Taliban hand over
Osama bin Laden and the other terrorist leaders to the United States.
It refused.

On October 7, U.S. planes backed by British cruise missiles began
bombing air-defense systems, weapons dumps, and training camps run
by the Taliban and al-Qaeda. After twenty-nine days of bombing, *Time*
reported, Northern Alliance and other anti-Taliban Afghan forces,
equipped with U.S. weapons, mounted a ground offensive, and on November 13, Kabul was liberated. Two weeks later, negotiators gathered
in Bonn, Germany, to fashion a post-Taliban Afghanistan.

On December 16, barely two months after the first bombs fell, the
remaining al-Qaeda forces surrendered, and the war was over. Or was
it? Osama bin Laden was still at large, and an unknown number of
Taliban fighters had escaped capture. A disappointed President Bush
declared, "When the dust clears, we'll find out where he is, and he'll
be brought to justice."[9] But it would be another nine years before the
dust cleared and Bush's successor was able to announce that Osama bin
Laden, the architect of the 9/11 attacks, had received a just punishment.

In March 2003, President Bush carried out the other part of his
two-pronged offensive against terrorism, delivering an ultimatum to
Iraqi leader Saddam Hussein and his two sons that they leave Iraq in
forty-eight hours or the United States and its allies would remove them.
When Saddam refused, Operation Shock and Awe was launched with a
wave of air strikes on selected military and civilian targets in Baghdad.

U.S. troops crossed the border from Kuwait, and a second Iraqi war began.

The president argued that Saddam must be removed because (1) Iraq was building weapons of mass destruction; (2) there were links between Saddam and the al-Qaeda terrorist network; and (3) bringing democracy to a brutal police state was a laudable goal. All three reasons were challenged by opponents of the war, and the first two were proved to be based on faulty evidence.

Unable to secure a UN resolution authorizing the use of force against Saddam (as his father had in the first Iraqi war), George W. Bush declared that such authorization was unnecessary because "we really don't need anybody's permission" to defend U.S. interests.[10]

Heritage agreed. Research fellow Jim Phillips outlined why Saddam should be removed from power, arguing that he was "a serial mass murderer responsible for the deaths of thousands of Iraqis" and had stockpiled, according to UN weapons experts, "more than 600 metric tons of chemical agents such as mustard gas and nerve gas."[11] Research fellow John Hulsman advocated a new strategy for American-European operations, such as case-by-case "coalitions of the willing." Research assistant Carrie Satterlee exposed the financial ties between France, Germany, Russia, and other nations and Saddam's regime. Her paper received national attention. Once the war began, Heritage initiated the Iraq Briefing Room, an online collection of daily news updates, analysis, and commentary edited by the deputy director of the Davis Institute, Helle Dale.

Addressing the question of whether the Iraq war was a just war, conservative icon William F. Buckley, Jr., recipient of Heritage's highest honor, the Clare Boothe Luce Award, listed the criteria: "It had to be that the offense was critical, that the defense was appropriate, that the violence was proportional."

Buckley accepted Bush's descriptions of U.S. action in Afghanistan and Iraq as "proportionate to the offense" and said that the president now had "history itself to point to, to the effect that what needs to be done to target terrorists and their supporters we can do without open, or unspoken, or furtive fear that superseded canons of moral restraint will enfeeble our resolution, and distract our purpose." To put it more simply, the Iraq war was a just war.[12]

Along with other conservatives, Bill Buckley became increasingly skeptical about the conflict—especially after it was established that Iraq had no weapons of mass destruction—and the Bush notion of nation building. "Knocking off Saddam" is one thing, he wrote, "rebuilding Iraq [is] quite another." Nation building is utopian, he said, and therefore unconservative.[13]

However, in a September 2007 column, Buckley asked a critical question then confronting Congress: What would happen in Iraq if America withdrew? He concluded his column with these words: "If the vote were mine, I'd say: Stick it out."[14] His counsel to "stick it out" was Bill Buckley's last public comment about the war.

Heritage had no doubt that staying the course was the right course in Iraq, echoing what Secretary of Defense Donald Rumsfeld told American troops on an April 2003 visit to Baghdad: "You've liberated a people, you've deposed a cruel dictator, and you have ended his threat to free nations." A week later, speaking aboard the USS *Abraham Lincoln* in the Persian Gulf, beneath a giant banner reading "Mission Accomplished," President Bush declared that "major combat operations in Iraq have ended" and "the United States and our allies have prevailed."[15]

But in Iraq as in Afghanistan the fighting was not over, and it remained to be seen how and if the United States and its allies had prevailed.

• • •

But first came the 2004 presidential election. Heritage does not engage in electoral politics, but policy making is materially affected by elections, and the foundation watched with close interest the challenge of Democrat John Kerry and Republican George W. Bush's response.

Kerry won at least one of the three televised presidential debates with Bush and campaigned hard from coast to coast. But his gaffes political and personal were too many, especially his explanation of why he voted against the authorization of $87 billion for postwar Iraq: "I actually did vote for the $87 billion before I voted against it." Commented Bush adviser Karl Rove after the election: "[It was] the gift that kept on giving."[16]

Election Day exit polls revealed that Bush led Kerry among white males, 61–38 percent; married women, 54–45 percent; veterans, 57–42 percent; and once-a-week churchgoers, 58–41 percent. Among those who said moral values were the most important issue, Bush led Kerry 79–18 percent.

In the end, President Bush won the popular vote by 51–48 percent and the electoral vote by a slim margin of 286–251. America remained a red and blue nation, with the president prevailing across the South, the

Midwest, and the Mountain states while the challenger carried almost all of the East and West Coast states. Nevertheless, the elections gave Republicans a rare trifecta of power in the White House, the Senate, and the House of Representatives.

When liberals conducted their postelection analysis, they concluded that what the Left needed was "a Heritage Foundation of our own." They had high hopes for the Center for American Progress (CAP), launched the year before, with John Podesta, President Clinton's former chief of staff, as its president. CAP signaled it would be a different kind of think tank—a "do" tank—by starting at the same time CAP Action Fund, a 501(c)(4) lobbying group.

While flattered by the liberal emulation, Ed Feulner commented that what the Left really needed was "new ideas and a core of well-grounded principles." The Heritage Foundation's success, he said, flowed from "one set of principles—those of the Founding Fathers" and a vision of an America where freedom, opportunity, prosperity, and civil society flourished.[17]

• • •

Throughout 2004, Heritage research helped to preserve American freedom by (1) persuading Congress to reject attempts to cut the core defense budget; (2) helping the Pentagon to divide responsibilities between the U.S. Southern Command and the new Northern Command (delegated to defend North America from attack); (3) preserving vital antiterrorist tools provided by the Patriot Act; and (4) blocking efforts to ratify the proposed Law of the Sea Treaty, which threatened U.S. sovereignty on the high seas.

Senior legal research fellow Paul Rosenzweig, senior researcher James Carafano, and research assistant Alane Kochems wrote *The Patriot Act Reader: Understanding the Law's Role in the Global War on Terrorism,* which debunked many myths about the law, including the misconception that it allows FBI agents to set up roving wiretaps without judicial authorization and to search public library records.

Heritage published its first serious examination of immigration policy with a *Backgrounder* by Edwin Meese III and Matthew Spalding that articulated basic principles of citizenship and rejected the proposals of open-borders advocates. It also released a history of the thirty-year battle of the Right for civil liberties—*Bringing Justice to the People: The Story of the Freedom-Based Public Interest Law Movement.*

The foundation was able to continue its comprehensive analysis of foreign policy because of a $10 million endowment from Heritage trustee Douglas Allison and his wife Sarah, which created the Allison Center for Foreign Policy Studies. Among the center's initial speakers was Secretary of Defense Donald Rumsfeld, who said: "We will have to wage a war of ideas to win the allegiance of a new generation that needs to see that freedom is a vastly better choice than terrorism and hatred."[18]

To help further prosperity at home, Heritage proposed a school choice initiative for some two thousand low-income students in Washington, D.C., and a market-based health insurance plan for residents of the nation's capital.

In the field of taxation, foundation analysts continued to refute liberal charges that the Bush tax cuts were responsible for the record federal deficits. To the contrary, Heritage research showed that the tax cuts had stimulated the economy and led the nation out of recession. From 2003 through 2007, following the second Bush tax cuts, employment rose 8.1 million—an average of 148,000 new jobs each month. The true threat to prosperity was runaway federal spending such as Congress's proposed pork-laden highway bill, which Heritage research helped defeat—saving the U.S. taxpayers some $300 billion.

Research fellow David John paved the way for postelection Social Security reform with three major papers. In his November study, "How to Fix Social Security," John identified three key ingredients for successful reform:

- A voluntary Personal Retirement Accounts (PRA) program, funded in part by existing payroll taxes that would allow all workers a chance to build a significant nest egg.

- A simple, low-cost administrative structure for the PRAs that would use the current payroll tax system and professional investment managers.

- A carefully controlled set of investment options that would include an appropriate default option.

- An adjustment of promised Social Security benefits to sustainable levels.

One member of Congress who expressed strong interest in the Heritage plan was Representative Paul Ryan (R-WI), author of the widely debated Ryan Plan to control federal spending and manage entitlements and the GOP's 2012 vice-presidential nominee.

Heritage urged Congress to adopt a federal Taxpayers' Bill of Rights, modeled after the formula in place in Colorado, that would limit the growth of federal spending to the inflation rate plus population growth. Rather than grow 6.4 percent annually (the average over the past five years), federal spending under the Heritage plan would increase about 3.3 percent annually, saving taxpayers more than $4 trillion in the first decade.

Heritage rallied the conservative movement at the annual Resource Bank—which set a new attendance record with more than six hundred people from forty-five countries—and other venues by defending American values such as traditional marriage, religious freedom, free speech, and open government.

Once more in the middle of the public policy fray was the resolute Robert Rector, who argued that poverty could be reduced by promoting abstinence education and reauthorization of 1996's successful welfare/workfare reforms.

• • •

"Children should be educated and instructed in the principles of freedom," wrote Founder John Adams. It is an injunction that Heritage and Matthew Spalding, director of the B. Kenneth Simon Center for American Studies, take seriously, particularly with regard to foundational documents like the U.S. Constitution.

In 2004, Spalding finished editing a multiyear project—*The Heritage Guide to the Constitution,* containing 180 essays by 110 of the nation's constitutional experts and scholars. It was the first examination of each and every line of the Constitution since Joseph Story's definitive study in the middle of the nineteenth century. The need for the *Heritage Guide* was proven by its becoming a bestseller (at 450-plus pages) with more than forty thousand copies sold and its status as a required textbook at many of the nation's law schools. In 2012, Heritage released an online edition of the *Heritage Guide*; in the first month, it had nearly forty thousand visitors.

Always alert to the latest technology, Heritage adjusted quickly to the Internet, and more than 4.6 million people visited Heritage.org in 2004. Its *Daily Briefing* became a full-blown blog, attracting more than 100,000 readers in its first months. Townhall.org, another Heritage web property, was converted into a separate and more action-oriented entity in 2005. In its last year as a part of Heritage, Townhall.org set records, receiving 41.8 million visits from around the globe, especially to its commentary pages that offered seventy columnists, an online chat room, a virtual bookstore, and links to 114 conservative groups (all members of the fabled "vast right-wing conspiracy").

Members enabled Heritage to meet and surpass its 2004 budget of $37.4 million, the largest in its thirty-one-year history. John Van Kannon and his development team responded with heartfelt thank-yous by letter, e-mail, newsletter, and nearly six hundred face-to-face meetings.

Reflecting the shared vision between Heritage and members was a letter to Ed Feulner from Dean Webster, who said: "No organization more deserves such support as Heritage, and I send along with it my enthusiasm for the work that you and your associates do, day in and day out, in the cause of freedom and good government."[19]

John Von Kannon says that the foundation "got more serious" about direct marketing in 1988, when it hired a young man named Carsten Walter to run the program. The year before Heritage had a total income of $11.5 million, with $3 million coming from some 100,000 members.

By 2004, under Walter's direction, membership had nearly tripled to 272,000. Membership income alone had risen five-fold to $15.4 million. Noting that a Chay McQueen national survey had identified 17.5 million households "who are aligned with The Heritage Foundation mission," Walter argued that Heritage should set a goal of one million members. Feulner, the perpetual optimist, embraced the idea and the goal.[20]

• • •

On July 4, 2004, Ed Feulner was where he always liked to be—on the beach at Bethany, happily overdecorating the Feulner house with American flags and lots of red, white, and blue bunting. He looked forward to watching the annual tiny parade through the town along with Linda, E.J. and his wife Wendy, Emily and her husband Christian, and little Elizabeth Jane Feulner, the first grandchild. In a couple of years, Elizabeth would be joined by Sara Wade Feulner and William Barrett Lown.

In the summers to come, Grandpa would lead the three grandchildren down to the beach, where he would teach them to dive through the waves, build intriguing sand castles, and fly colored kites. "The beach puts everything in perspective for Ed," says Linda. "It's made us close to the grandkids and vice versa. We all love it, and it's good for him."[21]

The beach is also a good place to recover from surgery. During Ed's annual physical in 2004, they discovered a malignant prostate. At first, says Linda, he was shocked but was reassured when his doctors said they had caught it in time. Since the operation, there has been no recurrence of cancer. As Feulner likes to say, "Don't worry until there's something to worry about."[22]

At work, although not a worrywart, he expects to be apprised of everything, large and small, that affects Heritage and the conservative movement. If Frieda or Dorothy at the reception desk is home sick, he wants to know. If another think tank president is having problems with his board, he wants to know the details. If there is tension within the House leadership, he expects to be kept informed because, as his former chief of staff Derrick Morgan says, "he is a creature of the Hill. You can see him drawing energy from meeting with members of Congress. He sympathizes with them, he understands them." But no matter how busy he is, or how crowded his schedule might be, he finds time to talk informally with his chief of staff or his research assistant or his intern, "training them up to carry out conservative ideals."[23]

• • •

The foundation opened 2006 with the launch of a center named in honor of a political leader second only to Ronald Reagan in Heritage's eyes—former British prime minister Margaret Thatcher. Funded with a $3 million grant from the Thatcher Foundation and $6 million in additional gifts from Heritage members, the Margaret Thatcher Center for Freedom is committed to examining and promoting U.S.-British relations as well as America's strategic role in Europe. Nile Gardiner, a former foreign policy adviser and researcher to Thatcher, was named the center's director. Later that year Lady Thatcher visited Heritage, causing Ed Feulner to say, "The walk is a little slower, the talk is a little softer, but the magic is still there."[24]

Meanwhile in 2006, five thousand miles from Washington, a group of Hawaiians were pushing the Native Hawaiian Government bill that would have created a subgovernment in Hawaii based on race and ethnicity. Heritage analysts produced *WebMemos* and hosted public events that exposed the bill as "a piece of politically correct humbug." Several U.S. senators, reported Feulner, credited Heritage as "instrumental" in defeating the bill.

Much of what Heritage does on Capitol Hill is done beneath the waterline, in face-to-face meetings with members of Congress and their staff. In just the first three months of 2006, for example, foundation experts held briefings for four senators, twenty-eight congressmen, forty-four House aides, and fifty-five Senate staffers. Heritage analysts also testified twelve times before congressional committees and commissions.

Major policy addresses at Heritage were delivered by Vice President Dick Cheney, Secretary of State Condoleezza Rice, Homeland Security secretary Michael Chertoff, the prime minister of Pakistan, and the foreign minister of Afghanistan (although not on the same day). The annual Conservative Members Retreat in Baltimore drew a record sixty-six members of Congress, who heard such speakers as columnist George Will, prison evangelist Chuck Colson, and former House Speaker Newt Gingrich.

Heritage set a record for op-ed article placements in major outlets—logging 1,089 on high-traffic websites and in newspapers with circulation of more than 50,000. The foundation's clipping service recorded 7,750 Heritage stories, representing publications with a combined circulation of nearly 800 million readers.

"When you consider our television and radio appearances," said Ed Feulner, "our research publications, our briefings with members of Congress, our lectures and panel discussions, the speeches that major political figures deliver at Heritage, and the extent to which we multiply all of these through out Internet sites, you find a volume of conservative communications that truly boggles the mind."[25]

Heritage also carefully monitored the Hill's legislative actions. In May, the Senate opened hearings on an immigration reform bill supported by the administration. While senators debated the proposal, Robert Rector did something most of them had not done—read the bill. He concluded the bill would fling wide the border gates, potentially admitting a staggering 103 million immigrants over the next twenty years. Aside from the huge budget costs, Rector said, "the character of the nation would differ dramatically from what exists today."[26]

Rector's startling research hit Capitol Hill like a "perfectly timed statistical bomb," wrote the *San Francisco Chronicle,* placing the bill's sponsors on the defensive. Rector and Senator Jeff Sessions (R-AL) held two packed news conferences. News media quoted Rector and his "103 million immigrant" figure night and day. Proponents changed the immigration cap to "just" 60 million, but thanks to Heritage research and marketing, opponents ensured that the legislation did not go beyond the Senate.

• • •

Ed Feulner believes deeply in the power of books, recalling what Abraham Lincoln wrote: "The things I want to know are in books." Feulner's life had been fundamentally changed by what he read at Regis College, transforming him into a thinking not just an instinctive conservative. So when a New York publisher asked him to coauthor (along with Townhall chairman Doug Wilson) a book on how to get America back on track, he quickly agreed.

Bill Buckley, author of more than fifty books, called *Getting America Right* "a unique, insightful handbook on civil obligations good for the next fifty years." Margaret Thatcher said, "It reminds us that the greatest nations are those rooted in a moral code of belief, from which policy and action subsequently flow."[27]

To hold the government accountable, Feulner and Wilson suggested six practical questions that every citizen and every policy maker should ask about every government action.

"Is it the government's business?" What Americans want, the authors said, is the least possible involvement, with federal action kept within the limits of constitutional authority. "We believe," they wrote, "that local solutions are the best solutions in all forms of public activity but particularly in education, transportation, and welfare reform."

"Does it promote self-reliance?" Individual freedom and self-reliance must be promoted to wean people from the government trough. America's future "depends on reducing the demand side of government."

"Is it responsible?" The American people must demand greater transparency in government, clear and fair rules and regulations, and mechanisms that help legislators and bureaucrats control their "irresponsible impulses."

"Does it make America more prosperous?" America must preserve and strengthen its economic freedom by lightening the tax and regulation burdens, abolishing trade barriers, and forming a global alliance of countries committed to free trade.

"Does it make us safe?" American must contain rogue nations, using diplomacy when possible but recognizing "our military strength might have to be called into play to deter aggression and keep rogue nations from threatening us and our neighbors."

"Does it unify us?" The unity we once prized and encouraged our immigrants to embrace "is eroding in a dangerous trend toward cultural relativism and the cult of diversity that threaten our very survival."

In the epilogue, Feulner urged Americans to participate more actively in the American experiment, to breathe new life into "the Founders' constitutional vision," and to seek practical solutions based on the ideas that have molded America for over two hundred years. He was optimistic about the future, but only if citizens summoned the courage to act.

"It's up to us," he wrote. "This is our republic to cherish and nourish. Let's get to work."[28]

Feulner took his own advice and set to work promoting the book with a national book tour in the spring of 2006 that led him to thirty cities over the next month. Accompanying him was Michael Needham, his new chief of staff and the future head of the foundation's lobbying affiliate. In addition to book-signing events, Feulner met with Heritage members and kept up with Heritage via the Internet and the telephone.

While on the road, the sixty-four-year-old foundation president and his twenty-four-year-old chief of staff intently discussed the central issues of the day, including Social Security, the mounting congressional earmarks, and the nomination of Harriet Miers to the Supreme Court. President Bush was "trying to do a bold thing in terms of reforming Social Security," says Needham, "but in the political environment then you couldn't have an adult conversation about Social Security."

As for earmarks, he remarks, "you saw the waste that was going on in Washington and the frustration that people had with the Republican Congress, with Tom DeLay saying there's no fat left in the federal government." What he really meant was that "every single dime in the federal budget had been spoken for by some special interest."

The Harriet Miers nomination highlighted what Ed Meese had been saying for years about the true meaning of the Constitution. A Supreme Court nomination, says Needham, "is not about outcomes, how a justice may vote on this or that issue, but his or her fidelity to the Constitution. Even if Harriet Miers voted the right way on all of the allegedly key cases, she wasn't doing it because of a deep grappling with the constitutional issues that the conservative movement had built up."

The conversations helped Mike Needham to crystallize his thinking about the need for a principle-driven organization that can tell a conservative politician who is used to being told he's a 100 percent conservative, "Sorry but we score you at 70 percent." "I think it would be incredibly dishonest for us," he says, "for us to do a scorecard that says everybody in Congress gets 100 percent this year just because they're doing the best they can."[29]

Back in his Heritage office after the book tour—which helped make *Getting America Right* a *New York Times* bestseller—Feulner described to colleagues the widespread public frustration he had encountered everywhere he traveled. They're very unhappy with the direction of the country, he said, and may very well take out their frustration on the party in power—the Republicans.

CHAPTER 21

LEADERSHIP FOR AMERICA

Almost two years before the 2006 elections, in which voters decisively rejected Republicans and gave Democrats control of the U.S. Congress for the first time in over a decade, GOP political strategist Karl Rove issued a warning:

> The GOP's progress during the last four decades is a stunning political achievement. But it is also a cautionary tale of what happens to a dominant party . . . when its thinking becomes ossified, when its energy begins to drain, when an entitlement mentality takes over, and when political power becomes an end in itself rather than a means to achieve the common good.[1]

Republicans failed to heed Rove on all counts and, in Ed Feulner's words, turned their stunning achievement of 1994 into a "stunning political defeat." Writing after the November 2006 elections, Feulner said that too many congressional conservatives forgot they were conservatives and remembered only that they had a majority. They lost their energy and their commitment to principled politics. "They settled into the comfortable mentality of entitlement. And now they've paid the price."

And they deserved to, said Feulner, who proceeded to list explicitly what congressional Republicans had failed to do.

- They did not tackle immigration reform. The best they could do was to authorize a fence along one-third of the U.S.-Mexico border.

- When President Bush stumped the nation in the first half of 2005 promoting Individual Retirement Accounts (IRAs) under Social Security, congressional Republicans sat on their hands and waited for him to close the deal with the American public. "Backing him up was too much of a risky scheme for them," Feulner lamented. Instead, they passed a Medicare drug benefit that will leave future generations with *trillions* of dollars in liabilities.

- In the twelve years since they achieved a congressional majority, "Republicans have more than *doubled* the size of the federal government."[2]

The Heritage president stressed that the election was a defeat not for conservatism but for "once-upon-a-time conservatives" who had abandoned conservatism. And they did so when most Americans remained conservative in their beliefs and in their practices.

Postelection polls showed that 59 percent of Americans still wanted smaller government. Eighty-five percent belonged to a church or synagogue. Over the last thirty years, the number of adults 18–25 who described themselves as conservative increased 143 percent. Feulner quoted Representative Mike Pence of Indiana, who told his colleagues, "We did not lose our majority, we lost our way. . . . The American people did not quit on the Contract with America, we did."[3]

It remained for conservatives, said Feulner, to follow the example of Ronald Reagan, who, after he lost the 1976 battle for the presidential nomination to Gerald Ford, did not quit but quietly resolved to run again. Reagan had recalled the words of an old Scottish ballad:

I am wounded, but I am not slain.
I shall lay me down and bleed awhile;
Then I shall rise and fight again.[4]

The November 2006 election, Feulner said, showed that political parties will forget their constituents and betray their principles. Not so

Heritage, Feulner asserted. Think tanks like Heritage have thrived precisely "because conservatives want to know that they can trust someone to stand by their principles and advance the cause."[5]

Liberals offered a different explanation for the Republican defeat. Senator Chuck Schumer (D-NY) said it meant that "we're about at the tail end of the Ronald Reagan era, where his *ideas* . . . have just lost steam, lost resonance." By "resonance," Feulner explained, Schumer meant "relevance." That is, Reagan's ideas were no longer applicable to America's problems. But that would be like saying, Feulner argued, "that the *ideas* of the Founding Fathers were no longer relevant."

And that would mean that the Constitution was no longer relevant, free enterprise was no longer relevant, traditional American values were no longer relevant. That was not only wrong but dangerous, for what would take the place of conservative ideas and principles? Liberal ideas like the welfare state, a "living" Constitution, secular humanism, U.S. servicemen serving under a UN flag?

"Conservatives aren't lacking in ideas and principles," Feulner insisted. "We don't need redefining. What *is* lacking is intellectual and political leadership—*inspiring* and *energizing* leadership."[6]

• • •

At age sixty-five, Feulner was conscious that the time for him to step down was not too far away, perhaps when he turned seventy. He wanted to leave Heritage in the strongest possible condition for his successor and enable him to further the foundation's vision for America regardless of who was in the White House or who controlled the Congress. The need to act dramatically was compounded by the Democrats' impressive 2006 victory and what it might portend for the 2008 elections.

At the December 2006 board of trustees meeting, Feulner introduced the idea of a major new campaign by the foundation. He said flatly, "We cannot count on politicians or universities to address America's problems—it is time for Heritage to leap forward to another level." He asked permission to outline what he and other senior managers had in mind at the next board meeting in the coming spring.

In April 2007 an ebullient Feulner proposed to the Heritage board of trustees a national campaign—Leadership for America—"to save America from its future. To get our country back on course, we believe it is time to recall the nation to its First Principles." The latter phrase was significant—Heritage intended to base the proposed campaign on permanent things like the Declaration of Independence and the Constitution, not the transitory musings of *The Washington Post* or *The New York Times*.

This is bigger than anything we've tried before, he told the board, bigger than anything any think tank has tried before. He referred to his remarks to the Reform Club in London earlier in the year. "It is possible to win the war of ideas," he had said, "but fail to change the way the world works. Ideas do have consequences. But ideas are not self-implementing or self-sustaining—they must be linked to action."[7]

He informed the trustees he had asked senior management to think about what they wanted America to look like ten years from now and what they wanted Heritage to have accomplished in ten years. Why ten years? Because it was five times the average congressman's time horizon; longer than any president's vision; and beyond the time that much of senior management and many of the trustees would still be at Heritage. Think of this campaign, he said to his colleagues, "as our legacy to Heritage, our legacy to America."[8]

To dramatically change America, the senior management team had come up with eight "big ideas" ranging from "restore the family to its central role in civil society" to "advance American leadership and freedom in the world." The list would later be expanded to ten "initiatives" regarding the country's most critical problems.

What might America look like if Heritage did nothing? Feulner asked the board.

If we do nothing about entitlements, he said, "our tax rates will look like those of France or Germany." If we continue on the current spending trajectory, "the entire U.S. budget will go to pay for the big three—Medicare, Medicaid, and Social Security." Our military will be "hollowed out" from overuse and underfunding. The world will become "a much more dangerous place if we allow terrorist states to develop nuclear weapons."

"I will leave it for you to imagine what America will look like in 20 years," Feulner said, "if we don't secure our borders or if the decay of the family continues."

Therefore, he said, "we must renew our will—we must reestablish America's sense of greatness—and we must convince more Americans than ever before of the rightness of our cause."[9]

The Washington of 2007 is vastly different from the Washington of 1973, he said, when Heritage came on the scene. Then, conservative Members of Congress—a minority within a minority party—had convictions, "but they needed the facts, information, and data. Today, conservative Members of Congress have the information, but too often they seem to lack the will to do the right thing."

We need a campaign, Feulner said, "that will re-teach the principles of the Founders to the American people and then encourage principled Americans to demand that their government live by those principles. . . . It is no longer enough to provide policymakers with the *right* ideas," he argued, "*they must be encouraged by the public to implement them*" (emphasis added).

This was said three years before CNBC commentator Rick Santelli's impassioned call for a new "tea party" that gave birth to a political movement against uncontrolled federal spending and debt that produced the tsunami-like results of the 2010 elections.

It is no longer enough, Ed Feulner emphasized to the Heritage board of trustees, "to take our research directly to Congress. We must send our message directly to the American people so that *they* will demand Leadership for America rather than interest group politics or a congressional reaction to the latest news cycle.

"Only by engaging, educating and mobilizing a larger majority of America's citizens," he said, "can we hope to be successful in this endeavor."[10]

The use of the word *mobilizing* anticipated Heritage's decision four years later to form for the first time in its history a 501(c)(4) lobbying group—Heritage Action for America.

What will a Leadership for America campaign require? asked Feulner. It will take more of what the foundation was already doing; it will take restructuring; it will take new strategies such as "virtual think tanks"; it will take new products as revolutionary as the *Backgrounder* was in 1977 and new communications techniques to shape the national debate.

It will take innovation, planning, brainpower, and yes, money, he said. But we're ready to embark upon this campaign "to give our children and grandchildren a better America, one where freedom, opportunity, prosperity and civil society flourish."

He asked for and received the approval of the board of trustees to proceed.[11]

• • •

Leadership for America puzzled some Heritage staffers. The foundation was doing fine, membership was up, income steadily increased year by year, members of Congress looked to Heritage for legislative analysis, talk radio and cable news channels featured Heritage experts night and day, even liberals admitted that Heritage was one of the most influential think tanks in Washington. Why mess with success?

That attitude was why Feulner and his senior colleagues decided to initiate Leadership for America. They had read and absorbed the opening lines of Heritage trustee Robert Herbold's cautionary book, *Seduced by Success:*

> *When leaders of organizations experience meaningful levels of success or periods of stability, they tend to believe that they are entitled to continued success into the future. In many cases, managers become complacent, comfortable, and mediocre when, in fact, they should be building on all the things they have done well in the past. They should be probing to uncover fresh approaches, improving their products and services, and staying lean and agile. . . .*
>
> *Success . . . can destroy an organization's or an individual's ability to understand the need for change and can also destroy the motivation to creatively attack the status quo.*[12]

Feulner and the other senior managers were unwilling to settle into a plush-lined rut. They determined to increase the foundation's influence, strengthen the conservative movement, and lead the nation in a more conservative direction despite the Democratic Congress and its liberal leadership. That meant that Heritage would have to go outside Washington in a far more aggressive way to create a more receptive climate for conservative ideas and develop grassroots leadership committed to First Principles.

Starting in 2008, Heritage bought time at an annual cost of $2.5 million on the radio programs of Sean Hannity (weekly audience of 12.5 million) and Laura Ingraham (audience of 5 million) under the theme, "What Would Reagan Do?" Listeners were reminded of how the fortieth president had governed through low taxes, a strong national defense, traditional values, free markets, and individual freedom and responsibility. The campaign increased Heritage's Web traffic by almost 90 percent. In November alone one million unique visitors came to Heritage.org—an unprecedented volume of traffic for a think tank.

Listeners were invited to ask for a free pocket copy of the Declaration of Independence and the U.S. Constitution. In the first week, the foundation mailed forty thousand copies and a total of 1.5 million for the year. Over the next five years, Heritage distributed more than four million copies of the Constitution.

In 2009, Heritage launched a new radio campaign with talkmeister Rush Limbaugh (weekly audience, fifteen million) and Sean Hannity. The two conservatives invited their millions of listeners to visit a new site—AskHeritage.org—that outlined innovative, Reagan-style solutions for the issues of the day. Heritage Web traffic soared. The foundation's principal website, Heritage.org, logged a total of 9.3 million unique visitors in 2009, a 22 percent increase over the previous year. Traffic at the for-members-only website, MyHeritage.org, logged 1.03 million visitors, nearly doubling the previous year's total. These numbers exceeded the total Web traffic of the next three think tanks—Brookings, AEI, and Cato—combined.

• • •

The Democratic Congress, headed by House Speaker Nancy Pelosi, presented so many targets of opportunity in 2007 and 2008 that Heritage analysts hardly knew where to begin. They calculated that in forty years, Medicare, Medicaid, Social Security, and the interest on the national debt would consume the entire U.S. budget—unless Congress, in concert with the executive branch, overhauled the programs. That was the arresting theme of the "Fiscal Wake-Up Tour," a national series of events organized by the liberal Concord Coalition and involving Heritage, the Brookings Institution, and other policy groups along with David M. Walker, the U.S. comptroller general. Led by Heritage vice president Stuart Butler and Brookings's senior fellow Alice Rivlin, the tour visited nineteen cities in 2007, warning community leaders, journalists, college students, and ordinary citizens about "the tidal wave of red ink that threatens to swamp future generations."

At year's end, Heritage kicked off a new phase of the program, "the Conservative Fiscal Wake-Up Tour," with Alison Acosta Fraser, the director of the Thomas A. Roe Institute for Economic Policy, and other speakers stressing the need to get America's fiscal house in order without raising taxes. "We got ourselves into this mess by over-spending and over-promising," Fraser said. "Over-taxing will only compound the problems, not solve them."[13]

In 2008, Heritage began producing a series of film documentaries, starting with *33 Minutes: Protecting America in the New Missile Age*. Conceived by communications vice president Rebecca Hagelin, the film tells the story of the nuclear threat currently posed by hostile nations and rogue dictators. It stresses two sobering facts: no matter where an enemy may launch a missile from, it will strike a U.S. target in thirty-three minutes or less, and the United States has no comprehensive defensive system to knock down incoming missiles.

The foundation expanded its network of Community Committees, started in 2006, to eight communities: Atlanta, Chicago, Dallas/Fort Worth, Minneapolis/St. Paul, New York City, Omaha, Southern California, and Tucson. Made up of civic and business leaders, the committees recruited new members, reached out to young people, developed programs and events, met with local and state officials, contacted local media, and educated people about Heritage research and the First Principles of America's Founders—all without a single copy of Saul Alinsky's *Rules for Radicals*.

The committees garnered considerable local publicity and brought in new members, but they were expensive and required extensive administration by the Heritage staff in Washington. In 2012 it was decided to close them and use Heritage Action and its Sentinel program to hold more than twenty local events to "educate" members of Congress about issues.

Heritage set a goal of one million members by 2017 "so that no Member of Congress can ignore the voices of Heritage Foundation constituents back home." Membership grew to 320,000 in 2007 and to 400,000 by the end of 2008. Income experienced similar remarkable growth, reaching $45.6 million in 2007 and $52.3 million in 2008, almost double what it had been in 2000. By the end of 2012, Heritage had close to 600,000 members and an expected income of $75 million.

During the late 2000s, there was a direct correlation between the foundation's rapid ascent and the Republicans' rapid descent. Conservatives, feeling abandoned by the GOP, sought Heritage for reassurance that all was not lost, America's best days were not behind her, and Heritage led by Ed Feulner could save the movement and the nation.

The foundation's most enduring response was to restructure Heritage around the ten initiatives of Leadership for America. While other think tanks like AEI give their analysts nearly free rein to research and write what they want, Heritage selects the issues to be examined and then gives its analysts the freedom to find and develop the conservative arguments for and against possible solutions. Leadership for America was a logical extension of the top-down approach and added something—from now on, analysts would work across disciplines and departments. Heritage would follow a horizontal rather than a vertical model. Except in rare cases, there would be no more silos where analysts discussed their research only with their immediate boss or a senior manager.

The ten LFA initiatives were:

Revive a broad understanding and respect for constitutional principles.

Return the judiciary to its constitutional role and strengthen the rule of law.

Restore the permanent institutions of religion and family.

Provide future generations with educational choice.

Replace the culture of entitlement with the culture of mutual responsibility.

Ensure that every American has freedom of choice in health care.

Provide energy and environmental solutions to keep America safe, free, and prosperous.

Make federal taxes low, flat, simple, and fair—and unleash the pent-up energies of America's entrepreneurs.

Protect America and Americans from freedom's enemies.

Restore the United States as a respected and influential world leader.[14]

All ten initiatives were important, but one was *more* important—the revival of a deep understanding of and respect for the Constitution and the founding principles of the American Revolution, for what constitutional scholar Matthew Spalding called "first principles."

Genevieve Wood, with nearly twenty years of experience in mass communications, was promoted to vice president of strategic operations and placed in charge of Leadership for America. She sees LFA as drawing together all the parts of Heritage and providing a united conservative vision that will "keep the country strong and moving ahead." "Success comes when you are prepared for opportunity," says Wood, who regards LFA as the way to prepare Heritage for whatever the future holds.[15]

In a letter to Heritage members outlining Leadership for America, Ed Feulner promised that "however much your elected 'leaders' might let you down, your Heritage Foundation will never forget and never forsake the conservative principles we share."[16]

• • •

Understanding that the support of congressional conservatives for Leadership for America was essential, Feulner addressed in August 2007 members of the Conservative Opportunity Society, a group formed by Jack Kemp, Newt Gingrich, and other congressmen, including a young John Boehner in the 1970s. Knute Rockne would have approved Feulner's fighting spirit.

He began by asking, "Why is a party that looked so stable in 2005 now the minority in both the House and Senate? I believe the answer is much simpler than some might have you believe. Republicans are now the minority party because they became distracted by the need to govern and get reelected, which in turn moved them away from that solid base of conservative ideals."

This is the time to return to basics, he said, a time to return to the conservative ideals that a majority of Americans have proven again and again they overwhelmingly support. If the Republican Party wants to recapture the confidence of this nation, he said, "it needs to return to what our country's founding principles promote: an America where freedom, opportunity, prosperity, and civil society flourish. Some of you may recognize that as our Heritage mission statement."

But, Feulner insisted, "I believe it can serve as much more than as a motivational phrase for The Heritage Foundation"—it can serve as a platform for congressional action on a wide variety of issues.[17]

Citizens should be "free from a burdensome federal government" that dictates how and where a large portion of their paycheck is spent. There should be "equal opportunity for all, not equal outcomes for all." Societies that embrace free markets, low taxes, and deregulation will prosper. Conversely, nations that move toward a centralized economy, high tax rates, and more government regulations and interference "will invariably experience stagnation and poverty." A civil American society is dependent "on traditional American values and individual responsibility."

Freedom, opportunity, prosperity, and civil society are America's pillars, Feulner said. Remove any one of the four, and the others will topple. "It is only when all of them stand firmly together that they are able to support the weight of a free society like ours."

The Democrats' victory in November 2006 could be reversed, he insisted, but only "if the Republican Party returns to its core conservative principles and continues to focus the debate on the reckless liberal policies the [Democratic] majority is trying to force through Congress."[18]

The congressmen present assured the Heritage president of their strong support. Feulner took them at their word but knew that Heritage would have to keep reminding them of their pledge and convincing them that the ideas of Leadership for America were the right ideas for America's future—and their own.

A month later Ed Feulner was on the *Sea Dream II* in the middle of the Aegean Sea giving trustees and major donors an update on LFA and pointing out that when the campaign was finished, Heritage would be almost half a century old. Increasingly he and Phil were being asked, "What happens when you and Phil and John retire?"

Acknowledging that keeping faith with donors is essential, Feulner described the steps being taken regarding donor intent. For the first time since 1973, when the foundation was established, the bylaws were amended to include both the vision and the mission statements. Second, present board members would discuss with prospective board members their commitment to Heritage's founding principles. Third, once a year at the dinner preceding a board meeting there would be a discussion of the vision and mission of the foundation.

"We are going to do everything an organization can do," Feulner said, "to recommit Heritage to those principles on which we were founded."[19] Left unsaid was the history of once-conservative foundations like MacArthur and Pew that had strayed far from the original intent of their founders.

Taking up LFA, Feulner reminded everyone that Thomas A. (Tom) Saunders III, who had joined the board in 2005, had agreed to become the general chairman of the Leadership for America campaign. Saunders's commitment and energy so impressed the trustees that in 2009 they elected him chairman of the board.

In less than two weeks, Feulner informed board members, senior managers would hold their annual three-day retreat on the Eastern Shore of Maryland, where they would focus on ways to keep LFA on track, such as making sure silos were broken down, bureaucracy did not take over, and Heritage remained "as lean and mean and principled as ever."

So, he asked, what do we want America to look like in 2017, when LFA comes to a close?

- We want to have "a fully deployed missile defense system."

- We want the freest economy in the world—"the best place in the world for entrepreneurs."

- We want "a simpler, fairer, flatter income tax system."

- We want regulation to be "slowed down, stopped and rolled back."

He promised that Heritage would measure not just outputs—how many *Backgrounders* and *WebMemos*, how many conferences, how many radio-TV-cable interviews—but outcomes: "What actually happened as a result of the LFA initiatives? What has changed?"

To bring about real change, Feulner said, they would have to reach not just the 535 members of the House and Senate but the people who influence them, "so that in Denver or Hartford or wherever, we have a cadre of people who can impact Congress and congressional staffs directly." Heritage would have to build what he called an "infrastructure of influence." He was confident it could be done: in fact, Heritage had been building such an infrastructure from the beginning.[20]

Looking back on his thirty years as a Heritage trustee and fifteen years as board chairman, Dr. David Brown says he is proud of the foundation's critical role in creating the network of state think tanks—an idea pushed hard by fellow trustee Tom Roe. He also believes that Heritage is responsible, in part, for the Tea Party movement, because the foundation has pursued a "grassroots strategy" from the beginning.

One of Heritage's "crucial steps" in communications was taking over Townhall. "That was a tough decision Ed and I wrestled with," recalls Dr. Brown. "It was a leap of faith. But we felt it was needed" by the conservative movement. Today Townhall is a powerhouse of conservative communications with an incredible eight hundred-plus columnists and contributors, more than any other website in America (and probably the world).

Ed Feulner, says Dr. Brown, "is the persona of Heritage, the leader who we tried to help every way we could. He runs a tight ship, well organized on sound business principles. He doesn't have many flaws, or we wouldn't be where we are. He's an All-American quarterback."

Brown is an enthusiastic supporter of Heritage Action, which has made a real difference in a short time with its scorecard and issue ads in a congressman's district.

Deeply concerned about the direction of the country under President Obama, he says, "I shudder to think what if Heritage had not existed." On the other hand, he describes the president as "the best development officer we have ever had—people are coming forward who never before have done so."[21]

• • •

There were two great debates in 2007 and 2008, one political, the other fiscal. The first revolved around the political question "Whom should the Democrats and the Republicans nominate for president?" The second addressed a fiscal crisis that extended from Wall Street to Main Street: "How should the federal government deal with the financial meltdown?"

The Democrats dominated the political debate with the intense contest between the early front-runner and former first lady Hillary Clinton, and Barack Obama, the charismatic African American and first-term U.S. senator from Illinois. Those Democrats who did not have a favorite felt that the party could not lose—they would nominate and elect as president either the first woman or the first African American in American politics. After all, hadn't they just won a great congressional victory in 2006? Despite the worrisome political signs, ten Republican candidates showed up for their party's first presidential debate in New Hampshire in June 2007, almost eighteen months before Election Day 2008, making it the longest race in history.

Obama surprised and then impressed the political establishment by raising more money than anyone else, campaigning for convention votes in the caucus as well as the primary states, and captivating large crowds with his call for fundamental change in Washington and the nation and an end to the Iraq war. On the Republican side, McCain stumbled in the early going and was counted out by voters and donors. But the one-time POW in Vietnam reorganized his campaign and went on to win a crucial South Carolina primary and succeeding contests as Rudy Giuliani, Mike Huckabee, and Mitt Romney all faded.

McCain electrified the Republican convention and conservatives everywhere by selecting as his running mate the beautiful, outspoken, evangelical Alaska governor Sarah Palin. Her acceptance speech, which drew an impressive forty million viewers, mixed humor, pathos, and strong rhetoric.

Calling herself a "hockey mom," she added, "they say the difference between a hockey mom and a pit bull [is] lipstick." The delegates roared with laughter. She proudly said that her nineteen-year-old son Track would shortly deploy to Iraq. The delegates stood and applauded. She said how blessed she and her husband felt when she gave birth in April to their "special needs" son Trig, who was in fact a Downs infant. Convention delegates, led by right-to-life supporters, again rose to their feet. She aimed barbs at the Democratic nominee, pointing out that he had "authored two memoirs but not a single major law or even a reform." There are candidates, she said, "who use change to promote their careers. And then there are those, like John McCain, who use their careers to promote change."[22] As good a communicator as Republicans had seen in many years, Palin was seemingly unfazed by the intense pressure placed on her, not even when her TelePrompTer went black—she kept speaking as though nothing had happened.

Following her speech, a national poll found that 40 percent of Americans believed Sarah Palin was ready to be president. McCain's standing in red states and among conservative Republicans shot up, but a financial bubble based on easy money and ever-rising home prices and sustained by "leverage" was about to burst.

In mid-September, on the day that Lehman Brothers disintegrated, precipitating a financial crisis, McCain was 2 points ahead of Obama. When *The Wall Street Journal* asked voters who was better on taxes, McCain beat his younger, untested opponent 41 percent to 37 percent. Over the next month as the crisis intensified, there was a sharp reversal of opinion, until Obama led McCain 48 percent to 34 percent.

The Obama campaign relentlessly exposed McCain's weakness in economics. "The fundamentals of our economy are strong," McCain had often said during the late summer and again just a few days before Lehman's collapse. As the need for governmental action of some kind became more urgent, McCain was quoted, accurately, as having told *The Wall Street Journal,* "I am fundamentally a deregulator."[23]

In the last month of the campaign, Obama used his fund-raising prowess to present in prime-time TV a political "documentary" that told his Hollywood-like story of a mixed-race child of a single mother who graduated from Harvard Law and taught at the University of Chicago before being elected to the Senate at age forty-four.

On November 2, 2008, Barack Obama handily defeated John McCain by 53 percent to 46 percent in the popular vote and by 365 electoral votes to 173 electoral votes, winning a majority of men, 56 percent of women, 54 percent of Catholics, 66 percent of Latinos, and—important for the future of both parties—68 percent of new voters. He brought with him larger Democratic majorities in both houses of Congress, setting the stage for the president-elect to implement a radical change in the lives of every American.

• • •

Meanwhile, Heritage had been hewing to conservative principles throughout 2007 and 2008, earning plaudits from the Bush administration.

In a televised November 1987 address in the foundation's packed Allison Auditorium, President Bush declared: "I really want to thank Heritage. . . . The folks here have been tireless advocates, tireless champions of liberty and free enterprise and democracy and religious freedom."[24]

Following the principle of "peace through strength," the foundation strengthened homeland security with a proposal—shepherded by James Carafano—that requires the Department of Homeland Security to undergo a top-to-bottom performance review every four years. Todd Gaziano and other scholars in the Center for Legal and Judicial Studies advised members of Congress how to update the Foreign Intelligence Surveillance Act (FISA) and strengthen the National Security Agency's terrorist surveillance program without compromising constitutional rights.

The foundation provided research that enabled lawmakers to block the attempt to turn a government health program for poor children—SCHIP—into an entitlement for the middle class. One key finding of Robert Moffit and other Heritage analysts was that more than half of the children who would "gain" government coverage under the bill were already covered. The Democratic Congress tried to override President Bush's veto twice before conceding defeat.

Heritage, in the person of Grover Hermann Fellow Brian Riedl, made a significant difference in the debate over earmarks—a device used by congressmen to fund pet projects for their constituents. After promising greater transparency in the budgeting process, House Appropriations Committee chairman David Obey (D-WI) said that earmarks would be made public only *after* the House approved them. Riedl let loose a barrage of papers, commentaries, and TV interviews showing how earmarks contribute to massive federal spending. Finally and reluctantly, Obey reversed himself and made proposed earmarks public *before* they became law.

• • •

Heritage research played an active role in one of 2007's critical debates—the battle over a complex eight-hundred-page bill promising "comprehensive immigration reform" but really creating a path to citizenship for illegal immigrants. It is a story of duplicitous legislating by liberal members of Congress and firm conservative opposition led by Heritage.

The bill was crafted behind closed doors by a few Democratic senators and their aides, who held its release until late on a Friday night when lawmakers had left Washington for the weekend. The Democratic leadership scheduled a vote the following Monday—barely forty-eight hours later—when the Senate was due to reconvene. "It was a clever plan, but not clever enough," said Ed Feulner.

Heritage managed to get a copy of the bill at two a.m. Saturday morning and immediately posted it on Heritage.org, giving Americans and most members of Congress their first look at the legislation. "Thank goodness [Heritage] did make it public," said Senator Jeff Sessions (R-AL). It gave "the American people the opportunity to know what's involved."[25]

Coordinated by Ed Meese and Matthew Spalding, more than thirty Heritage analysts began going over the proposed law line by line. They discovered numerous serious defects that would have:

- Granted amnesty to nearly all of the approximately 12 million illegal immigrants in America—including those who had committed serious crimes.

- Increased incentives to enter the country illegally, further eroding U.S. border security.

- Cost U.S. taxpayers an estimated $2.6 trillion [*sic*] in welfare and other "support services" for low-skilled immigrants over the next twenty years.

Heritage flooded the mass media with more than two hundred appearances on national radio and TV and dozens of print interviews.

The foundation zeroed in on one jaw-dropping fact: under the bill every illegal immigrant household would receive about $21,000 a year in government benefits. To the sound of a revving car engine, a Heritage radio spot—part of a significant advertising campaign—announced: "That's like buying them a brand-new Mustang convertible each year!" Listeners were directed to Nofreemustang.com, a Heritage website with the latest research and commentary about the issue.

Capitol Hill switchboards were shut down by the wave of calls generated by Rush Limbaugh, Sean Hannity, Laura Ingraham, Mark Levin, and other radio talk show hosts. An early key event—devastating to proponents of the bill—was a Capitol Hill news conference held by senior analyst Robert (Pit Bull) Rector, who documented that low-skill immigrants receive nearly three times as much in government services as they pay in taxes.

Over the next month, liberals would propose amendments, and conservatives with the aid of Heritage research would rebut them. In mid-June President Bush visited Capitol Hill to urge senators to resurrect the bill. Demonstrating again that it was a conservative institution independent of any political party, Heritage responded with a paper reiterating essential reforms still missing from the proposal.

Spalding and national security expert James Carafano wrote "A New Strategy for Real Immigration Reform" that recommended (1) enforcing the existing laws, (2) regaining control over the southern border with Mexico, (3) emphasizing legal immigration along with the "Americanization" of new citizens, and (4) creating flexible work opportunities in the United States.

On June 28 the bill died 53–46 in the Senate on a procedural vote. Heritage president Ed Feulner urged Congress to drop its unrealistic "comprehensive" approach and work "one bite at a time" on immigration issues while enforcing existing law. Two months later the White House unveiled administrative reforms in line with Heritage's recommendations. "Comprehensive immigration reform" died a deserved death, and the foundation's Leadership for America campaign proved its worth.

Heritage's work on immigration, Ed Feulner pointed out, did not begin on May 19, 2007, when it publicly exposed the secret Amnesty bill. Three years earlier Ed Meese published a paper on the principles of immigration policy that served as a guide for the foundation's later work. The Center for Data Analysis spent a decade developing the massive databases that enabled Heritage to reveal the true cost of the

Amnesty bill. Analysts like Rector, Carafano, and Spalding were not creatures of coincidence but examples of a Feulner rule—"Find the best people you can and let them do their best."

Whether on immigration or other issues, Feulner said, too many of our elected leaders "have sold their conservative principles as the price of staying in office." Understanding how disturbing that was, Feulner pledged personally to Heritage members that "no matter how far the politicians might stray off course, The Heritage Foundation will never forget and never forsake the principles that you cherish. . . . You can count on Heritage," he said, echoing Ronald Reagan, "to stay the course."[26]

CHAPTER 22

FORCE FOR GOOD

Heritage is used to honors but was very pleased to be recognized as one of only a dozen "Forces for Good" in America in the authoritative book of that title. The authors found that Heritage had "revolutionized" the think tank world with its reader-friendly reports that explain how policy proposals would affect everyday lives and had built "a grassroots constituency and a large base of individual donors who are actively engaged in its work."[1]

Forces for Good, published in 2007, identified six practices that explain the success of great nonprofits, regardless of mission or cause, including:

They build and nurture nonprofit networks, treating other groups as allies rather than competitors. Which is what Heritage does with its annual Resource Bank and constant sharing with other conservative groups.

They master the art of adaptation. Which is what Heritage did with *Policy Review,* handing it off to the Hoover Institution after a quarter-century of publication, and with Townhall, splitting it off as an independent operation and enabling it to become one of the most visited conservative websites in the country.

They invest heavily in people and infrastructure to advance their mission. Which is what Heritage does in accordance with Feulner's first law, "People are policy."

"Out of some 1.5 million nonprofits in America," Feulner said, the "Heritage Foundation emerged as one of the 12 most effective at advancing its mission. . . . I'd be less than human if I didn't get a little glow from that."[2]

Following the Great Recession of 2008, the authors decided to publish a new edition of *Forces for Good* to determine how the dozen nonprofits had survived the crisis. They discovered that most of them, including Heritage, had in fact thrived because the six practices outlined in the first edition, especially the ability to influence others and to help partners committed to lasting change, still held up, albeit in a far different context.

Among the lessons drawn from the recession by the twelve nonprofits was "Stay Close to Your Donors." Ed Feulner instructed his development staff to call every one of Heritage's major donors. But, he said, "don't ask for money or confirmation of their support. Instead, ask: 'How are you doing? How will the downturn affect you?' " From the conversations, Heritage deduced that major gifts would be down about 10 percent in the upcoming year. The foundation announced a hiring freeze and a cap on all salary increases but stepped up its direct marketing to such an extent that the 2009 budget almost reached $72 million, 13 percent higher than the previous year. "We didn't want to show weakness," explained Feulner.[3]

• • •

In 2008, the year of the great mortgage meltdown, Heritage expanded its publishing, producing *Liberty's Best Hope: American Leadership for the 21st Century* by Kim Holmes, who outlined a U.S. foreign policy of both soft and hard power; and *A Parent's Guide to Education Reform,* which presented "action points" for parents seeking to reform local schools, such as reporting a public school's test scores to parents, and allowing talented people from other professions who did not have an education degree to become public school teachers.

One piece of legislation that particularly aroused Heritage was the Climate Security Act that would have crippled the U.S. economy in the name of being "green." Senators Joseph Lieberman (I-CT) and John Warner (R-VA) introduced the bill—better known as the "cap and trade" act—to strictly limit greenhouse gas emissions, mainly carbon dioxide. Heritage experts (using CDA analysis) immediately pointed out that the proposal would increase the average household's yearly utility bill by nearly $500, erase half a million jobs annually, and reduce the GDP by at least $155 billion each year.

When the bill died in the Senate, with the help of Heritage research, the EPA quickly stated its intention to regulate CO_2 under the Clean Air Act. Heritage calculated that the EPA approach was even more expensive and more intrusive than the Lieberman-Warner bill, giving the agency the power to regulate almost anything with a combustible engine—from cars and ships to lawn mowers and tractors. Such bureaucratic authority would mean a $600 billion loss in the gross domestic product and 800,000 fewer jobs annually, according to the foundation.

A determined Heritage led a coalition against the EPA proposal and created StopEPA.com to educate citizens about the agency's overreach and encourage them to submit their comments to EPA. More than fourteen thousand people went to the site and expressed their opposition.

In the field of energy, a series of studies by research fellow Jack Spencer addressed practical concerns about nuclear energy such as how to manage spent nuclear fuel and rebuild the nuclear industry without government subsidies. At present, nuclear power generates 19.2 percent of America's energy needs. Ironically, the state with the highest percentage of nuclear-generated electricity is one of the most liberal states—Vermont, with 72.5 percent. Due to the meltdowns at the Fukushima Daichi plant in Japan and Chernobyl in Ukraine as well as the near-accident at the Three Mile Island plant in Pennsylvania in March 1979, the Nuclear Regulatory Commission had not approved a permit for a new nuclear reactor for three decades—until it okayed construction of two reactors in February 2012.

While some hailed the NRC's action as the start of "a nuclear renaissance," Spencer was more cautious. Calling the decision "noteworthy" and "welcome," Heritage's nuclear expert argued that "the United States does not need the government to dictate how it produces energy." Government bureaucrats, he said, "should step aside and allow market forces to determine the future of the nuclear industry."[4]

• • •

To Ed Meese and his associates in the Center for Legal and Judicial Studies, the rule of law in America is under serious attack and in danger of being fundamentally altered.

Too many judges stray from the Constitution by acting as policy makers rather than as judicial arbiters.

The trend to "overcriminalize" or impose severe federal penalties for minor actions that deserve only a civil fine is accelerating.

Our legal system suffers from frivolous lawsuits and astronomical damage awards.

Through its legal center, Heritage works to restore constitutional fidelity, reverse the overcriminalization trend, and restore the civil justice system to its traditional role.

The center, for example, opposed the Justice Department when it sought to coerce corporations into waiving their corporate and employees' attorney-client privilege—a basic right of our criminal justice system. The department announced it would stop the practice.

The center's Supreme Court Advocacy Program, headed by Todd Gaziano, helped secure a landmark victory for Second Amendment rights—*Heller v. District of Columbia*—in which the Supreme Court ruled that the Second Amendment protects the right of all Americans to possess guns and that Washington, D.C.'s, total ban on all handguns violated that constitutional right.

Visiting legal scholar Hans von Spakovsky, a former member of the Federal Elections Commission, detailed in a series of reports and commentaries that fraud remains a real problem in modern elections. "If an election is close," he wrote in *The Wall Street Journal*, "the possibility exists that the winner may be decided not by the American people, but by fraudulent votes cast by individuals exploiting the weaknesses in our current system."[5]

• • •

In the fall of 2007, Heritage and the Federalist Society cosponsored five book-signing events around the country featuring Supreme Court associate justice Clarence Thomas talking about his just-published memoir, *My Grandfather's Son*.

When introducing Justice Thomas, Ed Feulner explained that Heritage is not only a public policy think tank but "the institutional leader of the conservative movement in America." To succeed in restoring and preserving America's founding ideals—a major purpose of Heritage's Leadership for America campaign—"all of us need to pause now and then and reflect on what is required of us as *individuals*. Clarence Thomas has given us a rare opportunity to do that" with his book.

Feulner recalled that back in 1998 Heritage had marked its twenty-fifth anniversary with a series of lectures on public policy that included a talk by Clarence Thomas, who spoke about the importance of character in a free society. He defined character as composed of "moral strength, self-discipline, fortitude" and a person of character as "a pillar of his family and community" and someone who leads by example.

That is what is needed today, Feulner said—pillars of character "who lead us by [their] example." And we find that example in Thomas's story in which he refused to back away from his political beliefs to ease the pressure from his ideological opponents. "When we meet a person like Clarence Thomas we owe them our full recognition, our heartfelt gratitude, and our highest respect." And that is why Heritage was proud to host Justice Thomas, Feulner explained, and introduce his book to "as many Americans as we possibly can," resolved never to give up on our principles.[6]

• • •

The 2008 financial crisis was a perfect storm, created by easy money, mountainous debt, governmental overstimulus, perfunctory congressional oversight, and runaway Wall Street greed.

For twenty years—from Bill Clinton to George W. Bush—financial institutions had gambled that the price of assets, especially houses, would never fall. With congressional approval, the government-chartered companies Fannie Mae and Freddie Mac made mortgage loans to tens of thousands of first-time home seekers with low incomes. At last, real estate prices stopped climbing. Many subprime borrowers found their homes were worth less than their mortgages. Defaults spread, and prices sank.

In the summer of 2007, as *Time* reported, two mortgage funds operated by the investment bank Bear Stearns became insolvent. By the end of the year, the market for mortgage securities had dried up, and other markets followed suit, sparking a credit crisis.

That set the stage for a series of shocks across the economy, akin to a financial horror show, "as if Stephen King were channeling Alan Greenspan to produce scary stories full of negative numbers"—with narration by Rod Serling.[7]

In September 2008 the Lehman Brothers investment bank went under. The same month the government forced the merger of Bank of America and the sorely stretched Merrill Lynch; then Washington came up with $182 billion to prop up the insurance giant AIG.

The institutions that received priority attention, however, were the government-chartered Fannie Mae and Freddie Mac, which held or guaranteed about half the nation's mortgage loans, some $5.2 trillion in mortgage debt, slightly less than the total U.S. debt. Confronted with tighter credit, falling home prices, and rising foreclosures, Fannie and Freddie faltered and began to fail. The federal government solved the problem the Keynesian way—they seized control of the mortgage titans.

Heritage had foreseen the danger of runaway mortgage debt and the inevitable consequences as early as 2005, when senior research fellow Ronald Utt wrote: "With such market power concentrated in the hands of only two companies, the stability of U.S. financial markets could be undermined by financial problems in just one of them." And, he prophesied, "if a bailout ever becomes necessary, the taxpayers could end up paying the bill."[8] As taxpayers did and still are.

And yet, as Ed Feulner pointed out, Fannie and Freddie—"the major culprits in the meltdown"—successfully evaded attempts to regulate them, assisted by powerful congressional Democrats. In 2003, for example, Representative Barney Frank of the House Banking Committee denied the two institutions were facing any kind of financial crisis. The more people exaggerate these problems, Frank warned, "the more pressure there is on these companies, [and] the less we will see in terms of affordable housing." Whether people could "afford" the house did not matter—Fannie and Freddie would guarantee the purchase.[9]

By the fall of 2008, it was clear that something had to be done to avoid a financial crash as serious, in the minds of many economists, as the one that triggered the Great Depression. President Bush and his economic team, in concert with Democratic and Republican leaders in Congress, came up with a $700 billion rescue plan for Wall Street. The plan was immediately labeled a "bailout," and despite bipartisan support and the tepid endorsement of presidential candidates Obama and McCain, the House voted it down.

In response, the Dow Jones industrial average plunged 778 points, scaring everyone in Washington except hardcore Ayn Randians. As America's troubles rippled across the world, Congress passed and the president signed in early October the $700 billion TARP, the Troubled Assets Relief Program.

In deciding its position, Heritage went through one of the most intense debates in its history. TARP violated four of the foundation's five basic ideas. It expanded rather than limited government. It ignored a fundamental principle of free enterprise that if a company makes the wrong decision, it and not the government should pay the price—even that of bankruptcy. It undercut the notion of individual freedom and responsibility. And it mocked traditional American values such as prudence and thrift.

Voices were raised, doors were slammed, and there were even threats of resignation, but in the end Heritage reluctantly endorsed TARP out of fear that the core financial institutions of the U.S. economy would fail. A failure to actively stabilize the financial markets would have precipitated a huge crisis that would have fed on itself for many years. A *WebMemo* by Stuart Butler, Alison Fraser, and James Gattuso made a critical point: "When government fails to carry out this role [of assuring the integrity of the market's infrastructure] in critical times, such as its failure to maintain liquidity after the stock market crash of 1929, the results can be catastrophic."[10]

In an official *WebMemo* titled "The Bailout Package: Vital and Acceptable," coauthors Stuart Butler and Edwin Meese III wrote that in "a crisis of this scale" swift action was needed. "The core technical parts of the negotiated package," they said, "are acceptable." If action is not taken, "it is only a matter of time before the fallout hits Main Street, with potentially devastating economic effects for typical American households."

Butler and Meese listed several "troubling" provisions of TARP. The measure granted extraordinary powers to the treasury secretary "without providing sufficiently specific direction." And the oversight board had members not subject to or removable by the president, making TARP "less democratically accountable." But they did not count the provisions so troublesome as to prevent Heritage's reluctant endorsement.

"The situation is so grave," Butler and Meese wrote, "that we must take unusual measures now and accept some negotiated arrangements that remain very troubling, provided they are limited in extent and time and are not accepted as a permanent part of our government."[11]

Pragmatism prevailed over principle in a real-time application of the often-cited Feulner Law—"Do not let the perfect be the enemy of the good." In the following weeks, the foundation, led by its president, kept issuing warnings and expressing objections to the implementation of the measure, but in fact The Heritage Foundation—the champion of the free market—endorsed a $700 billion governmental bailout.

Other conservative institutions followed suit but without enthusiasm. *National Review* called it "a necessary measure" but complained it did not address the problem that "got us into this mess," Fannie

Mae and Freddie Mac, which ought to be put "on the road to full privatization."[12]

Cato Institute chairman Robert Levy cautiously wrote that in the current crisis, "extraordinary measures might be in order. . . . Maybe the bailout is necessary. Maybe it will even work. But . . . [it] is unconstitutional." It is a precedent, he warned, that will "rear its ugly head every time there's serious trouble that the federal government thinks it can fix."[13]

In his usual crisp, uncompromising way, Cato senior fellow Daniel Mitchell (who had served Heritage as its senior expert on taxes for seventeen years) explained why the bailout was bad for America: (1) it rewarded executives and companies for poor choices; (2) it would encourage future "imprudent risk"; (3) it would reduce economic efficiency and retard economic growth; (4) it repeated the mistakes Japan made in the 1990s when it tried and failed to "stimulate" its economy through government spending; and (5) it would increase Washington corruption.[14]

Conservative columnist George Will pointed out that such thoughtful congressional Republicans as Eric Cantor of Virginia and Paul Ryan of Wisconsin supported TARP because they had substantially improved it by requiring financial institutions to help finance their bailout, giving Treasury equity in firms revived by public funds, and eliminating "a slush fund" for Democratic activists. "The public wanted catharsis," Will wrote, "and respect for its center-right principles, and got both" with the House vote for the program.[15]

Onetime neoconservative columnist Charles Krauthammer wrote that TARP revealed the different economic philosophies of the two parties. Republicans saw the $700 billion rescue as an "emergency measure to save the financial sector lest credit dry up and strangle the rest of the economy." Democrats regarded it as an opportunity to initiate a massive industrial policy, starting with the auto industry. Consider the effects, he said, of bureaucrats issuing production quotas to fit five-year plans to meet politically mandated fuel-efficiency standards—all "to lift us to the sunny uplands of the coming green utopia."[16]

• • •

Ever sanguine, Ed Feulner was pressed to the utmost to be positive in the dark days following Obama's election and the Democratic capture of both houses of Congress. His office was besieged with e-mails and telephone calls from despairing members asking what could be done—besides moving to Canada or perhaps Australia. As in the past, he took it upon himself to rally Heritage members and fellow conservatives.

In a special letter to the President's Club, he wrote that while conservatives are entitled to be unhappy about the Republican Party betraying conservative principles, "we are not entitled to despondency and pessimism." Although liberal Democrats controlled the White House and both houses of Congress and talked openly of launching "New Deal 2," things had been no less bleak in the late 1970s under the Carter administration.

But rather than accepting what seemed like our destiny at the time, wrote Feulner, the American people had turned to Ronald Reagan, who provided "principled conservative leadership . . . courageous leadership. Weary of the darkness, we opted for sunrise."

Now, following the 2008 elections, Feulner agreed that the Republican Party was in trouble, "serious trouble of its own making," but "the conservative movement is not in decline" but "in robust good health and growing stronger." Consider the following, he said:

Conservatives have achieved a "staggering" presence on the Internet. Townhall.com, for example, provides links to several hundred conservative columnists.

There are more conservative think tanks, "idea factories," than ever. In addition to Heritage, AEI, Cato, CSIS, and other national research organizations, there are fifty-five state think tanks in fifty states with a combined budget approaching $60 million.

America "remains essentially a center-right nation." When asked whether government should redistribute wealth or improve the overall economy to create jobs, 84 percent of Americans chose the latter.

Heritage increased its 2008 operating budget by almost 50 percent in order to deliver "our ideas to wider audiences" through ads on national radio programs like Rush Limbaugh and Sean Hannity and with more on-the-ground events that engage local leaders and "build grassroots demand for accountability in Washington."

Now is a time not for despondency but for commitment, Feulner insisted. It is time to stand by conservative principles, to stand up for America's heritage and to stay the course.[17]

• • •

In late December, Ed Feulner reiterated there had been good reasons earlier in the year to believe that the entire global financial system was at risk. TARP was supposed "to buy up troubled assets so our nation's banking system wouldn't collapse."

But it was not intended, Feulner said bluntly, that TARP money would be used "to guarantee securities backed by student loans and credit card debt" and "to prop up the unprofitable segments of the auto industry." He called on Congress to reassert its constitutional responsibilities and end the TARP program.[18]

As disturbing as the misuse of TARP money was, Feulner's greater concern was President-elect Barack Obama and his intention to press for what he called "a stimulus package." In his first postelection news conference, Obama said, "I want to see a stimulus package sooner rather than later." His chief of staff Rahm Emanuel explained that America needed "a short-term economic recovery act" that put Americans to work "building our roads, our bridges, our schools, our water systems."[19]

The Obama "stimulus," Feulner said, came from "the old liberal playbook" and was based on the idea that you "can make the economy better by simply mailing checks to taxpayers." It didn't work with the Bush stimulus package in 2001, he said, and it wouldn't work in 2008 or 2009.

What would work as it had in the past, Feulner said, was tax cuts. The 2003 Bush tax cuts created incentives for growth, "and Americans cashed in." In the next eighteen months, the stock market climbed by one-third and the economy created some 300,000 new jobs. In the next two years, five million more new jobs were added, and overall economic growth rates doubled.[20]

Would this history make any difference to the president-elect, or was he committed to "fundamentally transforming the United States of America"—a promise he made just before Election Day 2008? The answer was swift in coming.

Imitating the first days of the New Deal in 1933, the Obama administration pushed through an economic stimulus package of $787 billion, proposed a "cap and trade" energy plan, and introduced a government-run health system controlling one-sixth of the nation's economy. General Motors became Government Motors, and a ballooning budget deficit of $1.3 trillion in 2010 caused jaws to drop all over Washington.

The White House did not neglect social issues like abortion that mattered to its liberal supporters. On January 23, 2009, President Obama revoked the Mexico City Policy, first laid down by President

Reagan in 1984. The policy prevented U.S. funds from going to nongovernmental organizations (NGOs) that performed abortions or actively promoted abortion as a method of family planning in other countries. President Clinton had voided the policy in 1993, but President George W. Bush restored it in 2001. Obama declared that the policy was "unwarranted" and undermined "voluntary" family planning programs in foreign nations. Planned Parenthood and NARAL applauded the president's action, as did the Chinese Communist regime, seeking justification for its infamous "one-child" policy.[21]

At the same time, the administration downgraded the war on terrorism to "overseas contingency operations" and reclassified terrorism as "man-caused disasters." It unilaterally reneged on an agreement to build ten interceptor sites in Poland and deploy missile-defense radar in the Czech Republic. And the president practiced friendship diplomacy with the world's most anti-American rulers—Mahmoud Ahmadinejad of Iran, Bashar al-Assad of Syria, and Hugo Chávez of Venezuela.

It was change, but change so sweeping and revolutionary that it soon alarmed not just conservatives but independents, who found themselves, to their surprise, forming a new kind of political party.

CHAPTER 23

A MODERN MACHIAVELLIAN

Every new president believes he has the answer for whatever is troubling the nation—be it a recession, a war, or public pessimism. Even those who win by the narrowest of margins claim a mandate and act quickly as they know they must in the first months of their presidency. Sometimes they are proven right, and sometimes they are proven wrong—in the latter case the whole country suffers.

Ever the realist, Richard Nixon—the first president of the Heritage era—initiated wage and price controls but was forced to lift them and never again asserted, "Now we are all Keynesians." Gerald Ford proudly displayed a WIN button on his lapel (Whip Inflation Now) but could not win against Jimmy Carter, that most self-righteous of all modern presidents.

Carter made mistake after mistake at home and abroad, culminating in the taking of sixty-six Americans as hostages in Iran, but he never accepted responsibility for any of his missteps, choosing to blame the American people for the mess in which the nation found itself.

Ever the optimist, Ronald Reagan said that in the present crisis government was not the solution but the problem and sparked the longest period of economic growth in peacetime with his across-the-board income tax cuts. He ended the Cold War at the bargaining table rather than on the battlefield, using SDI and Heritage research. George H. W. Bush coasted into the White House on Reagan's popularity but defeated himself by violating a "no new taxes" pledge.

Bill Clinton sought the nomination no one else wanted and triangulated himself into a second term by declaring an end to big government and signing a historic welfare reform bill—drafted in part by Heritage's Robert Rector—after vetoing it twice.

After winning the closest presidential election in U.S. history, George W. Bush emphasized his compassionate conservative credentials, until 9/11 turned him into a wartime president determined there would be no more 9/11s, an objective that took him and America halfway around the world to a war in Afghanistan.

Throughout these forty years, The Heritage Foundation focused on Congress as its prime constituency but accepted the necessity of working with or opposing every president, sometimes doing both. While there was little in the Carter years that Heritage could endorse, the foundation wrapped both arms around Ronald Reagan and embraced him, perhaps too tightly, as Ed Feulner later conceded, reluctant to criticize the first conservative president since Calvin Coolidge.

George H. W. Bush led the United States and its allies to swift victory in the Persian Gulf War. Understanding the core importance of the Constitution, he named the first black conservative jurist, Clarence Thomas, to the Supreme Court, almost but not quite canceling out his reversal on taxes, which even Feulner, the most forgiving of conservatives, could not overlook. Bill Clinton presented Heritage with an ever-moving target, producing more balanced budgets than any president since Dwight D. Eisenhower and keeping America out of war. At the same time he revealed an ideological side with his proposed radical reform of the nation's health care system and his vetoes of welfare reform legislation that was a point of special pride to Heritage.

There was a good deal for Heritage to like about George W. Bush, feisty, fine-tuned, and publicly appreciative of the foundation despite its criticism of his No Child Left Behind education plan and his multibillion-dollar drug prescription program. It was difficult for a steadfast anti-Communist like Ed Feulner to censure a politician who delivered the dedication speech for the Victims of Communism Memorial on Capitol Hill, just four blocks from the foundation's headquarters.

Barack Obama offered different challenges. From his entry into politics, political observers and ordinary citizens have attempted to discern the real Obama.

What is he—a committed progressive or a deferrer to left-wing Democrats in Congress? A disciple of the radical Saul Alinsky or the big-city boss Richard Daley? The most liberal Democrat in the U.S. Senate or the shrewd pragmatist who upset the favored Hillary Clinton for the Democratic nomination? An antiwar activist or a condoner of deadly drones targeted at America's overseas enemies? A supporter of same-sex marriage or a devoted family man? A secular humanist or a churchgoing Christian? A unifier or a divider? The most brilliant occupant of the White House since Thomas Jefferson—the consensus of the White House staff and many in the media—or an arrogant know-it-all unwilling to admit mistakes?

Is he, to borrow from Winston Churchill, a riddle wrapped in a mystery inside an enigma? Or is he a modern Machiavellian?

On January 13, 2009, barely a week before he was inaugurated as America's first black president, Barack Obama sat down to dinner with a group of Reaganite journalists at George Will's Chevy Chase home. All of them were familiar with what candidate Obama had said just before Election Day: "We are five days away from fundamentally transforming the United States of America."[1] When Obama left the Will home three hours later, the writers—all of them experienced observers of the Washington scene—confessed that they had been charmed by his humor and willingness to listen and impressed by his quick intelligence and prudent observations, but were uncertain as to his governing philosophy.

Eighteen months later, Will would write that President Obama was advancing "lemon socialism." Lawrence Kudlow said that he was presiding over a government of "crony capitalism at its worst." Michael Barone called it "Gangster Government." Rich Lowry said that Obama was "the whiniest president ever." Peggy Noonan wrote, "He is not a devil, an alien, a socialist. He is a loser." The most stinging criticism came from Charles Krauthammer, who described him as "sanctimonious, demagogic, self-righteous, and arrogant."[2]

In his first joint address to Congress in January 2009, Obama outlined what Krauthammer called the "boldest social democratic manifesto ever issued by a U.S. president." He set forth three goals—universal health care, universal education, and a new green energy economy "highly funded and regulated by government"—all calculated to move the "relatively" modest American welfare state toward "European-style social democracy."[3]

• • •

When Obama entered the White House in January 2009, his Gallup approval rating stood at 68 percent, the highest for any newly elected president since John F. Kennedy in 1961. He immediately set in motion the transformational change he had promised as a candidate, starting with a $787 billion economic stimulus package.

The plan included $275 billion in federal contracts, grants, and loans and $152 billion for infrastructure improvements, what the president called "shovel-ready" projects. There were confident predictions that the money would arrive quickly and that unemployment would drop significantly. But on October 1, 2009, the Bureau of Labor Statistics reported that unemployment had risen to 9.8 percent, the highest rate since June 1983. Three years later, in late 2012, unemployment was close to 8 percent, while GDP growth sputtered along at an annual rate of barely 2 percent. (No president seeking reelection has ever won when the GDP was at 2 percent or less.)

At the height of the stimulus debate, Heritage led a nonpartisan coalition calling for less not more federal spending and retention of the Bush tax cuts. One congressman in particular got the message. When Representative Paul Ryan (R-WI) wrote his landmark "Roadmap" legislation to fix entitlements and reform the tax code, he turned to Heritage analysts for recommendations and sophisticated analysis of his plan's prescriptions.

Trying to highlight how much spending had increased, Heritage pointed out that between 1965 and 2008, "mandatory" federal spending—driven by Social Security, Medicare, and Medicaid—more than quadrupled, from $3,000 per household to nearly $14,000 per household. In 2009, because of TARP and other federal spending, it jumped almost 30 percent, to $18,000 per household.[4] The national debt reached an alarming $14 trillion—more than the gross domestic product of China and Japan together.

Such runaway spending could not continue, Heritage warned, or America would become another bankrupt nation like Greece. Someone had to speak up.

In February 2009, while discussing the federal bailout on CNBC's *Squawk Box*, the fiery analyst Rick Santelli boiled over: "If you read our

Founding Fathers—people like Benjamin Franklin and Jefferson—what we're doing in this country now is making them roll over in their graves."

To applause from other brokers on the floor of the Chicago Board of Trade, Santelli escalated the rhetoric: "We're thinking of having a Chicago Tea Party in July. All you capitalists that want to show up to Lake Michigan, I'm gonna start organizing."[5]

Aided by the Internet, Tea Parties began popping up all over the country. One website reported more than six hundred organizations from Cottage Grove, Oregon, to Concord, New Hampshire. Thousands of people turned out on July 4 at various rallies, and on September 12 one million Tea Partiers marched on Capitol Hill. Their signs fairly shouted: "Stop Saddling Our Grandchildren with Debt!" and "Start Acting Like Responsible Adults!"

Among them, and without orders from anyone, were Heritage people whose observations Ed Feulner passed along to Heritage members:

One saw Middle America at its best. These were ordinary, hard-working people. They bought their own bus and plane tickets, paid their own hotel tabs, and made their own signs. Many came as families: parents, grandparents, and children. . . . They radiated good cheer among themselves and outrage toward their government. They were fed up with politicians squandering their taxes and appropriating powers not found in the Constitution. And they said so, all day long.[6]

The protests confirmed Tocqueville's observation, said Ed Feulner, that when roused to action, Americans unite in voluntary associations. "Like no other people on Earth," he said, "Americans will *join causes* for common purposes."[7]

Polls showed that 41 percent of Americans identified themselves as conservative on the issues of taxes, government spending, and business regulation. Only 12 percent called themselves liberal. The same polls showed independent voters moving toward conservative positions. In October, for the first time since President Obama took office, a majority of respondents, almost two-thirds, said America was on the wrong track—a statistic that would persist for the next three years.[8]

Feulner quoted Michael Barone on the core difference between "Obama liberals" and the Tea Partiers. The liberals see an America, Barone wrote, "in which ordinary people cannot fend for themselves, where they need to have their incomes supplemented, their health care insurance regulated and guaranteed, their relationships with their employers governed by union leaders." It is a culture of dependence.

The Tea Partiers see things differently. They are not necessarily looking for lower taxes—half of them think their taxes are fair—but recognize that the Obama Democrats "are trying to permanently enlarge government and increase citizens' dependence on it." They believe "this will destroy the culture of independence that has enabled Americans over the past two centuries to make this the most productive, prosperous and charitably generous nation in the world."[9]

As a discontented public, led by the Tea Party, sought alternatives, Heritage provided them with Leadership for America, centered on the idea that the American people must rediscover and apply the First Principles of the founding—equality, natural law, and the consent of the governed. These principles, the foundation argued, would save the American Dream.

The people's response amazed even Feulner. Heritage membership in 2009 increased by 45 percent, from 400,000 to 582,000. The connection between the exponential growth of Heritage membership and of the Tea Party was not coincidental. Led by external relations vice president Becky Norton Dunlop and her team, the foundation reached out to Tea Partiers at dozens of grassroots meetings and through the Internet.

Heritage revenues also soared, growing 13 percent over the previous year, reaching $71.6 million (up 60 percent over annual income a decade earlier). A typical comment came from Elizabeth Ann Ownbey: "Thank you from the bottom of my heart for your contribution to save America, to build on moral strength and decency. There are millions upon millions of us here looking for your exact type of leadership."[10]

Dismissing negative polls, President Obama set about transforming every part of the government, including exercising his power as commander in chief. He ordered the Joint Chiefs of Staff to cut the Pentagon's budget by at least 10 percent, including missile defense, new fighter jets, and the next generation of weapons. Heritage experts responded that an adequate defense required an annual budget of at least 4 percent of gross domestic product. Obama's budget was only 3 percent. To raise public consciousness, Heritage proclaimed Protect America Month, offering a series of lectures and other events showing the dangers of "penny-wise" policies that threatened to "hollow out" the armed forces. The kickoff speaker was former Massachusetts governor Mitt Romney (and future Republican presidential nominee), who identified serious global threats such as radical jihadism and rising authoritarian states and called for a robust military as a countermeasure.

At the opening of the 111th Congress, liberal leaders vowed to ram through a ruinous "cap and trade" climate bill in the first hundred days. It turned into a sustained five-month battle that ended in defeat for the Obama administration.

The Waxman-Markey "cap and trade" bill was in fact a massive cap-and-tax scheme. Even Obama had admitted while campaigning, "Under my plan . . . electricity rates would necessarily skyrocket." That was far from the whole story. Heritage's Center for Data Analysis ran an economic analysis that documented a host of costs the plan would inflict upon the economy—totaling an estimated $1.9 trillion over eight years. As it always tried to do, CDA broke down the costs, showing how much more an average person would have to pay for gasoline, electricity, and consumer goods. An average family's annual electric bill would go up $1,860, its natural gas bill $1,393. Gasoline prices would rise an estimated 58 percent, breaking the five-dollar-a-gallon ceiling.[11]

Subsequent Heritage research showed how much Waxman-Markey would cost each congressional district in economic productivity, jobs, and personal income. CDA estimated that nonfarm employment lost in 2025 would range from 63,000 in California to 41,000 in Texas to 30,000 in Florida.[12]

The House Energy and Commerce Committee invited testimony by Heritage experts David Kreutzer and Ben Lieberman, while a group of Capitol Hill energy policy staff asked Kreutzer to conduct a "mega-briefing" detailing "cap and trade" costs and explaining how the EPA and the Congressional Budget Office had greatly underestimated the costs.

"The Center for Data Analysis at The Heritage Foundation analyzed a proposal to cut CO_2 emissions by 70 percent," senior policy analyst Kreutzer testified. "Such a cut would have little impact on global temperatures. At best, the trade-off is trillions of dollars in lost income and hundreds of thousands of lost jobs vs. a fraction of a degree change in average world temperature eighty-five years from now."[13]

On June 26, Waxman-Markey barely passed the House, 219–212, making Senate passage unlikely. An alarmed administration instructed the EPA to get busy. The agency issued an "advanced notice" that it intended to designate CO_2—the gas that human beings exhale and that plants need to live and grow—as a "pollutant." Such a regulation would give EPA the ability to issue costly far-reaching new regulations.

Heritage was ready. By April 17, 2009, the energetic Bridgett

Wagner had assembled a foundation-wide working group of experts in law, public policy, and communications to craft a comprehensive conservative response. On a new website, StopEPA.com, David Kreutzer explained how the proposed EPA regulations would adversely affect the climate and the average citizen's pocketbook. CDA estimated that the EPA campaign would cause cumulative GDP losses of $7 trillion by 2029, along with job losses of 800,000.

"It is ironic," Ed Feulner wrote in his Townhall column, "that just a few months ago, lawmakers raced to pass a so-called stimulus package that would supposedly pull the country out of its first deep recession in two decades. Yet today they're trying to pass a bill that would destroy jobs, year-in and year-out for decades. Waxman-Markey is like a self-imposed, rolling recession."

And the American people wanted no part of it.

* * *

The most revolutionary initiative of the Obama administration—economically as well as politically—began in March, when the president proclaimed that "the stars are aligned" for health care reform, which, he predicted, would be approved by a heavily Democratic Congress before it adjourned for its summer recess. But as the far-reaching applications of Obamacare became clearer to members of Congress and the public, the early deadline was abandoned.

Few think tanks were as well prepared for the debate as Heritage, which had published its first paper on health care in the 1970s and had analyzed the Obama health proposal while he was a candidate. The foundation presented a steady stream of rigorous original research and precise analysis that exposed the multiple flaws and fallacies of the thousand-page House bill and the two-thousand-plus-page Senate proposal.

The administration, for example, stated that "if you like your current coverage, you can keep it." Heritage commissioned the Lewin Group—a nationally respected independent health research group it had used before—to analyze exactly how the House version of Obamacare would affect those already insured. Lewin's conclusion: 83.4 million *fewer* Americans would have employer-based coverage, with most ending up in a government-run plan. That would be a 48.4 percent reduction in the number of people with private insurance (currently 172.5 million people).[14]

Heritage's initial estimates were that the total cost (federal and state) of the Medicaid expansion would be between $400 billion and

$500 billion over the first seven years. Heritage analysts Edmund Haisl-maier and Brian Blase warned that enactment of the "massive" Patient Protection and Affordable Care Act would not only alter the relation-ship between individuals and the federal government but "alter the re-lationship between the federal government and the states . . . [which] would be reduced to mere agencies of federal authority."[15]

Members of Congress, intent on coming up with cost-effective reforms, relied on the CDA's analytical tools for their own proposals. Talking to a *Washington Post* blogger, Representative Paul Ryan cited the alternative health care plan of Heritage analysts and expressed confidence that "we can get to a market-based, patient-centered [plan] where we bring free-market principles" to help control costs, improve care, and reduce the debt.[16]

Again and again, Heritage challenged the president's assertions:

- *Claim: Obamacare will be fiscally responsible.* Fact: the ten-year price tag for various versions ranges from $900 billion to $2.5 tril-lion, with taxes starting years before the benefits begin, and adding significantly to the national debt.

- *Claim: Obamacare will save the typical family $2,500.* Fact: the act will increase total health care spending. Many Americans, es-pecially the young and healthy, will face higher health care costs to underwrite generous subsidies to lower-income citizens to purchase health insurance.

- *Claim: middle-class Americans making $250,000 or less will not see their taxes go up.* Fact: the individual mandate and new taxes on insurance plans, medical devices, and pharmaceuticals will in-crease taxes for many middle-class families and businesses. The total cost of Obamacare taxes from 2010 through 2019, according to Heritage research, is $502 billion.[17]

- *Claim: Obamacare is not a government takeover.* Fact: it will con-centrate decisions over private health care financing and delivery in the Department of Health and Human Services, and subject Medi-care to the Independent Payment Advisory Board. The board was established to make recommendations regarding payments to slow the growth of Medicare, but as Bob Moffit points out, it is "prohib-ited by law from proposing real structural reforms."[18]

By late 2009 the Senate and House were close to approving "two profoundly dysfunctional bills," in Feulner's words.[19] Frustrated conservative lawmakers turned to Heritage for advice on alternatives that would expand health care coverage and increase the options for affordable insurance while leaving decision making to consumers and physicians, not the government.

However, a determined president, with an eye on history, kept pushing, and on December 24, the Senate passed the Patient Protection and Affordable Care Act (PPACA) by 60–39, with all Democrats and two Independents voting for and all Republicans voting against. On January 19, 2010, Republican underdog Scott Brown of Massachusetts shocked the political world by winning the U.S. Senate seat long held by the Democratic legend Ted Kennedy. Brown campaigned on giving the Republican minority the forty-first vote needed to sustain a filibuster, even signing autographs "Scott 41."

It did not matter. Despite widespread public demonstrations and protests, especially by the energized Tea Party, the House passed the Senate bill by 219–212 in March 2010, with 34 Democrats and all 178 Republicans voting against it. House Speaker Nancy Pelosi stunned even cynical congressional observers by telling her colleagues, "We have to pass the bill, so that you can find out what is in it."[20]

Proponents were obliged to negotiate with pro-life Democrats to obtain their support and passage of the legislation. President Obama, the very model of a modern Machiavellian, pretended to go along, issuing an executive order purporting to reaffirm the principles of the Hyde Amendment, which prohibits federal funding of abortions. The president signed Obamacare into law on March 23, sparking a blistering reaction by Ed Feulner:

"We oppose this new law because it is a radical new intrusion into the daily lives of all Americans and a massive takeover of one-sixth of the U.S. economy. We view the President's health care law as inimical to our national interests and offensive to the historic American dedication to the principle of self-government." Feulner called it an "intolerable act," akin to the Townshend Act of 1767, which imposed taxes on many popular items, including tea, and sparked the first Tea Party and the American Revolution. Obamacare, he said, cannot be fixed—it must be "repealed."[21]

He was almost as upset when the president cited Heritage research in an attempt to sell his health care program as a "middle of the road, centrist approach." The insurance market "exchanges" that Heritage had proposed, Feulner explained, are a way to help families choose their personal and portable health insurance without tax or regulatory penalties, while the Obama "exchanges" are a vehicle "to introduce sweeping regulation and federal standardization of health insurance."

Immediately, a majority of states along with many conservative organizations filed actions in federal courts challenging the act's constitutionality. Legislators in some thirty states introduced measures to amend their constitutions to invalidate various parts of Obamacare. In 2011 the new Republican majority in the House approved repeal of the administration's health care proposal, but the still Democratic Senate voted it down. Following split decisions by federal appellate courts (with two upholding the act and one declaring the individual mandate to be unconstitutional), the Supreme Court held oral arguments regarding the constitutionality of the Affordable Care Act in March 2012.

In the November 2010 midterm election, with the Tea Party leading the opposition, Democrats lost more seats in Congress than any party in more than seventy years—with many of the losses attributed to the issue of health care. In February 2012 a USA Today/Gallup poll found that 72 percent of registered voters in twelve key states believed that the individual mandate in Obamacare was unconstitutional, while 56 percent of Americans nationwide agreed the mandate was unconstitutional. Both conservatives and liberals described the Court's ruling as a defining moment in American politics.[22]

On June 29, 2012, in a decision that surprised Left and Right, the Supreme Court "saved the heart" of the president's health care law by ruling 5–4, with Chief Justice John Roberts writing the majority decision, that the individual mandate was constitutional under Congress's authority to levy taxes. According to The Washington Post, the ruling prompted an emotional outburst in the White House with Obama and his aides embracing each other. Their elation was understandable, after a two-year battle over an act whose constitutionality was always in doubt.[23]

However, opponents of Obamacare noted that the Roberts decision also said that the mandate could not be justified under the Commerce Clause or the Necessary and Proper Clause, a far-reaching determination because progressives have persistently used the clauses to justify the growth of federal power embodied in the modern administrative state.

Within minutes of the court's decision, Heritage analysts led by Ed Meese and other members of the Legal and Judicial Studies Center (which would be renamed the Edwin Meese III Center for Legal and

Judicial Studies in late 2012) were on the Internet, radio, and television, rallying conservatives and reminding them "there are no permanent defeats" in politics. Calling 2012 "a pivotal point in American history," Ed Feulner urged Heritage members to become "part of the mission to repeal Obamacare" and to save "the American Dream for the next generation."[24]

The Supreme Court had had its say. Now it was the people's turn.

• • •

During the 2008 Democratic presidential nomination campaign, Barack Obama and Hillary Clinton both had proposed plans to cover the 45 million Americans said to be without health insurance. Consistent with her 1993 position, Clinton said she would require everyone to have coverage—in effect, an individual mandate for health insurance—while Obama said he would provide a subsidy but would not require all Americans to obtain health insurance. However, once elected, Obama changed his mind and included a mandate in his health plan, citing The Heritage Foundation as an "originator" of the health insurance exchange.

What are the facts about "HeritageCare"?

Stuart Butler, the father of Heritage's health care plan, explains that in the late 1980s and early 1990s, he believed that some kind of "requirement" to purchase insurance was needed. It was needed, he argued, to create as universal a market as possible and to avoid the serious instability that could be created by two factors: insurers that avoided bad risks and healthy people who declined coverage.

The Heritage approach, Butler says, was shared at the time by conservatives as well as liberals. Even the libertarian icon Milton Friedman spoke of replacing Medicare and Medicaid "with a [minimum] requirement that every U.S. family unit have a major medical insurance policy."[25]

However, several conservative health care experts strongly opposed the Heritage way, including Peter Ferrara (a Heritage alumnus), Grace-Marie Turner, head of the Galen Institute (another Heritage alumnus); Tom Miller of the Cato Institute; and Merrill Matthews of the National Center for Policy Analysis, which originated the idea of Medical Savings Accounts (MSAs).

Butler admits that he and Heritage have changed their position, in part because based on new health research and economic analysis, they have concluded that an insurance mandate is not needed to achieve stable, near universal coverage. Furthermore, the very meaning of the individual mandate that Heritage is said to have "invented" has changed. Today, says Butler, a mandate means that the government makes people buy comprehensive benefits for their own good rather "than our original emphasis on protecting society from the heavy medical costs of free riders" who can afford insurance but decline to buy it, then receive expensive emergency room care.

Regarding the constitutional argument against Obamacare, says Butler, he agrees with the later analysis of the foundation's legal center that the president's "mandate"—as well as the original Heritage "mandate"—exceeds the constitutional powers granted to the federal government. For example, *United States v. Lopez* in 1997 affirmed the correct interpretation of the Constitution that limited Congress's power under the Commerce Clause. The problem, as constitutional scholar John Eastman has pointed out, is that the lower courts continued to reject Commerce Clause challenges in hundreds of cases.[26]

Widely regarded as the foundation's most distinguished scholar, Butler explains Heritage's approach to research. Analysts inside and outside Heritage, he says, take part in a continuous and collegial discussion about major policy questions. "We read each other's research. We look at the facts. We talk through ideas with those who agree or disagree with us. And we change our policy views over time based on new facts, new research, or good counterarguments.

"I've altered my views on many things," says Butler. "The individual mandate in health care is one of them."[27] There are few scholars, in Washington or elsewhere, who would make such a public and candid confession.

• • •

In May 2011, Heritage filed its first-ever amicus brief in a federal court of appeals, in this case the Eleventh Circuit, in support of the State of Florida against the Department of Health and Human Services. The issue was Obamacare.

In its merits brief before the court, the foundation notes, the United States quoted a twenty-one-year-old lecture by a Heritage policy expert (Stuart Butler) as supporting "a government-enforced mandate." "If citations to policy papers were subject to the same rules as legal citations," stated the brief, "then the Heritage position quoted by the Department of Justice would have a red flag indicating it had been reversed." Whatever the government's purpose, the amicus brief said, "Heritage thinks resorting to abandoned and empirically repudiated ideas from another era is a sign of desperation and highlights the impotence of [the government's] current policy argument."[28]

In publications and statements over the last several years, the brief continued, Heritage health policy experts "have opposed on purely policy grounds a government-enforced mandate that individuals or families buy health insurance." In fact, Heritage experts had concluded that "an insurance mandate is unnecessary to expand health coverage significantly and, indeed, is highly undesirable."[29]

The Heritage amicus brief concluded:

> *Empirical and other policy research in the past two decades—and relevant legal analysis—confirm what in fact was always the case: (1) health insurance individual mandates will fail and are bad public policy; and (2) the federal government's attempt to force private citizens to purchase health insurance in [Obamacare] is unconstitutional.*[30]

CHAPTER 24

NO PERMANENT VICTORIES— OR DEFEATS

All during 2009 and 2010, Heritage felt like the little Dutch boy with his hand in the leaking dike, except that the foundation was concerned about not just one but a dozen holes in the dike that was the U.S. economy.

The foundation agreed with the liberal commentator who exulted that Obamacare created "a huge structural change in the relationship between the public, the economy, and the government."

Heritage pointed out that despite the president's $800 billion stimulus program, the number of jobless in the first six months of 2010 increased by more than 2.2 million.

It underlined that the national debt soared by $1 trillion in the last nine months of 2010, reaching an alarming total of $14 trillion, equal to the nation's annual GDP.

It noted that as many as 85 percent of the American people said the country was on the wrong track; that 58 percent supported repeal of Obamacare; and that three-fourths said the stimulus money was wasted money.

In this time of turmoil, Heritage significantly increased its activities on and off Capitol Hill.

In 2010 foundation experts testified at twenty-eight House and Senate hearings and conducted more than eight hundred briefings for lawmakers and staffs. They wrote more than 580 *Backgrounders*, executive memos, *WebMemos*, legal memos, and special reports. The Center for Data Analysis analyzed sixty-four draft legislative proposals for members of Congress at their request. During the midterm elections, the government relations team briefed 141 candidates, an all-time high.

Knowing there are no permanent victories or defeats in Washington, Heritage took measured steps that it believed would substantially increase its conservative policy impact in Washington and the nation.

It formed Heritage Action for America, a 501(c)(4) sister organization, to put direct political pressure on Congress to adopt Heritage solutions as the law of the land. Michael Needham, a former chief of staff to Ed Feulner and a Stanford business school graduate, was named president and CEO of the new lobbying organization. Tim Chapman, who had served Heritage in several different positions and had been director of communications for Senator Jim DeMint (R-SC), was appointed chief operating officer (COO) of Heritage Action.

Heritage created Libertad.org, a new website that presents Heritage research, analysis, and commentary in Spanish. Named editor of Libertad was bilingual Israel Ortega, a former legislative aide to Congresswoman Ileana Ros-Lehtinen, former chairman of the House Foreign Affairs Committee.

It transformed the Center for Media and Public Policy into a hub of investigative journalism with former reporter and Heritage analyst Rob Bluey as its director. The center immediately began producing print, broadcast, and digital media exposés of governmental wrongdoing such as Representative Nancy Pelosi's trumpeting of PAYGO as a tool to stop deficit spending.

Pay-as-you-go budgeting is a way of offsetting or paying for new spending or tax cuts with spending reductions or tax increases. Bluey pointed out that PAYGO covers only new spending on mandatory entitlement programs, about 6 percent of the annual budget. Discretionary spending, about 40 percent of the budget, is exempt. Examples of major legislation that have been exempted include the economic stimulus and Obamacare. Two of Heritage's most alert watchdogs, Alison Acosta Fraser and Brian Riedl, warned in December 2006 that "PAYGO would be a sham."[1]

Heritage started the Center for Policy Innovation, charged with designing the next generation of new policy ideas. The center was conceived and is headed by Stuart Butler, who describes it as a virtual think tank, consisting of Heritage insiders and outside individuals. In making the appointment, Ed Feulner said that the foundation was lucky to have Butler "keeping us on the cutting edge."[2]

"Think of the center," said Feulner, "as a freewheeling research laboratory dedicated to thinking 'outside the box' to devise landmark policy recommendations consonant with time-tested conservative principles."[3]

Taking Butler's place as vice president for domestic and economic policy in September 2010 was David S. Addington, whose long résumé includes stints as chief of staff for Vice President Dick Cheney and president of a political action committee. He was also general counsel of the Department of Defense and held senior posts at the CIA, at the White House, and on Capitol Hill. He was associated with several major Washington law firms and was president of a multicandidate political action committee.

"David understands how Washington works at both ends of Pennsylvania," said Ed Feulner, "and knows exactly what it takes to turn policy ideas into law."[4]

That Addington knows how Heritage works was proven only eighteen months later, when he was named senior vice president and deputy chief operating officer, joining the executive team of Ed Feulner and Phil Truluck, who had managed Heritage for thirty-five years.

He offers this insight about Heritage's vision: "Freedom and opportunity produce prosperity and civil society." Asked whether he is optimistic or pessimistic about America's future, Addington replies that as a student of U.S. history, he is optimistic because "the American people have never failed yet" in a time of crisis. In the long run, he says, echoing Ronald Reagan, "I believe in the American people." Counseling patience, he says, "We're self-correcting, not fast-correcting." And things are not so bad, he insists, that "we cannot correct them."[5]

• • •

The foundation renamed the Center for American Studies the B. Kenneth Simon Center for Principles and Politics in 2011 and promoted its director, Matthew Spalding, to a new senior management position—vice president for American studies.

When the Left derided Tea Party members as "terrorists," "racists," and "Nazis," Heritage pointedly cosponsored Ohio's state Tea Party convention in July 2011. There Spalding conducted a seminar for more than seventy Tea Party leaders, explaining the First Principles of the American founding. Over the year he led First Principles seminars for state activists and Tea Party members from Texas, Oklahoma, Louisiana, and Arkansas.

In Washington, the Simon Center began publishing *Constitutional Guidance for Lawmakers,* a series of papers to help members of Congress follow a new rule requiring lawmakers to file a statement of constitutional authority with every bill they sponsor. The center also started *New Common Sense,* an e-newsletter that links present policy debates to America's First Principles. By the end of 2011, *New Common Sense* had 22,250 subscribers, an impressive showing due in part to the lively writing of its young editors, David Azerrad and Julia Shaw.

On September 17, 2011, Constitution Day, Heritage partnered with Classical Conversations, a home-schooling support group, to distribute twenty thousand copies of the foundation's pocket Constitution and Declaration of Independence at events around the nation.

All these activities were part of Heritage's commitment to the American Dream, as enunciated by the Founding Fathers, that America is a nation founded not on raw power but on eternal principles—that all men are created equal, that they are endowed with God-given unalienable rights to life, liberty, and the pursuit of happiness.

• • •

Responding to the sharply rising cost of higher education, Stuart Butler published "The Coming Higher-Ed Revolution." Over the past twenty-five years, he reported, the cost of a college education, adjusted for inflation, has almost tripled, while inflation-adjusted median family income has risen by only 10 percent. The average annual cost for tuition, fees, room and board, and other expenses now exceeds $17,000 ($29,000 for out-of-state students) at four-year public colleges. It tops $38,000 at private nonprofit schools.

Graduates from public colleges have an average indebtedness of $19,000; graduates from private colleges owe $26,000. Looking ahead, Butler writes, "The college prospects of less affluent Americans are likely to become much bleaker if the system does not go through some significant change." Among the major reforms discussed by Butler, as head of the Center for Policy Innovation, are online education and innovative for-profit schools. Traditional colleges may resist such changes,

Butler concedes, but "for most young people today electronic friendships and networks are the norm."[6]

● ● ●

Honors continued to flow to Heritage and Ed Feulner. *Washingtonian* magazine named Feulner one of "45 Who Shaped Washington" over the last forty-five years. The other forty-four included *Washington Post* publisher Katharine Graham, President Ronald Reagan, and Brookings's Alice Rivlin. In 2007 and again in 2010, *The Daily Telegraph* of London placed Feulner on its list of "The Most Influential U.S. Conservatives," saying that under Feulner, Heritage had become "a powerhouse of conservative ideas." Fox News Sunday featured Feulner as its "Power Player of the Week." Political strategist and *Wall Street Journal* columnist Karl Rove picked Feulner as one of the "Seven Most Powerful Conservatives" in Washington—the only nonelected public official, along with columnist Charles Krauthammer, to make Rove's list.

Jennifer Marshall, director of domestic policy studies, was named one of "20 Power Players" by the *National Journal* for her role in the national debate on education policy. Distinguished fellow Jim Talent also won the "power player" title from the *Journal* for his work on national defense policy.[7]

Heritage membership soared again, from 580,000 in 2009 to 710,000 in 2010, a 22 percent increase, and more than double what membership had been in 2007. Contributions in 2010 reached a new high of $73 million, compared with $45.6 million just three years earlier. The Heritage endowment stood at about $100 million. Prudent stewardship enabled the foundation to weather the 2007 financial crisis better than most think tanks and foundations.

A major contributor to Heritage's success—aside from the expanded national awareness of the foundation through talk radio and cable television—was the phenomenon of the Tea Party, which, in Ed Feulner's words, "recognized Heritage as that rarest of all Washington institutions: a principled force that fought daily to uphold the ideals of our nation's founders." The Tea Party people knew, said Feulner, that "we weren't about to go wobbly in this time of choosing."[8]

To guide the foundation and the conservative movement philosophically, Heritage drafted the Mount Vernon Statement, a manifesto reaffirming "a Constitutional conservatism [that] unites all conservatives through the natural fusion provided by American principles." The statement was initially signed by more than eighty conservative leaders, including Tea Partiers, and subsequently by more than 230,000 people. The Mount Vernon Statement was widely described as the best statement of conservative principles since the 1960 Sharon Statement, which had been approved at the founding meeting of Young Americans for Freedom.

An in-depth examination of America's liberating ideas was provided by Matthew Spalding in his bestselling book, *We Still Hold These Truths* (as of mid-2012, some 46,000 copies had been sold). Representative Paul Ryan, chairman of the powerful House Budget Committee in the post–Tea Party Congress and the GOP's 2012 vice-presidential candidate, called the principles set forth in Spalding's work "the indispensable guides policymakers need now."[9] Matt Spalding shows why "the principles of our liberty are still fresh today," Feulner commented, "and why their revival is the *only* way to prevent America from becoming another dead culture like Europe."[10]

In recognition of its commitment to the American founding, the Tea Party was awarded the 2010 Henry Salvatori Prize for American Citizenship. With the party's concurrence, Heritage sent "First Principles Field Kits"—including the U.S. Constitution, *We Still Hold These Truths, The Founder's Almanac, The Heritage Guide to the Constitution,* and *Reading the Right Books*—to several hundred Tea Party leaders. Accepting the Salvatori Prize for the Tea Party was Billie Tucker, who said, "[We] just ask you to help us by giving us training, giving us material, and we'll give you the people to make it happen."

Spalding responded by pointing out the differences between the patriots of the first Tea Party in December 1773 and today's patriots:

> *Our task is different. It is not about fixed bayonets, but fixed principles; not about bullets but ballots. Our task is not to overthrow; it is not revolution; it is renewal and restoration of those self-evident truths of constitutional government at the heart of America.*[11]

• • •

However, given the progressive revolution initiated by President Obama and his allies on Capitol Hill, Heritage had to be practical as well as philosophical.

The American electorate was divided between mainstream voters and what pollster Scott Rasmussen called the "political class" over the necessary size and scope of government. Heritage's position as enunciated by Ed Feulner was clear: "The will of the American people cannot continue to be overridden by a political elite. Government must tax and spend less."[12] This became the Tea Party's mantra, resulting in the countrywide repudiation of Democratic candidates in the 2010 elections.

Brian Riedl, the foundation's Grover Hermann Fellow, became a Tea Party favorite when he documented that the Congressional Budget Office had understated the ten-year deficit by $7 trillion. Using a more realistic baseline, Riedl showed that the proposed Obama budget would add $16.3 trillion in new debt between 2009 and 2020. Talk radio host Rush Limbaugh read the Riedl report on the air, generating thousands of e-mails and phone calls to congressional offices.

When liberals sought to increase tax revenues through a value-added tax (VAT), Heritage stressed the "hidden" nature of a VAT and predicted it would not be a substitute for present taxes but would become an additional tax on an already overtaxed populace. When Senator John McCain introduced a resolution stating that a VAT would be "harmful" to the nation, he used the arguments of J. D. Foster, Heritage's Norman B. Ture Senior Fellow. The McCain resolution carried by a wide margin—85–13—and the Democrats abandoned VAT.

A major cause of America's Byzantine tax code is the fact that fewer and fewer Americans are paying federal taxes but still receive federal benefits. The result is that more and more people are trapped in a state of dependence on government to provide them with the basics of life. Heritage's annual *Index of Dependence on Government* (started in 2002) reported that dependence in 2009 increased 13.6 percent over the previous year.

The 2012 *Index*, prepared by the Center for Data Analysis, reported even more disturbing news: one in five Americans—67.3 million—now relies on the federal government for some benefit from housing, health care, and food stamps to college tuition and retirement assistance. The average beneficiary receives an estimated $32,748 annually. At the same time, nearly half of the U.S. population—49.5 percent—does not pay any federal income taxes. Feulner said bluntly: "This is a recipe for financial disaster and social collapse."[13]

Two years earlier, despite the findings of the 2010 *Index of Dependence on Government,* the Democratic Congress, with President Obama's concurrence, had pressed for more taxes—income taxes, capital gains taxes, dividend taxes, estate taxes—to take effect on January 1, 2011. Given the documented public opposition to tax increases,

Heritage analysts wondered whether congressional Democrats were possessed by a death wish.

A special CDA report showed that raising taxes on those earning above $250,000 would take jobs and income from all Americans. To drive the argument home, the report presented job and income loss by state and by congressional district, enabling members of Congress to see and to argue that raising taxes in a recession sinks all ships.

After the November 2010 elections, a lame-duck Congress, chastened and contrite, voted down the higher tax rates proposed by an unrepentant Nancy Pelosi and other liberal Democrats.

• • •

The federal government kept declaring so many things to be criminal that Heritage was obliged to ask: "Are we becoming one nation under arrest?"

Lindsay Brown, a high school senior, was jailed for having a butter knife in her car.

Cortez Curtis, a thirteen-year-old, was arrested for bringing a calculator that contained tools (including a tiny knife blade) to school.

Twelve-year-old Ansche Hedgepeth was handcuffed and detained for eating one French fry on the Washington, D.C., subway.

Sixty-one-year-old Kay Leibrand was booked for letting her hedges grow too tall.

In fact, the foundation discovered, the government is unable to say how many crimes are on its books—a condition accentuated by the increasing number of federal regulations that carry criminal penalties. The result: a blizzard of prosecutions and sentences.

Heritage came to the rescue with *One Nation Under Arrest,* edited by Paul Rosenzweig and Brian Walsh, which documents how, in the editors' words, "crazy laws, rogue prosecutors, and activist judges threaten [Americans'] liberty."[14] Representatives Bobby Scott (D-VA) and Louie Gohmert (R-TX) held a Capitol Hill news conference and a House hearing on overcriminalization that resulted in the introduction of legislation in May 2012.

No less troubling to the foundation was the state of the nation's defenses. Heritage recommended the establishment of an independent commission to review one of the Pentagon's most important responsibilities—its Quadrennial Defense Review. Congress adopted the foundation's suggestion regarding an outside commission and named Heritage distinguished fellow Jim Talent a commissioner.

National security studies fellow Mackenzie Eaglen followed up by putting together a coalition of think tanks and other groups committed to educating the public about "the need to reinvest in America's military." The coalition's first success was a *Wall Street Journal* column "Peace Doesn't Keep Itself" written by Feulner, AEI president Arthur Brooks, and *Weekly Standard* editor William Kristol. Eaglen was implementing the philosophy laid down by Feulner decades earlier that a strong conservative movement was in the best interests of the Heritage Foundation and of America.

Consistent with its belief in traditional American values, Heritage took special notice of the institution of marriage, which suffered several blows in 2010. *Perry v. Schwarzenegger* challenged California's voter-approved constitutional amendment (Proposition 8), defining marriage as between one man and one woman. When a trial court struck down Prop 8, Ed Meese wrote a *Washington Post* column arguing the ruling was "too extreme to stand" and praised the court of appeals for staying the lower court's order.

In *Gill v. Office of Personnel Management,* a Massachusetts federal judge ruled that the Defense of Marriage Act, passed by Congress in 1996, was unconstitutional, saying it had no "rational relationship to a legitimate government interest." Heritage forcefully rebutted the decision, demonstrating a wide range of benefits from marriage, including improved educational results for children in traditional families and the reduced likelihood of juvenile crime, pregnancy, and drug use.

Senior research fellow Robert Rector summarized the favorable economic impact of marriage: "Marriage remains America's strongest anti-poverty weapon, yet it continues to decline. As husbands disappear from the home, poverty and welfare dependence will increase, and children and parents will suffer as a result. Current government policies either ignore or undermine marriage," Rector wrote. "This needs to change."[15]

In July 2010, Rector published a definitive study documenting the failure of the forty-five-year-old War on Poverty, begun in 1965 by President Lyndon B. Johnson. The percentage of people living in poverty, Rector reported, remains essentially unchanged, despite seventy-one different federal programs and benefits that will cost taxpayers more than $10 trillion over the next decade.

The veteran analyst, author of more than a dozen major papers on welfare, called for a rethinking of federal strategy and outlined a more effective approach including:

- Making committed marriage a centerpiece of welfare policy and eliminating the "marriage penalty" inherent in many current programs.

- Capping aggregate spending on welfare programs.

- Treating a portion of aid to able-bodied adults as a loan to be repaid rather than a gift.

Members of the new Republican Congress—called the Tea Party Congress by some—drew heavily on Rector's research when they introduced sweeping welfare reform legislation in early 2011.

• • •

As important as Heritage's research, publications, films, radio-TV-newspaper interviews, legislative assistance, fund-raising, and grassroots activity were, the most far-reaching and controversial action of The Heritage Foundation in 2010 was the formation of Heritage Action for America, its sister 501(c)(4) "advocacy" group.

For thirty-three years Ed Feulner and Phil Truluck had resisted the suggestion that Heritage should get into the lobbying business while conceding that the foundation was more aggressive about promoting its ideas than research organizations of the past. Think tanks were overly cautious in deciding "just how far they can opine," Feulner told a historian. "The result was that their impact was not as effective as it should have been. We set out to change that, and we did."[16]

When he was Heritage's vice president for government relations in the early 1980s, Richard N. Holwill (who went on to head up Amway's Washington office) provided an explanation of what lobbying is and isn't that served Heritage well for more than three decades.

As a tax-exempt 501(c)(3) policy research organization, Holwill said, the foundation is not permitted to lobby for or against a specific piece of legislation. Heritage is allowed, however, to publish studies that address policy issues facing American lawmakers. The next step is crucial to understanding what a 501(c)(3) can and can't do.

Copies of the Heritage study are distributed to the appropriate members of Congress, congressional and committee staffers, White House officials, other executive branch people, and the media. "Though Heritage does not take a formal institutional position on any of these issues," Holwill explained, "we encourage our analysts to express their views in the clearest possible terms and to structure their arguments persuasively, logically. Naturally, we don't expect everyone to agree with our findings." And he added this critical point:

> We never ask anyone to vote one way or another on a particular proposal. The line between policy analysis and lobbying is very clear. It is a line we never cross.[17]

That Heritage never crossed the line into the mine-filled land of lobbying is attested by the fact that after three and a half decades of advocacy and frequent IRS audits, the foundation remained a tax-exempt think tank in good standing with the ever-vigilant Internal Revenue Service.

However, things radically changed in 2007 with congressional passage of the Honest Leadership and Open Government Act, an expansion of the 1995 Lobbying Disclosure Act. The 2007 legislation instituted much tighter reporting requirements for any group or individual that contacted a member of Congress regarding proposed legislation. Such contacts included personal visits, telephone calls, and e-mails. If the contacts totaled more than 20 percent of the individual's time, he had to register as a lobbyist. This meant that some of Heritage's most influential analysts who routinely spent many hours and even days working with a congressman or senator on a piece of legislation would have to register as lobbyists.

"When I first read the new lobbying act," Feulner said, "it scared the socks off of me with its unbelievable restrictions. Phil and I began discussing how to go about establishing a 501(c)(4) organization. We discovered it could be done easily and legally."[18]

In a memo to Feulner, Heritage lawyer Alan Dye summarized the rules regarding the relationship between a tax-exempt entity and a lobbying group:

- Each organization had to be truly separate with its own board of directors and officers, its own bank accounts, and its own financial operations.

- There could be overlap among the officers and directors of the two organizations and cooperation in their activities.

- If they shared office space, equipment and other services, the cost had to be reasonably allocated between the two organizations.

The legal issues, Dye said, "are relatively easy to manage." What he called "the issues of credibility" were more problematic. He predicted that critics of Heritage would suggest that "a lobbying affiliate" compromises the foundation's academic reputation. But there was a counterargument: "such an affiliate is merely a prudent way to assure that Heritage does not engage in advocacy."[19] Feulner and Truluck accepted the advice of their longtime legal counsel and added their own overriding argument regarding the formation of a 501(c)(4).

It was no longer enough to present the most persuasive policy paper in the world to a congressman or senator and expect him to vote the right way if (a) he was mainly motivated by the desire to stay in office, or if (b) he was easily intimidated either by his party leaders or by the liberal establishment.

In the permanent campaign world of contemporary Washington, Feulner concluded, something more tangible than logic and reason was required. He recalled what Ronald Reagan had said: "If you can't make them see the light, make them feel the heat." Feulner decided that Heritage should significantly raise the temperature. The vehicle he and Truluck developed was Heritage Action.

"The 1995 Lobbying Disclosure Act was well intended," says Phil Truluck, "designed to limit the influence of lobbyists, but think tanks shouldn't be considered lobbyists. We're not trying to sell anything. We deal in ideas. We're not trying to get special favors. No one can give us a subsidy or a government contract." But Heritage faced a new reality affecting contacts with members of Congress in the new act.

After exploring every possible consequence for a year, Feulner and Truluck finally decided to create Heritage Action for America in concert with the foundation's other senior managers. "The whole (c)(4) discussion took place in front of all senior management," says Truluck. "Everyone had their input. This was not something that Ed and I just sat down and said, 'Hey, we're going to do this.' That's not the way we operate.

"Our senior managers are not just important for running their departments," he says. "We depend on them to help us run Heritage and decide where Heritage is going in the future."[20]

Once the decision was made, Heritage determined that it was going to be the best (c)(4) in operation. There are institutional "ramifications," the COO concedes, "which are still being worked out and will take time. But we were not going to get into a situation where our analysts would be labeled lobbyists."[21] The proposal for Heritage Action for America was submitted to the Heritage board of trustees, which carefully considered and then approved the plan.

Feulner used the pages of *The Wall Street Journal* to announce the new independent advocacy organization. Pointing out that Heritage had been called "the beast" of all think tanks (by *The New York Times*), he said that "our beast [has] added new fangs. . . . Heritage Action for America." This new organization, he explained, "will be able to spend money to push legislation we think the country needs without the obstacles faced by a nonprofit like the Heritage Foundation."

Heritage Action would not get involved in electoral politics, Feulner said, but it would use "all the tools available in the American political system to ensure that congressmen face the same pressure to do the right thing as they face to do the politically expedient thing."[22] That meant taking on the Republican leadership if necessary.

Over the next two years—on an annual budget that went from $4.5 million to $6 million—Heritage Action lobbied successfully for the House to pass repeal of Obamacare legislation, promoted the foundation's *Saving the American Dream* as the guideline for serious reform of spending, taxes, and entitlements, and initiated a tough legislative scorecard that tracked not only key up-and-down votes but early procedural and amending votes. It also created a network of "sentinels," grassroots leaders trained to advocate conservative policies locally and nationally.

Led by two young "tigers," thirty-year-old Mike Needham and thirty-four-year-old Tim Chapman, Heritage Action unapologetically stepped on the toes of conservative congressmen accustomed to getting almost-perfect ratings from conservative organizations. A 65 percent or 75 percent score from Heritage Action shocked many of them. A few angry members said they would no longer cite Heritage Foundation research.

However, with the solid backing of the board of trustees, Ed Feulner kept urging Heritage Action on, and Needham and Chapman kept fighting for conservative ideas and policies. When a bipartisan group of lawmakers introduced the NAT GAS Act, Heritage Action explained that tax subsidies included in the act for natural gas vehicles would distort energy markets while benefiting only a few consumers. By the end of 2011, nineteen members had removed their names from the bill—a Capitol Hill record.

The House Republican leadership is still adjusting to the aggressive tactics of Heritage Action. They say "we're unreasonable and never want to compromise," remarks Tim Chapman. What "we're trying to do is message to them that we are dying, literally dying, to fight [alongside] them." But a big *if* is attached to the pledge: the Republican leadership must take on, not accommodate, the liberal Democrats.

Needham and Chapman worry that if Republicans do not "paint in bold colors," they could win elections but have no mandate to do anything significant with their newfound power.[23] To help Republicans move in the right direction, says CEO Mike Needham, Heritage Action will "take the conservative policies outlined by our sister organization and make them a reality."

Thirty years earlier Ronald Reagan called The Heritage Foundation the "feisty new kid on the block." Heritage Action was now "the tough new kid on the congressional block," eager to affect outcomes on Capitol Hill with the help of The Heritage Foundation's several hundred thousand members.[24]

CHAPTER 25

FIRST PRINCIPLES

From the beginning Heritage has stressed the need for accountability for itself and for public officials—which is behind its sharp criticism of President Obama. By any fair measure Obama has been one of the most unaccountable chief executives in recent history, despite his campaign pledge to once again make government "accountable" to the people. Ed Feulner offered the following examples:

Two weeks before his inauguration, Obama said, "We are going to ban all earmarks." The first spending bill he signed contained more than nine thousand earmarks.

Of the health care debate, he said, "We're going to do all the negotiations on C-SPAN, so the American people will be able to watch." Succeeding months of debate were conducted behind locked doors.

Obama ran against the idea of a mandate for Americans to buy health insurance—attacking Hillary Clinton for championing the idea—and then made the mandate a key provision of the bill that passed.

The president promised to reduce federal spending and effect "a net spending cut." He did precisely the opposite, presiding over the largest budget deficits in U.S. history.

Such broken promises, said Feulner, are at the core of what is infecting government today: "Too many elected officials are untrustworthy. Their promises just run through their fingers like water."[1]

"I don't predict election results," the Heritage president said about the 2010 elections, "but I'll be surprised if November 6 doesn't bring political shifts of historic proportions."[2]

• • •

The startling results of 2010 made it clear that American voters had had enough. "The people have sent an unmistakable message to [the president]," declared John Boehner, the new Speaker of the House, "and that message is, 'Change course.' " A subdued President Obama agreed that the Democrats had taken a "shellacking."[3]

Republicans picked up sixty-one seats in the House, exceeding the fifty-two seats captured in the 1994 Gingrich revolution and giving them a commanding majority. The GOP gained six seats in the Senate, drastically reducing the Democratic majority, and six new governorships. If you subtracted the states where Democrats lost badly—Virginia, Indiana, Ohio, Pennsylvania, Michigan, Wisconsin, Florida—*Time* reported, Obama's "2008 landslide evaporates into a dead heat."[4]

Neoconservative columnist Charles Krauthammer viewed the massive Republican swing as a reaction to "a ruling party spectacularly misjudging its mandate and taking an unwilling country through a two-year experiment in hyper-liberalism." But the president, he said, "remains clueless." When asked three times at a postelection news conference whether rejection of his policy agenda might have something to do with the drubbing he took, Obama looked "as if he had been asked whether the sun had risen in the West" and replied, No.[5]

A more philosophical explanation of the Republican sweep was offered by James Ceaser of the University of Virginia, who wrote that to the Tea Party, the inflated size of government and the extent of the federal debt "represented not only a burden on future generations and a threat to American power, but also a violation of the spirit and letter of the Constitution." This theme, Ceaser said, "is what connects the Tea Party to the American tradition and makes their concerns matters of fundamental patriotism."[6]

It was this connection and patriotism that persuaded Heritage to cooperate with the Tea Party and to encourage Tea Partiers to study the Constitution and understand its relevance to the current issues of the day. In his monthly letter from the President's Office, Feulner wrote that the election "set the elite political class against Middle Americans and the latter prevailed."

The Tea Party's phenomenal growth, he said, "suggests that in the months ahead Heritage and allied think tanks could exert more influence than ever." He pointed out that for months people "have been joining us at a rate of about 15,000 per month. . . . It's no coincidence that during the same period, the Tea Party was growing into a movement of national consequence."[7]

Heritage and the Tea Party are natural allies, Feulner said, insisting that government should be guided by First Principles, "not by the interests of career politicians feathering their political nests." As a result of the elections, he said, Congress is getting a "new wave of members committed to the politics of ideas, especially the founding principles of limited government." The foundation, he revealed, would welcome the new congressmen with a three-day new-member orientation. And it would continue talking with Tea Party leaders and providing them with Heritage materials "that [will] help them hone their messages and stay politically engaged." "This election," wrote Ed Feulner, "renews our faith in what is possible when we stand together and stay the course. Onward!"[8]

President Obama had a different plan, grounded in politics.

• • •

When you have suffered a major political defeat and you want a second term in the White House and you are a modern Machiavellian, what do you do?

Barack Obama had begun his presidency seeking to be loved not feared, accepting as his due the acclamation of his party and the nation and the world, certain he was the change America had been waiting for, and pointing to his decisive presidential victory as proof that the nation and its people shared his progressive vision. He was cool and cerebral on the outside but inwardly relishing the love bestowed on him by *The New York Times* and *The Nation*, Oprah and Arianna Huffington, German chancellor Angela Merkel and French prime minister Nicolas Sarkozy, Warren Buffett and Jon Stewart, and *Newsweek*'s Evan Thomas, who said in awe, "Obama's standing above the country, above—above he world. He's sort of God."[9]

But Obama was obliged, after the unexpected emergence of the Tea Party movement and the sweeping anti-Democratic results of the 2010 elections, to accept Machiavelli's counsel about choosing fear over love. He gave it a modern twist: he sought to be loved *and* feared—loved by fellow progressives but feared by conservatives who opposed his intention to transform America into another social democratic country like

Germany or France. Obama calculated that conservatives would resort to wild, inflammatory rhetoric that would push Middle America into supporting him.

As a resourceful Machiavellian, he used modern means to achieve political ends, including exploitation of the mass media, especially social media; the mass transfer of income to voting blocs through entitlement programs; and the use of executive orders and government regulations to satisfy special interests. His formula was money + organization + ideology + media = political success. He rarely played the race card—he did not have to. It was a very unusual African American who did not cast his ballot for Obama. At the same time, there existed what the black author Shelby Steele calls "white guilt." White Americans, conservatives as well as liberals, willingly vote for an African American to demonstrate that America is not racist.[10]

Still, the weak recovery from the Great Recession weakened Obama's reelection prospects, inspiring nine Republicans to seek their party's presidential nomination. Beginning in 2011, they began participating in an almost weekly series of debates that one wag likened to a TV reality show, *Meet the Challenger*. Over the course of twenty debates, viewers probably learned more than they needed to know about former governor Mitt Romney, ex-senator Rick Santorum, former House Speaker Newt Gingrich, Representative Ron Paul, Texas governor Rick Perry, businessman Herman Cain, former ambassador Jon Huntsman, Representative Michele Bachmann, and former governor Tim Pawlenty.

After months of debate and thousands of miles of travel and millions of dollars of advertising—most of it negative—former Massachusetts governor Mitt Romney won the most convention delegates by the spring of 2012 and gained the right to challenge the president.

Thus the American people were given the opportunity to vote for an incumbent president whom 25 percent of Americans did not believe had been born in America or a challenger whose father had been born in Mexico; a liberal turned moderate or a moderate turned conservative; a radical community organizer or a Wall Street millionaire; a Harvard graduate or a Harvard graduate; a president whose wife was 20 percentage points more popular than he or a challenger whose wife was also more popular than he; a president whose black pastor had publicly declared "God damn America!" or a challenger whose faith did not ordain black men to the priesthood of his faith until 1978.

The people had another option: to stay home. But given the stakes—who would be the chief executive officer of a stagnant but still-gigantic $16 trillion U.S. economy and the commander in chief of the remaining superpower in the world—that seemed an unlikely decision by most voters.

In such a supercharged electoral atmosphere, what could just one albeit influential research organization do? As from its beginning, a resolute Heritage took stock of where America was and proposed where it should be and how to get there.

America had become a scary place. Washington, D.C., spent billions of dollars it didn't have, Congress seemed frozen by partisanship, the president blamed his predecessor for America's economic woes, the national debt ballooned, federal regulators kept piling on new rules and regulations, employers delayed expansion plans, banks sat on their cash, housing prices still lagged far behind prerecession levels, and millions of unemployed wondered whether they would ever see a paycheck again.

A battle-hardened Heritage waded into key policy debates, like repealing Obamacare and providing for a necessary national defense. But, insisted Ed Feulner, "these challenging times demand even more." And so the foundation mapped out a vision for America's future. It was a future, Feulner said, where "hard work is rewarded not punished," where "our children and grandchildren are free of crushing national debt," and where "a social safety net protects the least among us."[11]

The road map was called *Saving the American Dream,* and it outlined how to fix the debt, cut spending, and restore prosperity. It was bold, comprehensive, and less than fifty pages—strikingly different from the 1,046-page *Mandate for Leadership I.* But Heritage had long since adjusted to the Age of the Internet. As called for by the times, *Saving the American Dream* was ambitious.

It eliminated the 72,000-page U.S. tax code, replacing it with a simple flat tax.

It downsized the federal government and increased the role of the states.

It brought decision making closer to the people rather than unelected bureaucrats, starting with the health care system.

It fully funded national defense, critical in a precarious world.

It balanced the nation's budget within a decade and showed how to keep it balanced.

It started paying down the national debt.

We have been in critical times before, Feulner said, "and every time the American people have risen to the occasion." We were told in 1776, he pointed out, that "no upstart colonists could defeat the strongest nation in the world," and we changed the course of history.

In 1860 we were told the Union could not hold and America was through, "and we brought forth a new birth of freedom."

In 1980 we were told that the American century was at an end, and "we launched a great economic expansion, rebuilt our military, and revived our national spirit."[12]

Quoting Ronald Reagan, Ed Feulner said what is required is "a willingness by all of us to believe in ourselves. Together and with God's help, we can and will resolve the problems which now confront us.

"Let us seize the moment," he urged, "change our country's course, and save the American Dream."[13] Heritage set about doing all three things.

Throughout 2011 and into 2012, Heritage (1) helped prevent the inclusion of tax increases in the Budget Control Act of 2011; (2) published a fifteen-paper series making the case for repeal of Obamacare—which the House of Representatives did in January 2011; (3) supported congressional ratification of free-trade agreements with Colombia, Panama, and South Korea, long-standing Heritage objectives; and (4) sponsored in November 2011 (along with the American Enterprise Institute and CNN) a nationally televised debate for Republican presidential candidates on foreign and defense policy.

More than nine million viewers watched the live foreign policy debate at Constitution Hall in Washington, D.C., while millions more viewed it on CNN en Español, CNN International, American Forces Network, and C-SPAN. It was generally conceded to be the most informative of the many Republican debates, with Heritage's David Addington being singled out for his probing question on Syria, "What are our interests in this region and what would you do to protect them?" Commented *The Wall Street Journal:* "The queries were much deeper and more substantive than those the candidates typically get from political journalists and handpicked 'regular voters.' "[14]

Congressional leaders joined the campaign to save the American Dream. Representative Jim Jordan (R-OH), chairman of the Republican Study Committee, and Senator Jim DeMint (R-SC), the immediate past chairman of the Senate Steering Committee, introduced bills to overhaul the nation's welfare programs based on Heritage research. Representative Paul Ryan, chairman of the House Budget Committee, and Senator Ron Wyden (D-OR) proposed a reform of Medicare similar to the foundation's recommendations.

Heritage was Washington's busiest think tank in 2011 with 188 public lectures, 131 *Backgrounders*, 346 *WebMemos*, forty-seven appearances before congressional committees, and thirty issues briefings for candidates. It held 3,508 radio interviews (an average of ten a day), 1,339 TV interviews, and more than fourteen thousand commentaries in major print outlets (newspapers, magazines, and journals). It stepped up its Internet activity with 9.6 million visitors to Heritage.org, 6.1 million visitors to the *Foundry* blog, 400,000 Facebook friends, and 162,000 Twitter followers. No other think tank has come close to generating this level of social media traffic.

Drawing on the foundation's Townhall experience, in July 2012 Heritage Action launched *Istook Live!* a daily three-hour radio talk show featuring distinguished fellow Ernest Istook, who hosted a popular radio interview program in Oklahoma before serving in Congress for fourteen years. "Our mission," explains Istook, "is to bring listeners smart, civil programming from a conservative perspective." Heritage Action will partner with broadcasting experts who will syndicate the show and sell advertising. Heritage COO Phil Truluck emphasized that the new venture would not "detract" from the long-standing successful relationship between Heritage and talk radio. *Istook Live!* he said, is another example of the foundation's entrepreneurial philosophy.

Consistent with Feulner's build-the-conservative-movement philosophy, Heritage seeks out the right people for its prestigious Clare Boothe Luce awards. Recent awardees have included Fox News Channel founder Roger Ailes, Pittsburgh publisher and Heritage board vice chairman Richard Scaife, former vice president Richard Cheney, social critic and Heritage trustee Midge Decter, and neoconservative author Norman Podhoretz. The foundation gave its 2011 Henry Salvatori Prize for American Citizenship to Dr. Hal Scherz, founder of Docs 4 Patient Care, and it hosted a tribute dinner for author-journalist-professor-epigrammatist M. Stanton Evans for his lifelong service to American conservatism.

The Salvatori Prize was the latest project of a decades-long relationship between Heritage and the late California industrialist Henry Salvatori, whose generosity made possible in 1991 the establishment of the Salvatori Center for Academic Leadership. As Salvatori Fellows, young academics and advanced graduate students came to Washington to learn about the foundations of American liberty. Among the dozens of recipients were UC Berkeley professor of law John Yoo, Lt. Col.

(USA-ret.) Wesley Allen Riddle, UCLA political scientist Timothy J. Groseclose, Radford University professor Matthew J. Franch, and Federal Elections Commission chairman Bradley Smith.

Heritage welcomed 100,000 new members in 2011, bringing total membership to about 685,000 while receiving contributions of just under $74 million, divided between individuals (78 percent), foundations (16 percent), and corporations (6 percent). Of the $80 million in operating expenses (as intended, Heritage withdrew $4.5 million from its reserve), research and education took $49 million, media $12 million, management and general expenses $3 million, and fund-raising $16 million. Donors noted and approved the low percentage allocated to fund-raising and Heritage's insistence that it be audited by a highly regarded independent firm of CPAs.

Outside Washington, Heritage hosted more than thirty-five events in twenty-six cities, attracting thousands of attendees and featuring prominent speakers such as former defense secretary Donald Rumsfeld, author Dinesh D'Souza, *Weekly Standard* editor Fred Barnes, author/scholar Victor Davis Hanson, *Wall Street Journal* editors Dan Henninger and Steve Moore, radio-TV host Sean Hannity, political strategist Karl Rove, Wisconsin governor Scott Walker, and Gen. Peter Pace, former chairman of the Joint Chiefs of Staff.

The foundation got as close to the grass roots as possible in January 2012 when it hit the road in partnership with the Family Research Council (FRC) on a yearlong bus tour of America under the theme "Your Money, Your Values, Your Vote." With Heritage emphasizing fiscal issues and FRC values issues, the two organizations calculated the forty-five-foot-long Values Bus would visit some thirty states right up to the November 6 election. In the first six months, the bus tour (personally supervised by Heritage vice president Genevieve Wood) hosted eighty events attracting over forty thousand people interested in the issues of the day and registering to vote if they had not already done so. "We're saving the American Dream one bus stop at a time," quipped Ed Feulner.[15]

Awards kept coming for Heritage people. Distinguished fellow Edwin Meese received the Family Research Council's Vision and Leadership Award, while Stuart Butler, director of the Center for Policy Innovation, was given one of Fox Business's John Stossel's Emmys for offering the best plan—according to a poll of viewers—to solve the nation's fiscal crisis. Butler's presentation on Stossel's program was based on *Saving the American Dream.*

• • •

There were accolades from inside and outside the conservative movement to Ed Feulner as the totality of his contributions through the decades seemed to strike everyone at the same time.

When Arthur Brooks, the dynamic president of the American Enterprise Institute, appeared at The Heritage Foundation in May 2012 to talk about his latest book—*The Road to Freedom*—he revealed that the foundation "has a lot to do with the things that have gone right in my professional life," such as inviting him to talk about every one of his "freedom" books. He appreciated that a Heritage audience understood the importance of a free society.

And that, he said, was due to "the visionary leadership of Ed Feulner, who has a unique place in the conservative movement and a unique place in designing an agenda of public policy" that "is our gift to America and America's gift to the world."[16]

Despite what he calls Heritage's "contribution" to Obamacare, Cato's longtime president Ed Crane does not stint in his praise of Ed Feulner: "He's a tireless worker and a smart guy, he knows his goals, he hires good people, he's principled." The man who headed the leading libertarian think tank in America—until announcing his retirement in the fall of 2012—calls Heritage "the leading conservative organization in the country. Ed has done a marvelous job."[17]

Ed Feulner has been able "to bridge ideas and action," says David Abshire, the former president of the Center for Strategic and International Studies, who has known Feulner since the early 1960s. He understands that "you can't ride on your oars. You must constantly seek a sense of renewal." Summing up Feulner, Abshire says, "Ed made Heritage."[18]

The past president of Brookings, Michael Armacost, concurs with Abshire's point about Feulner being a bridge builder. "Ed has a high regard for the power of ideas," says Armacost, "but is centered in the policy environment." Such melding will inevitably become more prevalent in research organizations as the pace of mass communications quickens. But there is a price to be paid, he says: Washington is now "a less reflective and more competitive place."[19]

Gerald Dorfman of the Hoover Institution observed Ed Feulner as chairman of the U.S. Advisory Commission on Public Diplomacy: "There is a force about him. You pay attention to what he has to say." Dorfman compares the Heritage president to Margaret Olivia Sage, founder of the Russell Sage Foundation, who helped shape social research and public policy during the Progressive Era. Among the many think tanks in this conservative era, Dorfman asserts, "Heritage has made the most national splash." Hoover director John Raisian is equally complimentary, saying, "I hold Ed Feulner on a pedestal in terms of being the most qualified and efficient producer of policy information to the broader public that exists in this country."[20]

Economist Jeffrey Eisenach, who has been a visiting scholar at AEI, Heritage, and the Hudson Institute as well as president of the Progress and Freedom Foundation, said that Feulner is successful because "he believes so deeply in what he is doing. . . . There is that flame inside him." Under his leadership, Heritage "has had far and away the greatest impact of any think tank on the political process."[21]

According to Will Marshall, president of the Progressive Policy Institute, which includes Bill Clinton as a founder, Heritage "pioneered a new kind of advocacy tank" that "broke the old mold" made by Brookings. He says that Ed Feulner was "generous with his time" and "even encouraging" when Marshall asked for his advice when getting started. Marshall was especially impressed with Heritage's marketing skills: it wrote the book on how to "popularize political ideas."[22]

Ed Feulner "has a vision and a passion for building the movement," says Larry Mone, the president of the New York City–based Manhattan Institute.[23] "Ed is one of the towering examples of a successful conservative organizational entrepreneur," remarks Morton Blackwell, founder and president of the Leadership Institute, which has graduated over 110,000 young men and women from its programs, including the Feulners' daughter Emily.

"Ed is the perfect head of the Heritage Foundation," says Phyllis Schlafly, the doyenne of the profamily movement in America. "He's led it with dignity and focus and good goals and excellent product. I'd give him an A-plus." "He's taken a concept and turned it into a powerhouse," says Ron Robinson of Young America's Foundation, which grew out of the activist Young Americans for Freedom.

"No conservative organization has been anywhere near as effective as Heritage," says *über*-fund-raiser Richard Viguerie, "in changing the culture not only here in Washington but also in the country. I hate to think where we would be without The Heritage Foundation."[24]

"Ed is an emotionally and intellectually secure person," says former U.S. senator Jim Talent, who has led several of the Osprey Point retreats for senior management. "That is a rare quality for a leader based in Washington." "He is both classical liberal and traditional conservative," remarks T. Kenneth Cribb, Jr., the former president of the ISI. "He embodies the idea of fusionism."

"He turned a storefront into a national institution," says Mike Franc, Heritage's veteran vice president for government relations. "Ed acts like a general in a lot of ways," says Vice President James Carafano, a retired army colonel and former West Point instructor who heads Heritage's Allison Center for Foreign Policy Studies. "He provides the vision and lets people do their thing." "He has an enormous ego," says Bridgett Wagner, who after thirty years at Heritage knows Ed Feulner as well as anyone. "But he would say he was a failure if Heritage closed down after he left."

"He is a true visionary," remarks Genevieve Wood, Heritage's vice president of marketing, who has worked with such conservative icons as Paul Weyrich, Morton Blackwell, and Jack Kemp. "And yet he has a far deeper understanding of all the parts of Heritage than I expected in a CEO."

"Nobody hates Ed," offers Hillsdale president and Heritage trustee Larry Arnn. "He is a really good man, a just man." "I do not know how you manage your infinite courtesies," wrote William F. Buckley, Jr., "so warm, so well-worded, so thoughtful. I wish I could say this freshly, but I have been a fan too long to get away with it." "He has an amazing love for God and for his wife and children and grandchildren and for his beliefs and his work," says his sister Joan Barry. "He's a very driven man," says his sister Barbara Lackey, "but I don't think his work is more important to him than his family or his faith is."[25]

"I am honored to become Patron of the Heritage Foundation," Margaret Thatcher wrote in 2006. "Your work ensures that the message of liberty—democracy, under a rule of law, with free enterprise—remains a powerful force in political argument around the world."[26]

Not only the high and mighty took time to express their thanks for Ed Feulner and the Heritage Foundation. Member Verna Shaub said: "When you write and thank me for supporting The Heritage Foundation, I always think—no, it is the other way round. I should be thanking you all at Heritage for all that you are doing to save our country." "You are the closest thing to having our original Founders' voices being accurately heard and represented in Washington, D.C., our Nation and the world," wrote another member, John S. LaMarr.[27]

Heritage people like to tell stories about the man who hosts the biweekly Friday morning "Paychecks and Donuts" when he is in town. "He loves chocolate chip cookies," reveals Heritage's front desk receptionist

Dorothy Hodo, "and he will come into the first floor kitchen and take one and say, 'Now, don't tell on me.' "

When his assistant and driver Kevin Germany lost his mother, Feulner pulled aside Freida Warren, who has been the face of Heritage at the reception desk for over twenty years, and asked, "Is he okay?" Heritage is like a family, Warren says, and "Dr. Feulner is the Big Daddy."[28]

• • •

"Heritage is a Colossus that is to be reckoned with on every public policy issue in our country," says Richard Allen, who brought Ed Feulner to Washington in 1966. "And Ed has been the architect and constructor of it."

Heritage trustee J. William Middendorf II, whose public service is as long and almost as impressive as that of George H. W. Bush, says, "The four greatest people I have worked with over the course of my [fifty-year] career are Eisenhower, Reagan, Maggie Thatcher, and Ed Feulner."[29]

In the fall of 2012, Feulner received a rare award at the general conference of the Mont Pelerin Society held in Prague—the Golden Medal of the President of the Czech Republic. In presenting the medal, President Václav Klaus described Edwin Feulner as "among the most distinguished members of the Mont Pelerin Society" and a tireless champion of freedom, individual liberty, and free markets. The award meant much to Feulner, coming at a Mont Pelerin Society meeting and from Klaus, who as prime minister and president helped turn the Czech Republic into a model of freedom and democracy in Eastern Europe.

The Czech president praised Feulner for transforming Heritage into "America's leading conservative institution" and for personally "expanding the ideas of the free society around the world." The two "classical liberals" first met in 1990, just after Communism collapsed in Central and Eastern Europe, and Klaus became the first Eastern European member of the Mont Pelerin Society. As he placed the medal around Ed Feulner's neck, President Klaus said, "You are among the friends I am proud to have."[30]

• • •

Following his lifetime habit of doing when most people are content with dreaming, Feulner published another book in 2012, *The American Spirit: Celebrating the Virtues and Values That Make Us Great*, with fellow Heritage trustee and motivational guru Brian Tracy, that

explored "the breadth and depth of what it means to be an American."
A key word in the subtitle, he said, was "virtues." Virtue involved more
than doing the right thing. Quoting Aristotle, he said that virtues like
courage and generosity developed "dispositions to do the right thing in
the right circumstances from the right motives."

That was what Ronald Reagan did at Reykjavik in 1986, when he
did not give up SDI as Gorbachev demanded at their summit meeting
on arms control, and what Rosa Parks did in 1955 in Montgomery, Ala-
bama, when she refused to let a white man have her bus seat. It was
courage, Feulner wrote, that made Reagan get up and leave the meeting, and it was courage that kept Rosa Parks in her seat. As a result of
their courageous actions, each built a bridge that delivered millions of
oppressed people to their birthright of freedom and dignity—"in Reagan's case, citizens of Central and Eastern Europe, and in Parks' case,
citizens of the United States.

"That is who we are. We are a people with the courage to do the
right thing."[31]

But since 2009, wrote Feulner, Obama liberals "have run hog-wild
with policies that undermine the American spirit. They are crippling
free enterprise with layer upon layer of new and excessive regulations.
They are amassing ruinous public debt that will burden the next several
generations of Americans."

Heritage has the policy innovations that can reverse this disastrous
course, he said, but it will take more than policy reforms to succeed.
It will take "the fighting spirit that is an integral part of the American
spirit." Heritage members, he said, are the very soul of the American
spirit.

"Never let that spirit die. Onward!"

CHAPTER 26

STEPPING DOWN

It seemed that Heritage would keep going from triumph to triumph under its seasoned energetic leadership for years to come. But the senior managers knew something that the rest of the Heritage staff and hundreds of thousands of supporters did not know. At the October 2009 senior management retreat, held at Osprey Point on Maryland's Eastern Shore, Ed Feulner had stunned his colleagues with a brief but game-changing announcement—he would not serve as president of Heritage beyond April 2013.

There was initial disbelief among the ten vice presidents, followed by prolonged rationalization. He must be joking, they thought. No, he never jokes, and besides his leaving would be no joke. Wait a minute, they said to each other, 2013 is four years away, an eternity in Washington. He'll change his mind. Heritage has been his life. It *is* his life. How could he give it up? What would he do? Sit on the beach? We may not have him forever, they thought, but with a little bit of luck, he'll be president long after 2013.

But Ed Feulner had made up its mind. He had seen too many in Washington who did not know when to step down. In the summer of 2012, as he approached his seventy-first birthday, he took stock of his thirty-five years of stewardship of Heritage and reflected that he had accomplished most of what he had set out to do.

Heritage was a permanent Washington institution whose influence extended across the country and the world, ranking among the top think tanks in the world. It had changed think tank culture with its quick, concise, reliable research, targeted marketing, and membership-driven direct-mail fund-raising. It had led the conservative movement into becoming a major and often a dominant factor in American politics, with things like the Resource Bank, a must-attend conference for movement leaders, and its encouragement of the State Policy Network. As *The Wall Street Journal*'s John Fund put it, Heritage was like Grand Central Station—everyone eventually passed through it. And it had always connected with the American people who knew that Heritage is *in* Washington but not *of* Washington.

It had crafted major initiatives in domestic and foreign policy from missile defense, homeland security, and free trade to welfare reform, immigration, and health care. It had counseled presidents, congressional leaders, cabinet secretaries, governors, and mayors and provided them with a major platform from which to announce headline-making programs. It had given influential authors like Charles Murray and Dinesh D'Souza their start. It had inspired hundreds of tomorrow's conservative leaders with its innovative intern program. It had made First Principles based on the American founding a major part of the national dialogue.

It had highlighted Asia as the most important part of the world for America when the nation was still Euro-centered. At the same time, it was the only American think tank to establish a research center in the name of Margaret Thatcher. It had become an automatic port of call for foreign leaders visiting Washington.

Of course, there had been disappointments and setbacks.

The Department of Education still existed. The tax code was bigger than the *Encyclopaedia Britannica*. The capital gains tax was too high, and the flat tax was still a talking point. The navy had less than half of the ships it should have, and air force pilots were flying planes older than they were. The missile defense system was underfunded, while food stamps remained a federal priority. Heritage had been slow getting involved in the cultural war, and it should have realized earlier the potential for building coalitions with Hispanics, blacks, Asians, and other minorities.

But just think, Feulner reflected, where the conservative movement and the nation would be if there had been no Heritage Foundation. He was proud of what he and his colleagues—for it had never been about him—had achieved.

All things considered, it was the right time to step down from the top slot and hand to his successor the keys of an institution at the peak of its influence. Still, questions about Heritage and the conservative movement and the nation kept coming to mind, questions the next president would have to answer.

Growth was good, no question about that, but was a payroll of more than three hundred employees too big, or was it necessary to accomplish the foundation's goals? Had Heritage expanded too quickly with the purchase of a third building in the 200 block of Massachusetts, N.E., a townhouse half a block away, and the three-story Pennsylvania Avenue building on the House side? Or were they prudent investments and necessary to accommodate the ever-expanding staff and number of public events?

Heritage appeared to be on track to reach an annual operating budget of $100 million before long—was it asking too much of the mighty Heritage development machine to raise that much money? Total expenditures for 2012 were an estimated $79 million, about the same total as the year before. Even Heritage members were feeling economically pinched. Membership had crested at more than 700,000 in 2011 and was now just below 600,000, because of the slow economic recovery and increased competition from other conservative organizations. Was a target of one million members realistic?

Was there a possibility of The Heritage Foundation being dismissed as too political because of the aggressive agenda of Heritage Action? Were members of Congress not using Heritage research because of their poor scores from Heritage Action? Did Heritage Action sometimes act more like a political action committee than a lobbying group?

Almost half the senior managers and many of the senior analysts, including Stuart Butler, Kim Holmes, John Von Kannon, Robert Rector, and Jim Phillips, were not far from retirement—who would replace them?

Was the conservative movement expanding or contracting? Was it still a major influence in American politics, or was it showing signs of decline, like so many other political movements in American history? And if the movement waned, what did that mean for Heritage?

Given that nearly 50 percent of Americans received significant help from or worked for the government, was America so near to becoming an entitlement society that the process could not be stopped, let alone reversed? Was it possible to save the American Dream for the next generations? Was Heritage's vision of an America in which freedom, opportunity, prosperity, and a civil society flourished achievable or utopian?

They were tough questions, difficult to answer, perhaps impossible to answer in some cases, at least in the short run. But Heritage had made its reputation taking on and solving what seemed insoluble problems, like welfare reform, health care, and saving the American Dream.

And it could call on something no one else could: Heritage was the only think tank, right or left, grounded in American political thought, properly understood.

For himself, Ed Feulner was not walking away from Heritage—he would remain a member of the board of trustees and consult for the foundation if asked. However, he would *not* follow the example of his good friend and mentor Glenn Campbell of the Hoover Institution, who after resigning retained his spacious office at the top of the Hoover Tower and continually second-guessed the personnel and other decisions of his successor. His model was the smooth transition at AEI, where Arthur Brooks had succeeded Chris DeMuth as president.

When he was no longer Heritage president, he would spend more time with Linda, paying back for all those times when he was on the road and she was raising E.J. and Emily. He reflected that it was harder today to raise a family because, for example, of the new media. Thirty years ago you only had to react once or twice a day, but now you were on call every hour every day.

He would be able to sit back at the beach house and watch old movies like *Chariots of Fire*. (Eric Little had been right not to run on Sunday.) He could spoil his grandkids as much as he wanted, although truth be told, they spoiled him by letting him be with them. He had taken E.J. and Emily when they were young on a foreign trip once a year—health permitting, he hoped to do the same with the "grans." He might even sleep in, although he was so used to six or seven hours of sleep that that might not happen very often. He would stay connected to the ISI because it was vital to convey the ideas of freedom and the rule of law and capitalism and optimism to future generations. And of course he would not neglect the Mont Pelerin Society or the other organizations on whose boards he served—such as the Acton Institute, the Lehrman Institute, and the Philadelphia Society. He was in line to become the president of the Philadelphia Society in 2014 when it celebrated its fiftieth anniversary.

He would not leave the arena but would continue to fight the good fight for an America where liberty and self-government are championed. And to be honest with himself, he knew he would keep an eye on Heritage to ensure that it remained true to its mission and to the movement.[1] In between, he might teach at universities that had already invited him and write the book he was outlining in his mind. And he would unpack his beloved HO Model Railroad from its boxes and rebuild it in that special room in the beach house.

· · ·

Who would succeed him? A succession committee had been in place since 2009, headed by Tom Saunders, the chairman of the board of trustees, and a short list of candidates from inside and outside Heritage had been compiled. By his choice, Phil Truluck was not one of the names but planned to stay on as COO to help the new president.

It was a daunting question: who could take Ed Feulner's place?

When asked that in the past, Feulner replied that before anything else, regardless of his or her managerial and fund-raising ability, a Heritage president must be a conservative and more traditional than libertarian in his philosophy. The foundation needs a person, he said, who understands economics but has "a deep religious commitment to a higher order." It is "essential," he said, "to remember our place. Politics is only a part—public policy is only a part of who we are."[2]

More than a decade later, Feulner listed the following traits his successor must have: "Number one, absolute commitment to our beliefs; number two, an ability to market effectively those beliefs to key target audiences and to know who those audiences are; number three, to motivate people both inside and outside Heritage to add and multiply, not divide and subtract."

A Heritage president, Feulner said, must be able "to take our ideas, develop them, and make them the universally declared objectives of the American people." That, he said, "is what we're all about."[3]

Tom Saunders agreed with Feulner's criteria, admitting it would not be easy to find the right person. As head of the investment firm of Ivor & Co., a longtime director of Dollar Tree, and formerly managing director of Morgan Stanley & Co., Saunders has been on several search committees. "This search is more difficult," he said, because the president of Heritage has to be so many different things.

Along with superior management skills, Heritage's president has to understand Washington, "the ins and outs of that political labyrinth." In this "very Machiavellian environment," Saunders said, "you have to function when your friends are in power and you have to function equally well when your friends are out of power."

He has to be "global in his thinking." Ed Feulner "has complicated the job," conceded Saunders, "because he's built this incredible group of relationships around the world which are important to Heritage.

"Our job," Saunders said, "is to make this transition seamless, and I think we can."[4]

• • •

Ed Feulner has changed since his first years as a thirty-six-year-old Heritage president—he will never weigh 225 pounds again, and what hair he has left is gray and thinning. But he still keeps two secretaries busy handling his correspondence—five hundred letters a month, maybe 200,000 letters over the years—and he bombards colleagues and friends with e-mails and telephone calls about the latest conservative initiative on Capitol Hill and what is going on between Representative X and Senator Y and is it time to unleash Robert Rector again? Sitting behind his desk piled high with Heritage studies, *The Economist,* other publications, and the latest book a friend says he *must* read, he goes over his introduction of a prominent congressman who will outline his road map to prosperity, confers with his chief of staff about the agenda for the weekly management meeting, meets with Phil Truluck to go over the foundation's receipts and expenditures for the last quarter, places calls to Heritage's golden donors, talks perhaps to the ISI president about a new educational initiative and to the Philadelphia Society president about its fiftieth anniversary, and lets Linda know when he will be home.

He follows the rules he has followed all his life:

Don't let the urgent overwhelm the important.

Never assume the competition or the enemy is standing still.

There are no permanent victories or defeats in Washington.

People are policy. Without the best people in place, even the best ideas don't matter.

Onward!

In all he says and does and plans and proposes, his goal is the same—to keep Heritage and the conservative movement and America moving forward on the road to liberty. He once wrote that "we must work not just to roll back the welfare state but to transcend the welfare state." That will happen, he said, not with "one mighty burst of legislation or a single dramatic event like the fall of the Berlin Wall" but through a series of discrete actions by:

- Intellectuals with the courage to speak the truth to power.

- Ordinary people who take responsibility for themselves and their families.

- Religious and community leaders who uphold and pass on their faith and example.

- Political leaders who love freedom and know that the common man can manage his own life better than any government can.[5]

"I'm always the optimist," Ed Feulner admits. "I'm the congenital optimist in Washington and in the conservative movement." He traces his optimism in large part to what Ronald Reagan often said: "Trust the people."

Heritage has always trusted the people and never stops looking for ways to inform the people, to rouse the people, to inspire the people. "If we do that," says Feulner, the people will respond by reminding Washington of another Reagan insight: "We are not a government with a people. We are a people with a government."

Washington elites come and go, he says, and sometimes they inspire you and sometimes they let you down. "But if you trust the people, our future is secure."[6]

• • •

The John F. Kennedy Center for the Performing Arts gleamed white in the late-afternoon June sun as four hundred of America's most distinguished citizens—intellectuals and policy makers, PhDs and JDs, journalists and think tankers, veterans of foreign wars and domestic political campaigns, elegant women in long dresses and loops of pearls, gray-haired men in Brooks Brothers navy blue and the occasional tux—gathered to honor the four winners of the 2012 Bradley Prizes—the conservative equivalent of the Nobel Prizes.

After musical entertainment by Broadway-Hollywood star Shirley Jones, still radiant at eighty and able to hit the high notes of "Oklahoma" and "God Bless America," AEI's Nicholas Eberstadt, the Institute for Justice's William (Chip) Mellor, and former attorney general

Edwin Meese III accepted their awards and a check of $250,000 with grace and humor, Meese approving the "balance" of the awardees—two economists and two lawyers.

The last honoree and speaker of the evening was Ed Feulner, no easy role given that his colleagues and the audience were accustomed to eloquence. Master of ceremonies George Will, as witty and urbane as an Oxford don, introduced Feulner by saying that under his stewardship, "Heritage has leavened the nation's civic discourse with sound philosophy supported by persuasive research." It has been "a great force in its own right," he said, and "an inspiration to think tanks all across the country." For "the innumerable services he has performed for liberty, Ed Feulner tonight receives a 2012 Bradley Prize."[7]

Standing before his peers, calm and commanding in black tie, Feulner recalled that coming to Washington in the 1960s was like arriving in a new and not-very-friendly world. As a conservative, he had felt more than a little like Indiana Jones entering the Temple of Doom.

He mentioned a few of the "laws" by which he tried to live:

"Pick the right people to get the right results.

"Don't let the perfect be the enemy of the good. If you can get 70 percent of what you want, take it and come back later for the other 30 percent."

He quoted his favorite political leaders:

"Freedom is a fragile thing and never more than one generation away from extinction. . . . It must be fought for and defended constantly by each generation."—Ronald Reagan

"It is the task of conservatives to revive a sense of Western identity, unity, and resolve."—Margaret Thatcher

And his favorite political thinkers:

"A true conservative will strive to conserve the three things that tie together our civilization—our Judeo-Christian faith, humane letters, and the social and political institutions that shape us."—Russell Kirk

"The really important ethical problems are those that face an individual in a free society—what he should do with his freedom."—Milton Friedman

He conceded that America's problems were serious—rogue states with nuclear missiles, ever-rising government spending and debt—but he rejected the prophets of doom and gloom. Seeking to rally the troops and in this case the generals, he said that more and more Americans identify themselves as conservative and endorse conservative ideas like limited constitutional government and a culture of responsibility.

"Many Americans may have lost faith in the future, but a greater number still believe in America, in its enduring principles and its unlimited promise."

He recognized all those who had guided and inspired him—father, mother, sisters, children, grandchildren, teachers, mentors, pastors, Heritage staff and trustees, fellow conservatives, the many political figures "I have been privileged to work with," and especially and most of all Linda. "I wouldn't be here tonight, dear, without you by my side all the way."

Remembering all of them and looking out at those who meant the most to him, he said, simply, quoting Shakespeare:

" 'I can no other answer make than thanks and thanks and ever thanks.' "

CHAPTER 27

WHAT NOW?

As Ed Feulner puts it, there are two kinds of politics—electoral and policy. Electoral politics consumes most of Washington most of the time. Policy politics is the province of The Heritage Foundation and other think tanks. But inevitably the two kinds intersect and interact, particularly in a presidential election year like 2012.

Behind the final returns—Obama with 51 percent and Romney with 47 percent of the popular vote; Obama with 332 electoral votes and Romney with 206 electoral votes—lie the five essential elements that determine victory or defeat in a political campaign. They are Money, Organization, the Candidate (as a campaigner), Issues, and the Media (MOCIM), a formula I use in my politics classes and at Heritage to analyze political campaigns.

In *Money,* President Obama raised an astounding $1-plus billion for his campaign while the challenger raised almost $1 billion, which would have set a record except for the president's Midas touch. Super PACs for both candidates raised another $1 billion, making the 2012 presidential election—at some $3 billion—the most expensive in history. Advantage: a tie.

In *Organization,* the Obama campaign put together one of the most effective get-out-the-vote efforts in modern politics, using technology that did not exist a decade before. It was called Operation Vote and was aimed at the constituencies—blacks, Hispanics, youth, and single women—that composed the Obama coalition. The operation cost an estimated $350 million and was possible only because of the president's phenomenal fund-raising prowess.

Advantage: Obama.

As to which was the better *Candidate,* Barack Obama remains one of the most fascinating campaigners in American politics, notwithstanding his limp performance in the first presidential debate. His radiant smile, vibrant voice, and lithe figure combine to project the image of a vital, confident leader. His victory speech on Wednesday morning, November 7, deserves study by politicians and political scientists.

Mitt Romney was a good campaigner, attractive and energetic, better by far than John McCain in 2008. But he was basically a New England moderate who was never comfortable with the principled conservatism that has characterized the GOP since the Reagan years.

Advantage: Obama.

In the realm of *Issues,* America's weak recovery from the Great Recession of 2008–09 favored Romney, the challenger. No president since FDR in 1936 had won reelection with a GDP (Gross Domestic Product) of less than 2 percent and an unemployment rate as high as 8 percent.

But while the macro-issues favored Romney, the micro-issues that developed during the campaign favored the president, including Hurricane Sandy, the modest uptick of jobs and consumer confidence in the last days of October, and verbal gaffes by the challenger. Sandy was particularly damaging to Romney as it froze the campaign for several days and afforded Obama the opportunity to act presidentially, visiting a decimated New Jersey with a grateful Republican governor Chris Christie at his side. Exit polls revealed that an incredible 42 percent of voters said that Obama's handling of Hurricane Sandy positively influenced their vote.[1]

Advantage: a tie.

As for the *Media,* the great majority of reporters, anchors, columnists, commentators, editors, bloggers, Twitters, Facebookers, and other communicators were openly sympathetic to Obama. As with Martin Luther King, Jr., and other civil rights leaders in the 1960s, many journalists—most of them white and liberal—felt it was their social responsibility to shade their coverage in favor of Obama, the first African American president.

Advantage: Obama.

There is one other factor: In a close election, the candidate with the highest IQ (Intensity Quotient) among his supporters can pick up enough votes to win. It seemed from the momentum created by the first debate and the large enthusiastic crowds in the closing days of the campaign that Romney's IQ was rising and could make the difference. But the Obama team stuck to its unprecedented get-out-the-vote campaign. While Obama's IQ was not as high in 2012 as in 2008—he received 4.5 million fewer popular votes—his organization got his supporters to the polls. They made the difference in every one of the battleground states but North Carolina.

Advantage: a tie.

In summary, Obama bested Romney in three of five categories—Organization, Candidate, and Media—and tied in Money and Issues. He deserved to win and he did.

Obama's "double" victory in the popular vote and the electoral college enabled him to promise a progressive agenda for his second term. In his postelection news conference, the president said he had received "a mandate" to help the poor and especially the middle class and that a majority of the voters had approved his approach to the economy.[2]

• • •

Pundits and politicians were quick to suggest what conservatives (and Republicans) should now do.

For traditional conservative George Will, it was imperative to accept the new demographics. Unless Republicans respond to accelerating demographic changes, led by the rise of the Hispanics, he wrote, "the 58th presidential election may be like the 57th, only more so." Still, he said, the argument over the proper scope and actual competence of government continues: Obama was able to convince only half the voters of his progressive position. "Americans still find congenial," he wrote, "conservatism's vocabulary of skepticism about statism." Next time, he suggested, Republicans should nominate someone "who tilts toward the libertarian side of the Republican Party's fusion of social and laissez-faire conservatism."[3]

For Catholic biographer George Weigel, "the American cultural war has been markedly intensified" as those who booed God and celebrated "unfettered abortion" at the Democratic National Convention will advance their lifestyle "through coercive state power." He proposed a recasting of FDR's four freedoms, including *freedom of religion:* "no government bureaucrat is going to tell your religious community how to conduct its affairs"; and *freedom from fear:* no tolerance of "the burning of American embassies and the torture and murder of our diplomats by the thugs of al-Qaeda and their jihadist allies."[4]

"Romney's loss is not an indictment of conservatism," said conservative radio talk-show host Laura Ingraham, who often substitutes for Fox News's Bill O'Reilly. "The Tea Party remains the most invigorating force in the GOP, and conservatism's core principles still deliver the greatest promise to a demoralized middle class." Neoconservative blogger Ron Radosh said, "It is essential that conservative intellectuals do not abandon the effort to change the culture." Republican Party regulars and Tea Party conservatives must bridge the divide between them and support whoever wins the nomination, wrote Fred Barnes, executive editor of *The Weekly Standard*. "Ignore the advice that Republicans must be less conservative," he counseled, "especially on social issues."[5]

Craig Shirley, a veteran Republican strategist and author of two excellent Reagan biographies, wrote that if Ronald Reagan, Bill Buckley, and Barry Goldwater were still living, they would be "shaking their heads in disbelief at the [Republican] party's devolution." They gave the modern GOP its intellectual and political underpinnings—federalism (limited federal government) and fusionism (the notion that business interests and social interests are united in their aversion to big government).

But this philosophy, he said, has been abandoned in favor of "Big Government Republicanism." It is past time to return to a philosophy of freedom, individual rights, and individual privacy. He quoted Reagan: "I do not want to go back to the past. I want to go back to the past way of facing the future."[6]

Neoconservative columnist and commentator Charles Krauthammer had a succinct answer for the doomsayers who said that Republicans must change not just ethnically but also ideologically—"Nonsense."

He pointed out that "the exit polls showed that by an eight-point margin (51–43) Americans believe that government does too much. And Republicans are the party of smaller government. Moreover, onrushing economic exigencies—crushing debt, unsustainable entitlements—will make the argument for smaller government increasingly unassailable." His advice to Republicans: "Do conservatism but do it better."[7]

• • •

Which is what The Heritage Foundation strives to do.

In the days following the election, Ed Feulner seemed to be everywhere, rallying conservatives and urging them to stand up and declare, "We will continue to fight against big government and for freedom."

In his "Morning Bell" message to the 600,000 Heritage members—

released at 9:51 a.m., November 7, less than twelve hours after President Obama's victory speech—he said that while the president won, "he knows that he lacks a mandate for [radically] changing our nation according to his progressive vision." It was a direct challenge to Obama's assertion that he had received a mandate.

Heritage will fight, Feulner said, by offering the right policy proposals—entitlement reform, a strong national defense, a comprehensive energy policy, a balanced budget. "Let's get to work to save America," he urged, "starting today."

At a special meeting of senior management later that morning, Feulner acknowledged that the results "were not what we hoped," but that Heritage had a special role to play as "the leading institution of the conservative movement." "If not Heritage," he asked, "who?" The senior managers sitting around the table in the Krieble Board Room were in accord: It was a Republican not a conservative defeat. As always, they agreed, Heritage must be principled yet realistic in its policy proposals. The endgame was clear: Obama's "fourth wave of progressivism"—after Woodrow Wilson's New Freedom, FDR's New Deal, and Lyndon Johnson's Great Society—had to be stopped.

At a jam-packed all-staff meeting in the Allison Auditorium that afternoon, Feulner regarded the solemn concerned faces before him and said, "Many of you may be looking around in despair and asking—where is the cavalry that can come galloping to our rescue and save us from disaster?"

Well, he said, he had news for everyone: "This time around, *we* are the cavalry.

"*We* are the flagship conservative organization that carries on the Reagan legacy.

"*We* are the people conservatives look to to stop the Obama Revolution in its tracks."

Reflecting on the four decades since Heritage opened its doors, Feulner said, "It seems to me that perhaps everything we have built up, slowly and sometimes painfully, has finally led us to this defining moment—for the great battle in which we are engaged."

And he had a special message for his younger colleagues.

"You may not know it, but I know that you are equal to the challenges that await us.

"You may not know it, but I know that you will acquit yourselves with honor and dignity and great effectiveness.

"You may not know it, but I know that you will bring distinction to yourselves, your families, your larger Heritage family, your conservative movement, and your country."

He concluded: "We are well armed—morally, intellectually, and materially—to carry on this struggle. And with God's help and in his own good time, we will take our country back!"

Some two hundred conservatives, young and old, veteran analysts and new researchers, vice presidents and mailroom staffers, rose spontaneously and gave Ed Feulner a thunderous ovation while he dabbed at his eyes with a handkerchief.

In his letter to President's Club members a week after the election, CEO Feulner recalled America's Founders, who had made enormous sacrifices "to establish this great nation. . . . We, as conservatives, bear a moral responsibility to defend" the principles they fought for.

He quoted Bayard Boyle, a good friend and longtime Heritage member, who had e-mailed him after the election: "The right attitude is increased determination to fight every inch of the damage they are doing, and I am confident that's what Heritage will do." Feulner's ready answer: "You bet we will!"[8]

That same week, he was the kickoff speaker at the Conservative Leadership Summit in northern Virginia that brought together the unhappy heads of nearly a hundred national conservative organizations. Who better than Ed Feulner to put things in perspective—thought the summit's organizers—and set a course for a new beginning?

Feulner reminded his fellow conservatives they had been here before: in 1964 when Barry Goldwater had been trounced in the presidential race, in 1976 when Ronald Reagan narrowly lost the Republican presidential nomination, in 2006 when Democrats won a majority in both houses of Congress, and in 2008 when Barack Obama won the White House decisively.

Each time conservatives came roaring back because of the ideas of Milton Friedman and Russell Kirk, the charismatic leadership of Ronald Reagan, and the steadfast support and sure strength of conservative organizations "like those represented here today."

Notwithstanding the election results, he said, over 50 percent of the American people continue to assert that the nation is headed in the wrong direction. "You and I and every other conservative leader," he said, "must stand up for these Americans and for the right principles and the right policies." Policies like real health care solutions, meaningful spending cuts, tax reform that spurs economic growth and creates jobs, a strong national defense for a still dangerous world, measures to rein in an out-of-control bureaucracy, a way to energy independence and a protected environment, commonsense immigration reform, protection of human life from conception to natural death, and preservation of the traditional family.

"If I may borrow from my favorite president," he said, "you and I have a rendezvous with destiny. Future generations will look back on us and either praise us or shake their heads at our failure to preserve for our children this, the last best hope on earth." He asked the assembled conservative leaders:

"Can we do it? Of course we can.

"Will it be easy? Of course not.

"Do we have a choice? No, we do not."

Let us here resolve, Feulner said, "that we will work together and commit ourselves to a new crusade for freedom." With God's help, he said, "we will resolve the problems which now confront us and secure the future of our beloved country."

And then Ed Feulner was off to Florida for the annual meeting of the State Policy Network—where he was the featured speaker—and anywhere else the conservative movement needed him.

• • •

One month after Election Day, Heritage's board of trustees selected Ed Feulner's successor, ending months of speculation within and without the conservative movement. It was Senator Jim DeMint (R-SC), whose "dedication to the principles of our nation's founding, and his ability to translate policy ideas into action," explained Heritage board chairman Tom Saunders, will "lead Heritage to even greater success."[9]

As a congressman and senator, DeMint worked with economic conservatives, social conservatives, and national security conservatives. He was ranked by the *National Journal* as one of the most conservative members of the U.S. Senate and the No. 1 Senator by the National Taxpayers Union. He was a leader of the Tea Party Caucus in Congress and delivered the keynote address at the 2011 Conservative Political Action Conference (CPAC), attended by some 10,000 conservative activists, just as President Ronald Reagan had done three decades earlier.

During his Senate tenure, DeMint took principled conservative stands on issue after issue. He opposed federal bailouts of banks and carmakers, introduced a balanced budget amendment to the U.S. Constitution, supported school prayer and opposed abortion except when the mother's life is in danger, backed the U.S. invasion of Iraq, and voted against Obamacare. He gained national prominence in 2006 for his successful campaign to stop congressional earmarks.

"I am a product of Heritage," DeMint said after he was introduced at an all-staff meeting as the new president. "It inspired me to run in the first place, and I went to Heritage before introducing every major legislative proposal. This is a dream job and a homecoming for me."[10]

Standing on the stage of the Allison Auditorium, a beaming Ed Feulner warmly welcomed his successor. He was confident that DeMint would lead his beloved Heritage and the conservative movement to new heights. He was content—he was leaving Heritage in good hands.

NOTES

INTRODUCTION

1   EJF, remarks at a news briefing about *Mandate for Leadership,* November 16, 1980.

2   EJF, in Heritage Foundation *Annual Report 1981,* 3.

3   Ed Meese to Lee Edwards, August 6, 2012.

4   Bernard Weinraub, "Conservatives Aid Transition Plans Behind the Scenes," *New York Times,* December 5, 1980; Ira Allen, "Conservative Think Tank Moves into Capital Spotlight," *Los Angeles Times,* December 21, 1980; Shirley Elder, Media General News Service; Heritage Foundation *Annual Report 1980,* i.

5   For Birch Bayh's and EPA administrator Douglas Costle's remarks, see Heritage Foundation *Annual Report 1980,* 11. For Vernon Jarrett's screed, see "A Right-Wing Jab to Minority Laws," *Chicago Tribune,* November 16, 1980.

6   Charles Heatherly, interview by author, August 19, 1996.

7   Edwin Meese III, interview by author, May 26, 2011; T. Kenneth C. Cribb, Jr., interview by author, June 8, 2012.

8   Heritage Foundation *Annual Report 1980,* 2.

9   For David Stockman and Newt Gingrich's quotations, see Heritage Foundation *Annual Report 1980,* 10, 12.

10   Weinraub, "Conservatives Aid Transition Plans."

11   Russell Kirk, "The Conservative Movement: Then and Now," Heritage Lecture no. 1, January 4, 1990.

12   Milton Friedman, remarks at black-tie dinner celebrating the dedication of new Heritage Foundation buildings, May 1980.

13   EJF, *The Quiet Revolution,* unpublished manuscript, 1991, 64, EJF Private Papers.

14   James Rosenthal, "The Second Generation Think Tank: Heritage Hype," *New Republic,* September 2, 1985.

CHAPTER I: GROWING UP RIGHT

1   See Thomas Sowell, *Ethnic America: A History* (New York: Basic Books, 1981), 43–68.

2   EJF, interview by author, August 17, 2011; Barbara Lackey and Joan Barry, interviews by author, September 28, 2011.

3   Ibid.

4   Ibid.

5   Bruce McEvoy, interview by author, July 3, 2012.

6   Ibid.

7   Ibid.

8   McEvoy interview; Barry interview.

9   EJF, acceptance speech, Immaculate Conception Distinguished Alumni Award, January 29, 2009, EJF Papers.

10   Lackey interview.

11   EJF and Brian Tracy, *The American Spirit: Celebrating the Virtues and Values that Make Us Great* (Nashville, Tenn.: Nelson, 2012), ix.

12   Ibid.; Lackey interview.

13   Ibid.; Barry interview.

14   EJF, Immaculate Conception acceptance speech.

15   James T. Patterson, *Grand Expectations: The United States, 1945–1974* (New York: Oxford University Press, 1996), 457.

16   Lee Congdon, "Erik von Kuehnelt-Leddihn," in Bruce Frohnen, Jeremy Beer, and Jeffrey O. Nelson, eds., *American Conservatism: An Encyclopedia* (Wilmington, Del.: ISI Books, 2006), 483.

17   Ibid; John Adams to Mercy Warren, quoted in Forrest McDonald, *Novus Ordo Seclorum: The Intellectual Origins of the Constitution* (Lawrence: University of Kansas Press, 1985), 72.

18   EJF, interview on C-SPAN, December 20, 1984.

19   Lionel Trilling, *The Liberal Imagination* (New York: Random House, 1950), ix.

20   Russell Kirk, *The Conservative Mind: From Burke to Santayana* (Chicago: Henry Regnery, 1953), 7–8.

21   EJF, foreword to Friedrich A. Hayek, *The Road to Serfdom: Special Abridged Edition,* ed. Jameson Campaigne (Washington, D.C.: Heritage Foundation, 2011), viii.

22   Friedrich A. Hayek, *The Road to Serfdom: The Definitive Edition,* ed. Bruce Caldwell (Chicago: University of Chicago Press, 2007), chap. 3, esp. 85–87.

23   Barry Goldwater, *The Conscience of a Conservative* (Shepherdsville, Ky.: Victor, 1960), 6.

24   Ibid., 11.

25   Ibid., 13–14.

26   Ibid., 23.

27   EJF, *The Quiet Revolution,* EJF Private Papers; EJF, interview by author, April 20, 1993.

28   "Feulner Board Reviews Progress," *Brown and Gold Review* 46, no. 3 (March 1963).

29   Richard V. Allen, interviews by author, June 7, 1996, and July 28, 2011.

30   "Feulner Board Reviews Progress."

31   Rev. Thomas F. Finucane, S.J., "The Role of the Moderator," Regis College Student Leadership Conference, ca. September 3, 1962, EJF Private Papers.

32   EJF, interview by author, August 17, 2011.

33   EJF, "Student's View on War," Letters to the Editor, *Denver Post,* November 18, 1961.

34   George A. Martelon to EJF, February 15, 1962, EJF Private Papers.

CHAPTER 2: GETTING DOWN TO BUSINESS

1   EJF, interview by author, August 17, 2011.

2   EJF to Kenneth C. Siedenstricker, February 28, 1965, EJF Private Papers.

3   EJF, interview by author, June 6, 1996.

4   Ibid.

5   Robert Ritchie, interview by author, April 30, 2003.

6   "By Way of Introduction," *Intercollegiate Review* 1, no. 1 (January 1965), 4.

7   Donald Lipsett, memorandum about the Stephen Decatur Society, Donald Lipsett Personal Archives.

8   Edwin J. Feulner, Foreword to "The President's Essay 2000: Four Essays by Leonard Read," Washington, D.C.: The Heritage Foundation, 2000, 5–6.

9   EJF, interview by author, September 17, 2012.

10   For details about President Johnson's "Anti-Campaign," see Lee Edwards,

Goldwater: The Man Who Made a Revolution (Washington, D.C.: Henry Regnery, 1995), 309–12.

11   EJF, interview by author, June 6, 1996.

12   Lee Edwards, "Forty Years of Defending Freedom," excerpted from the official program of the Philadelphia Society's fortieth anniversary, April 4, 2004.

13   Edwards, *Goldwater*, 344.

14   Frank Meyer, "What Next for Conservatism?" *National Review*, December 1, 1964, 1057.

15   For Trumbo quote, see M. Stanton Evans, *The Future of Conservatism* (New York: Holt, Rinehart & Winston, 1968), 135.

16   Ronald Reagan, *National Review*, November 17, 1964, 1055.

17   EJF, interview by author, April 20, 1993.

18   EJF to George Reinart, October 21, 1965, EJF Private Papers.

19   EJF to Rudy Sporcich, September 27, 1964, EJF Private Papers.

20   William F. Buckley, Jr., to Anthony Lejeune, December 1, 1964, EJF Private Papers.

21   EJF, interview by author, June 11, 1996.

22   EJF, interview by author, August 17, 2011.

23   Ibid.

24   EJF, interview by author, June 6, 1996.

25   Bruce McEvoy, interview by author, July 3, 2012.

26   Ibid.

27   EJF to Ralph Harris, October 25, 1965, EJF Private Papers.

28   EJF to Kenneth C. Seidenstricker, February 28, 1965, EJF Private Papers.

29   Richard V. Allen to EJF, May 5, 1965, EJF Private Papers.

30   EJF to Richard V. Allen, May 10, 1965; Allen to EJF, May 12, 1965, EJF Papers.

31   Lyndon B. Johnson, "The Great Society," remarks at the University of Michigan, May 22, 1964, *Public Papers of the Presidents of the United States: Lyndon B. Johnson, 1963–64* (Washington, D.C.: Office of the Federal Register, 1965), 1:704–7.

CHAPTER 3: THE CAPITAL OF THE WORLD

1   Lyndon B. Johnson, "The Great Society," remarks at the University of Michigan, May 22, 1964, *Public Papers of the Presidents of the United States: Lyndon B. Johnson, 1963–64* (Washington, D.C.: Office of the Federal Register, 1965), 1:704–7.

2   Samuel F. Clabaugh and EJF, *Trading with the Communists: A Research Manual* (Washington, D.C.: Center for Strategic Studies, 1968), 3.

3   EJF to his father, January 13, 1966, EJF Papers.

4   EJF to Patrick J. Buchanan, September 8, 1966, EJF Papers.

5   EJF to Milton Friedman, August 1, 1966, EJF Papers.

6   EJF to Leonard Read, August 6, 1966, EJF Papers.

7   EJF, interview by author, June 11, 1996.

8   Lev E. Dobriansky, *U.S.A. and the Soviet Myth* (Old Greenwich, Conn.: Devin-Adair, 1971), 19 et seq.

9   EJF to Lev E. Dobriansky, April 15, 1966, EJF Papers

10   EJF to Richard F. Ryan, S.J., June 6, 1966, EJF Papers.

11   Ibid.

12   EJF, "A Review," *Review of Social Economy,* March 1966, EJF Papers.

13   EJF to author, July 20, 2012.

14   John Lehman, interview by author, May 11, 2011.

15   Melvin R. Laird to Richard V. Allen, November 2, 1976, EJF Papers.

16   John F. Kennedy, inaugural address, January 20, 1961, *Public Papers of the Presidents of the United States: John F. Kennedy, 1961* (Washington, D.C.: Office of the Federal Register, 1962), l.

17   EJF, remarks at the Orlando National Convention of Alpha Kappa Psi Fraternity, August 23, 1968, EJF Papers.

18   Ibid.

19   Ibid.

20   Ibid.

21   Kevin Phillips, *The Emerging Republican Majority* (New Rochelle, N.Y.: Arlington House, 1969), 474.

22   EJF, interview by author, June 6, 1996.

23   Stephen F. Hayward, *The Age of Reagan: The Fall of the Old Liberal Order 1964–1980* (Roseville, Calif.: Prima, 2001), 230.

24   Linda Feulner, interview by author, September 5, 2012.

25   Ibid.

26   EJF, interview by author, September 27, 1996.

27   Emily Lown, interview by author, May 12, 2011.

28   Linda Feulner, interview by author, September 5, 2012; Lown interview.

29   EJF, interview by author, October 26, 2011.

30   Ibid.

31   Ibid.

32   EJF, "A Letter to My Son," *Alexandria Gazette,* July 4, 1979.

CHAPTER 4: ON THE HILL

1   EJF, interview by author, June 6, 1996.

2   EJF, "Freedom and Power," remarks at the ISI Western Summer School, Stanford University, August 1969.

3   Donald Lipsett to Philip M. Crane, November 26, 1969, EJF Papers.

4   Philip Crane, interview by author, July 25, 1996.

5   EJF to Edward E. Noble, August 8, 1969, EJF Papers.

6   EJF to Carl S. Wallace, January 6, 1970, EJF Papers.

7   EJF, *Quiet Revolution,* unpublished manuscript, 1991, 49, EJF Papers.

8   EJF, *Conservatives Stalk the House: The Story of the Republican Study Committee 1970–1982* (Ottawa, Ill.: Green Hill, 1983), 41.

9   William F. Buckley, Jr., *National Review* 22, no. 49 (December 15, 1970), 1330.

10   Roger Freeman, *The Growth of American Government: A Morphology of the Welfare State* (Stanford, Calif.: Hoover Institution, 1975), 115.

11   Allen Schick, "The Supply and Demand for Analysis on Capitol Hill," *Policy Analysis* 2 (Spring 1976), 228.

12   Stephen F. Hayward, *The Age of Reagan,* 241.

13   Daniel P. Moynihan to William F. Buckley, Jr., September 4, 1978, as quoted in *National Review,* September 29, 1978.

14   EJF, *Quiet Revolution,* 51.

15   EJF, *Conservatives Stalk the House,* 55.

16   Philip M. Crane, *The Democrat's Dilemma* (Chicago: Henry Regnery, 1964), 358–59.

17   Ibid., 59.

18   Ibid., 53.

19   Ibid., 70.

20   Robert Schuettinger to author, September 20, 2012.

21   EJF to Henry Manne, president of the Philadelphia Society, June 2 1975; EJF to Richard DeVos, June 9, 1975; EJF to Milton Friedman, November 19, 1975; EJF to William F. Buckley, Jr., September 3, 1975; EJF to Irving Kristol, February 27, 1975, EJF Papers.

22   EJF to Linda Feulner, June 2, 1974, EJF Papers.

23   Philip Crane, interview by author, July 25, 1996.

CHAPTER 5: A NEW KIND OF THINK TANK

1   Richard M. Nixon, TV interview, January 4, 1971, in *What They Said in 1971: A Yearbook of Spoken Opinion,* ed. Alan F. and Jason R. Pater (Beverly Hills, Calif.: Monitor, 1972), 191.

2   See Lee Edwards, *The Power of Ideas: The Heritage Foundation at 25 Years* (Ottawa, IL: Jameson Books), 3–5.

3   EJF, *The Quiet Revolution*, 56.

4   James A. Smith, *Brookings at Seventy-five* (Washington, D.C.: Brookings Institution, 1991), 14.

5   James A. Smith, *The Idea Brokers: Think Tanks and the Rise of the New Policy Elite* (New York: Free Press, 1991), 130–31.

6   EJF, *Quiet Revolution*, 48.

7   J. Frederic Rench, interview by author, April 12, 1996.

8   Paul Weyrich, interview by author, April 17, 1996.

9   Ibid.

10   Ibid.; Joseph Coors, interview by author, August 18, 1996.

11   Ibid.

12   Paul Weyrich, interview by author, July 18, 1996; Hearing of U.S. Senate Committee on Finance, February 1, 1972, Roger Freeman Papers, Hoover Institution Archives, Stanford University.

13   Joseph Coors, interview by author, August 18, 1996; Weyrich, interview by author, April 17, 1996.

14   EJF to Joseph Coors, September 28, 1973, EJF Papers.

15   See EJF to David Hulett, Office of Management and Budget, October 22, 1973, for description of Schuchman Center for the Public Interest; EJF to Philip Crane, November 19, 1973, EJF Papers.

16   Weyrich, interview by author, April 17, 1996.

17   Jack Wilson, memorandum to the staff, August 14, 1973, EJF Papers.

18   Dan Joy, interview by author, May 17, 1996.

19   Jack Wilson, memorandum to EJF and Paul Weyrich, January 31, 1974, EJF Papers.

20   Ibid.

21   Fritz Rench, e-mail to author, May 24, 2012.

22   Ibid.

CHAPTER 6: WATERGATE WAVES

1   Lee Edwards, *The Conservative Revolution: The Movement That Remade America* (New York: Free Press, 1999), 180–81.

2   Heritage Foundation, "Prospectus for 1974," included in a letter from Jerry James to Roger Freeman, inviting him to serve on Heritage's board of advisers. Roger Freeman Papers, Hoover Institution Archives, Stanford University.

3   EJF to Walter Mote, October 18, 1974, EJF Papers; see also *The Power of Ideas*, 12–30.

4   Ben Blackburn, interview by author, June 22, 2012.

5   Ibid.

6   Richard A. Viguerie, *The New Right: We're Ready to Lead* (Falls Church, Va.: Viguerie, 1980), 63.

7   George Nash, *The Conservative Intellectual Movement in America Since 1945* (New York: Basic Books, 1976), 314–15.

8   Theodore White, "The Action Intellectuals," *Life*, June 9, 1967, 35.

9   EJF, interview by author, January 30, 2012.

10   EJF, interview by author, June 6, 1996.

11   Lee Edwards, *Ronald Reagan: A Political Biography* (Houston: Nordland, 1981), 178.

12   Ronald Reagan, "Speech at Republican National Convention," Kansas City, KS, August 19, 1976.

13   Milton R. Copulos, interview by author, June 3, 1996.

14   Stuart M. Butler and Eamonn F. Butler, *The British National Health Service in Theory and Practice: A Critical Analysis of Socialized Medicine,* Public Policy Studies no. 4 (Washington, D.C.: Heritage Foundation, 1976), 4, 37.

15   Ibid., 50.

16   Jeffrey St. John and Jeremy Rifkin, *The Great Bicentennial Debate: History as a Political Weapon* (Washington, D.C.: Heritage Foundation, 1976), 46.

17   EJF, interview by author, September 27, 1996.

18   Stephen Isaacs, "Coors' Capital Connection: Heritage Foundation Fuels His Conservative Drive," *Washington Post*, May 7, 1976.

19   Heritage Foundation, *Communique II*, no. 1, January 1977, 3.

20   Richard Odermatt, interview by author, March 15, 1996.

CHAPTER 7: INTELLECTUAL ENTREPRENEUR

1   Richard A. Viguerie, *The New Right*, 76–77.

2   Ibid., 79.

3   Heritage Foundation, "Desired Job Qualifications," February 25, 1977, EJF Papers.

4   Fritz Rench, interview by author, April 12, 1996; Joseph Coors, interview by author, August 18, 1996.

5   EJF to Frank Walton, November 5, 1975; EJF to Frank Walton, December 1, 1975; EJF to Tom Cantrell, October 18, 1976; all in EJF Papers.

6   EJF to Karen Davis, November 5, 1975; EJF to Tom Cantrell, October 18, 1976; in EJF Papers.

7   Phillip Truluck, interview by author, May 21, 2012.

8   Bernard Weinraub, "Heritage Foundation 10 Years Later," *New York Times,* September 30, 1983.

9   EJF, *Quiet Revolution,* 60.

10   Orrin Hatch to EJF, April 7, 1977; Peter Bauer to EJF, April 18, 1977; Svetozar Pejovich to EJF, March 4, 1977; all in EJF Papers.

11   EJF, interview by author, June 11, 1996.

12   EJF, *Quiet Revolution,* 62.

13   Richard Allen, interview by author, June 7, 1996.

14   EJF, *Quiet Revolution,* 84–85.

15   Ibid., 64.

16   Ibid.

17   Ibid., 68.

18   Ibid.

19   Robert Schuettinger to author, September 20, 2012.

20   As recalled by EJF in comments to Heritage Foundation senior management, July 2, 1990, EJF Papers.

21   Heritage Foundation *Annual Report 1977,* 12.

22   Christopher DeMuth, interview by author, July 9, 1996.

23   "Message from the Chairman and President," Heritage Foundation *Annual Report 1978,* 3.

24   Heritage Foundation *Annual Report 1977,* 1, 3.

25   Heritage Foundation *Annual Report 1983,* 3; Heritage Foundation *Annual Report 1988,* 3.

26   Heritage Foundation *Annual Report 1993,* 5.

27   Pat Williams with Jim Denney, *How to Be Like Rich DeVos* (Deerfield Beach, Fla.: Health Communications, 2004), 31–32.

28   EJF, All-Staff Meeting, Heritage Foundation, December 13, 2011.

29   EJF, interview by *Wharton School Review,* Summer 2012, 11–13.

30   Ibid.

31   EJF, "Building the New Establishment," *Policy Review,* Fall 1991.

32   "Cultivating Freedom for Future Generations: Dr. G. L. Carter, Jr.'s Legacy for America," Heritage Legacy Society, April 2012, 3.

33   Matthew Spalding, *We Still Hold These Truths: Recovering Our Principles, Reclaiming Our Future* (Wilmington, Del.: ISI Books, 2009), 239.

34   Tod Zeigler, "Best U.S. Think Tank Websites," *Bivings Report,* May 16, 2010.

35   John Von Kannon, interview by author, March 8, 1996.

36   Richard Larry, interview by author, August 1, 1996.

37   Heritage Foundation *Annual Report 1981,* 15.

38   Heritage Foundation *Annual Report 1997,* 45–46.

39   John Van Kannon to author, January 25, 2012.

40   EJF, *Quiet Revolution,* 218–19.

41   EJF to Heritage Board of Trustees, February 14, 1978.

42   Amy Wilentz, "On the Intellectual Ramparts," *Time,* September 1, 1986, 22.

43   I am indebted for this section to James A. Smith and his definitive study, *The Idea Brokers: Think Tanks and the Rise of the New Policy Elite* (New York: Free Press, 1991).

44   Robert Dreyfuss, *Nation,* March 1, 2004, 4.

45   EJF to Tom Cantrell, March 9, 1977, EJF Papers.

46   Phillip Truluck, interview by author, April 26, 2011.

47   EJF to Phillip Truluck, May 3, 1977; EJF to List Committee, April 25, 1977; EJF to Phillip Truluck, May 31, 1977; all in EJF Papers.

48   EJF, memorandum to Messers. Truluck, Schuettinger, Newton, Cantrell, and Mesdames Johnson and St. John, June 22, 1977, EJF Papers.

49   EJF, memorandum to the files, August 1, 1977, EJF Papers.

50   EJF to Nancy DeMarco, August 5, 1977, EJF Papers.

51   Phillip Truluck, interview by author, April 26, 2011.

CHAPTER 8: "DR." FEULNER

1   EJF, memorandum to Edinburgh file, December 8, 1977, EJF Papers.

2   EJF, interview by author, October 26, 2011.

3   EJF, "Public Policy, Politics and Power," address delivered in Chicago, August 22, 1977, EJF Papers.

4   Austin Ranney, *The American Elections of 1980* (Washington, D.C.: American Enterprise Institute, 1981), 31; Jimmy Carter, "Address to the Nation on Energy and National Goals: The Malaise Speech," July 15, 1979.

5   Council on Environmental Quality and the Department of State, "The Global 2000 Report to the President: Entering the Twenty-First Century," 1977, 1.

6   James Phillips, "The Iranian Oil Crisis," Heritage Foundation, February 28, 1979.

7   Robert Schuettinger and Eamonn Butler, *Forty Centuries of Wage and Price Controls: How Not to Fight Inflation* (Washington, D.C.: Heritage Foundation, 1979), 147.

8   Heritage Foundation *Annual Report 1979,* 1.

9   Lindsey Burke, "School Choice in America 2009: What It Means for Children's Future," *Backgrounder* no. 2332, November 4, 2009.

10   Stuart M. Butler, *Enterprise Zones: Pioneering in the Inner City* (Washington, D.C.: Heritage Foundation, 1980); quote on the back cover.

11   Stuart Butler, "The Enterprise Zone Tax Act of 1982: The Administration Plan," Heritage *Issue Bulletin,* March 29, 1982, 12.

12   Jilian Mincer, "Turning a Town from Gloom to Boom," *New York Times,* February 26, 1989.

13   "Enterprise Zones," *Encyclopedia of Business,* www.enotes.com/biz-encyclopedia/enterprise-zones.

14   Stuart Butler, "Time to Enact Real Enterprise Zones," Executive Memorandum, Heritage Foundation, October 24, 1995.

15   Stuart Butler, interview by author, September 21, 2010.

16   Phillip Truluck, interview by author, January 30, 1997.

17   Samuel T. Francis, "Cost Estimates of the Carter Welfare Reform Proposal," *Backgrounder,* November 11, 1977, 1, 3, 5.

18   Martin Anderson, "Why Carter's Welfare Reform Plan Failed," *Policy Review* 5 (Summer 1978), 37–39.

19   Heritage Foundation *Annual Report 1978,* 11.

20   Heritage Foundation *Annual Report 1979,* 3.

21   James Phillips, "Afghanistan: The Soviet Quagmire," *Backgrounder,* October 25, 1979, 1, 14–15, 17.

22   Ibid., 18.

23   EJF, *The Quiet Revolution,* 79.

24   Heritage Foundation *Annual Report 1979,* inside front cover.

25   Ibid.

26   Heritage Foundation *Annual Report 1989,* 22–26.

27   Heritage Foundation *Annual Report 1983,* 13.

28   "Always the Optimist, Feulner Has High Hopes for Conservatism," *Foundry: Conservative Policy News Blog from The Heritage Foundation,* November 25, 2008.

29   Heritage Foundation *Annual Report 1981,* inside front cover.

CHAPTER 9: THE BIG GAMBLE

1   Lee Edwards, *Ronald Reagan,* 188.

2   Lou Cannon, *President Reagan: The Role of a Lifetime* (New York: Simon & Schuster, 1991), 247.

3   Minutes, Heritage Foundation Board of Trustees meeting, October 9, 1979; EJF, interview by author, May 17, 2011.

4   Bernard Weinraub, "Conservatives Aid Transition Plans Behind the Scenes," *New York Times,* December 15, 1980.

5   Phillip Truluck, interview by author, April 26, 2011.

6   Charles Heatherly, interview by author, August 19, 1996.

7   Ibid.

8   EJF, Foreword to *Mandate for Leadership: Policy Management in a· Conservative Administration,* ed., Charles Heatherly, Washington, D.C.: Heritage Foundation, 1981, vii.

9   Heatherly interview.

10   Ibid.

11   Ibid.

12   James E. Hinish, "Regulatory Reform: An Overview," *Mandate for Leadership,* 704.

13   Truluck interview.

14   Ibid.

15   Ibid.

16   Hinish, "Regulatory Reform: An Overview."

17   EJF to Chuck Heatherly, March 6, 1980, and April 25, 1980, EJF Papers.

18   EJF to Chuck Heatherly, June 11, 1980; EJF to Phillip Truluck and other department heads, June 11, 1980, EJF Papers.

19   EJF to Jeff Gayner, May 1, 1980, EJF Papers.

20   Ibid.

21   Ronald Reagan, "Address Accepting the Presidential Nomination at the Republican National Convention in Detroit," July 17, 1980.

22   Ibid.

23   Jeff Greenfield, *The Real Campaign* (New York: Summit Books, 1982), 235–41.

24   Ibid.

25   "Time to Pull Together," *US News & World Report,* November 10, 1980, 100ff.

26   "Start of a New Era," *US News & World Report,* November 17, 1980, 90–110; "The Tidal Wave," *Washington Post,* November 6, 1980, 18.

27   Meese quoted in Robert Timberg, "What the Think Tank Thought," *Baltimore Evening Sun,* April 26, 1981; James quoted in Joanna Omang, "The Heritage Report: Getting the Government Right with Reagan," *Washington Post,* November 16, 1980; Stockman and Lott quoted in Heritage Foundation *Annual Report 1980,* 10–11.

28   David M. Abshire to EJF, December 5, 1980; Richard Nixon to EJF, December 8, 1980, EJF Papers.

29   Omang, "Heritage Report"; Gannett and *Globe-Democrat* quoted in Heritage Foundation *Annual Report 1980,* i.

30   "Defense," *Mandate for Leadership,* 117.

31   Robert L. Terrell, "The Department of the Interior," *Mandate for Leadership,* 333–403.

32   *Mandate for Leadership,* 630–31.

33   EJF, *Quiet Revolution,* 112.

34   Norman B. Ture, "The Department of the Treasury," *Mandate for Leadership,* 662.

35   Joe O. Rogers, "Office of Management and Budget," *Mandate for Leadership,* 957.

36   Tidal W. McCoy and Sven Kraemer, "The Department of Defense," *Mandate for Leadership,* 90.

CHAPTER 10: PEOPLE ARE POLICY

1   EJF, *Quiet Revolution,* 117.

2   Phillip Truluck, interview by author, April 26, 2011.

3   Bernard Weinraub, "Conservatives Aid Transition Plans Behind the Scenes," *New York Times,* December 15, 1980.

4   Ronald Reagan, "The President's News Conference," January 29, 1981, Public Papers of President Ronald W. Reagan, Ronald Reagan Presidential Library.

5   Peter Goldman, Thomas M. DeFrank, Eleanor Clift, John J. Lindsay, Gloria Borger, and Howard Fineman, "RWR's Own New Deal," *Newsweek,* March 2, 1981.

6   Hedrick Smith, "U.S. Priorities: A Basic Reversal," *New York Times,* March 5, 1981.

7   Ronald Reagan, "Remarks at the Conservative Political Action Conference Dinner," March 20, 1981, *Public Papers of President Ronald W. Reagan,* Ronald Reagan Presidential Library.

8   Thomas M. Humbert, "An Analysis of the Reagan Tax Cuts and the Democratic Alternative," Heritage *Issue Bulletin* no. 60, July 13, 1981.

9   Ronald Reagan to EJF, August 14, 1981, EJF Papers.

10   EJF, *Quiet Revolution,* 128.

11   Ibid., 129.

12   Ibid., 130.

13   Heritage Foundation *Annual Report 1981,* 4, 7.

14   Jeffrey G. Barlow, ed., *Reforming the Military* (Washington D.C.: Heritage Foundation, 1981); quote is from Monograph Summary, May 10, 1981.

15   Burton Yale Pines, "The Case for Ignoring the World Court," Heritage Executive Memorandum, April 12, 1984; also see *The Power of Ideas*, 58–60.

16   *Washington Post*, October 3, 1983.

17   Burton Yale Pines, interview by author, May 8, 1996.

18   Charles Murray, *Safety Nets and the Truly Needy: Rethinking the Social Welfare System* (Washington, D.C.: Heritage Foundation, 1982), 25.

19   Phillip Truluck, interview by author, April 26, 2011.

20   Phillip Truluck, interview by author, May 22, 2012.

21   Phillip Truluck, interview by author, January 30, 1997.

22   Antonio Martino, interview by author, September 4, 2012.

CHAPTER II: THE MOST IMPORTANT INITIATIVE

1   "New National Strategy Based on U.S. Lead in Space Recommended to Reagan Administration and Congress," Summary of *High Frontier*, March 3, 1982.

2   Ibid; see also *The Power of Ideas*, 63–65.

3   Martin Anderson, *Revolution* (New York: Harcourt Brace Jovanovich, 1988), 94–95.

4   Edwin Meese III, *With Reagan: The Inside Story* (Washington, D.C.: Regnery Gateway, 1992), 193.

5   Anderson, *Revolution*, 97.

6   George A. Keyworth, interview, September 28, 1987, Oral History Project, Ronald Reagan Presidential Library, Simi Valley, Calif.

7   Ronald Reagan, "Address to the Nation on Defense and National Security," March 23, 1983, *Public Papers of President Ronald W. Reagan*, Ronald Reagan Presidential Library; "Nuclear Facts, Science Fiction," *New York Times*, March 27, 1983.

8   EJF, *Quiet Revolution*, 187.

9   Peter Schweizer, *Reagan's War: The Epic Story of His Forty-Year Struggle and Final Triumph over Communism* (New York: Random House, 2002), 152; Daniel O. Graham, *Confessions of a Cold Warrior* (Fairfax, Va.: Preview Press, 1995), 153.

10   John O'Sullivan, *The President, the Pope, and the Prime Minister: Three Who Changed the World* (Washington, D.C.: Regnery, 2006), 284.

11   EJF, *Quiet Revolution*, 189; "Russians for SDI," *Wall Street Journal*, October 22, 1991.

12   Ken Sheffer interview with EJF, Hong Kong, January 15, 2012.

13   Ibid.

14   Taiwan Relations Act, Public Law 96–8, April 10, 1979.

15   EJF interview, January 15, 2012.

16   EJF, interview by author, March 28, 2012.

17   Ibid.

18   Ibid.

19   EJF, "Building the New Establishment: Edwin J. Feulner Jr. on Heritage and the Conservative Movement," *Policy Review,* Fall 1991, 14.

20   Author's interview with Midge Decter, October 29, 2010.

21   Midge Decter interview, April 13, 1996; see also *The Power of Ideas,* 66.

22   "A Nobel Winner Assesses Reagan," *New York Times,* December 1, 1982.

23   F. A. Hayek, "Our Moral Heritage," Heritage Foundation Lecture no. 24, 1983.

24   Conversation between President Ronald Reagan, EJF, and Fredrich von Hayek, November 17, 1983, transcribed video.

25   Ronald Reagan, "Special Message to the Heritage Foundation," Heritage Foundation *Annual Report 1981,* 1.

26   Richard N. Holwill, ed., *The First Year* (Washington, D.C.: Heritage Foundation, 1982), 2, 3.

27   Ibid., 4.

28   Ronald Reagan to EJF, February 8, 1982, Ronald Reagan Presidential Library, Simi Valley, Calif.

29   EJF, interview by author, December 21, 2011.

30   EJF, interview by author, September 27, 1996.

31   Tom Korologos, interview by author, November 22, 2011.

32   Ibid.

33   Helle Dale to author, April 19, 2012.

CHAPTER 12: "STUNNING" IMPACT

1   Heritage Foundation *Annual Report 1983,* 20.

2   Phil McCombs, "Building a Heritage in the War of Ideas: The Tigers in the Think Tank Celebrate 10 Years," *Washington Post,* October 3, 1983.

3   EJF, memorandum for the file, September 1984, EJF Papers.

4   EJF, interview by author, June 26, 1996.

5   Heritage Foundation *Annual Report 1983,* 2–3, 8.

6   Linda Feulner, interview by author, September 5, 2012; EJF, interview by author, June 23, 2011.

7   EJF, interview by author, June 23, 2011.

8   Heritage Foundation *Annual Report 1986,* 26.

9   Ronald Reagan, "Remarks at Heritage's Tenth Annual Dinner," April 22, 1983.

10   Heritage Foundation *Annual Report 1983*, 20.

11   Heritage Foundation *Annual Report 1986*, 2.

12   President's Council on Jobs and Competitiveness, "Road Map to Renewal," Year-End Report, 2011, 37.

13   Peter J. Ferrara, "The Social Security System," *Mandate for Leadership III: Policy Strategies for the 1990s* (Washington, D.C.: Heritage Foundation, 1989), 274.

14   Ibid., 275.

15   Ibid., 276.

16   Heritage Foundation *Annual Report 1984*, 4.

17   John Palffy, "Saving $111 Billion: How to Do It," *Backgrounder*, July 24, 1983.

18   George Easterbrook, "Ideas Move Nations: How Conservative Think Tanks Have Helped to Transform the Terms of Political Debate," *Atlantic Monthly*, January 1986, 66.

19   Ibid., 9.

20   *National Security Record*, no. 87, January 1986, 2.

21   "Summit Excitement," *New York Times*, November 27, 1985; Heritage Foundation *Annual Report 1985*, 14; and Lou Cannon, *President Reagan: The Role of a Lifetime* (New York: Simon & Schuster, 1991), 751.

22   Heritage Foundation *Annual Report 1985*, 14.

23   EJF to Heritage Foundation Board of Trustees, April 30, 1986; Heritage statement, April 29, 1986; EJF, interview by author, July 15, 2011.

24   EJF, interview by author, May 17, 2011.

25   EJF, *Quiet Revolution*, 191.

26   Ibid., 192.

27   EJF, "Keeping LOST Underwater," April 21, 2009, Townhall.com.

28   Richard Bernstein, "U.S. Aide Suggests Members Take the U.N. Elsewhere If Dissatisfied," *New York Times*, September 20, 1983.

29   EJF, "How a Think Tank Works," Trendleaders Club, Gaithersburg, Md., March 7, 1985, EJF Papers.

30   Heritage Foundation *Annual Report 1983*, 8.

CHAPTER 13: CONTINUING THE REVOLUTION

1   Stuart Butler, Michael Sanera, and W. Bruce Weinrod, *Mandate for Leadership II: Continuing the Conservative Revolution* (Washington, D.C.: Heritage Foundation, 1984), 5–8.

2   Ibid., 224–28.

3   "Washington Talk: Mandate and the Sequel," *New York Times,* December 5, 1984, "Mandate for Leadership II," book review, *Saturday Review,* February 1985.

4   "Washington Talk: Scores on State of Union," *New York Times,* February 22, 1985.

5   Richard Corrigan, "A National Agenda," *National Journal,* January 12, 1985, 105.

6   EJF, "Ideas, Think-Tanks and Governments," Heritage Foundation Lecture no. 51, August 18, 1985.

7   Ibid.

8   EJF, interview by C-SPAN, December 20, 1984.

9   EJF to Joseph Coors, March 7, 1985, EJF Papers.

10   Lou Cannon, *President Reagan: The Role of a Lifetime* (New York: Simon & Schuster, 1991), 656, 661.

11   Burton Yale Pines, "Policy on Iran: Right and Wrong," *New York Times,* December 5, 1986.

12   Edwin Meese III, *With Reagan,* 271.

13   Ibid., 286.

14   U.S. Senate, 100th Cong., 1st Sess., *Report of the Congressional Committee Investigating the Iran-Contra Affair,* November 13, 1987, 437–38.

15   EJF, interview by author, June 18, 2012.

16   John Andrews and Byron Lamm, interviews by author, April 26, 1996.

17   Thomas A. Roe, interview by author, April 13, 1996.

18   Terrence M. Scanlon, interview by author, August 5, 1996.

19   EJF, remarks to Catholic Center for Free Enterprise Graduate Program, Chicago, Ill., September 10, 1984, EJF Papers.

20   Marvin Olasky, interview by author, July 25, 1996.

21   Ibid.

22   Clarence Thomas, "Why Black Americans Should Look to Conservative Policies," Heritage Foundation Lecture no. 119, August 1, 1987.

23   "Clare Boothe Luce Quotes," About Women's History: http://womens history.about.com/cs/quotes/clarebootheluce.htm.

24   EJF, remarks to Clare Boothe Luce Award Dinner, September 23, 1991.

25   Heritage Foundation *Annual Report 1987,* 1.

26   Heritage Foundation *Annual Report 1991,* 5.

27   EJF to E.J. Feulner, October 1, October 9, October 12, 1987, EJF Papers.

CHAPTER 14: BEYOND REAGAN

1   Stuart Butler and Anna Kondratas, *Out of the Poverty Trap: A Conservative Strategy for Welfare Reform* (New York: Free Press, 1987), 243.

2   Robert Rector and Michael Sanera, eds., *Steering the Elephant: How Washington Works* (New York: Universe Books, 1987), 338, 344.

3   Ibid.

4   Heritage Foundation *Annual Report 1987,* 2.

5   EJF, interview by author, May 17, 2011.

6   Linda Feulner, interview by author, October 18, 1996; see also *The Power of Ideas*, 210.

7   EJF, interview by author, June 26, 1996.

8   EJF, "Conservatism After Reagan: Ideas," remarks at annual meeting of the American Political Science Association, Washington, D.C., August 28, 1986, EJF Papers.

9   Ibid.

10   Tom Korologos, interview by author, November 22, 2011. See, for example, Steven Roberts, "Preserving Reagan's Legacy," *New York Times,* May 7, 1987.

11   Charles L. Heatherly and Burton Yale Pines, eds., *Mandate for Leadership III: Policy Strategies for the 1990s* (Washington, D.C.: Heritage Foundation, 1998), xi; Peter Osterlund, "Homework for Mr. Bush," *Christian Science Monitor,* December 8, 1988; Tom DeLay, memorandum to the Heritage Foundation, January 10, 1989.

12   Ibid., 14.

13   Ibid., 15–16.

14   *Mandate for Leadership III,* xii.

CHAPTER 15: THE YEAR OF MIRACLES

1   EJF, "Conservatism in a New Age," essay distributed by Heritage Foundation, January 1991.

2   Linda Feulner, interview by author, September 4, 2012.

3   Phil Truluck, interview by author, May 22, 2012.

4   EJF, sermon in Kiev Baptist Church, Kiev, Ukraine, October 2, 1990, EJF Papers.

5   EJF, "Conservatism in a New Age."

6   Ibid.

7   EJF, "The Conservative Movement: Where We Are, Where We're Going," remarks to Lincoln Club of Orange County, Irvine, Calif., September 11, 1989.

8   Ibid.

9 EJF to George H, W. Bush, January 22, 1988; George H. W. Bush to EJF, January 30, 1988; in EJF Papers.

10 George H. W. Bush to EJF, August 1, 1988, EJF Papers.

11 EJF to George H. W. Bush, February 17, 1989, EJF Papers.

12 President George H. W. Bush, interview with members of the White House Press Corps, April 20, 1989.

13 EJF, memorandum to the files, November 21, 1989, EJF Papers.

14 Stuart Butler, interview by author, February 26, 1997.

15 Robert Rector to Stuart Butler, impact statement, May 18, 1989; see also *The Power of Ideas*, 107–108.

16 Robert Rector, interview by author, May 23, 1996.

17 Heritage Foundation *Annual Report 1989,* 17.

18 Ronald Reagan, address to the Heritage Foundation Annual Board Meeting and Public Policy Seminar, Carmel, Calif., June 1990.

19 Edwin Meese III, "The Reagan Legacy," address to Heritage Foundation Annual Board Meeting and Public Policy Seminar, Carmel, Calif., June 1990.

20 "Economics Panel Labels Tax Hike 'Unnecessary,' " Heritage Foundation release, May 30, 1990.

21 EJF to President Bush, May 11, 1990, EJF Papers.

22 EJF, "The State of Conservatism 1991: Fashionably Out of Fashion Again," January 7, 1991; "The State of Conservatism 1992: Bush Recession Needs Conservative Cure," January 23, 1992, Heritage Foundation.

23 EJF, interview by author, June 23, 2011.

24 Ibid.

25 Ibid.

26 EJF, "State of Conservatism 1992."

27 Russell Kirk, "Prospects for Conservatives Part III: The Behemoth State: Centralization," Heritage Foundation Lecture no. 293, September 19, 1990.

28 EJF, "State of Conservatism 1992."

29 Ibid.

30 Ibid.

31 Scott Hodge, interview by author, April 5, 1996.

32 Ibid.

33 Phillip Truluck, Hugh Newton, Jack Kemp, Don Lipsett, Stuart Butler, Chuck Heatherly, John Von Kannon, Kim Holmes, excerpts from the Heritage Foundation twentieth anniversary party, Metropolitan Club, Washington, D.C., February 16, 1993.

CHAPTER 16: A PERMANENT PLACE

1   Michael Needham, interview by author, September 16, 2011.

2   Tim Chapman, interview by author, May 8, 2011.

3   Ibid.

4   Linda Feulner, interview by author, September 4, 2012.

5   Phillip Truluck, interview by author, April 26, 2011.

6   John Von Kannon, interview by author, April 15, 2012.

7   T. Kenneth Cribb, interview by author, June 8, 2012.

8   EJF to author, August 10, 2003.

9   Steve Moore to author, January 26, 2012.

10   Christopher Long to author, December 3, 2011.

11   Brent Bozell to author, November 4, 2011.

12   Heritage Foundation *Annual Report 1990,* 3.

13   Frank Staar, "What Will the U.S. Fight For?" *Baltimore Sun,* January 20, 1991.

14   Heritage Foundation *Annual Report 1991,* 17.

15   "Editorial," *National Review,* August 12, 1991, 10; David Lauter and Edwin Chen, "Health Care for All—Three Plans Compete," *Los Angeles Times,* November 11, 1991.

16   William J. Bennett, "The War over Culture in Education," Heritage Foundation Lecture no. 341, October 19, 1991.

17   William J. Bennett, *The Index of Leading Cultural Indicators* (Washington, D.C.: Empower America, Heritage, and Free Congress Foundation, March 1993), i–iii.

18   EJF, "The Hegemony of Ideas," Heritage Foundation Lecture no. 999, May 3, 2007.

19   Kim R. Holmes, ed., *A Safe and Prosperous America: A Foreign and Defense Policy Blueprint* (Washington, D.C.: Heritage Foundation), 9–12.

20   Russell Kirk, "Prospects for Conservatives Part I: Prospects Abroad," Heritage Foundation Lecture no. 274, June 14, 1990.

21   EJF, foreword to Holmes, *Safe and Prosperous America,* 2.

22   EJF, "A New Conservative Internationalist Foreign Policy," remarks at a Windsor Group Conference, Pultusk, Poland, November 12, 1994.

23   Ibid.

24   Heritage Foundation *Annual Report 1993,* 18.

25   Baker Spring, "Clinton's Defense Budget Falls Far Short," *Backgrounder Update,* March 15, 1994; Spring, "The Army's Budget Choice: A Force Too Small or Hollow," *Backgrounder Update,* March 28, 1994.

26   John Luddy, "This Is Defense? Non-Defense Spending in the Defense Budget," Heritage *F.Y.I.*, March 30, 1994; Luddy, "More Non-Defense Spending in the Defense Budget," *F.Y.I.*, December 30, 1994.

27   Kim Holmes, interview by author, March 8, 1996.

28   See Heritage Foundation *Annual Report 1986* for comments in *Kommunist* and Mezdunarodnaya *Zhizn,* 10. On his 1996 conversation with Alexander Yakovlev, see Holmes interview.

29   Heritage Foundation *Annual Report 1991,* 5.

30   Heritage Foundation *Annual Report 1993,* 11, 17; see also *The Power of Ideas,* 127.

31   Yevgeny Volk to author, January 21, 2011.

32   Margaret Thatcher, remarks to Clare Boothe Luce Award Dinner, Heritage Foundation, September 23, 1991.

CHAPTER 17: NEW DEMOCRATS AND NEWT REPUBLICANS

1   Lee Edwards, "Why Bush Lost—and What It Means," *The World & I,* February 1993, 28–29.

2   EJF, "A New 'Mandate' for Limited Government," from "The State of Conservatism 1993," January 4, 1993, distributed by Heritage Foundation.

3   Ibid.

4   Ibid.

5   Ibid.

6   Lydia Saad, "Conservatives Remain the Largest Ideological Group in U.S.," Gallup Poll, January 12, 2012.

7   Heritage Foundation *Annual Report 1993,* 6.

8   Robert Rector, "The Poverty Paradox: How America Spent $5 Trillion on the War on Poverty Without Reducing the Poverty Rate," September 22, 1993.

9   Theda Skocpol, *Boomerang: Clinton's Health Security Effort and the Turn Against Government in U.S. Politics* (New York: W.W. Norton, 1996), 1.

10   Ibid., 2.

11   Ibid., ix.

12   EJF, "Good for What Ails You?" *Chief Executive,* May 1991; see also *The Power of Ideas,* 137–47.

13   "Tax Credits for Health: Wrong Rx," editorial, *New York Times,* December 16, 1991.

14   James J. Kilpatrick, "A Good Idea—for Health Care," *San Diego Union-Tribune,* June 15, 1989; Michael Kinsley, "The Right Cure," *New Republic,* July 29, 1991, 4.

15   John Hood, "Healthy Disagreement: The Struggle to Offer a Politically Palatable Alternative to Hillarycare," *Reason,* October 1993, 30.

16   Ed Crane quoted in Ruth Shalit, "The Wimp-Out," *New Republic,* February 14, 1994; Grace-Marie Turner, "Setting the Record Straight on the Individual Mandate," *Galen Institute Newsletter,* February 7, 2012.

17   Robert Moffit, interview by author, March 22, 1996.

18   Robert Moffit, "A Guide to the Clinton Health Plan," Heritage *Talking Points,* November 19, 1993, 1–5.

19   "The Clinton Health Plan: A Prescription for Big Government," Heritage Foundation Special Report, November 1993.

20   "Towers of Babble," *The Economist,* December 25, 1993, 72.

21   Robert Rector, "Combatting Family Disintegration, Crime and Dependence: Welfare Reform and Beyond," *Backgrounder,* April 8, 1994, 3.

22   Robert Rector, "Understanding the Welfare Reform Bill," Heritage *F.Y.I.,* August 7, 1996.

23   Stuart Butler, interview by author, September 15, 2012.

24   Kim R. Holmes, preface to Bryan T. Johnson and Thomas P. Sheehy, eds., *The Index of Economic Freedom* (Washington, D.C.: Heritage Foundation, 1995), vi.

25   Ibid.

26   Terry Miller, Kim R. Holmes, and EJF, eds., *2012 Index of Economic Freedom: Promoting Economic Opportunity and Prosperity* (Washington, D.C.: Heritage Foundation and *Wall Street Journal,* 2012), 429.

27   Ibid., 1.

28   Ibid., xii.

29   EJF, in Heritage Foundation *Annual Report 1994,* 2.

30   Ibid.

31   Ibid.

32   Ibid., 3.

33   Ibid., 8.

34   Ibid.

35   Peter F. Drucker, *Managing in a Time of Great Change* (New York: Truman Talley Books/Dutton, 1995), 306.

36   EFJ, "Moral Reflections on Life Inside the Beltway," Acton Institute, March 1995.

37   Heritage Foundation *Annual Report 1998,* 15.

38   William Beach, interview by author, June 15, 2000.

CHAPTER 18: TURNING SPLENDID

1   Patrick F. Fagan, "Why Religion Matters: The Impact of Religious Practice on Social Stability," *Backgrounder,* January 1996, 1, 28.

2 George W. Bush, "Executive Order: Establishment of White House Office of Faith-Based and Community Initiatives," January 29, 2001, georgewbush -whitehouse.archives.gov/news/releases/2001/01; George W. Bush, "Second Inaugural Address," January 20, 2005, Bartleby.com.

3 EJF, "Did We Win or Lose?" Heritage column, April 11, 1996.

4 Ibid.

5 Ibid.

6 Ibid.

7 R. W. Apple, Jr., "Nation Is Still Locked onto Rightward Path, Leaving Liberals Beside Road," *New York Times,* November 5, 1996.

8 EJF, remarks at President's Club Meeting, December 3, 1996.

9 Ibid.

10 Mortimer Smith, "Individualism Talks Back," *Christian Century* 62 (February 14, 1945), 202.

11 Richard Cockett, *Thinking the Unthinkable: Think-Tanks and the Economic Counter-Revolution, 1931–1983* (London: HarperCollins, 1994), 104.

12 EJF, "We Are All Liberals Now—or Are We?" presidential address, Mont Pelerin Society, April 12, 1997.

13 Ibid.

14 EJF, "Renewing the Free Society," presidential address to the 1998 Golden Anniversary meeting of the Mont Pelerin Society, August 30, 1999, Heritage Foundation Archives.

15 Kenneth Minogue, interview by author, September 3, 2012.

16 Stuart M. Butler and Kim R. Holmes, eds., *Mandate for Leadership IV: Turning Ideas into Actions* (Washington, D.C.: Heritage Foundation, 1996), xvi.

17 Ibid., 79, 80, 102, 154–55, 263, 291, 561–62.

18 Ibid., 279, 282, 295.

19 Donald Lambro, "Learning from Last Year's Errors," *Washington Times,* January 16, 1997.

20 John Godfrey, "Clinton Proposes $1.7 Trillion Budget," *Washington Times,* February 3, 1998; James K. Glassman, "Budget Whoppers," *Washington Post,* February 3, 1998.

21 Rich Lowry, *Legacy: Paying the Price for the Clinton Years* (Washington, D.C.: Regnery, 2003), 164.

22 "Getting the Story Behind the Story," *Heritage Today,* Summer 2000, 6.

23 Mike Franc to author, November 16, 2000.

24 Becky Norton Dunlop to author, November 20, 2000.

25 EJF to President's Club members, July 10, 2001.

26   Edwin Meese III quoted in "Heritage Foundation Creates Center for Legal and Judicial Studies," Heritage Foundation release, November 6, 2000.

27   Heritage Foundation *Annual Report 1999*, 21.

28   Ibid., 17.

29   EJF, "Tiananmen Square and Taiwan: Reform and Accountability," Heritage Foundation Lecture no. 202, delivered at the Institute for International Relations, Taipei, Republic of China, August 1, 1989.

30   EJF, remarks at concluding banquet of Leadership for America campaign, December 8, 1999; Heritage Foundation *Annual Report 1999*, 8, 31.

31   Heritage Foundation *Annual Report 1999*, 4, 31, 33, 35, 42, 49, 31.

32   Ibid., 3.

33   EJF to President's Club Members, December 1, 1999.

34   Ibid.

35   Ibid., 7.

36   Phillip Truluck, interview by author, July 3, 2012.

CHAPTER 19: 9/11

1   Barry Toiv, "The Media," Heritage Foundation Roundtable on the Presidency, March 16, 2000.

2   Alvin S. Felzenberg, "How to Ease into the Oval Office," *Austin American-Statesman*, April 30, 2000.

3   Ken Herman, *Austin American-Statesman*, October 28, 1999, as reported in Heritage Foundation *Annual Report 2000*, 20.

4   EJF to President's Club members, February 7, 2001.

5   EJF to President's Club members, March 19, 2001.

6   Ibid.

7   George W. Bush, *Decision Points* (New York: Crown, 2010), 141–42.

8   Ibid., 147–48.

9   James Phillips, "Defusing Terrorism at Ground Zero: Why a New U.S. Policy Is Needed for Afghanistan," *Backgrounder* no. # 1383, July 12, 2000.

10   EJF, interview by author, September 27, 2001.

11   Kim R. Holmes, "At Issue: The Aftermath of the Terrorist Attacks on U.S.," *WebMemo* no. 35, September 12, 2001; Ariel Cohen, "Intelligence Disaster, Bureaucratic Sclerosis," *Commentary*, September 16, 2001; James Phillips, "Uproot Bin Laden's Terrorist Network and Taliban Allies in Afghanistan," Executive Memorandum, no. 776, September 17, 2001; Brett Schaefer and Michael Scardaville, *Backgrounder* no. 1474, September 18, 2001; James Phillips, *Commentary*, September 18, 2001; "Terrorist Attack on America," *WebMemo* no. 40, September 18, 2001; Baker Spring, "Talking Points: Terrorist Attack on America Confirms the Growing Need

for Missile Defense," *Backgrounder* no. 1477, September 20, 2001; Jack Spencer, "A Defense Agenda for 21st Century Warfare," *Backgrounder* no. 1476, September 20, 2001; Larry Wortzel and Michael Scardaville, "The New Agenda for Homeland Security," Executive Memorandum no. 779, September 28, 2001; Kim R. Holmes and Edwin Meese III, "The Administration's Anti-Terrorism Package," *Backgrounder* no. 1484, October 3, 2001; Kim R. Holmes, "America Strikes Back: Looking Ahead," *WebMemo* no. 46, October 8, 2001.

12   Lee Edwards, as quoted by Fox News, September 14, 2001.

13   EJF, "Declare War," *Commentary*, September 14, 2001.

14   EJF, "Now More Than Ever," *Commentary*, September 21, 2001.

15   EJF, memorandum to friends and supporters, September 17, 2001.

16   EJF, Phillip Truluck, and Kim Holmes, interviews by author, September 27, 2001.

17   James Phillips, interview by author, October 18, 2010.

18   Heritage Foundation *Annual Report 2002*, 8–9.

19   Heritage Foundation *Annual Report 2001*, 16.

20   Ibid., 18.

21   Ibid., 20.

22   George W. Bush, "Remarks at the Citadel in Charleston, South Carolina," December 11, 2001, *Public Papers of President George W. Bush.*

23   George W. Bush to EJF, January 23, 2002, EJF Papers.

24   George W. Bush remarks at the Citadel.

25   Heritage Foundation *Annual Report 2001*, 29.

26   Ibid.

27   EJF to President's Club, February 25, 2002.

28   Heritage Foundation *Annual Report 2001*, 33–34.

29   Ibid., 36.

30   Dani Doane, interview by author, April 19, 2010.

31   EJF to Heritage Foundation members, March 3, 2010, Heritage Foundation Archives.

32   EJF to President's Club, April 25, 2003.

CHAPTER 20: GETTING AMERICA RIGHT

1   Bill Beach, "What Is 'Reality-Based Scoring'?," Heritage Foundation *Annual Report 2003*, 6–7.

2   Ibid., 3.

3   Mike Franc, interview by author, September 18, 2012; Stuart Butler, interview by author, September 13, 2012.

4   Ibid.; Heritage Foundation *Annual Report 2003*, 9–10.

5   Robert Moffit, interview by author, September 17, 2012.

6   Heritage Foundation *Annual Report 2003*, 12.

7   George W. Bush, "Remarks at the Heritage Foundation President's Club Luncheon," November 11, 2003, *Public Papers of President George W. Bush.*

8   EJF to President's Club members, May 31, 2002.

9   "America Strikes Back," *Time Annual 2002*, 41–46.

10   "Bombs Along the Tigris," *Time Annual 2004*, 56.

11   James Phillips, "Defusing Iraq's Ticking Timebomb," *Commentary*, September 6, 2002.

12   Lee Edwards, *William F. Buckley Jr.: The Maker of a Movement* (Wilmington, Del.: ISI Books, 2010), 172.

13   Ibid., 175.

14   Ibid., 178.

15   "Bombs Along the Tigris," 57.

16   *Time Annual 2005*, 26.

17   Heritage Foundation *Annual Report 2004*, 3.

18   Ibid., 5.

19   Ibid., 21.

20   John Von Kannon, interview by author, March 8, 2010; Carsten Walter, memorandum to John Von Kannon about Chay McQueen survey results, March 4, 2010.

21   Linda Feulner, interview by author, September 4, 2012.

22   Ibid.

23   Derrick Morgan, interview by author, September 14, 2012.

24   EJF to President's Club members, February 28, 2007.

25   Ibid.

26   "Getting America Right . . . With Immigration Reform," Heritage Foundation *Annual Report 2006*, 20.

27   Margaret Thatcher, quote on back cover of EJF and Doug Wilson, *Getting America Right* (New York: Crown Forum, 2006).

28   Ibid., 226.

29   Michael Needham, interview by author, September 16, 2011.

CHAPTER 21: LEADERSHIP FOR AMERICA

1   EJF to Heritage Foundation members, November 20, 2006.

2   Ibid.

3   Ibid.

4   Lee Edwards, *The Essential Ronald Reagan: A Profile in Courage, Justice, and Wisdom* (Lanham, Md.: Rowman & Littlefield, 2005), 76.

5   EJF to Heritage Foundation members, November 20, 2006.

6   EJF to Heritage Foundation members, February 4, 2008.

7   EJF, "The Hegemony of Ideas," presentation to the Political Committee of the Reform Club, London, February 20, 2007.

8   EJF, remarks to the Heritage Foundation Board of Trustees, April 2007, Heritage Foundation Files.

9   Ibid.

10   Ibid.

11   Ibid.

12   Robert J. Herbold, *Seduced by Success: How the Best Companies Survive the 9 Traps of Winning* (New York: McGraw-Hill, 2007), 3.

13   Heritage Foundation *Annual Report 2007*, 20.

14   EJF to Heritage Foundation members, February 4, 2008.

15   Genevieve Wood, interview by author, December 18, 2009.

16   Ibid.; EJF to Heritage Foundation members, February 4, 2008.

17   EJF, "Leadership for America," presented to the Conservative Opportunity Society, Capitol Hill Club, Washington, D.C., August 1, 2007, Heritage Foundation Files.

18   Ibid.

19   EJF, "Leadership for America Campaign," Heritage Foundation Cruise, Aegean Sea, October 2, 2007.

20   Ibid.

21   David R. Brown, interview by author, April 9, 2011.

22   Sarah Palin, Vice Presidential Acceptance Speech, September 3, 2008, C-SPAN.

23   "Black Monday," *New York Times*, September 15, 2008; "I'm Always for Less Regulation," *Wall Street Journal*, March 3, 2008.

24   George W. Bush, "Remarks at the Heritage Foundation President's Club Luncheon," November 1, 2007, *Public Papers of President George W. Bush*.

25   Heritage Foundation *Annual Report 2007*, 12.

26   EJF to Heritage Foundation members, July 11, 2007, Heritage Foundation Files.

CHAPTER 22: FORCE FOR GOOD

1   Leslie R. Crutchfield and Heather McLeod Grant, *Forces for Good: The Six Practices of High-Impact Nonprofits* (San Francisco: John Wiley & Sons, 2008), 114.

2   EJF to Heritage Foundation members, November 20, 2007, Heritage Foundation Files.

3   EJF quoted in Crutchfield and Grant, *Forces for Good*, 261–62.

4   Jack Spencer, "Is a Nuclear Renaissance Approaching?" *Foundry*, February 15, 2012.

5   EJF to Heritage Foundation members, November 20, 2007.

6   EJF to President's Club members, October 26, 2007.

7   "Farewell, Free Lunch," *Time Annual 2009*, 44.

8   Ronald D. Utt, "Time to Reform Fannie Mae and Freddie Mac," *Backgrounder* no. 1861, June 20, 2005, Heritage Foundation Files.

9   EJF, "Financial Forensics," October 14, 2008, Heritage Foundation Files.

10   Stuart Butler to author, July 24, 2012.

11   Stuart M. Butler and Edwin Meese III, "The Bailout Package: Vital and Acceptable," *WebMemo* no. 2091, September 29, 2008.

12   "The Week," *National Review*, September 29, 2008, 10.

13   Robert A. Levy, "Is the Bailout Constitutional?" Cato Institute, October 20, 2008, also *Legal Times* on the same date.

14   Daniel J. Mitchell, "Mislead," Cato Institute, October 1, 2008, also *National Review Online*.

15   George Will, "A Vote Against Rashness," *Washington Post*, October 1, 2008.

16   Charles Krauthammer, "A Lemon of a Bailout," *Washington Post*, November 14, 2008.

17   EJF to President's Club members, November 14, 2008.

18   "Bale Up the Bailouts," EJF, commentary, December 29, 2008, Heritage Foundation Files.

19   "Shun the 'Stimulus,' " EJF, Townhall.com., November 19, 2008.

20   Ibid.

21   Barack Obama, "Mexico City Policy—Voluntary Population Planning," White House, January 23, 2009.

CHAPTER 23: A MODERN MACHIAVELLIAN

1   Barack Obama, "Address to supporters at University of Missouri," October 20, 2008.

2   Ryan Lizza, "The Obama Memos: The Making of a Post-post-partisan Presidency," *New Yorker*, January 30, 2012.

3   Charles Krauthammer, "Obama Proposes a European U.S.," *Washington Post*, February 27, 2009.

4   " 'Mandatory' Spending Soars Nearly 30% in 2009," Heritage Foundation *Annual Report 2009*, 24.

5   "Getting 'Hope and Change' Right," Heritage Foundation *Annual Report 2009*, 2.

6   EJF to President's Club members, October 16, 2009.

7   Heritage Foundation *Annual Report 2009*, 2.

8   "Right Direction or Wrong Track," *Politics*, May 30, 2012.

9   Barone quoted in EJF to President's Club members, May 28, 2010.

10   Heritage Foundation *Annual Report 2009*, back cover.

11   Nicolas Loris, "EPA's Flawed Cap and Trade Analysis," *Foundry*, May 22, 2009.

12   "Non-Farm Employment Lost, by State, in 2025 Due to S.2191," Map 3b, CDA 02–02, May 12, 2008.

13   David W. Kreutzer, "The Economic Impact of Cap and Trade," testimony before the Energy and Commerce Committee, April 22, 2009.

14   Lewin Group, "Analysis of the July 15 Draft of The American Affordable Health Choices Act of 2009," July 17, 2009, revised July 23, 2009.

15   Edmund Haislmaier and Brian C. Blase, "Obamacare: Impact on States," *Backgrounder* no. 2433, July 1, 2010.

16   Jennifer Rubin, "Exclusive: Paul Ryan Talks to Right Turn," *Washington Post* blog, March 30, 2012.

17   "Taxed Enough Already? Just Wait Until Obamacare Kicks In," Heritage Infographic, March 23, 2012.

18   Robert Moffit, "Obamacare and the Independent Payment Advisory Board: Falling Short of Real Medicare Reform," *WebMemo* no. 3102, January 19, 2011.

19   Ibid., 8.

20   Nancy Pelosi, "Remarks at the 2010 Legislative Conference for National Association of Counties," March 9, 2010.

21   EJF, "Heritage President Ed Feulner Responds to President Obama's Claims," *Foundry,* March 30, 2010; "Opposing an Intolerable Act," Townhall.com, April 1, 2010.

22   Jeffrey H. Anderson, "*USA Today*/Gallup Poll: Swing State Voters Want Obamacare to Be Repealed," *Weekly Standard* blog, February 27, 2012.

23   Robert Barnes, "Health-Care Law Upheld," *Washington Post*, June 29, 2012.

24   EJF, "Morning Bell: Join the Fight to Repeal Obamacare," Heritage Foundation, June 29, 2012.

25   Stuart Butler, "Don't Blame Heritage for ObamaCare Mandate," *USA Today*, February 6, 2012.

26   For an examination of the Commerce Clause debate, see John Eastman, "The Revival of Federalism," in Lee Edwards, ed., *Bringing Justice to the*

People: The Story of the Freedom-Based Public Interest Law Movement (Washington, D.C.: Heritage Foundation, 2004), 183–204.

27   Ibid.

28   See below.

29   *Brief of Amicus Curiae The Heritage Foundation,* U.S. Court of Appeals for the Eleventh Circuit, May 11, 2011, 3–4.

30   Ibid., 6.

CHAPTER 24: NO PERMANENT VICTORIES—OR DEFEATS

1   Rob Bluey, "Pelosi's PAYGO Ploy: Budgetary Gimmick Provides Cover for Liberals," *Foundry,* October 15, 2010.

2   EJF, "Heritage Launches the Center for Policy Innovation," *Foundry,* August 27, 2010.

3   Ibid.

4   "Heritage Board Confirms Addington as VP for Domestic Policy," Heritage Foundation news release, September 17, 2010.

5   David Addington, interview by author, July 8, 2011.

6   Stuart Butler, "The Coming Higher-Ed Revolution," Heritage Foundation Commentary, January 13, 2012.

7   "45 Who Shaped Washington 1965–2010," *Washingtonian,* October 5, 2010; Toby Harden, "The Most Influential U.S. Conservatives," *Telegraph,* January 4, 2010; Matthew Cooper, Major Garrett, et al., "The New Power Players," *National Journal,* November 15, 2010.

8   Heritage Foundation *Annual Report 2010,* 2.

9   Matthew Spalding, *We Still Hold These Truths,* back cover.

10   EJF to Heritage Foundation members, November 6, 2009, Heritage Foundation Files.

11   Billie Tucker, remarks at Heritage Foundation Resource Bank, April 22, 2010; remarks by Matthew Spalding; ibid.

12   Heritage Foundation *Annual Report 2010,* 12.

13   Ibid., 14.

14   Ibid., 15.

15   Ibid., 25.

16   James A. Smith, *The Idea Brokers,* 201.

17   Heritage Foundation *Annual Report 1992,* 12.

18   EJF, remarks at Heritage Foundation Osprey Point Retreat, October 5, 2009, author's notes.

19   Alan P. Dye to EJF, October 1, 2009, Heritage Foundation Files.

20   Phillip Truluck, interview by author, April 26, 2011.

21 Ibid.

22 EJF and Michael Needham, "New Fangs for the Conservative 'Beast,' " *Wall Street Journal,* April 12, 2010.

23 Ramesh Ponnuru, "Action Report," *National Review Online,* October 17, 2011.

24 Michael Needham, interview by author, September 16, 2011.

CHAPTER 25: FIRST PRINCIPLES

1 EJF to President's Club members, April 15, 2010.

2 EJF to President Club members, September 15, 2010.

3 "Changing Course," *Time Annual 2011,* 20.

4 Ibid., 21.

5 Charles Krauthammer, "A Return to the Norm," *Washington Post,* November 5, 2010.

6 James W. Ceaser, "The Great Repudiation," *Claremont Review of Books,* Fall 2010, 9.

7 EJF, letter from the President's Office, November 10, 2010, Heritage Foundation Files.

8 Ibid.

9 Charles Krauthammer, "Hovering on High: Obama Surveys the World," *Washington Post,* June 12, 2009.

10 Barack Obama, *The Audacity of Hope: Thoughts on Reclaiming the American Dream* (New York: Three Rivers Press, 2006), 247; Shelby Steele, *White Guilt:How Blacks and Whites Together Destroyed the Promise of the Civil Rights Era* (New York: HarperCollins, 2006), 5.

11 EJF, "Saving the American Dream," Heritage Foundation *Annual Report 2011,* 1.

12 EJF, foreword to Stuart M. Butler, Alison A. Fraser, and William W. Beach, *Saving the American Dream* (Washington, D.C.: Heritage Foundation, 2011), 2.

13 Ibid.

14 "Defending the Dream," Heritage Foundation *Annual Report 2011,* 13.

15 EJF, "Heritage, FRC Set Bus Tour to 'Save Dream,' " Heritage Foundation news release, January 16, 2012.

16 Arthur Brooks, "The Road to Freedom: How to Win the Fight for Free Enterprise," lecture at Heritage Foundation, May 21, 2012.

17 Ed Crane, interview by author, July 22, 2011.

18 David Abshire, interview by author, July 15, 1996.

19 Michael Armacost, interview by author, June 21, 1996; see also *The Power of Ideas,* 199.

20   Gerald Dorfman, interview by author, August 23, 1996; John Raisian, interview by author, August 2, 2011.

21   Jeffrey Eisenach, interview by author, June 3, 1996.

22   Will Marshall, interview by author, May 20, 1996.

23   Larry Mone, interview by author, October 29, 2011.

24   Mone interview; Morton Blackwell, interview by author, August 15, 2011; Phyllis Schlafly, interview by author, October 7, 2011; Ron Robinson, interview by author, September 26, 2011; Richard A. Viguerie, interview by author, June 7, 2011.

25   Jim Talent, interview by author, November 4, 2011; Kenneth Cribb, interview by author, August 5, 2011; Larry Arnn, interview by author, July 1, 2011; James Carafano, interview by author, January 20, 2010; Mike Franc, interview by author, January 27, 2010; Bridgett Wagner, interview by author, March 20, 2011; Genevieve Wood, interview by author, September 18, 2012; Joan Barry, interview by author, September 28, 2011; Barbara Lackey, interview by author, September 28, 2011; William F. Buckley, Jr., to EJF, April 20, 2007; EJF Papers.

26   Margaret Thatcher to EJF, October 16, 2006, EJF Papers.

27   All quotes are taken from the 2011 files of Heritage Development.

28   Dorothy Hodo and Freida Warren, interviews by author, April 23, 2012.

29   Richard V. Allen, interview by author; J. Willliam Middendorf II, interview by author, July 31, 2011.

30   Václav Klaus to EJF, September 7, 2012.

31   EJF to President's Club members, June 15, 2012.

CHAPTER 26: STEPPING DOWN

1   EJF, interview by author, June 18, 2012.

2   EJF, interview by author, September 27, 1996.

3   EJF, interview by author, July 15, 2011.

4   Thomas Saunders III, interview by author, May 11, 2011.

5   EJF, "The Hegemony of Ideas," Heritage Foundation Lecture no. 999, May 3, 2007, originally delivered at the Reform Club, London, February 20, 2007.

6   EJF, interview by author, June 18, 2012.

7   George Will, remarks at the 2012 Bradley Prize awards ceremony, June 7, 2012.

CHAPTER 27: WHAT NOW?

1   Scott Wilson and Philip Rucker, "Victory Begins with a Strong Ground Game and Ends with a Perfect Storm," *Washington Post*, November 7, 2012.

2   Scott Wilson, "Meet the Press, Taking a Victory Lap," *Washington Post,* November 15, 2012; "President Barack Obama's Press Conference Transcript," *Politico,* November 14, 2012.

3   George Will, "The Status Quo Prevails," *Washington Post,* November 8, 2012, and "Still the Party of Principles," *Washington Post,* November 11, 2012.

4   George Weigel, "Sifting Through the Wreckage," National Review Online, November 8, 2012.

5   Laura Ingraham, "The Meaning of the Drubbing," lauraingraham.com, November 7, 2012; Ron Radosh, as quoted in EJF letter to President's Club members, November 15, 2012; Fred Barnes, "The Survivor in Chief," *Wall Street Journal,* November 8, 2012.

6   Craig Shirley, "A Revival Guide for the Republican Party," *Washington Post,* November 11, 2012.

7   Charles Krauthammer, "The Way Forward," *Washington Post,* November 9, 2012.

8   EJF to President's Club members, November 15, 2012.

9   Thomas A. Saunders, Heritage news release, December 6, 2012.

10   Jim DeMint, remarks to Heritage staff, December 6, 2012.

ACKNOWLEDGMENTS

I have been fortunate to have known and written about the signal leaders of the modern conservative movement—Ronald Reagan, Barry Goldwater, and William F. Buckley, Jr. I have described their physical and political courage, their prudence in times of crisis, their desire for justice for all, and most of all their wisdom, their ability to see what others could not see. These three men shaped American conservatism and thereby much of U.S. history in the last five decades.

In this book, I tell the story of another conservative, Ed Feulner, and the organization he has headed for more than thirty-five years. I believe he has made as enduring a contribution to the conservative movement as the above triumvirate. Without Ed Feulner and The Heritage Foundation, American conservatism would play a far less significant and continuing role in our nation's policy making and politics.

While writing *Leading the Way,* I was struck again that writing biography or history is a constant process of selection—of deciding what to include and what to exclude, whom to highlight and whom to leave in the shadows. You are obliged constantly to make choices between what is important and what is only interesting, what is consequential and what is merely arresting. My choices have been influenced by the fact that I was a conservative activist in the 1960s and 1970s and have been a conservative historian and biographer for the last quarter-century. That gives me an advantage not possible for a liberal or "objective" biographer. I bring a conservative's perspective to the examination of the last four decades.

Those seeking pure objectivity will not find it in these pages. But then they will not find it in Arthur Schlesinger, Jr.'s, history of Franklin D. Roosevelt's presidency or William Manchester's biography of John F. Kennedy. Both were liberals writing about liberals. The difference between them and me is that I admit my philosophical bias.

Let us be honest: pure objectivity is impossible. We all have our biases, prejudices, and beliefs, and we carry them with us wherever we go or whatever we do. Our duty as historians is to be as fair and factual as possible. This biography is a work of careful scholarship—with several hundred endnotes—judicious selection, and prudent judgment about a young man of unbounded energy and an entrepreneurial spirit from the South Side of Chicago who hoped to build a permanent and influential Washington institution—and succeeded.

• • •

There is no such thing as too much research. I adhere to the iceberg principle that what the reader sees is only the tip, perhaps one-eighth, of the research, writing, and rewriting on which the finished work rests. The more that the writer digs into the correspondence and the memos, conducts interviews with the principals and others, and reads relevant speeches, articles, and books, casting as wide and deep a net as possible, the better the book will be.

I conducted more than one hundred interviews with Ed Feulner and his family, friends going back decades, Heritage staffers and trustees, think tank competitors, journalists, members of Congress, fellow conservatives, and even a couple of liberals. I am especially grateful to Linda Feulner, who shared many wonderful stories about more than forty years of marriage and partnership. I thank Dr. Feulner's children E.J. and Emily, his sisters, Barbara Lackey and Joan Barry, and his lifelong friend Bruce McEvoy for their willingness to answer my many questions. Among the Heritage people I wish to single out for their assistance are Phil Truluck, John Von Kannon, Stuart Butler, Kim Holmes, and Genevieve Wood as well as Heritage trustees Tom Saunders, Midge Decter, Bob Pennington, Fritz Rench, and Bill Middendorf.

Among the interns and research assistants who assisted me, I want to pay special tribute to Leslie Grimard, ever ready to track down a quotation or confirm a fact. I would not have been able to complete this book without the archival help of the Bell sisters, Leigh, Heather, and

Rebecca, who have catalogued Ed Feulner's voluminous files as well as the papers of the Mont Pelerin Society

Without Dana Perino's help, I would not have Crown as my publisher and Sean Desmond as my superb editor.

As always, I have depended upon my wife Anne for daily and sometimes nightly editorial advice and counsel.

Last I am grateful to Ed Feulner for giving me the opportunity to write his truly remarkable story and that of The Heritage Foundation.

.—Lee Edwards
November 2012

INDEX

ABOUT THE AUTHOR

LEE EDWARDS is a leading historian of the conservative movement, having written *The Conservative Revolution, The Power of Ideas*, and acclaimed biographies of William F. Buckley, Jr., Ronald Reagan, Barry Goldwater, and Edwin Meese III, among many other books. He is the distinguished fellow in conservative thought at The Heritage Foundation, an adjunct professor of politics at the Catholic University of America, and chairman of the Victims of Communism Memorial Foundation.